QUEER
BANGKOK

Queer Asia

The Queer Asia book series opens a space for monographs and anthologies in all disciplines focused on non-normative sexuality and gender cultures, identities and practices in Asia. Queer Studies and Queer Theory originated in and remain dominated by North American and European academic circles, and existing publishing has followed these tendencies. However, growing numbers of scholars inside and beyond Asia are producing work that challenges and corrects this imbalance. The Queer Asia book series—first of its kind in publishing—provides a valuable opportunity for developing and sustaining these initiatives.

Other Titles in the Queer Asia Series

Undercurrents: Queer Culture and Postcolonial Hong Kong
Helen Hok-Sze Leung

Obsession: Male Same-sex Relations in China, 1900–1950
Wenqing Kang

Philippine Gay Culture: Binabae to Bakla, Silahis to MSM
J. Neil C. Garcia

As Normal as Possible: Negotiating Sexuality and Gender in Mainland China and Hong Kong
Edited by Yau Ching

QUEER BANGKOK

Twenty–First–Century Markets, Media, and Rights

Edited by

Peter A. Jackson

香港大學出版社
HONG KONG UNIVERSITY PRESS

SILKWORM BOOKS

Hong Kong University Press
14/F Hing Wai Centre
7 Tin Wan Praya Road
Aberdeen
Hong Kong
www.hkupress.org

ISBN 978-988-8083-04-6 *(Hardback)*
ISBN 978-988-8083-05-3 *(Paperback)*

British Library Cataloguing-in-Publication Data
A catalogue copy for this book is available from the British Library

Silkworm Books

ISBN 978-616-215-014-2 *(Paperback)*

The Southeast Asia edition published in 2011 by
Silkworm Books
6 Sukkasem Road, T. Suthep, Chiang Mai 50200, Thailand

www.silkwormbooks.com
info@silkwormbooks.com

10 9 8 7 6 5 4 3 2 1

Printed and bound by Condor Production Ltd, Hong Kong, China

Contents

Contributors

Aren Z. Aizura (Ph.D., Melbourne University) is a postdoctoral fellow in gender studies at Indiana University. He has published in the journals *Inter-Asia Cultural Studies, Asian Studies Review*, and *Medical Anthropology*. His research interests include trans and queer theory, and transnational studies.

Alex Au has been a gay activist in Singapore since 1993, when he began working with People Like Us, a gay and lesbian rights group with which he remains associated. He was the main shareholder in a gay sauna that operated in the city-state from 2000 to 2005, and among Singaporeans he is best known for Yawning Bread (www.yawningbread.org), a web site that has been on-line since 1996 and which enjoys a reputation for independent commentary on social, political, and gay issues.

Nikos Dacanay completed an M.A. degree in Southeast Asian studies, with Thailand as his focus, at the Asian Center of the University of the Philippines, Diliman. He was a fellow in the Southeast Asian Studies Department of Thammasat University, Bangkok, from 2003 to 2006. He is currently conducting a research on Internet usage by Burmese ethnic women migrants in northern Thailand with support from the Amy Mahan Fellowship Program to Assess the Impact of ICT Public Access Venues.

Brett Farmer (Ph.D., Griffith University) teaches in the Faculty of Arts, Chulalongkorn University, Bangkok. He is the author of *Spectacular passions: Cinema, fantasy, and gay male spectatorships* (Duke University Press, 2000) and numerous essays on film and cultural studies. He is currently working on a study of sexual modernities in Thai film.

Peter A. Jackson (Ph.D., Australian National University) is professor of Thai cultural studies in the ANU's College of Asia and the Pacific. He has written extensively on modern Thai cultural history with special interests in religion and sexuality. He is editor in chief of the *Asian Studies Review* and founder of the Thai Rainbow Archives Project, which is collecting and digitizing Thai gay, lesbian, and transgender magazines and community organization newsletters. See http://thairainbowarchive.anu.edu.au/index.html.

Ben Murtagh (Ph.D., School of Oriental and African Studies) is a lecturer in Indonesian and Malay at SOAS, the University of London. He is managing editor of the journal *Indonesia and the Malay World*, and his current research interests focus on gay, lesbian, and waria representations in Indonesian cinema and literature.

Pimpawun Boonmongkon (Ph.D., University of California, San Francisco–Berkeley) is an associate professor in the Department of Society and Health and director of the Center for Health Policy Studies at Mahidol University, Salaya. She is a founding member of the Southeast Asian Consortium on Gender, Sexuality, and Health, and her research focuses on sexual and reproductive health, HIV/AIDS, gender-based violence, and cyberspace and sexuality.

Stéphane Rennesson (Ph.D., Université Paris Ouest Nanterre La Défense) is a researcher at the Laboratoire d'Anthropologie Urbaine (Institut Interdisciplinaire d'Anthropologie du Contemporain, CNRS–EHESS) in Paris. He previously held a postdoctoral fellowship at the Musée du quai Branly and was an assistant professor of anthropology at the University of Versailles Saint Quentin. His work has been published in numerous French journals, and he is currently researching competitive games and sports in Thailand.

Ronnapoom Samakkeekarom (M.A., Mahidol University) is a researcher in the Center for Health Policy Studies at Mahidol University, Salaya. He was a founding member of the Health and Opportunities Network in Bangkok and is an advisory board member of the Thai Transgender Alliance. His research focuses on gender-based violence, cyberspace and sexuality, and sexual health.

Douglas Sanders is professor emeritus in the Faculty of Law, University of British Columbia. Beginning as a pre-Stonewall activist in Canada, he was later one of the first scholars to write on LGBT issues in that country. He represented the International Lesbian and Gay Association at the United Nations in the early 1990s and currently teaches in the human rights programme at Mahidol University, Salaya.

Megan Sinnott is an assistant professor of women's studies at Georgia State University. She previously conducted ethnographic research in Thailand for ten years and authored the 2004 ethnography, *Toms and dees: Transgender identity and female same-sex relations in Thailand*.

Serhat Ünaldi is currently enrolled in a doctoral programme at Humboldt University in Berlin, where he is researching the socio-political functions of Bangkok's Siam/Ratchaprasong shopping district. He holds a B.A. degree in area studies from Humboldt University and an M.A. in international studies from the University of Leeds.

Sam Winter (Ph.D., the University of Hong Kong) is associate dean for research and an associate professor in the Faculty of Education at the University of Hong Kong. He is a director of WPATH (the World Professional Association for Transgender Health), runs the TransgenderASIA Centre, teaches a sexual and gender diversity course, and has published in a wide variety of journals.

A Note on Thai Transcription
and Citation of Thai Names

There is no generally agreed system of representing Thai in roman script, and all current systems have some limitations. In this book we follow a modified version of the Thai Royal Institute system. This system makes no distinction between long and short vowel forms; and tones are not represented. We differ slightly from the Royal Institute system as follows: "j" is used for the Thai consonant *jor jan*, not "ch", and "eu", "eua", "euay" (not "ue", "uea", "ueay") are used for these vowels and diphthongs. Dashes are used to separate the units of Thai compound expressions that are translated as single terms in English, such as *khwam-pen-thai* for "Thainess".

We follow the Thai norm of referring to Thai authors by given names, not surnames, and all citations by Thai authors are in alphabetical order in the bibliography and elsewhere according to given names.

Queer Bangkok after the Millennium

Beyond Twentieth-Century Paradigms

Peter A. Jackson

Introduction

Sexual and gender cultures change constantly in response to shifts in social, political, and economic forces. This book details major changes that have taken place in the lesbian, gay, bisexual, and transgender/transsexual (LGBT) cultures and communities in Bangkok in the first decade of the twenty-first century. The capital of Thailand since 1782, Bangkok is a sprawling metropolis of more than 10 million people, and, as home to almost one-sixth of the country's population, it is the unrivalled centre of national economic, political, and cultural activity. Highly visible gay, lesbian (*tom-dee*), and transgender/transsexual (*kathoey*) cultures emerged in the city in the decades after World War II, and Bangkok is also unrivalled as the centre of Thai queer life. As shown in the studies collected here, the first years of the new century have marked a significant transition moment for all of Thailand's LGBT cultures, with a multidimensional expansion in the geographical extent, media presence, economic importance, political impact, social standing, and cultural relevance of Thai queer communities, which were already among the largest in the region—and, indeed, the world.

This book traces the roles of the market and the media, notably cinema and the Internet, in the recent transformations of Bangkok's queer communities and considers the ambiguous consequences that the growing commodification and mediatization of LGBT lives have had for queer rights in Thailand. The studies here consider Bangkok queer cultures until mid-2008, just before the onset of the global financial crisis in the second half of that year and before the intensification of political conflicts between supporters and opponents of the September 2006 military coup that toppled former Prime Minister Thaksin Shinawatra. The impact on Bangkok queer scenes of the dramatic changes in Thailand's economic and political circumstances since 2008 awaits future analysis.

Beyond Stereotypes

Outside Thailand, the country's queer cultures are often known primarily by way of stereotypes of a supposed "gay paradise" (Jackson 1999a), a prevalence of transgender *kathoeys* or "ladyboys", the widespread presence of both male and female sex work, and a supposedly queer-accepting culture where almost anything goes. Insider views that challenge these exoticizing stereotypes are surprisingly rare. In part this is a consequence of the fact that the international sectors of Bangkok's queer scenes that are visited by most foreign tourists are linguistically compartmentalized and spatially separate from the much larger number of venues in other parts of the city that are frequented by Thai queers. By analysing what has been happening in the domestic Thai and intra-Asian sectors of Bangkok's queer scenes, the chapters here correct widespread misrepresentations presented by monolingual foreign commentators for whom the large Thai LGBT worlds beyond international tourist zones such as Silom Road remain all but invisible.

This book brings together a genuinely transnational range of perspectives on twenty-first-century queer Bangkok; the authors come from Thailand, the Philippines, Singapore, Australia, the United Kingdom, France, Germany, Canada, and the United States. This reflects the significant extent of academic interest in queer Thailand in the West and in other Asian countries. This collection emerges from papers presented in the genders and sexualities stream of panels convened as part of the Tenth International Conference of Thai Studies at Thammasat University in Bangkok in January 2008. More than half the papers presented in that conference stream were on LGBT topics, reflecting the rapid growth as well as the increasing mainstream relevance of research on queer Thailand. A significant proportion of the papers in that conference stream were presented by younger scholars at the M.A. and Ph.D. levels. Several chapters here showcase the path-breaking research that younger scholars in Asia and the West are conducting on queer Thailand. It is only in the past decade that research programmes at the Ph.D. level, using Thai as their medium, have expanded across the country's tertiary education sector. It is still the case that the most advanced level of research undertaken by many Thai scholars is at the M.A. level. While this level of research is more focused in scope when compared with doctoral research, a growing body of M.A. work on queer themes has emerged in recent years, and it has increasingly challenged the pathologizing, biomedical focus of much twentieth-century Thai research on LGBT topics (Jackson 1997; Sinnott in this volume). As Timo Ojanen has observed:

> The recent literature [on Thai LGBTs] . . . seems almost universally accepting of the sexual/gender identities of study participants; unlike

earlier research, current studies no longer call for curing or preventing such identities. Today's researchers, both Thai and foreign, seem to hold that society should adapt to the needs of these minorities, rather than vice versa. (2009, 17)

The studies here draw on a range of academic and other approaches, including anthropology, cinema and literary studies, political analysis, and the narrative reflections of an Asian gay activist. While methodologically diverse, all analyses in this book are united by a shared commitment to expose, resist, and challenge the heteronormative assumptions that marked much earlier research on queer Thailand and which continue to restrict the lives and opportunities of Thailand's gay, *tom-dee*, and *kathoey* citizens.

The Languaging of "Queer" in Thailand

In this book the term "queer" denotes sexual and gender practices, identities, cultures, and communities that challenge normative masculine and feminine gender roles and/or transgress the borders of heterosexuality. "Queer" here also labels a critical theoretical stance that analyses all genderings and sexualities as emerging from contingent historical conditions. Queer studies views both hegemonically normative and minority genders and sexualities as interrelated components of an overarching gender/sex system in which notions of heterosexuality are constructed in relation to ideas of homosexuality and in which understandings of transgenderism/transsexuality emerge in opposition to notions of normatively gendered and sexed behaviour.

However, the English-language term "queer" as such is not used in Thailand's LGBT cultures. Rather, the Thai term *phet*—which incorporates ideas of sex, gender, and sexuality—is a master concept that is central to all legal, academic, and popular discourses of gender and sexuality. In Thai, heteronormative identities (e.g. "man", *phu-chai*; "woman", *phu-ying*) and queer subjectivities (e.g. *kathoey, gay king, gay queen, tom, dee*) are all regarded as varieties of *phet*. While all identities are imagined as blending different degrees of masculinity and femininity—and a gender binary underpins Thai understandings of sexual identity—the discourse of *phet* is not as such a binary construct. Rather, Thai discourses of *phet* reflect an understanding of proliferating diversity. When Thai scholars, journalists, and others write of *phet*, whether in formal or popular contexts, they typically do so by listing several, not just two, identities.

The proliferating diversity of Thai gender/sex categories

The growth of Bangkok queer scenes in the second half of the twentieth century was paralleled by a proliferation in the number and diversity of categories to label distinctive gay, transgender/transsexual, and lesbian identities. This explosion of Thai queer identity categories (Jackson 2000) began in the late 1950s and early 1960s and continued through the 1970s and early 1980s, with discourses of Thai queer identity undergoing yet further changes in the past decade. The proliferation of queer identities appears to have resulted from a range of influences, including these:

- A nineteenth- and early twentieth-century state project to "civilize" normative Siamese genders by accentuating the differentiation of masculine and feminine fashions, hairstyles, and names. This instituted a regime of biopower (Foucault 1980) over Thai genders that has, in turn, contributed to an incitement of transgenderism and new sexualities (Jackson 2003a).
- The emergence of new understandings of masculine and feminine gendering as a consequence of the spread of market capitalism in Thailand and the commodification of both urban and rural labour across the twentieth century (Jackson 2003b, 2009a, 2009b).
- Beginning in the 1950s, vernacular print capitalism (newspapers, magazines, books) supported the growth of imaginings of national-level queer cultures and communities (Jackson 2009a).
- In the late twentieth and early twenty-first centuries, globalizing capitalism, new electronic media, and transnational influences from Hong Kong, Taiwan, Japan, Australia, Europe, and the United States (Altman 2001) brought previously isolated homosexuals into contact with each other (Berry et al. 2003).

Thai lesbian culture reflects the continuing linguistic dynamism of the country's LGBT communities in the early twenty-first century. Until recently, the single term *tom* (from "tomboy") has encompassed all variations of female masculinity. However, Ojanen (2009, 7) notes that the binary gendering of female homosexual couples between a masculine *tom* and feminine *dee* (from "la_dy_") is being challenged, with the term *les* (from "lesbian") now being used by women who seek to break out of gendered role play in their romantic and sexual relationships with other women. Megan Sinnott here notes that the Internet is providing a medium for younger *ying rak ying*, "women who love women", to coin a range of new labels that more appropriately reflect the gendered diversity of their lives. Sinnott shows how young women who love women are creating hybrid categories such as *les king* and *les queen* that draw on established notions of *gay king* (sexually active partner) and *gay queen* (sexually receptive partner) in Thai gay cultures to create more nuanced ways to refer to female same-sex experience and sexual preference. The ready accessibility of the Internet to younger Thais from all socio-economic backgrounds has provided a medium to renegotiate identity categories that emerged in the second half of the twentieth century, a period when imaginings of Thai queerness were predominantly mediated through print media (Jackson 1995, 2009a).

Attempts to translate Western understandings of "queer" have had an unusual outcome in Thailand. In the context of helping organize the First International Conference of Asian Queer Studies in Bangkok in July 2005, Prempreeda Pramoj Na Ayutthaya, a transgender-identified researcher and activist, coined the compound expression *kham-phet* in an attempt to render notions of gender/sex fluidity into Thai. *Kham* means "to cross over", and Prempreeda's intent was to convey a sense of the blurring of identities within understandings of *phet*. Informed by her readings of Western queer theory, Prempreeda's neologism of *kham-phet* was an attempt to disrupt the apparent stability of the many identities labelled within Thai discourses of *phet*. However, *kham* is also used to translate the English prefix "trans", as in *kham-prathet*, "transnational". Most Thai readers interpreted Prempreeda's neologism as an attempt to render the English terms "transgender" and "transsexual" into Thai, and since 2005 *kham-phet* has quickly become a generally recognized translation of these two terms, which nonetheless are not always clearly differentiated in Thai.

Prempreeda's attempt to translate "queer" into Thai quickly slipped beyond her control and became appropriated to local notions of transgenderism/transsexuality. Thai still lacks an agreed academic rendering of "queer", and authors who wish to refer to Western ideas of "queer" often write the word in roman script within their Thai texts—a common practice adopted by Thai authors when no local equivalent term is available. Hence, "queer theory" may be rendered as *tharitsadi queer*. In crossing the linguistic/discursive/cultural divide from the Anglophone West to Thailand, "queer" itself has been subjected to localized processes of queering, reflecting both the significant autonomy of Thai discourses in representing sex/gender/sexuality, even at the height of early twenty-first-century globalization, as well as demonstrating the centrality of notions of transgenderism/transsexuality in contemporary Thai understandings of gender and sexual difference.

While Thai lacks a precise local rendering of "queer", terms for "gender" and "sexuality" have been coined. Since the 1990s, the English-language term "gender" has been variously rendered as *sathanaphap thang-phet*, *phet-sathan*, *phet-phawa*, *phet-saphap*, and *phet-saphawa* (all denoting "*phet* condition" or "*phet* status"), with *phet-saphap* ultimately emerging as the most commonly accepted translation among Thai feminist scholars. Over the past decade, the term "sexuality" has been translated as *phet-withi* ("*phet* orientation").

Given the diversity and dynamism of Thai queer terminologies, Thai academics and LGBT activists have struggled to find an agreed-upon, overarching term for all the country's queer genders and sexualities. The need for such a common term emerged in 2007 with the formation of a united front of lesbians, gays, and *kathoeys* to lobby the Thai government on a range of human rights issues. As Douglas Sanders details here, these efforts focused on attempts to enshrine an anti-discrimination clause in the Thai constitution, to permit male-to-female transgenders and transsexuals to have their feminine status recognized on identity cards and passports, and to overturn the Thai army's definition of *kathoey* conscripts as mentally ill. Since 2007, the expression *khwam-lak-lai thang-phet*—which can be rendered variously as "gender/sexual diversity" or "diverse genders/sexualities"—has emerged as the banner under which Thailand's diverse queer communities have come together in common political cause and remains the closest Thai equivalent to Western understandings of "queer". The language of "queer rights" has been translated formally into Thai as *sitthi khorng khon thi mi khwam-lak-lai thang-phet*, literally "The rights of people who possess *phet*-diversity". More popularly, the Thai term for "rainbow" (*si-rung*) has become a much more concise and locally evocative marker of diverse queer identities and cultures. The queer connotations of the term *si-rung* now circulate in the wider community; a 2009 Thai TV soap opera about a gay man's problematic relations with his adopted son was entitled *Phra Jan Si-rung*, or "Rainbow Moon".

While writing their contributions in English has often required this book's authors to draw on Anglophone terminologies such as "lesbian", "transgender", "transsexual", "LGBT", and "queer", all the studies here emphasize the distinctiveness of Thai discourses of sex, gender, and sexuality. English terms and concepts are used for linguistic convenience and should not be taken to indicate any identity, or convergence, between Thai and Western discourses. Most of the authors here conduct their analyses through the lens of Thai terminologies, and a glossary of key terms is included at the end of this book as a reference guide for readers.

Glocal Queering and Thai Vernacular Queer Modernity

Think Bollywood (not Hollywood)

The role of international (Euro-American) versus domestic factors in the explosion of Thai queer *phet* categories and the historical growth of Bangkok queer communities in the second half of the last century has been a matter of some discussion. The studies here reflect a growing consensus among students of modern Asian queer cultures of the need to challenge simplistic accounts of global queering that emphasize the causative influences of either "unique local essentialism", on the one hand, or Westernizing "global homogenization" on the other (McLelland 2006, 159). Like Eng-Beng Lim (2005) and Fran Martin et al. (2008), this book traces the transformations of early twenty-first-century queer Bangkok to complex hybridizing processes inflected by "transnational capital, and regional, inter-Asian diasporic circuits and exchanges" (Lim 2005, 384). Drawing on Dennis Altman's (1996b) influential notion of "global queering", Lim labels this emphasis on hybridizing processes the study of "glocal queering". I suggest that a comparison with the history of South Asian cinema provides insight into the nature of the intersecting relationship between Thai and Western queer cultures in processes of glocal queering, and that it also gives a sense of the distinctive character of Thai vernacular queer modernity as an alternative modernity that differs both from premodern Thai "tradition" and modern Western queer cultures.

In describing trends in contemporary Indian popular culture, Bhaskar Mukhopadhyay (2006) distinguishes between folk traditions and vernacular modernisms. In his study here of recent Thai queer cinema Brett Farmer also engages the notion of vernacular modernity as a frame for understanding the distinctiveness of Thai queer cultural production within a global context of expanding and intensifying cross-border interconnections. Farmer describes Thai queer cinema as a popular cultural artifact that has helped naturalize new forms of sexual and gender identity within a Thai cultural context. Indeed, Thai queer identities—such as *gay king, gay queen, kathoey, tom,* and *dee*—can be seen as vernacular modernisms of *phet* that have emerged out of premodern notions of gender and sexual difference. These modern Thai queer identities relate to Western queer cultures in a way somewhat similar to the manner in which India's Bollywood cinema industry relates to the American cinema capital of Hollywood. While drawing on the same film and digital technologies, the market, and advertising, Bollywood has nonetheless forged a distinctive cinematic idiom that remains largely independent of Hollywood. Mukhopadhyay notes, "One of the key questions raised by the 'new' film studies was how cinema came to assume an Indian identity" (2006, 281). In a similar vein, one of the key questions for Asian queer studies is how queerness has come to assume a Thai identity, a Chinese identity, an Indonesian identity, and so on.

Mukhopadhyay describes Bollywood as having constituted "something like a 'nation-space' without the backing of the state" (2006, 280). Modern Thai vernacular queer identities similarly constitute something like an imagined national space of gender and sexual diversity that has emerged, and found an increasingly secure space for existence, without the backing of the state.

Vernacular print and electronic media have been central historical forces in this queer cultural development. With regard to Indonesia, Tom Boellstorff argues:

> It appears that print media, television, and movies have been crucial to the formation of gay and lesbian subject positions . . . This seems more consequential than either the historically rare consumption of Western gay and lesbian media or publications produced by [gay and lesbian] Southeast Asians themselves . . . (2007, 213)

In Thailand, Thai-language print and electronic media have also been central to the emergence of national-level queer cultures (Jackson 1989, 1995, 1999b). In this context, Cindy Patton's comments on Benedict Anderson's argument in his influential *Imagined communities* (1983) have relevance to understanding the origins of Thai vernacular queer modernity:

> [T]he development of a semi-independent print capitalism allowed people who were widely dispersed to see themselves existing in a coexisting time . . . This enabled the development of cross-regional consensus about politics among the literate middle classes and enhanced the sense that a nation was a community, even if that national identity—called 'imagined community' by Anderson—existed only in a hypothetical space. (Patton 2002, 200–201)

Nationally distributed commercial print media were central to Thai gay identity formation in the decades from the 1960s to the 1980s (Jackson 1995). Anderson has characterized the Thai press from the 1960s onward as being "an ally of the new bourgeois political ascendancy" (1990, 41). As an originally middle-class phenomenon, the Thai national press has been a key vehicle for disseminating non-state views of Thai gay identity. That is, a vernacular press that voices largely middle-class concerns has disseminated middle-class political and cultural ideas, including originally middle-class ideas of gay sexual identity, across the country.

Waves of queer cultural development in Bangkok

Modern gay/*kathoey*/*tom-dee* cultures in Thailand are now half a century old and have gone through several stages of development as the country's market economy and new media emerged and grew, albeit unevenly and at different rates and intensities, through different geographical regions and socio-economic sectors. Queer communities and commercial scenes have been marked by periodic spurts of growth, as they have expanded into new sectors and classes:

- The 1960s: The first public "outing" of Bangkok's emerging gay, *kathoey*, and *tom-dee* cultures with sensationalist coverage in the national Thai- and English-language press (Jackson 1999b).
- The 1970s: The first small-scale openings of gay bars in Bangkok and publication of the first gay-themed Thai-language books.
- The 1980s: Publication of the first commercially successful gay magazines, *Mithuna Junior* and *Neon* (Jackson 2009a), the opening of the first gay saunas, the first wave of Thai queer cinema (Serhat Ünaldi in this volume), and the emergence of a more diversified gay commercial sector. In the wave of queer cultural development in this decade, Thai gay men, lesbians, and *kathoeys* began to take control of print and cinematic media to produce representations of and for themselves.
- The 1990s: Further expansion of Bangkok's commercial gay sector targeting the urban middle class.
- The 2000s: The rapid expansion of Thai queer modernity among youth and working-class men and women, accompanied by the mainstreaming and massification of representations of sexual and gender diversity.

New electronic and digital media and the continuation of rapid economic growth in East and Southeast Asia in the first decade of the new century have contributed to further waves of modern Thai queer cultural development, and this book looks at how one of Asia's oldest modern queer cultures is being transformed by these twenty-first-century processes. As in India, Thailand's vernacular modern queer cultures reflect "the maturity of consumerism due to the opening up of the economy" (Mukhopadhyay 2006, 288). Several chapters here consider the maturing of Thai queer consumerism, which emerged in the 1970s and early 1980s with the first commercially successful gay magazines and the development of a distinctive culture based on saunas, bars, pubs, and discos that targeted a Thai gay middle-class market (Nikos Dacanay in this volume).

Western queer cultures are known and recognized by Thai queers, but they are neither looked to as exemplary models to be imitated nor resisted or critiqued as paths to be avoided. Despite the presence of large numbers of Western gay tourists, the circulation of dubbed and subtitled Western gay movies, the reproduction (often via unlicensed pirating) of Western gay pornography and images from Western gay magazines, the relationship with the West cannot be categorized in simplistic terms as either "neocolonial" cultural imperialism or "postcolonial resistance". As Rachel Harrison and I have noted elsewhere, the fact that Thailand was never colonized by a Western power places this society in an ambiguous relationship with accounts of Euro-American imperialism (Harrison and Jackson 2010). Indeed, I have argued that the fact Thailand and

Japan remained politically independent during the era of Western imperialism is one reason Asia's first modern LGBT cultures emerged in Tokyo and Bangkok and not in the capitals of former European or American colonies in the region (Jackson 2009a, 366–367). A distinctive Thai vernacular queer modernism has emerged and found an increasingly secure foothold by forging a distinctive sense of identity within the commodified spaces of Thai popular culture, as well as by drawing on international discourses of human rights, to claim a space within the Thai polity (Megan Sinnott and Doug Sanders in this volume). Internationally circulating Western discourses of sexuality, homosexuality, gayness, queer, and so on have not led to unmediated "cultural borrowing" of Western sexualities in Thailand so much as a new repertoire of ways to retell local stories and alternative ways to remember local histories. As Fran Martin et al. (2008) point out in a comparative study of queer cultural developments across East and Southeast Asia, notions of cultural hybridity that foreground the power of local agency and the resilience of local discourses provide a more fruitful lens for conceptualizing what has been happening in queer Asia, including queer Bangkok, over recent decades.

Rethinking Globalization and Capitalism in the Asian Century

The following chapters are assembled into three thematic sections: Part I concerns markets and media in Bangkok's queer cultural transformations; Part II explores queer Bangkok in twenty-first-century global and regional networks; Part III illuminates LGBT activism, rights, and autonomy in Thailand.

The evidence and analyses presented in each section require us to rethink a range of issues in transnational queer studies, including the pattern of relations between Asian and Western queer cultures; the forms and direction of queer cultural globalization, and the role of capitalism in advancing LGBT rights and the emergence of spaces of queer cultural autonomy in Asia.

Part I: Markets and media in Bangkok's queer cultural transformations

In the immediate aftermath of the end of the Cold War and the collapse of the Soviet Union, much critical analysis tended to assume Western, or American, dominance and hegemony in processes of capitalist globalization. Globalization was seen predominantly in terms of Westernization, while most critical analysts envisioned capitalism as a Western-controlled force for exploiting and subjecting the non-West. However, with the rise of economies across East, Southeast, and South Asia, the unipolar world of the 1990s has given way to an increasingly complex international pattern of multiple economic, political, and cultural powers. While the chapters here do not directly address the geotectonic shifts now taking place in global markets and political arrangements, they nonetheless reflect the impact of contemporary geopolitical transitions. As I detail in my two later chapters here, among the analytical challenges for early twenty-first-century queer studies are the need to rethink both globalization and transnational capitalism in an era when the West is no longer an unchallenged global hegemon.

Focusing on different queer genders and identities, the chapters in Part I provide insights into why, in the early twenty-first century, the LGBT cultures of Southeast Asia's "gay capital" have developed in somewhat different directions from those in some Western countries. Bangkok's queer scenes boomed over the same period that gay and lesbian scenes of comparable age in some Western cities have appeared to decline. I consider this phenomenon in detail in the following chapter, where I also consider the evidence that the other chapters in Part I provide on the intersecting impact of media and commodifying processes on Bangkok's transgender/transsexual and gay communities.

Part II: Queer Bangkok in twenty-first-century global and regional networks

The chapters in Part II detail Bangkok's role as a major nodal point of global queering (Altman 1996a, 1996b, 2001). The border-crossing impacts of expanding markets, new electronic media, and consumerist lifestyles are key forces in cultural globalization, including the globalization of LGBT cultures. However, in contrast to some accounts that have equated globalization with Westernization or Americanization (e.g. Waters 1995), the chapters in the middle section of this book reflect Bangkok's role as a source of radiating influences in queer cultural transformations across both Asia and the West. This challenges and reverses Eurocentric narratives of global queering that posit the West as the originating site of major transformations in modern Asian queer cultures (Wilson 2006). As Aren Aizura details here, Western male-to-female transsexual communities are increasingly drawing upon Thailand as a source, and resource, of both physiological and cultural feminization. In the early twenty-first century, transnational queer cultural flows are also advancing from Thailand to the West—that is, they are not unidirectional from the West to Thailand. In their chapters, Alex Au and Ben Murtagh show that Bangkok's queer cultures have also had powerful influences on the emergence of gay identities in neighbouring Southeast Asian countries, from economically developed Singapore to the emerging democracy of Indonesia.

The chapters in this and other sections of this book reveal that in the early twenty-first-century intra-Asian flows have become more important than cultural and other influences from the West in the emergence of a regional network of interconnected Asian queer cultures. This network links LGBT communities in a growing number of regional metropolises—notably Bangkok, Singapore, Hong Kong, Tokyo, and Taipei—with Asianization and regionalism now the dominant directions of queer cultural change.

Part III: LGBT activism, rights, and autonomy in Thailand

As noted above, the studies here require us to rethink the power dynamics of capitalism in the early twenty-first-century world system. As we enter a period when a range of Asian societies, or at least the elites and middle classes of a range of Asian societies, are arguably beneficiaries rather than victims of transnational capitalism, we need to rethink twentieth-century views that equate the progressive marketization of social life with subjection to Western dictates. Capitalism undoubtedly remains a force for the production of inequality. As Aren Aizura highlights, Thai m-t-f transsexuals have been disadvantaged by the internationalization of the country's cosmetic-surgery industry. At the same time, however, LGBT communities across Asia, including those in Bangkok, have often found the market to provide a refuge from politically repressive and culturally heteronormative governments. As Asian economies have grown, gay men, lesbians, and transgenders/transsexuals across the region have used their increasing disposable incomes to purchase spaces of at least partial queer autonomy. Bangkok's queer cultures are highly commercialized, but the central place of the market in the city's LGBT communities should not be read in solely negative terms as a subjection to the dictates of capital. Bangkok's commercialized queer scenes also need to be seen in more positive terms as a negotiation with the market to craft zones of autonomy from the gender-conformist policies of the Thai state and bureaucracy.

In the past, some Western commentators have asserted that, while Bangkok may have extensive commercial gay, lesbian, and transgender scenes, it lacks "genuine" forms of LGBT community organization as found in cities such as San Francisco. This perhaps reflects an unduly negative view of the market as a domain for community development, and Bangkok queers do not have such a disparaging perception of their own situation. Expressions such as *chum-chon gay* ("gay community") and *sangkhom gay* ("gay social life", "gay scene") have long denoted a sense of shared queer cultural life and collective identity in Thailand. In this book, expressions such as "Bangkok's LGBT community" reflect Thai, rather than Western, understandings of shared collective life. The chapters in the final section of this book document advances that community-based activism achieved in institutionalizing gay, lesbian, and transgender/transsexual rights in Thailand in the first decade of the twenty-first century while also highlighting the persistence of discrimination and the limitations of LGBT activism in the country's highly volatile and unstable political culture.

Future Directions for Research on Queer Thailand

Regional, class, and ethnic divides

The following chapters focus on urban queer cultures and communities in Bangkok and its immediate hinterland, including the nearby resort city of Pattaya. Thailand's culturally and linguistically distinctive Southern (Tai), Northern (Lanna), and Northeastern (Isan) regions, and the many rural communities across the country where a large proportion of the Thai population continues to live, are not studied here. While "queer Bangkok" can in no way be equated with "queer Thailand", the country's mega-capital is, in geographers' terms, a primate city that dominates the nation economically, politically, and culturally. This is also true for the country's LGBT communities; Bangkok's queer cultures have powerful influences across the nation. Nonetheless, the ways that regional and rural queer communities relate to, and perhaps differ from, those in the capital remain topics for future research. The differentiation of Thai queer scenes along class and ethnic lines also remains poorly researched. Nikos Dacanay here takes us behind the doors of Bangkok's gay saunas to reveal the ethnicized and class-inflected patterns of sexual interaction that structure male-male casual sex in the city. However, much remains to be done on the questions of how Thai queer cultures and communities in the country's culturally and linguistically distinct regions differ from those in Bangkok, and how religious affiliation (e.g. for Thailand's Muslim minority) and ethnic status (e.g. for non-Thai "hill tribe" groups in the North and ethnic Khmer in the Northeast) influence patterns of queer culture and identity.

Women who love women

Bangkok's gay, *kathoey*, and *tom-dee* communities are not equally represented in the chapters presented here. This does not denote their relative size or cultural significance but rather is a further reflection of the uneven character of current research on queer Thailand. Considerably more research has been conducted on gay men and *kathoeys* than on Thai women who love women. This book is, then, a mirror of the incomplete and imperfect state of academic knowledge of queer Bangkok; it does fully reflect the scope and diversity of all the queer lives lived within that city.

HIV/AIDS

A further topic in need of urgent research is the social, cultural, and economic impact of the HIV/AIDS health crisis among Bangkok gay men and *kathoeys*. From 2003 to 2005, the rate of HIV prevalence among men who have sex with men (MSM) in Bangkok increased from 17 percent to 28 percent (van Griensven et al. 2005), rising to almost 31 percent in 2007 (van Griensven et al. 2009). These alarming figures have led both the Thai Ministry of Public Health and a range of international agencies to fund HIV/AIDS education and prevention initiatives through local non-governmental organizations such as the Rainbow Sky Association of Thailand, Bangkok Rainbow, MPlus, and SWING (Sanders in this volume). While at the time of writing the results of recent interventions in containing the HIV/AIDS epidemic are not yet clear, this increased Thai and international funding for NGOs has had a significant positive impact in facilitating community-building and collective, organized lobbying on human rights issues. As Megan Sinnott and Douglas Sanders detail here, some of the newly funded gay and *kathoey* NGOs have joined forces with lesbian organizations to establish a united front, the Sexual Diversity Network, to lobby for the overturning of institutional discrimination and call for institutional recognition of LGBT rights in Thailand's halls of power.

I

Markets and Media
in Bangkok's
Queer Cultural Transformations

1

Bangkok's Early Twenty-First-Century Queer Boom

Peter A. Jackson

Queer Bangkok and the West in the Early 2000s: A Study in Contrasts

In this chapter I contrast the boom in Bangkok queer cultures over the past decade with the sense of decline in some Western LGBT scenes, and I argue that in the early twenty-first century continuing processes of queer cultural globalization have produced contrasting patterns of cultural change in Asia and the West, as opposed to a transnational homogenization of LGBT cultures and communities.

In recent years, commentary in the gay press, and academic studies in some Western countries such as Australia and the United States, has lamented an apparent decline in the public forms of homosexual community and activism that marked the last three decades of the twentieth century. Gay, lesbian, and transgender/transsexual legal rights have continued to advance, if slowly and unevenly, and virtual queer communities have boomed on the Internet since the late 1990s. However, in Sydney local commentators have asked, "What happened to gay life?" (Reynolds 2007), while others in the same city have reported a "tarnishing of the golden mile" (Ruting 2007), with the closing of many gay businesses and a decline in the visible queer presence on Sydney's previously iconic queer precinct of Oxford Street, venue of the internationally famous annual Gay and Lesbian Mardi Gras parade. In the United States, a mood of nostalgia is apparent in some established gay ghettoes where, as in Sydney, the visible queer presence has declined as straight customers and businesses have increasingly colonized what, from the 1970s to the 1990s, had been predominantly queer business precincts. Alexei Barrioneuvo contrasts the rapid growth of Buenos Aires' gay scene since the end of Argentina's military dictatorship in 1983 to the sense of decline in some North American gay capitals:

> In other parts of the world, such as San Francisco's Castro district, gays have struggled recently to maintain cultural relevance in the face of gentrification. In the Castro, the largest U.S. gay neighborhood, San Francisco's most popular Halloween party was cancelled, striking a blow to the neighborhood's identity. (Barrioneuvo 2007, 2)

No definitive analysis of the sense of decline in public participation in some older Western gay locales has yet emerged. However, anecdotal reports suggest possible causes as the rise of queer Internet cultures, with LGBT people increasingly networking through virtual spaces, and a decline in overt expressions of homophobia such that queer people no longer feel a need to congregate in ghettoes for safety.

In Asia, Bangkok is second only to Tokyo in the historical depth, size, and broader social impact of its diverse gay, lesbian, and transgender/transsexual cultures. Widely known as the "gay capital" of Southeast Asia, Bangkok is home to one of the world's older, more established gay scenes; gay bars opened in the city some years before those in Sydney, Australia's self-proclaimed gay capital. However, in contrast to the sense of decline that has affected public queer life in early twenty-first-century Sydney and San Francisco, Bangkok's queer cultures and "rainbow" communities and markets have boomed. All Thai queer identities—gay, *kathoey* (transgender/transsexual), and *tom-dee* (lesbian)—participated in this early twenty-first-century boom, which marked all dimensions of queer life in Bangkok. These features of the phenomenon were most notable:

- An increase in the number of commercial gay venues in the city—including gay pubs, bars, discos, and saunas—from 165 in 2003 to 216 in 2007; gay saunas doubled in number over this period, to more than fifty (Nikos Dacanay in this volume).[1]
- An expansion in the number and geographical spread of gay entertainment zones across the city. Three new Thai gay zones emerged outside the downtown commercial district in suburban locations: Lam Salee, also called Ramkhamhaeng, a zone of pubs and discos in eastern Bangkok established in the early 2000s; Or. Tor. Kor.,[2] also called Jatujak, a new zone of gay pubs in the north of the city that grew rapidly from about 2003–04, and Ratchada, Bangkok's newest zone of gay pubs, which dates from 2006–07 and which is located in the city's inner north.
- The publication of ten new Thai-language commercial gay magazine titles in 2007 alone. In January 2008, Thailand's first commercial magazine for *tom* (butch lesbians), *Tom Act*, was launched.

- The publication of almost forty Thai-language, queer-themed paperback books in each of the past few years, rising from a handful of titles per year before 2000.
- The production of a growing number of queer-themed Thai films, including some that have broken new ground by portraying masculine-identified gay relationships instead of an historical focus on comedic transgender *kathoey* characters (Serhat Ünaldi and Brett Farmer in this volume).
- An expansion in Thai-language academic research on queer issues, mostly among postgraduate M.A. students (Megan Sinnott in this volume). The first Thai-language sexuality studies (*phet-withi seuksa*) conference, with a considerable queer content, was held in Bangkok in January 2008.
- The emergence of Bangkok as one of the hubs of a network of East and Southeast Asian cities hosting gay circuit parties, reflecting the rapid expansion of intra-Asian gay travel networks linking Bangkok with Taipei, Hong Kong, Singapore, Kuala Lumpur, Tokyo, Manila, and Jakarta (Alex Au and Ben Murtagh in this volume).
- The establishment of a range of new gay, lesbian, transgender, and male sex-worker community groups and non-governmental organizations (NGOs) (Megan Sinnott and Douglas Sanders in this volume).
- Thailand's emergence as a major international centre for gender reassignment surgery, or GRS, and related cosmetic and medical tourism (Aren Aizura in this volume).
- The mainstreaming of LGBT rights issues on the Thai political scene. Debates about "gender/sex diversity" (*khwam-lak-lai thang-phet*) took centre stage in public consultations leading up to the revision of the Thai constitution in 2007, a process that, ironically, took place under the watch of a military-appointed government (Douglas Sanders in this volume).
- An explosion in Thai queer web sites and Internet-based LGBT networking (Ronnapoom Samakkeekarom and Pimpawun Boonmongkon in this volume).
- Regular queer-penned columns in mainstream magazines and newspapers.
- Gay radio and television programmes, the latter typically on cable rather than free-to-air stations. Nonetheless, free-to-air TV talk shows and game-show programmes now regularly include gay, *kathoey*, and *tom-dee* personalities. In the early 2000s, Thailand's first gay media organization, Cyberfish Media, was established.

The recent Thai queer boom has also had a darker dimension. In the first years of the new century there was extremely rapid growth in rates of HIV infection amongst *chai rak chai*, "men who love men", in Bangkok (van Griensven et al. 2005, 2009; Centers for Disease Control and Prevention 2006). And despite an expansion in businesses, magazines, web sites, and organizations catering to queer markets and communities, homophobic attitudes and transphobic discrimination nonetheless remain prevalent and continue to cast shadows over the lives of Thailand's queer people (Sam Winter in this volume).

Sources of Bangkok's Twenty-First-Century Queer Boom

The diverse dimensions of Bangkok's recent queer boom suggest that no single factor has been the source of the growth of queer spaces, markets, discourses, organizations, and politics. However, this convergence over a short period of time raises the question of why the LGBT scenes in one of Asia's oldest gay capitals should have boomed at the same time that public participation declined in some Western gay and lesbian scenes of a similar historical vintage. An especially noteworthy feature of Bangkok's early twenty-first-century queer boom is the fact that it took place in the context of the political instability in Thailand since the September 2006 military coup that toppled former Prime Minister Thaksin Shinawatra. Another feature has been the fact that the "international" sector of the Bangkok gay scene, that most frequented by Western gay tourists, has remained comparatively stable over the past decade. The multidimensional expansion summarized above has overwhelmingly been in sectors oriented towards Thai and other Asian queer people, and it has been mediated predominantly through the Thai language rather than through English. This means that Bangkok's recent queer boom may not have been apparent to visitors or residents who do not speak Thai or who have not had access to Thai-language-mediated circuits in the city.

Other major cities in neighbouring countries, notably Singapore, Hong Kong, Taipei, Shanghai, and Beijing, have also seen a rapid expansion in their queer scenes and cultures over the past decade (Berry et al. 2003). However, in these cases the expansion has been from a low base in countries historically regarded as having less tolerant mainstream cultures. What distinguishes Bangkok's recent queer boom from others in Asia is that there has been a major expansion in LGBT scenes that were already large and well established by both regional and international standards. Mark McLelland (2006) has described two periods of gay boom (*gei bumu*) in Japan, first in the 1950s and subsequently in the 1990s. This apparent pattern of waves of queer cultural expansion in Asia's most established modern LGBT communities provides opportunities for potentially fruitful future comparative research.

The early twenty-first-century Thai queer boom appears to have emerged from a confluence of several factors, including the opportunities provided by new electronic media; the rise of intra-Asian gay tourism; the expansion of local Thai gay and lesbian markets; the political successes of Thai queer NGOs, and the contributing role of international HIV/AIDS agencies. I expand on these factors below by drawing on the findings of this book's contributors, on my own research on Thai queer cultures and communities, and on interviews conducted with Thai gay entrepreneurs and expatriate men working in HIV/AIDS education and prevention who have detailed knowledge of LGBT life in Bangkok. The names of all interviewees have been changed.

Power of the "Purple Baht"

Targeting the Thai gay market

To set the scene, Table 1.1 provides data on the growth of the Thai economy for the years 2005, 2006, and 2007.

Table 1.1   Thai Economic Performance[3]

	2005	2006	2007
GDP Growth	4.5%	5.1%	4.8%
GDP (US$bn)	176.2	206.6	245.5
GDP per capita (US$)	2,715	3,186	3,720
Unemployment Rate	1.8%	1.5%	1.4%

While average incomes in Thailand are one-fifth to one-sixth of those in developed economies, living standards have nonetheless risen consistently since the end of World War II. The data in Table 1.1 indicate that in the years immediately before the onset of the 2008 global financial crisis, the Thai economy expanded at a constant rate of approximately five percent per annum, unemployment was low (below two percent), and, most significantly, average incomes rose at a rapid rate of 16 percent to 19 percent annually, significantly outstripping the rate of growth of the economy and reflecting significant wage gains by Thai workers throughout this period.

One of the most significant factors supporting Bangkok's queer boom has been the growth in the number of mainstream businesses that have recognized the significance of the gay and lesbian market and taken advantage of this sector's purchasing power by a combination of targeted niche marketing and crossover marketing for both women and gay men, notably in fashion magazines. In the early 2000s, the borrowed English term "metrosexual" became a code word for products and services targeted to Thailand's middle-class gay market. In the West expressions such as "the pink dollar" and "the pink pound" refer to the purchasing power and market significance of gay and lesbian consumers. In Thailand a parallel expression denoting the economic significance of queer consumers is "the purple baht". Purple (*si-muang*) is widely known as the queer colour, and the expression "purple people" (*chao si-muang*) is one commonly used expression for *kathoeys*, gay men, and lesbians collectively.

In the twentieth century, Thai gay capitalism was often an underground phenomenon, linked to a black market in illegal pornography and reflecting the need to pay off the police in order to operate. While these features have by no means disappeared, Thai gay, *kathoey*, and lesbian capitalism has increasingly become a legitimate, above-ground phenomenon. In late 2007, Johnny, the Thai owner of a chain of gay saunas in Bangkok and northeast Thailand, provided an anecdotal indication of the rapid growth in mainstream investment in the gay scene when he noted that a decade earlier, in the 1990s, almost all gay-oriented businesses in Bangkok were both gay-owned and gay-managed. He stated that, in contrast, in the early 2000s, gay businesses with non-gay owners began to appear. The owners of these businesses nonetheless relied on gay management for their day-to-day operations. However, according to Johnny, the latest boom, since early 2007, has been marked by an increasing number of gay-oriented businesses with both non-gay ownership and management (interview, 6 November 2007).

The Increasing Openness of Bangkok Gay Men

Johnny observed that one factor contributing to increased mainstream investment in Bangkok's gay market has been a rapid change in the culture of gay men in the city. He stated that gay men in Bangkok are now much less closeted than in the 1990s and that it is increasingly possible for gay men to come out to straight friends and co-workers without suffering discrimination. According to Johnny, it has become increasingly "OK to be gay" in recent years; Thai gay men have become much less concerned about being seen in public at entertainment venues that are generally known to be gay. He said that being gay is increasingly "appreciated", using a borrowed English term that in Thai means to be approved of. Another informant, Joey, editor of a gay magazine and manager of a Bangkok gay pub, agreed with this view, stating that one of the biggest cultural changes in the Bangkok gay scene in the period 2006–07 had been the increasing preparedness of Bangkok gay men, of all ages, to frequent newer gay venues that are highly visible and located close to main roads; an older generation of venues, by contrast, were often obscured from public view and located in lanes, called sois in Thai. Joey also noted that it is becoming common for Bangkok nightclubs and pubs to have a mixed clientele and no longer be exclusively gay. He stated that 80 percent of the customers at the popular new pub that he manages in Bangkok's Ratchada area were gay, but he said there were also customers of "every gender/sex" (*thuk phet*), including straight men and women, *kathoeys*, and *tom* and *dee* couples. He observed that as the market for gay and gay-friendly entertainment has grown, so, too, has the size of new venues. Bangkok's newer gay pubs are often significantly larger than the gay bars of the 1970s, 1980s, and 1990s. They also feature crossover entertainment, with locally and regionally famous straight DJs performing. As with fashion magazines, there has been a trend towards crossover marketing that targets gay men as well as gay-friendly straight women, along with these women's heterosexual boyfriends.

However, this expansion of Bangkok's LGBT markets is not simply an economic phenomenon, and to a significant extent resulted from a range of non-market factors, as well as a dramatic transformation in the socio-economic and age structures of gay consumers. I now turn to the political, cultural, technological, and transnational forces that also contributed to the rapid expansion of queer markets in early twenty-first-century Bangkok.

Political Factors: Military-Installed Government and Bangkok's Queer Boom

The populist policies of former Prime Minister Thaksin Shinawatra (2001–06), in particular his government's Social Order (*jat rabiap sangkhom*) Campaign of 2004–05, led to the closure of significant numbers of both heterosexual and gay entertainment venues because of a marked drop in patronage. The enforcement of early closing times and police raids of pubs, discos, and some gay saunas (Nikos Dacanay in this volume) so as to administer compulsory urine tests for recreational drug use, especially Ecstasy (Thai: *ya E*), among both Thai and foreign patrons led to a mid-decade slump in the entertainment industry across the country. The Social Order Campaign was motivated by anxieties about wayward youth and was a response to middle-class concerns about teenagers engaging in pre-marital sex, consuming party drugs, drinking alcohol, and staying out late at discos, karaoke bars, and pubs. Janet Jakobsen (2002) notes that "family values" may be emphasized by states as a response to the perceived undermining of the family structure by capitalism, and Thaksin's Social Order Campaign has parallels to bourgeois moral panics in other societies. Johnny, the gay entrepreneur, observed that under the Social Order Campaign police raids of gay saunas, pubs, and bars caused investors to shy away from the gay market. Joey, the gay magazine editor and pub manager, confirmed that the gay market dropped considerably during the period of the Thaksin government, with an especially sharp decline in the number of Asian gay tourists visiting

Bangkok. This coincided with rapid growth in the number of new gay venues in Singapore and Hong Kong, which provided potential gay tourists from these cities with more opportunities for socializing and entertainment at home.

However, both Johnny and Joey concurred that gay businesses in Bangkok boomed in 2007 as a direct result of the military coup in September 2006. Historically, military governments in Thailand have not restricted queer communities, and the country's LGBT cultures have continued to grow under military regimes. There are two main reasons military governments have not always been bad news for Thai gays, lesbians, and transgenders. First, homosexuality and transgenderism have not been political issues because they have not been illegal. Issues of queer gender and sexuality have been outside of, and hence not directly affected by, the field of political conflict. Second, Thai military governments since World War II have been strongly pro-capitalist and pro-market, and their members have often enriched themselves by nurturing special relationships with commercial interests. These have included semi-legal as well as technically illegal commercial activities in the entertainment industry. Thailand's commercial gay culture has at times grown on the coat tails of the much larger heterosexual sex and entertainment industries, which the military, when in power, has milked for profits.

Thailand is not unique in Asia in that queer cultures have been able to grow under authoritarian governments, even in countries such as Singapore, where male homosexuality remains technically illegal. Across Asia, authoritarian governments that are committed to market capitalism—even where, as in China and Vietnam, they remain nominally socialist—have often permitted commercial gay cultures to develop. This was the case in the Philippines under the dictatorship of Ferdinand Marcos in the 1980s, and it has been the case in Singapore and China, and to a lesser extent Malaysia and Vietnam, since the 1990s. Indeed, in many countries with authoritarian political regimes the commercial gay scene may constitute a zone of relative queer autonomy. I return to this theme in a later chapter, where I contend that the anti-capitalist, anti-commodification arguments of some queer critics in Western liberal democracies undervalue the importance of the market as a space of queer autonomy in authoritarian Asian societies.

The overthrow of the Thaksin government, and especially the end of its morally interventionist Social Order Campaign, saw the emergence of an atmosphere of increased cultural liberalization. While the military coup of 2006 was widely condemned as undemocratic both in Thailand and internationally, the interim military-appointed government and the committee assigned to revise the country's constitution proved more receptive to calls for LGBT rights than the previous, elected government. As Douglas Sanders and Serhat Ünaldi detail in this volume, the fact that the military-appointed government was not democratically elected meant that it faced a crisis of legitimacy. One response to this was the military's claim that the coup was launched, in part, to protect human rights in Thailand. To give some credence to the tenuous claim that democratic political institutions were overthrown to protect human rights, the post-coup government and its agencies sought to be seen to be promoting human rights, a situation that created opportunities for rights activists and their supporters to gain a voice in a range of fields to which they had previously been denied access. Queer rights have also been supported by some other governments in Asia in attempts to legitimate their rule. Fran Martin (2003) has described how, in the 1990s, some Taiwanese politicians, seeking to promote the international standing of their society, supported local LGBT communities because of their perception that tolerant and liberal attitudes towards queer people had become an internationally recognized marker of an open, globalized society. By detailing occasions on which Thai LGBT community representatives became active participants in mainstream processes under the military-appointed government, Douglas Sanders shows in a later chapter here how Thai queer communities took advantage of the more liberal cultural spaces that were opened up by the politically authoritarian 2006 military coup to promote their calls for legally instituted anti-discrimination legislation and other measures.

Rising Intra-Asian Gay Tourism

Another factor supporting the recent expansion of gay markets has been a rapid increase in gay tourism to Bangkok, and other Thai cities, from neighbouring Asian countries. During the first decade of this century, these countries achieved even faster economic growth than Thailand, but they often had less tolerant sexual cultures and legal systems. With the growth of a gay middle class in cities such as Singapore, Hong Kong, Taipei, Kuala Lumpur, Jakarta, and Manila, Bangkok has emerged as a popular tourist destination for increasingly well-off Asian gay men; in short, the city became a playground for middle-class gay East and Southeast Asians. This is reflected in Ben Murtagh's analysis in this volume of the Indonesian gay novel *The Beautiful Man*, whose middle-class protagonists from Jakarta feel that they are only able to develop their relationship outside of Indonesia in the sexually liberal atmosphere of Bangkok. In his chapter, Alex Au makes an even stronger point, arguing that in the 1990s Bangkok was one of the crucibles in which contemporary gay Singapore culture was forged. Au observes that many gay Singaporeans first came to know each other, and to explore their sexuality, while on vacation in Bangkok; connections made in Thailand with other holidaying Singaporeans provided a basis for the development of more open gay networks back in the city-state. Murtagh and Au thus reveal how modern gay identities in Southeast Asia have emerged from intra-Asian flows of images and bodies.

In another chapter, Aren Aizura notes that queer practices of consumption and tourism remain insufficiently theorized, particularly in relation to neocolonialism and transnationality; queer-tourism discourses most often privilege white, middle-class, affluent gay tourist practices while relegating Asian men, women, and transgenders to the status of desired objects. Alex Au and Ben Murtagh break through the Eurocentrism of many studies of queer tourism (e.g. Clift et al. 2002) by providing accounts of Southeast Asian gay men as tourists in Bangkok. Interestingly, their analyses of Singaporean and Indonesian gay men's sexual self-explorations in Bangkok indicate that similar stereotypes of Bangkok as an imagined space of sexual liberality circulate among both Asian and Western gay men. Aizura's note, following Annette Hamilton (1997), of the place of Thailand in Western literature has strong resonances with the Indonesian novel studied by Murtagh and with Au's account of Singaporean gay men's sexual awakenings in Bangkok. As Aizura puts it, English-language expatriate novels represent Thailand as a transformative space, where Bangkok's purported exoticism and strangeness present an opportunity for Euro-American protagonists to become themselves and fully express their deepest desires. Similarly, for some Asian men from less liberal sexual cultures Bangkok may be a site within which their identity as gay men can find expression and take form.

The Babylon Sauna is one focus of Nikos Dacanay's study here of Bangkok gay men's sexual networks, and he notes that even at this venue—often characterized as catering to a Western gay market—by far the majority of patrons are Thai and other Asian gay men who seek to socialize with and cruise for Asian, not Western, partners. The predominantly Asian clientele of this venue is at odds with the perceptions of many Western visitors, who mistake its international ambiance as an iconic indicator of the extent to which the Thai gay scene caters to a Western gay market. An expatriate American who has lived in Bangkok for some years observed that the originally intended market of The Babylon Sauna was Thai; the venue's popularity among Western gay men was more accidental than intended:

> The owner of The Babylon went to university in America. He was a trained architect so the design of the first Babylon was high style . . . of course the later one was even more so. The vision he had was that The Babylon should be a kind of finishing school for young professional gay Thais. He wanted to give them a working knowledge of international culture, especially the gay sensibility, so that they could then travel by

themselves to the US and Europe and know the ropes. For example, the restaurant at The Babylon served all the classic American dishes: hamburgers with french fries, southern fried chicken, pasta with al fredo sauce, New York style cheese cake, pecan pie, and so on, so that his regular clients knew what to order when they visited the US. Also the music there was often live and included a pianist playing the Scott Joplin ragtime style, or Broadway show tunes with a singer . . . so that the Thai clients would be able to be familiar with American music. Many *farangs* [Westerners] would go to The Babylon and say, 'Oh, they are making me feel at home', but that was not the real motivation. (Interview, 12 May 2009)

As already noted, the commercial gay scene in Bangkok emerged first to meet the demands of the local Thai market, and only subsequently did it become intermeshed with international gay tourism.

It is not only the opportunity to visit a gay sauna or pub that attracts gay Asian tourists to Bangkok. The growth of regional, gay circuit parties is a further indicator of the accelerating integration of gay scenes across East and Southeast Asia. Bangkok has become one centre for these regional, gay circuit parties, in part as a result of the success of the Nation dance party, organized by fridae.com in southern Thailand's resort island of Phuket in late 2005. As Alex Au observes in his chapter, fridae.com (www.fridae.com) is a commercially successful, Singapore-based gay and lesbian web portal that for several years in the early 2000s organized large gay dance parties called "Nation" on the resort island of Sentosa on Singapore's National Day public holiday, 9 August. However, in 2004 the Singapore government banned the fridae "Nation" party. As a result, in 2005 fridae went offshore and organized the "Nation" party, which had rapidly become a magnet for gay tourists from across Southeast and East Asia, in Phuket. The success of "Nation" in Phuket, which was held there again in 2006, demonstrated the viability of Thailand as a site for regional circuit parties, and other entrepreneurs have since organized semi-regular gay dance party events advertised via multilingual web sites. For example, gCircuit has organized gay dance parties in the events halls of major downtown shopping malls in Bangkok since 2007; information on its web site is presented in Thai, English, Chinese, and Japanese. The "Sparkle Party", held on 19 October 2007, advertised "DJ Victor Cheng from Taiwan", who was described as having "created the first ever monthly gay party in Taiwan called 'Paradise Party' in 1995". The advertisement continued: "He has been one of the most important DJs for Taiwan's gay and straight club scene throughout the past 10 years" (www.gcircuit.com, accessed 19 October 2007).

The Thai Queer Internet Increases Real Queer Spaces in Bangkok

The almost exponential proliferation of Thai-language queer web sites, chat rooms, web boards, and e-mail lists, along with the use of SMS texting and mobile phones, is another major phenomenon of the past decade, the scope of which has been outlined only in the most cursory of terms in research to date. While undoubtedly a central contributing factor to the recent queer boom, the dimensions of the Thai queer worlds in cyberspace remain to be explored in future research. In recent years, the Internet has increasingly superseded print media as the preferred medium of communication among younger Thai gay men. Nonetheless, the expansion of the Internet has not yet led to any decrease in print media; both print and on-line queer media have expanded in parallel over the past decade. Megan Sinnott and Ronnapoom Samakkeekarom and Pimpawun Boonmongkon here provide studies of the ways the Internet is expanding opportunities for sexual expression among both women who love women and men who love men.

Broader expansion of Bangkok's LGBT markets has also been aided by the rapid increase in Internet accessibility and a related growth of social networking web sites; many, such as Camfrog, which is studied here by Ronnapoom and Pimpawun, offer direct and uninhibited expression of gay sexuality. Dan, an American from San Francisco now providing consultancy support for HIV/AIDS education and prevention in Southeast Asia, observed:

> I think in Thailand the Internet is actually driving new 'in person' live venues. More and more Thai [gay] people know where gay venues are, what they specialize in, what big party is happening and when, mostly from the net. I am sure that 'meeting for sex' dates are also happening at high rates from the Internet, but here [in Bangkok] they have not replaced the live venues, but rather have in fact increased them. (Interview, 10 May 2007)

Alex, a Dutch HIV/AIDS educator working for an international agency in Bangkok, stated:

> Young gay people—say, under 30—predominantly use the Internet, including lower- and middle- and higher-class men, although they may use different web sites and networks. The Internet cafes have become so cheap now that lower-class men can also afford them. (Interview, 10 May 2007)

Witthaya, a medical-research technologist working with Bangkok MSM communities stated:

> The numbers of gay venues in Bangkok have increased since 2000. The Internet is also booming, lots of web boards and chat rooms, especially Camfrog. It opens more opportunities to flirt around and meet people. . . . Although the capability of owning a personal computer is not as high in Thailand as in the US or Australia, there are many net cafes that these boys can go to and log on to Camfrog. You can see them on camera and notice that they are in a net café. (Interview, 5 October 2007)

It is not only gay men who are taking advantage of the opportunities provided by the Internet. Megan Sinnott shows here that Thai women who love women are also avid users of new digital technologies. Sinnott also reveals that the Internet is leading to a reconfiguration of lesbian identity categories that emerged in the era of print media in the twentieth century. Interactive digital media provide opportunities for novel explorations of desire, which, in turn, are shifting the terrain of the queer cultural landscape and producing a high degree of fluidity in popular queer discourses.

It may seem counterintuitive that the growth of on-line queer networking has led to more face-to-face networking and that queer virtual spaces have supported the proliferation of real spaces and venues in Bangkok. One suggested reason for the decline of older gay ghettoes in some Western cities is that the increasing use of Internet social networking sites has permitted gay men and lesbians to socialize and cruise for sexual and romantic partners on-line rather than in bars and sex venues. If that is the case, why should the rapid growth of on-line networking among Thai gay men and lesbians have had the opposite effect of supporting an expansion in the number of pubs and saunas in Bangkok? The answer, perhaps, lies in the different socio-economic situations of Western and Thai gay web users and the different nature of the relationship that Western and Thai gay men have with their families.

Significant numbers of Western gay men and lesbians have the economic means to rent or buy their own homes or apartments, or to share with other queer-friendly people. Many Western gay men and lesbians also have somewhat fraught relationships with their families and leave home to have the freedom to develop an independent homosexual lifestyle. In contrast, many of the working-class Thai gay men who now have access to on-line dating and cruising web sites such as Camfrog in cheap Internet cafes do not have the means to live independently and often share rooms with a number of other people, typically relatives or co-workers. Even adult middle-class gay men who can afford to live by themselves often remain at home because of the strength of cultural expectations that unmarried children should continue to provide financial and immediate social support for aging parents. Traditionally, unmarried daughters fulfilled this role of parental support, as cultural expectations meant that young men either married and established their own separate households or entered the Buddhist monkhood. However, since the 1970s and 1980s, increasing numbers of Thai gay men have resisted the expectation to marry. Attitudes as to whether gay men should marry have also changed dramatically in Thailand over the past thirty years. In the 1970s and 1980s, "agony aunt" and "agony uncle" columnists in newspapers and popular magazines typically advised gay male correspondents to marry to fulfil heteronormative social expectations and to seek out gay sex on the side, such as with a male sex worker (Jackson 1995). However, since the 1990s, Thai women have become increasingly vocal about the problems that arise from an often loveless and sexless marriage with a gay man. The theme of avoiding the trap of marrying a gay man has become an often repeated refrain in Thai women's magazines and was the focus of a successful 2006 movie, *Metrosexual* (directed by Youngyooth Thongkonthun), whose much more evocative Thai title, *kaeng chani kap ee-aep*, uses Thai gay idioms and translates as "The girl gang and the closet queen". In this comedy, a group of Bangkok career women suspect that the fiancé of one of their friends is gay and, with the intention of helping her avoid the fate of marrying a "closet queen" (*ee-aep*), enlist the help of a gay friend to determine whether the man is a straight "metrosexual" or a closeted gay man. The movie concludes with the man discovering his homosexuality, finding a boyfriend, and leaving the woman to seek out a compatible romantic and sexual relationship with a "real man" (*phu-chai thae*). As fewer Thai gay men marry, and as the average number of children in Thai families has decreased from six or seven a generation ago to just one or two today, it is now increasingly the case that it is unmarried adult gay children, not only unmarried daughters, who take on the filial duty of caring for aging parents.

It is not only filial expectations that keep many adult Thai gay men at home. In comparing representations of homosexuality in modern Australian and Thai novels, Isaraporn Pissa-ard observes:

> [F]or most Thai homosexuals, being ostracised by one's parents or leaving one's biological family in order to pursue one's sexuality are both highly undesirable because the ability to fulfil family obligations is highly crucial to one's self-worth. . . . Thus, the Anglo-American model of gay identity which advocates the quest for an alternative family to replace biological family can be problematic in a Thai context. Interestingly, while admitting that family can be a great source of oppression for a large number of homosexual and transsexual males, many of them unfailingly struggle to find a space for homosexuality or transgenderism within a family through the ability to take care of or support elderly parents or other close relatives. In many cases, the

ability to perform filial duties well and support family members can be a way in which homosexuality and transgenderism are rendered unproblematic. . . . Thus, unlike the Western model of gayness, which largely separates gayness from family and relies on alternative community as a means to find a space for gayness or normalise it, in Thailand blood family is crucial to gay and transgender males' negotiation for recognition and acceptance. (2009, 257–258)

Isaraporn's account contrasts with Western narratives of the emergence of gay identity as requiring a break with the heteronormative expectations of families. In critically assessing the work of John D'Emilio, Miranda Joseph observes that his account of gay identity formation involves, "the liberation of individuals from their kinship structures when they moved to urban centres created by/for capitalist production" (2002, 88). Ann Pellegrini similarly notes, D'Emilio "produces a homosexual coming-out narrative that seems to require a coming out of family. . . . [H]e implies that leaving family behind is a non-negotiable condition of gay identity" (2002, 139). Rather than being formed in isolation from the family, Isaraporn presents a model of Thai gay identity as being formed through a negotiation of familial expectations in which the autonomy to live a non-heteronormative life is legitimized by a demonstrated capacity to care for one's parents. This may not necessarily be felt as a burden; for Thai gay men, pride in the self derives in part from their capacity to care for their family members. Serhat Ünaldi and Brett Farmer both note in this volume that this theme of gay identity emerging in the context of family life recurs in Thai queer cinema. However, Ünaldi notes that in contrast to gay men, *kathoeys* are more commonly represented in Thai films as forging lives and identities separately from their families.

The mix of factors outlined above means that both working-class and middle-class Thai gay men may lack the independent living arrangements that most gay men in the West take for granted. While Thai gay men of all social strata now have access to web-based social networking sites, they may not have access to a private home space in which to meet a partner whom they have met on-line. In this situation, gay men may need to meet their on-line date at a gay venue to pursue a romantic or sexual relationship. That is, the boom in on-line gay cruising and dating has produced a demand for more gay-friendly private locations in which to meet. The distinctive socio-economic and cultural settings of both working-class and middle-class gay life in twenty-first-century Bangkok mean that the expansion of Thai gay worlds into virtual domains has been a driving force for a parallel expansion in real gay spaces. This situation offers an example of the way that one of the driving forces of cultural globalization— the despatializing interconnectivity made possible by the Internet—may have dramatically different impacts in different gay scenes around the world. Rather than leading to a transnational homogenization of gay cultures operating in lock-step with presumed Euro-American standards, at the beginning of the twenty-first century the expansion of Internet access has produced significantly different outcomes in the gay scenes of Bangkok when compared with those in many Western cities.

A New Mass Market for Thai Gayness

Cut price gay culture for the masses

Boellstorff notes that given the central place of capitalism in the emergence of modern Southeast Asian queer cultures and identities, their values and perceptions are strongly linked with the sensibilities of the iconic representatives of capitalism, namely, the middle classes:

> Across Southeast Asia, the rise of a substantial middle class seems to have played an important role in the formation of gay, lesbian, tomboy, and femme subject positions. Even for those who are poor, a middle class sensibility shaped by consumerism and advertising appears to have had a significant effect upon senses of sexual selfhood. (2007, 210)

Since its inception in Bangkok in the 1960s, Thai gayness (*khwam-pen-gay*) has indeed had a middle-class caché of modernity, fashionability, and consumerist lifestyle. Thailand's first gay boom, from the late 1970s to the early 1990s, during which the first gay bars, magazines, and saunas were established, paralleled the rise of the economy out of post-World War II doldrums and the rapid expansion in the size, wealth, and influence of the Thai middle class. Yet despite this middle-class caché, not all Asian gay men come from educated or wealthy backgrounds. As Boellstorff observes, "In reality, gay men can come from any socio-economic level, and since most Southeast Asians are not rich, it should not be surprising that few gay Southeast Asians are wealthy either" (2007, 198). Nonetheless, one needs a disposable income to live the Thai gay dream of an autonomous homosexual lifestyle. Thailand has a much bigger gap between rich and poor sectors of the population than many other countries in the region. While, overall, Thailand is wealthier than Indonesia or the Philippines, the extent of inequality between the incomes of the top and bottom sectors of the population, as measured econometrically by the Gini Index, is significantly greater in Thailand than among its Southeast Asian neighbours.[4]

The above discussion might seem to suggest that, as market-mediated phenomena, the expansion of queer identities and cultures will be restricted by a society's level of economic development and by the distribution of national wealth across the population. However, economic growth and redistribution are not the only avenues to expanding opportunities to be gay, *tom*, *dee* or *kathoey*. New market practices and efficiencies can make commodified sex cultural forms such as gayness more affordable, and hence more widely available, even in the absence of significant economic growth or a redistribution of wealth from rich to poor. In certain circumstances the number of gay consumers can increase even in a relatively stable economy and without new redistribution policies. This seems to have happened in Bangkok in the first years of the twenty-first century.

The rapid increase in the number of gay venues in recent years has led to increasing competition among venue owners, which, in turn, has led to lower entry prices, especially in suburban gay saunas and clubs. This has meant that gay entertainment has become much more affordable for lower-income men, as well as for middle-class high school students and teenagers. In other words, a new market for the Thai gay lifestyle has opened up among middle-class gay teenagers and adults in lower socio-economic strata; a cut-price version of the originally middle-class Thai gay identity has thus become available to the masses. Johnny was one of the first gay entrepreneurs to start the trend to lower entry prices to gay venues. A decade ago, the first generation of Bangkok gay saunas, such as The Babylon, Obelisk, Chakran, and Colony, all had entry prices of around 200 baht, which at the time was equivalent to the income that manual labourers would earn for two or more days' work. When he opened his first sauna in Bangkok's eastern suburbs in 1999, Johnny charged an entry fee of 99 baht. The initial arrangement in the changing rooms, which included five hundred lockers, proved inadequate to cope with demand, and Johnny subsequently increased the number of lockers to a thousand, but he said that queues still formed, especially on weekends. In an interview, Johnny laughingly confessed that he was "to blame" for the recent rapid growth in the number of saunas, as the low entry price at his venue had led to a large increase in sauna attendance in Bangkok and also to a subsequent proliferation of similarly priced gay saunas across the city. The Internet has also permitted groups previously excluded from the bourgeois, middle-class nature of twentieth-century Thai gay culture to participate in a cut-price form of gay life. Both middle-class teenagers and working-class men have been brought into the Thai gay world because of the ubiquity of Internet access in middle-class homes and in cheap Internet cafes across Bangkok and in most regional centres.

Competitive market practices in the Thai gay scene, together with the spread of information on gay venues via the Internet, have opened formerly elite and middle-class lifestyles to the city's gay masses and gay youth in a cut-price form. A comparison can be made with the impact of low-cost carriers on the airline industry. In many Western societies in the 1990s and early 2000s, the discounted airfares of low-cost airlines led to a rapid increase in the numbers of people flying; with the rate of increase in numbers of airline passengers exceeding the growth rate of the rest of the economy in these countries. In a similar way, the arrival of low-cost gay service providers in Bangkok has opened up the formerly middle-class gay lifestyle to a mass market of lower-income gay consumers. Over the past decade, Bangkok's gay spaces have expanded at a much faster rate than the overall Thai economy, and the Bangkok gay scene is now somewhat like the international airline industry. On the one hand, established, more expensive "full service" venues cater to one market sector, while, on the other hand, lower-cost venues cater to other market sectors. Nikos Dacanay, in a later chapter, details the distinctive, class-based sexual cultures that have emerged in Bangkok's high-end and cut-price gay saunas, respectively. Established, more expensive forms of gay entertainment have not died out; rather, they have been augmented by low-cost imitators.

Bangkok's first queer boom in the 1980s was one dimension of the emergence of the Thailand's middle class. The city's second queer boom, in the early 2000s, has in part resulted from the massification of this originally middle-class gay culture. The newer, low-cost, mass-market gay spaces are mostly on the city's periphery, away from the established and still comparatively expensive downtown gay scene. This massification is also reflected in the marketing of gay, *kathoey*, and lesbian autobiographies and pulp fiction nationwide by the 7-Eleven chain of convenience stores, which have become a ubiquitous feature of suburban and regional urban centres over the past decade. The awareness that gay youth now constitute a significant social sector, and a new market, has also infiltrated popular culture. As Brett Farmer details here, the 2007 film *Love of Siam* dealt with the romance of two middle-class teenage boys in Bangkok.

Political Successes of Thai LGBT Activism

Beyond the economic changes and market-based developments outlined above, early twenty-first-century queer Bangkok has also been marked by a growing mood of collective self-confidence and of social and political presence. The boom of the early 2000s also reflected the fact that the two decades of LGBT activism that started in the late 1980s began to produce concrete results during this period. As noted above, under the military-appointed government installed after the September 2006 coup, gay, lesbian, and transgender individuals and organizations achieved greater recognition and social and political legitimacy. In the twentieth century, Thailand was a queer-tolerant but not queer-accepting society (Jackson 1999a), with limited queer activism and no institutionalization of LGBT rights. The early twenty-first century has seen rapid growth in queer activism on rights issues and the beginnings of recognition in law and by state agencies. Johnny cited the liberalization of both official and general public attitudes to gays, lesbians, and *kathoey*s as a key factor in the rapid expansion in the number of gay-oriented businesses in Bangkok since 2006. This is reflected in the serious consideration LGBT rights issues are now given in a range of public and official contexts. As an example, Johnny noted that the Rainbow Sky Association of Thailand, a prominent NGO concerned with LGBT issues, had been invited by the Election Commission of Thailand to send a representative to sit on a sub-committee monitoring the conduct of the national election held on 23 December 2007.

These advances have been achieved as a result of a greater and more coordinated degree of LGBT organizational development compared with earlier decades. While the dramatic rise in HIV infections among Bangkok MSM in recent years constitutes a health emergency, it has nonetheless led to a growth in both international and Thai government support for LGBT organizations, which, in turn, have proved increasingly effective in voicing broader queer-community interests. It is no longer the case, as it was in the twentieth century, that Thailand lacks LGBT movements. Thai queers are no longer silent or invisible; rather, they are increasingly vocal and highly visible participants in the country's dynamic civil society.

From Social Outcasts to National Icons

Kathoeys *as queer cultural warriors*

The growing numbers of entertainment venues, magazines, and other services that cater to gay men reflect the significant numbers of masculine-identified men in Bangkok who seek out other men as sexual and romantic partners. Nevertheless, it is the transgender *kathoey* who continues to dominate public imaging and representations of queer Thailand, both internationally and inside the country. More than gay men or lesbians, the *kathoey* is the iconic face of queer Thailand. Brett Farmer and Serhat Ünaldi note in their respective chapters here that the stereotype of the tragicomic *kathoey*—as an ugly, cross-dressing buffoon perpetually doomed to lose out to "real women" (*phu-ying thae*) in romantic contests for the heart of a man—has been a staple of Thai cinema and TV since the 1980s. In his chapter, Sam Winter deconstructs the myth of Thailand as accepting of transgender people, revealing the persistent discrimination that *kathoeys* suffer in everyday life, despite their iconic role in both local and international representations of the country as a supposed home of sexual tolerance.

However, *kathoeys* are far from being passive victims who suffer their second-class status in silence. Of all Thailand's queer communities, *kathoeys* are the most vocal in claiming the right "to be themselves" and in demanding recognition of their distinctive gender status. While Thai cinema and TV perpetuate images of an ugly "fake woman" (*phu-ying thiam*), large numbers of *kathoeys* spend considerable time and money drawing on medical technologies and cosmetics to realize their ideal of feminine beauty. Indeed, while prepared to laugh at comedic stereotypes of *kathoeys* in movies and on TV, the Thai populace is also fascinated, even entranced, by *kathoeys* who are able to embody cultural norms of beauty. Stéphane Rennesson here details the Thai public's fascination with the transgender kickboxing sensation *Norng* Tum, who excelled in the hypermasculine sport of Muay Thai and used prizefight winnings to fund gender reassignment surgery. Since the late 1990s, annual beauty contests staged by nationally and internationally known transgender revues, such as Tiffany and Alcazar in Pattaya and Calypso in Bangkok, have been broadcast on national TV. Like the forms of feminine beauty to which they pay homage, Thailand's transgender beauty contests are a thoroughly modern phenomenon and their proliferation and growing mediatization on national TV over the past decade represent yet another dimension of Bangkok's recent queer boom. These national-level transgender beauty contests—and a host of smaller-scale events staged across Thailand as integral parts of local and regional festivals—reflect a form of cultural activism by *kathoeys* in which they collectively challenge the demeaning stereotypes that still dominate other fields of Thai popular culture. While arguably reflecting a subjection to commodified notions of feminine beauty, the money, time, and effort that many *kathoeys* invest to participate in these events nonetheless also reflect a claim for recognition and status in a beauty-obsessed society (Van Esterik 2000). Thailand's *kathoeys* have skilfully manipulated the country's mass media to promote positive images of their claimed feminine status and to achieve an increasingly recognized place in Thai society.

In a later chapter, Aren Aizura looks behind the public spectacle of *kathoeys*' performance of feminine beauty to study the financial and racial dynamics of gender reassignment surgery, or GRS, in Thailand. Unfortunately, there are no accurate statistics on either the number of GRS procedures performed each year in Thailand or the number of clinics offering the procedure. However, since the 1990s, Thailand has become one of the global centres of GRS and a major destination for Western and other transwomen seeking surgical interventions to align their physiology with their feminine gender identity. Thailand's emergence as a global centre for cosmetic surgery of all forms, including GRS, represents yet another dimension of the multi-sectoral queer boom of the past decade. As Aizura describes in detail, this boom has not always been good news for Thai *kathoeys*, as the internationalization of GRS has led to an increase in the price of the procedure and a movement of medical skill and resources towards catering to wealthier foreign clients, leaving many Thai transwomen to receive poorer quality procedures and a low level of post-operative care. The health implications of this lower standard of medical support for Thai transwomen undergoing GRS is an understudied issue in need of urgent investigation.

As I have argued elsewhere (Jackson 2009a), Thailand's modern queer cultures emerged predominantly through local processes of capitalist transformation and cultural self-modernization, subsequently coming into contact with and becoming intermeshed with similar phenomena in the West and other parts of Asia. Aizura cites Ara Wilson in confirming this pattern in his account of the historical development of GRS in Thailand:

> The development of Thai gender reassignment technologies as a market also predates the larger medical tourism industry by a number of years. Indeed, it is possible to regard gender reassignment surgery as the earliest medical tourism niche market in Thailand and a precursor to, or model for, the later development of medical tourism in Thailand generally. (Wilson, forthcoming)

While Thai transwomen use feminizing hormones, surgery, and cosmetics to embody femininity, not all seek to become indistinguishable from natal women. Many Thai *kathoeys* are proud of their capacity to embody and enact feminine beauty while retaining a sense of their distinctiveness as a "third gender/sex" (*phet thi-sam*). Indeed, in recent years some prominent transwomen have literally fought against men to achieve public recognition as a distinctive type of gendered being. *Nong* Tum, the Muay Thai kickboxer, reflects the pugnacious individual activism of many *kathoeys*, who are increasingly prepared to confront masculinist norms publicly and to break out of cultural stereotypes. While Thai lesbians have been the most active in engaging the state to seek to institutionalize queer rights (see the chapters here by Megan Sinnott and Douglas Sanders), and Thai gay men have been the most successful in exploiting the opportunities presented by capitalism to carve out commodified spaces of queer autonomy, *kathoeys* have arguably distinguished themselves as Thailand's most prominent queer cultural warriors, actively challenging norms of both masculinity and femininity.

Conclusions

Recent advances do not mean that Thailand's queer communities are fully accepted members of Thai society who enjoy rights and recognition equal to the rights and recognition enjoyed by heterosexuals. Far from it, as Douglas Sanders notes here, despite gaining a voice in some human-rights and political forums and achieving some victories in challenging heteronormative policies in the bureaucracy, much remains to be achieved to enshrine LGBT rights legally in Thailand. And as Sam Winter details in his chapter, while the transgender *kathoey* may have become an iconic symbol of modern Thai cultural liberality, the country's transgender and transsexual people continue to suffer from systematic institutional discrimination and cultural transphobia. Indeed, a factor in the rise in HIV infections among Bangkok gay men over the past decade has been discriminatory official attitudes, with the consequence that gay men have been less well-served by government prevention interventions than other at-risk groups. This is the case not only in Thailand. As noted by one international agency in 2008, "Globally, men who have sex with men are 19 times more likely to be infected with HIV than the general population".[5]

Researchers face significant methodological challenges in fully mapping the contours of the multidimensional growth of Thai queer worlds in the first years of the twenty-first century. We also face analytical challenges in interpreting the relative importance of different causal factors and in evaluating the consequences of this intersecting mosaic of phenomena for our understandings of queer cultural globalization. Here I offer some preliminary conclusions.

Market processes and socio-economic development remain central influences on the growth of queer communities. However, there is no simple relationship between economic growth and the expansion of Asian queer worlds. Restrictive political policies, such as populist responses to perceived moral panics about wayward youth, may dramatically affect the behaviour of both gay "consumers" and the confidence of investors, leading to a decline in the gay market sector even when the rest of the economy may be experiencing solid growth. Conversely, a liberalization of cultural policies may instil confidence in the market sectors directly relevant to gay men, leading to an expansion in the commercial gay scene that exceeds the growth rate of the rest of the economy. Furthermore, in the complex political economy of modern queer worlds, there is no immediately apparent relationship between the nominal political stripe of an Asian government—whether it is democratically elected or military installed, socialist or neoliberal capitalist—and the nature or impact of its policies regarding queer people. Under authoritarian political regimes—whether they are termed "socialist" as in China and Vietnam, "military" as in Thailand, or "democratic" as in Singapore—the commodified spaces of commercial gay scenes may provide zones of genuine queer autonomy.

In the first decade of the twenty-first century, an especially notable transnational phenomenon has been the emergence of an East–Southeast

Asian regional network of queer cultures. While connections with Western gay cultures have not declined in absolute terms when compared with earlier decades, the great expansion in regional gay tourism and intra-Asia gay flows means that, in relative terms, Western queer worlds now have a diminished role in Bangkok. The economic rise of Asia has meant a relative decline in the significance of influences from the West, with the result that Bangkok's queer worlds have become more Asian and less Western over the past decade. The spectre of a supposed homogenizing Americanization of Asian queer worlds as the cultural outcome of global queering has been revealed to be a phantom of mistaken twentieth-century imaginings.

Queer political activism in Asia has a genuine capacity to change public attitudes, to institutionalize queer-friendly bureaucratic procedures, and to see the enactment of legal measures that provide a basis for guaranteeing equality of opportunity and freedom from discrimination. However, queer political activism may achieve these successes under both authoritarian and democratic governments. While the emergence of modern queer worlds seems to require a civil society that is at least partially autonomous, a relative degree of press and media freedom, and a market unfettered by moralistic interventions, there is no direct relationship between Western-styled political democracy and the growth of new LGBT cultures and communities in Asia. Democratically elected governments that respond to moral panics may institute conservative anti-queer policies, while unelected governments seeking to construct an image of legitimacy may court LGBT support. Thai queer activists have achieved some degree of success by avoiding direct association with, or support for, any individual political player or form of government. This continued to be the case in the confrontations, at times violent, initiated by yellow-shirted opponents and red-shirted supporters of ousted Prime Minister Thaksin Shinawatra in 2008, 2009, and 2010. In the closing years of the decade, LGBT activism took a back seat to the much larger and at times bloody political contests that polarized Thai society.

In Thailand's highly volatile and unpredictable political environment, where the fortunes of any given politician or political party may change overnight, LGBT activists have advanced their cause by carefully avoiding tying their rainbow flag to the mast of any political grouping. Instead, significant effort has been put into building strategic alliances with queer-friendly media figures, reporters, and bureaucrats, with the last at times able to maintain comparatively stable policies and administrative arrangements in government agencies despite almost constant and polemically intense political instability.

The view that Thailand has lacked LGBT "political" activism until relatively recently in part emerges from a Eurocentric misperception of what constitutes queer politics. Given the long history of political instability in Thailand, Thai queers have put considerably more energy into lobbying the bureaucracy and counteracting negative media stereotyping than in lobbying politicians, whether they be elected members of parliament or military appointees. When Thai LGBT activism is seen in terms of the fields of local power that are most immediately amenable to the influence of Thai queers, rather than through Western conceptions that equate queer politics with engaging legislatures and changing legal statutes, Thailand is revealed as having a considerable history of queer engagement with and resistance to the forms of institutional power that have negatively affected the lives of lesbians, *kathoeys*, and gay men. In this, Thai queer NGOs present a microcosm of the much larger development of extra-governmental civil society organizations and movements in Thailand over the past two decades. When governments have been paralyzed or, as so often, in crisis, progressive social movements have turned to the mass media, the Internet, and sympathetic scholars, public intellectuals, and bureaucrats to build coalitions that have at times achieved real successes—despite, and not because of, governments.

The studies in the following chapters reflect the dramatic impacts of intensifying capitalist penetration, growing cross-border human movements, accelerating Internet-based communications, and expanding access to visual media in providing a collective impetus for the expansion of Bangkok's queer cultures and communities. This expansion has not made queer Bangkok a mirror image of queer New York, queer Sydney, or any other Western LGBT world. In the early twenty-first century, global queering in Bangkok has produced new forms of queer cultural difference at the same time that it has further integrated Thailand and its queer peoples into an expanded network of exchanges with the LGBT cultures of both Asia and the West. The forces that are changing the face of twenty-first-century Asian queer capitals such as Bangkok are at times producing unexpected and, in terms of the last century's understandings, counterintuitive results. The scale of early twenty-first-century Bangkok's queer boom are as challenging to the West-centred notions that dominated twentieth-century queer studies as the statistics of Asia's twenty-first-century economic growth challenge the last century's notions of Western global hegemony. Twenty-first-century Asian queer identities, cultures, and communities continue to be marked by the production of diversity and the sign of difference. It is perhaps in this fundamental process of queering—the displacing and refracting of local heteronormative expectations—that we should look for common links among LGBT people across borders, not in the presence or absence of any specific signifier such as "gay", "lesbian", or "queer".

Figure 1 Cover of January 2010 issue of *Max Magazine*, a free bilingual Thai-English magazine distributed from gay entertainment venues in Bangkok, featuring the "Coyote Boys" dance troupe, which performs at gay venues in the city's new Ratchada entertainment district. As Peter Jackson details here, since the 2006 military coup that ousted former Prime Minister Thaksin Shinawatra, Bangkok gay venues have increased in number and opened in several new areas of the city. (Source: Maxima Presentation)

Figure 2 Cover of February 2010 issue of *Thai Puan,* a free bilingual Thai-English magazine distributed from Bangkok gay venues and featuring a selection of previous issue covers. *Thai Puan* is one of half-a-dozen new free magazines oriented at Bangkok's increasingly well-healed gay men that began publication in the early 2000s, a period during which the city's gay market expanded rapidly.

2

Competing Cultures of Masculinity
When Thai Transgender Bodies Go Through Muay Thai

Stéphane Rennesson

In this chapter I consider the factors that have led to the national success of a number of male-to-female (m-t-f) transvestite *kathoey* Muay Thai boxers in Thailand. This is to a large extent a preliminary study, and I present a range of perspectives that stand as guidelines to be followed in future research on this topic. My data here come chiefly from ethnographic fieldwork on Thai kickboxing, or Muay Thai, carried out from 1999 to 2001 in the development of a Ph.D. thesis in anthropology (Rennesson 2005).[1]

Muay Thai can be defined as a truly gendered activity that places a strong emphasis on masculine behaviour. Peter Vail (1998) sees Muay Thai as one of the wombs of hypermasculinity, along with the monkhood and the status of a *nakleng* (an influential man, to put it succinctly), two other alternative masculine roles (1998, 320–328). Pattana Kitiarsa sees in Muay Thai a "true game of true men", as "manhood is judged by victorious conquests over opponents through physical superiority, cunning, wit, mental strength and prowess" (2005, 67). Given this, I wish to consider the apparently paradoxical success of two cross-dressing boxers, *Norng* Tum and his emulator, *Norng* Tim, who has not become as famous as the former. I draw on recent developments in gender analysis in Thailand that are embedded within contemporary critical theory. Peter Jackson (2003a), for instance, shows how the performative norms of masculine and feminine gendering have been altered and emphasized by the Thai state since the middle of the nineteenth century as part of a process that needs to be conceived as a self-civilizing response to the critiques of European colonial powers in Southeast Asia. For these powers, the androgyny of the premodern Siamese population was taken to be a sign of the country's semi-barbarous backwardness. According to Jackson (2003a), we have to acknowledge the human body in the Thai context as marked by gender behavioural performative norms. Furthermore, Bernard Formoso (1987, 2001) has shown how Thais, especially from the Lao-speaking northeast region of Isan, think of different social groups at every level as following metaphors of the human body. This analysis provides a tool of discrimination to think through the boundaries of social and cultural bodies. What should also be mentioned here is the great importance of the human body as a means for Thais to manage their relations to foreigners.

Drawing on these lines of research, I shall explore here the hypothesis that the intense mediatization of *Norng* Tum, and particularly its resonances among the broader Thai population, is related to the self-civilizing management of Thai bodies both within Thailand but also, and primarily, at the international level.[2] The broad context of my study is the enthusiasm of Thais for *kathoey* kickboxers in the context of the emphasis that local media put on the coverage of male boxing programmes. The question here is: In what particular ways do cross-dressing boxers bring something special with their bodies into such a masculine-oriented discipline as Muay Thai?

First, I present some biographical features of the two cross-dressing boxers: Aphinya So Phumrin, who is usually called by his nickname, *Norng* Tim, or "Young Tim" (and whose real name is Songrit Homwan), and Parinya Kiatbusaba, whose real name is Parinya Jaroenphol and who is generally known in Thailand by his nickname, *Norng* Tum, or "Young Tum". The former appeared in the media for a short period in 2004, when he fought victoriously against an American boxer at the Lumphini Stadium in Bangkok, and is generally acknowledged to be a simple emulator of the latter. [3] *Norng* Tum is much more famous. He fought Muay Thai bouts, with a male body, from 1994, when he was just twelve years old. His image became omnipresent in the national media from February 1998, when he fought for the first time in Bangkok at Lumphini Stadium,[4] until early 2000, just after he had undergone gender reassignment surgery in December 1999[5] that forced him out of the Muay Thai ring. As a woman, she came back for a few "freak" fighting exhibitions against female wrestlers and boxers in Thailand and in Japan until 2006. She then challenged a male Muay Thai boxer.[6] We do not know what happened to *Norng* Tim after his brief breakthrough in 2004, but the whole country still gets regular news about his elder. No Thai is unaware of the fact that, in her new female persona, *Norng* Tum is nowadays trying to make her way as an entertainer in show business and has also become a commercial agent for Fairtex, a health complex that combines a sports and tennis club with a luxury boutique hotel, a spa, and a dedicated Muay Thai training camp. *Norng* Tum's national, if not international, success was captured in a 2003 film called *Beautiful Boxer*, directed by Ekachai Uekrongtham, which delineated *Norng* Tum's biography. (See also Serhat Ünaldi's analysis of this movie in this volume.) The movie emphasized the reasons a young boy from a northern Thai village, who realizes his feminine identity during a stay at a Buddhist monastery, decides to become a boxer. The story as presented informs us about two main motives. First, *Norng* Tum sees apprenticeship in Muay Thai as a means to defend himself against his male peers, who tease and bully him because of his effeminate behaviour as a *kathoey*. This word is used to refer to effeminate men and male-to-female transvestites or transsexuals, who, from a Thai perspective, are often regarded as a "second kind of woman" (*phu-ying praphet sorng*). Second, and as *Norng* Tum made it widely known through the media during his short career, boxing was a way to earn the money necessary to undergo gender reassignment surgery to make "his body and heart go in the same direction" (*rang-kai kap hua-jai pai thit-thang diao-kan*).

As young country boys reared in impoverished families of Northern Thailand, both *Norng* Tum and *Norng* Tim epitomize the sociological forces at work behind every boxing career in the country. Prizefighting enables Thai boxers, most of whom come from poor backgrounds, to repay their parents for having raised them by earning money to help their families step out of the low socio-economic status that is characteristic of most rural peasants. Nonetheless, *Norng* Tum and *Norng* Tim's filial debts were peculiar, since being a *kathoey* is sometimes regarded as bestowing "demerit" (*bap*) upon parents; according to customary beliefs, children, especially boys through their ordination as Buddhist monks, are supposed to give their parents religious merit (*bun*). Hence, the quests of both *Norng* Tum and *Norng* Tim to achieve an ultimate feminine self-transformation by means of the hypermasculine path of Muay Thai prizefighting takes on a unique quality.

As others (Jackson, 2003a; Van Esterik, 1999) have explained, performative gender roles rely much on the body, notably its control in the course of everyday life. According to these studies, self-definition is essentially body-based in Thailand, and drawing on this dynamic perspective of the embodied and gendered Thai personal identity, one can consider Muay Thai to be a supreme form of bodily discipline and somatic control. Following Vail and Pattana's analyses, there is no question that Muay Thai provides young boys with an embodied curriculum in Thai manhood. The development of a strong, manly physique, the mastering of one's strength and of violence, and learning to be self-reliant are among the Muay Thai skills that lead to the mastering of manhood. Boxing furthermore concerns the maintenance of one's "boxing form" (*rup muay*), a criterion that informs the appreciation of bouts and of individual pugilists' abilities. The boxers are not supposed to express their feelings, sensations of pain, or fatigue; they should remain "indifferent" (*choey*) throughout matches. Muay Thai also carries moral values such as courage, tenacity, and self-composure, all of which refer to the ethical principles of a dominant Buddhist ideology.

These values, which constitute goals and tools during the socializing process of boxers in Muay Thai training camps, are closely linked to the Buddhist ideals of overcoming oneself in the spiritual search for "detachment" (Pali: *upekkha;* Thai: *khwam-choey*). Throughout training sessions and while in the ring, boxers have to be "courageous" (*jai-kla*) and refrain from expressing emotion as they endure terrible physical suffering. The work on the body, especially its comportment and presentation, that Muay Thai requires makes it a suitable tool to reveal oneself, or by "subsuming" oneself in the Buddhist way of thinking, and to live in accord with one's "destiny" (*kam*).

Moreover, in training camps young men experience a great variety of interactions following the double pattern of both equals or peers (*pheuan*, "friend") and the hierarchical relationships that structure Thai society (Formoso, 1994). Professional pugilists are first engaged in stable, dyadic relations with their trainers and promoters; these involve reciprocal moral obligations, as the former have to obey and respect the latter in exchange for protection and education. According to a common pattern of social organization in Thailand, boxers are enmeshed in hierarchical networks centred in and oriented towards Bangkok, where one finds the most prestigious camps and stadiums and the most influential promoters. In addition, an important part of the training is relegated to the more fluid and ambiguous relationships between equals in the world of Muay Thai, as two boxers can fight professionally and publicly only when their weights and levels of achievement are similar. Interactions among equals are organized on an axis of tension comprising competition and cooperation. This balance is to be negotiated when sparring during training and when fighting in the ring. Accomplished boxers know better than anyone what it means to be equals. This point applies to both those who are intimate—that is, those within a boxer's camp and in the same network and whom he will not be able to fight—and also those who are not intimate and who belong to other networks and whom a boxer is predisposed to fight in the ring. As Muay Thai capitalizes on the ambiguity of physical violence, the entirety of the professional boxing device acts as a genuine educational institution. The camps provide boxers with an alternative meritocratic way to social advancement separate from the monkhood and school-based education.

Putting an individual to the test through rough physical experience is related to a man's performative role, which makes boxers hypermasculine males, even though Muay Thai as practised by women has developed significantly over the past decade. From this point of view, while *Norng* Tum and *Norng* Tim began their careers in male bodies, in the Thai idiom these physical "housing bodies" (*reuan kai*) possess the hearts of women. This incongruity echoes the fact that many *kathoeys* in the countryside, to judge by those I met during my fieldwork in Isan, often have a stronger masculine body build than the typical Thai rural-dweller. At the same time, and again accoassociationrding to people in the Isan rural areas that I know the best (the provinces of Khon Kaen, Mahasarakham, Kalasin, and Roi-Et), think that *kathoeys* can in some way compete with men in terms of physical force as much as they can compete with women sexually for male partners. Without searching for causal explanations, which has not been my purpose, one can assume that the biographies of some up-country *kathoeys*, conceived as long-term processes of interaction with one's environment, both social and natural, bring the discrepancy between "physical appearance" (*hun phai-nork*) and "interior" (*phai-nai*) reality to its height. From this perspective it is quite interesting to investigate the case of *Norng* Tum, whose hardship during training and in the ring is widely understood in Thailand as having been his/her chosen path towards the future attainment of a woman's body.

Strangely enough, neither *Norng* Tum nor *Norng* Tim is directly associated with either of the two categories of boxing styles, described below, by which Muay Thai aficionados traditionally assess Thai boxing practice. A difficulty in classifying boxing styles is not restricted to these two boxers, but the question nonetheless brings us to a sharp contrast between these two transgender boxers and other pugilists. Muay Thai aficionados distinguish between two different kinds of boxers. On the one hand, there are those who are "artists" (*nak-muay fi-meu*, "skilful boxer"; *nak-muay cherng*, "artful boxer", or simply *bokser,* from the English "boxer"), and, on the other hand, those who are "attackers" (*nak-muay buk* "attacking boxer"; *nak-muay thorahot* "tough boxer", or *faither,* from the English "fighter"). The same binary classification of boxers exists in the world of international boxing and is expressed in English, such that a distinction is made between "stylists", "boxers", or "counterpunchers" on the one hand, and "brawlers" or "bangers" on the other. The findings of four anthropologists who have investigated Muay Thai ethnographically—Catherine Choron-Baix (1995); Peter Vail (1998); Pattana Kitiarsa (2005, 2007); and myself (Rennesson 2005)—show that the "artist" is one who uses counterattack, who models his rhythm and tactics on those of his opponent, who fights intelligently by dodging and side-stepping, and who masters the better part of Muay Thai technique with effectiveness and stylishness. On the other hand, the "attacker" is a boxer who always moves forward, relies on his stamina and strength, endures many blows, and whose technical register is more limited than that of the artist. The attacker's style, in short, is not as aesthetic as the artist's. The boxing stance of the latter refers, if indirectly, to the notion of "art" (*sinlapa*). It is not a question of terminology so much as the way the stylishness of the artists fits in the aesthetic realm of "beauty" (*khwam-suay-ngam*), and, from a Buddhist perspective, what is beautiful is considered to be virtuous and righteous. The artist's style underlines the "civilized" aspect of Thai boxing, which is why it is considered part of the national cultural heritage.

Furthermore, Muay Thai boxers belong to a group of local performers, including comedians, dancers, and singers, who are renowned for their stylishness and grace, be they women or men. These aesthetic expectations hold for all performers of both genders. Like any other performer, pugilists have to prepare themselves and their bodies to be presentable to the public. Trainers add olive oil to the massage oil with which they treat boxers before a fight. They explain that by doing so they intend to lend an agreeable colour to the boxer's skin and add a shine to it. To please audiences, from ordinary wage-earners up to the king and the gods, it is said that male boxers have to look *suay-ngam* ("beautiful") before being *lor* ("handsome"). Training-camp owners, as well as relatives of the boxers, are very sensitive about this aesthetic aspect of the boxing exhibition. The good appearance of a fighter is a source of great pride and honour. It is even more important during the "paying homage to the [Muay Thai] teacher dance" (*ram muay wai khru*) that all boxers perform before every fight. The *ram muay wai khru*, which each boxer also performs at the beginning of his apprenticeship, is characteristic of the ritualistic bonds that link pugilists to their elders, the people to whom they must pay respect—that is to say, their parents, teachers, trainers, owners, promoters and, last but not least, the King of Thailand, the ultimate moral reference.

Each camp owner is thought to teach his own stylized version of the ritual *ram muay wai khru* dance, even if, nowadays, boxers tend to develop their own interpretations. This was the case with *Norng* Tum and *Norng* Tim, who became famous for their very stylish way of performing the *ram muay wai khru*. Among the several different standard patterns of dancing that may be performed as part of this pre-fight ritual, they chose a movement that used to be famous but which is now not so much employed in Thai boxing rings. It is called "The Young Lady Who Powders Herself" (*sao noi pa paeng*), which is celebrated as the most graceful pattern when skilfully executed. There are many other types of movements, the most famous being "The Swan's Flight (*hong hern*), "Rama (Vishnu) Follows the Deer" (*Phra Ram tam kwang*), and "Narai (Indra) Throws the Discus" (*Narai khwang jak*). These are named either after prominent scenes related to war and hunting from Thai classical literature, especially the local version of the Indian Ramayana epic (Thai: *Ramakien*), or after everyday activities. "The Young Lady Who Powders Herself" falls into the latter category. While it may be true that this movement is the only one that is based on an activity not traditionally carried out by men, it remains the case that Muay Thai audiences view aesthetic mastery of this dance as a sign of a boxer's finesse.

While boxers who are not cross-gendered have chosen the "The Young Lady Who Powders Herself" pattern of ritual dance, the makeup and powder that both *Norng* Tum and *Norng* Tim applied to their faces before stepping over the ropes into the ring (even the lipstick on many occasions for *Norng* Tum and on all occasions for *Norng* Tim) reinforced their interpretation of the dance in a demure and sophisticated fashion, exaggerating the way in which Thai women are supposed to control their body movements. While other boxers execute the movements to produce an appealing display in honour of their elders and to warm up their bodies, *Norng* Tum and *Norng* Tim went beyond this by pushing the refinement of self-presentation further than other pugilists and gave it an explicit feminine gendered nuance. As I noted during my fieldwork, this was widely discussed and often appreciated by the Thai public, both inside and outside the world of Muay Thai aficionados and practitioners. In my view, *Norng* Tum and *Norng* Tim, more than other boxers, have disturbed routines and given the Thai public grounds to reflect as much on the ambiguous meaning of violent contact as on its manly essence.

A beautiful dance performance presented as a gift to the gods and one's elders is a concept that is without question relevant to the Thai boxing ring. But both *Norng* Tum and *Norng* Tim became famous for their fluid and graceful movements, not only when performing the opening ritual dance but, even more significantly, during their fierce battles in the ring. Their artfulness, as with any other boxer, was not interpreted as a sign of weakness. More than anything else, pugilists fight for somebody else's "honour" or "reputation" (*kiat*). Moreover, a Muay Thai fight has to be *run-raeng di*, that is, "pleasantly violent", or sufficiently violent but still fought within the rules of the contest. Aesthetics play a significant role in Muay Thai as a violent encounter between two male bodies, but on another level from that discussed above. The execution of combative techniques in the ring is one of the main criteria by which observers judge whether the violence expressed is mastered or not—that is, legitimate or not—and whether the encounter fits within the Muay Thai framework or is simply a vulgar street fight. Even the most fearsome boxers satisfy these criteria of aesthetic combat. Beyond the visual appreciation of the refinement that boxers are able to evoke when fighting, the beauty of the bout is considered moral because the male-upon-male violence is controlled. Boxing "artists" are considered to possess greater control of themselves and of their art than "fighters".

Interestingly, both *Norng* Tum and *Norng* Tim also achieved renown as fierce fighters who could defeat their opponents by relying on the strength of their punch. They were especially appreciated for the immediate and devastating effectiveness of their "roundhouse kick" (*te wiang*),[7] which is the trademark of Muay Thai as a masculine activity of mutual challenge.[8] Such features of their styles associate them to some extent with the "attacking" approach to boxing. "Fighters" embody the endurance and the fighting skills of the Thai people. They are conceived as representing a less sophisticated practice of Muay Thai associated with the poor and less civilized margins of the country, at least according to the stereotypes widely used in the boxing world, the influence of which on press and media representations should not be underestimated.

More broadly, *Norng* Tum's and *Norng* Tim's media coverage, especially their numerous interviews on television talk shows, also drew on the fact that Thai people like to think about *kathoeys* as a national idiosyncrasy that is constructed on a comparative standpoint—that is, of Thai versus foreigner. Indeed, the mediatization in Thailand of *Norng* Tum and *Norng* Tim concentrated much more on their fights against foreigners, especially Westerners (*farang*) and Japanese. Before *Norng* Tum went on to fight in Japan, most of his opponents in Thailand in 1998 were, in fact, foreigners.

In the context of intercontinental boxing bouts, whether in Muay Thai or international boxing, when Thai fighters meet foreigners, the local pugilists are either identified as artists, and then are represented in terms of the skilfulness and the elegance of Thais, or as attackers, who are taken to demonstrate the strength and the martial potential of the Thai people—or, indeed, they are portrayed as representing both of these attributes at the same time. Genuine pugilistic excellence, indeed, depends upon a harmonious combination of the two styles. Such a symbiosis is a reference to the unity of the Thai people and makes of the perfect boxer, whatever the fighter's regional background, an ideal representative of the country. In a way, this is the kind of icon the two cross-dressing boxers came to personify, since they were widely recognized as both fierce and skilful boxers. As an excellent pugilist, *Norng* Tum essentially embodied the self-defence potential that is thought to characterize the Thai nation (*chat thai*) (Rennesson, 2007).

Unambiguously gendered Thai bodies, whether women who are engaged in international beauty contests or male boxers fighting with foreigners, provide support for defining what is thought of as the "Thai people's nature" (*thammachat khorng khon thai*) and what is "Thainess" (*khwam-pen-thai*). Discussion of the perfect national representative is often passionate. When national pugilists are chosen to confront foreigners in the ring, the results are more often than not an opportunity to discuss the kind of "Thainess" or "Thai manliness" (*kan-pen-phu-chai Thai*) that best represents the country and shows the world a national superiority in fighting. To put it in simple terms, discussion focuses on whether Thailand should send rough-and-tough country guys, whom foreigners find hard to fight, or artists, who risk being knocked out by well-built Westerners. A combination of the two profiles—artful and attacking—lowers the risk in a Thai-Western bout. We can thus understand how cross-dressing fighters draw on such a stimulating discourse, for they invite the public to focus on the gender issue.

In this perspective, the framing of discourses about nationhood in socio-biological terms, both for male and female representatives of Thailand who are engaged in international competition, usually draws upon body stereotypes. While boxers may be caught between discourses of whether they have a family background in the central region of the country or in its geographical and cultural margins, females representing Thailand at international beauty pageants are enmeshed in a no-less-reified set of alternatives between being seen as either having an upcountry origin or being of "mixed ancestry" (*luk-khreung*)—that is, having both a Thai and a Western parent. In the latter case, the question is, roughly: "Will we be better or more effectively represented by an explicit and authentic native of the country, or by a mixed-race person who is increasingly the aesthetic model in contemporary Thailand?"

We may ask what kind of opportunistic socio-biologization *Norng* Tum and *Norng* Tim provided to the different segments of the Thai society. To do so, we need first to take a closer look at how their careers developed in an historical context. Even though the two cross-dressing boxers' talents as genuine pugilists are beyond doubt when compared with their peers (especially *Norng* Tum, who, according to many commentators, is a breathtaking pugilist), it also seems that they were unusual in their rocketing from village-fair fights to the limelight of the international boxing programmes without going through the normal intermediary stages of an ordinary boxing career. It took a little more than twenty bouts before *Norng* Tum was catapulted to prominence in Bangkok's rings, which is a half or one-third the usual number of fights a regional boxer must contest before achieving fame in the national capital. But one also has to bear in mind that by that time, *Norng* Tum had won twenty of his twenty-two fights and had knocked out his opponents eighteen times. More significantly, *Norng* Tum's prize win for his first fight at the Lumphini Stadium in Bangkok (a forty thousand baht purse) was at least four times greater than what most newcomers are able to take. Nevertheless, what is clear is that following the 1997 Asian economic crisis, which hit professional Muay Thai critically, the main investors in the business were highly gratified to bring a new light on the national rings, which had largely been deserted by gamblers, by propelling a kind of freak boxer, *Norng* Tum. Promoters did everything to shine a media light on *Norng* Tum as they tried to bring people back to the stadiums, while also appealing to a potential public beyond the traditional circle of Muay Thai aficionados.

Muay Thai promoters realized *Norng* Tum's advertising potential after his first fight in Bangkok, on 24 February 1998, when the media publicized a dramatic incident that occurred during the public weigh-in that morning.[9] *Norng* Tum refused to take off his underwear before stepping onto the scales. His heartbreaking crying finally persuaded officials to accept his special request, and this became the basis of his fame. But very few promoters exploited *Norng* Tum in the media to serve the cause of the national boxing community. According to one of his managers, Wichit Prai Annan, there appeared to be no general agreement among the various network leaders who share the huge professional Muay Thai business about what to do with him. *Norng* Tum's repeated victories brought interesting outcomes, not only in Thai society but also across the world. In a short time, coverage of *Norng* Tum's life advanced him as a media star the equal of any other, and he appeared in mainstream talk shows and in television and news magazines; oddly, it must be noted, he was barely noted in the boxing press. *Norng* Tum first became famous because of his success as an impressive fighter. Then, from the end of 1998 onward, his presence in the media was much more related to his regular declarations concerning his thoughts in the matter of changing sex. His sporting achievements were by this time largely instrumental parts in the broader narrative of his life that was developing. Again oddly, press accounts of his actual fights are almost impossible to find, all the more so after his first fight at Lumphini in 1998. Nevertheless, it seems that he did fight some thirty more times, from February 1998 to November 1999—half of these bouts in Thailand and half abroad—and that he was victorious much more often than he was defeated, even though he suffered more losses at the end of 1999 as the feminizing hormones he was taking slowly reduced his strength.

One measure of the commodification of his life was the fact that he became a main focus of the Tourism Authority of Thailand's 1998–99 advertising campaign, branded with the slogan "Amazing Thailand". It was not only that some *kathoeys* recognized themselves in *Norng* Tum and *Norng* Tim. From that moment on, Thai people more than ever saw Muay Thai as one of their primary national cultural assets. Cross-dressing boxers firstly personified the overcoming of "a life of hardship" (*chiwit lambak*) more effectively than other fighters. Not only did they have to work diligently to improve their economic situations, like other boxers; they also had to struggle with the ambiguous situation of being a *kathoey* in Thai society. In addition, their biographies showed that pugilists could manipulate the boxing system to their benefit, in contrast to the widespread view of the boxing community as one that crushes individuals. The mediatization of *Norng* Tum and *Norng* Tim made Muay Thai more acceptable and took the sport well beyond the traditional circle of the Thai boxing community (*sangkhom muay* or *wong-kan muay*), which is dominated by a hypermasculine ethos. The Thai middle-class view of the Muay Thai world consisted, and still consists, largely of images of a highly corrupt system wherein the most powerful exploit the weakest, namely, poor young boys and youths. During my periods of fieldwork, in 1999 and 2000, it was apparent that the middle classes were one of the key new audiences that Muay Thai promoters had in mind when they decided to push *Norng* Tum onto the media scene; foreigners were another. I would not say, however, that this strategy was particularly successful on the national scale. *Norng* Tum and *Norng* Tim undisputedly helped the development of Muay Thai practice as an amateur sport and as a self-defence technique, but the professional network is still largely despised by the middle classes for the same reasons as previously.

If we take a closer look at the empirical grounds for *Norng* Tum's success as a performer in a masculine world such as Muay Thai, we find that his mediatization reflected two factors. On the one hand, and primarily, it rested on his progressive efforts to come to terms with himself as a *kathoey* while in the ring; on the other hand, there was also his debate within himself as to whether to have an operation that would transform his male body into a female one. As time went on, *Norng* Tum stylized his makeup more and more; in 1999, he decided to proceed to take female hormones on a daily basis to enlarge his breasts. This transformation could not be ignored when he began to reference women's outfits in the ring by wearing a strap cloth across his chest to cover his emerging female form. This physical and very public evolution was not uniformly regarded, whether in Thailand generally or in Muay Thai circles, as I shall now explain.

From information I gathered through the testimonies of some of *Norng* Tum's boxing companions, whom I interviewed in a Chonburi camp that he had frequented just before his sex reassignment and his retirement, his process of physical transformation presented no problems, either during the workout or in daily life among intimates in the camp. This was because they were all linked by close relationships based on the sharing of hardships and the common goal of bringing honour and pride to the group and its leader. *Norng* Tum brought fame to the camp, and he was respected for this. Even more to be remarked, his comradeship with his boxing mates was not endangered by his identity as a *kathoey*. While training and in daily life, small accommodations were made so that all in the camp would feel at ease: *Norng* Tum, for instance, was allowed to train wearing upper-body clothes (particularly during wrestling sparring); he was also permitted to shower on his own without being disturbed, which is a considerable privilege in a boxing camp.

At the same time, as a prizefighter and a public icon, far away from the daily routines and intimacy of the training camp, *Norng* Tum's radical transformation began to put him at odds with the principle of man-to-man challenge that is the root of competitive practice. *Norng* Tum increasingly stylized his womanly outfits after his first win at the Lumphini Stadium, and this posed more problems than his makeup and his womanly movements. This became even more acute for the more conservative Muay Thai aficionados as *Norng* Tum repeatedly beat his male opponents. As his gender transition progressed, it rapidly overshadowed his role as a boxer, which had been to provide an agreed-upon opportunity among Muay Thai promoters to renew and modernize the sport's image on the domestic scene. The ambiguity of *Norng* Tum's gender identity, which initially permitted different points of view to co-exist and to be discussed in a single stream of mediatization, progressively vanished as he increasingly approached the embodiment of the feminine ideal he desired. From interviews within the Muay Thai community, we know that he began to draw more and more criticism. Promoters became increasingly reluctant to advance him in traditional boxing programmes in Bangkok. Beyond traditional Muay Thai circles, *Norng* Tum was still very popular, once again especially among the Thai middle class, but this was far from the boxing ring. This declining local appeal is perhaps what encouraged Muay Thai officials to organize a circus-like fight between *Norng* Tum and a Japanese woman wrestler in Japan at the end of 1998. He readily accepted the situation in which he found himself—and took advantage of it. *Norng* Tum undoubtedly made big money in the Japan exhibition. From that time on, up to his gender reassignment surgery at the end of 1999, he fought only abroad, mostly in Japan and against both male and female fighters in different kinds of competitions. Fragmented and not fully consistent information collected from informants suggests that he won the greatest part of his twenty international outings.

Norng Tum, and to a lesser extent *Norng* Tim, at a certain moment of their careers, bestowed a peculiar opportunity for Thais to test among themselves and, more significantly, with foreigners, the continuum of the performative gender roles pervasive in Thailand. We can conclude that these cross-dressing boxers came to symbolize the country and all Thais, as well as the three genders—male, female, and *kathoey*. The narratives came to be recounted throughout Thai culture. More than any other boxers, they conveyed a complex, polymorphous, and fluid gender picture of themselves, an image that Thais want to claim for themselves and advance to the rest of the world. At a particular moment in its modern history, Muay Thai needed the ambiguity expressed in the cross-dressing bodies of both *Norng* Tum and *Norng* Tim. Their presences made available a range of possible masculinities. These possibilities, in turn, highlighted the moral haziness of physical violence as it exists between grace, on the one hand, and fierceness on the other—the tension, that is to say, that characterizes Thai cultural attitudes to masculinity. Who better to personify that ontological tension of Thai masculinity than cross-dressing boxers? A complementary question, which goes beyond the scope of the present analysis, concerns the extent to which some segments of the Thai cross-dressing community may regard Muay Thai as a political tool. I suggest that the whole range of Thai performative gender roles is not merely a symbolic landmark of national identity. Rather, this fluid system of gendered being needs alien bodies—to be confronted by them and compared with them—to function properly on the domestic scene. Future research would benefit from comparative work by putting side-by-side the success of the two cross-dressing boxers considered here and the very famous national and international transsexual beauty pageants, such as Miss Tiffany's Universe and Miss International Queen, that also catch the attention of Thais at large. In contrast to *Norng* Tum and *Norng* Tim, the candidates in these contests of feminine beauty are evaluated on a regime of self-presentation that fits more immediately with what is more generally expected of them in Thailand as m-t-f transvestites and transsexuals. The criterion to judge competitors in transgender beauty contests draws more on physical and behavioural compliance with a feminine ideal, a device entirely other than the Muay Thai's system, based as it is on the direct confrontation of bodies.

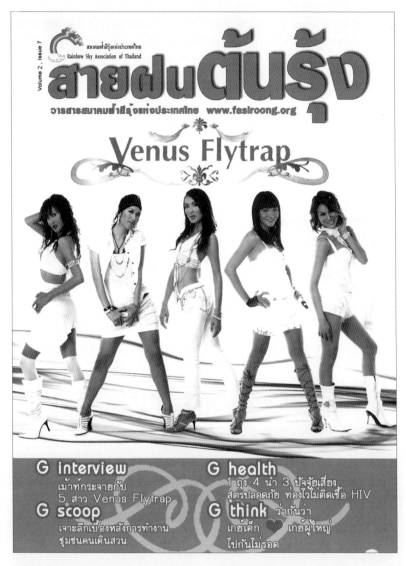

Figure 3 Members of the all-transsexual Thai pop band, Venus Flytrap, who released a self-titled CD and music video in 2006. As discussed here by Stéphane Rennesson and Serhat Ünaldi, male-to-female transgenders and transsexuals have become increasingly prominent figures in national-level sport and in the Thai entertainment industry in recent years. (Source: Rainbow Sky Association of Thailand)

Figure 4 Images of young Thai transgenders, or "second type of woman" (*sao praphet sorng*), on the cover of a 2008 "TG" (transgender) edition of the newsletter of the Rainbow Sky Association of Thailand.

3

Back in the Spotlight

The Cinematic Regime of Representation
of *Kathoeys* and Gay Men in Thailand

Serhat Ünaldi

Introduction

When, in July 2005, the First International Conference of Asian Queer Studies was held in Bangkok, Peter A. Jackson, as co-organizer, pointed to one of the thematic highlights, namely, the analysis of the media representations of homosexuality. "The stereotyping of gays remains a major issue [in Thailand]," Jackson said. "To analyze and criticize the media is important for the promotion of [LGBT] rights" (cited by Veena 2005). In Thailand, the visual representation of queerness has long been dominated by transgender *kathoey* characters. An analysis of the sources of this representational emphasis and of alternative developments of queer representation in Thai cinema may shed light on possibilities for the emergence of a movie scene that better reflects the diversity of queer life in Thailand. As will be shown, below the surface the Thai movie scene is becoming increasingly dynamic in its depictions of modern gay and *kathoey* lives. Most notably, alternative filmmakers are pushing the boundaries to make visible once-hidden facets of Thai gender and sexuality.

Shortly after the emergence of the so-called Thai New Wave Cinema[1] in 1997, movies dealing with lives of *kathoeys* became a major part of the country's cinematic culture. More recently, films about gender-normative masculine gay men have appeared. But whereas the former are products of the mainstream film industry, the latter, with some recent exceptions, are rooted in an increasingly strong community of independent Thai filmmakers. Below I consider how and why this gap between the representations of transgender and gay minorities came into being and what it reveals about Thai society and its relation to the groups described.

Jackson has outlined the concept of the Thai "regime of images", understood as the greater exertion of state control over the public sphere, as opposed to the private realm, to present positive images of the nation (Jackson 2003a, 2004a, 2004b). This analysis of the public imaging of minority groups also highlights the underlying power relations and hegemonic interests of elite sectors that try to dictate the dominant frameworks of representation.

The fact that the gap between images of *kathoeys* in mainstream cinema and alternative gay representations began to narrow in recent years, at a time when Thailand was under a military-appointed government, may reveal something about the tactics that anti-democratic forces in the twenty-first century use to give themselves a liberal veneer. As Doug Sanders also details in his chapter here, tolerance towards homosexuals increasingly becomes a marker of a state's degree of liberalism and democracy. Thus in the Thai case, an unelected government seeking national and international acceptance opened liberal spaces where these least hurt its conservative political agenda. Producers of the first mainstream, gay-themed films, as opposed to *kathoey* movies, strategically used these opening spaces of ambiguous liberality.

The movies considered here have been chosen for their commercial success, for the discussion they provoked, and also for their original approach to the subject matter. The focus is on representations of male-to-female transgender *kathoeys* and male homosexuals, although *tom-dee* lesbians[2] also appear in a number of the films. Generally, these female characters tend to occupy positions of leadership—a sports team coach or a company boss—and derive social acceptance from their professional success. With few exceptions, screenwriters deny them private lives, let alone erotic relations, and their cinematic roles are limited to intellectual anti-poles and advisers to emotionally struggling male homosexual protagonists. A detailed study of the representation of female homosexuality in Thai cinema has still to be done.

The movies considered here are divided, first, into a group of mainstream films produced by Thailand's major studios—*Iron Ladies 1* and *Iron Ladies 2* (Youngyooth Thongkonthun, 2000 and 2003), *Saving Private Tootsie* (Kittikorn Liasirikun, 2002), *Beautiful Boxer* (Ekachai Uekrongtham, 2003), *The Last Song* (Phisan Akraseranee, 2006), *Metrosexual* (Youngyooth Thongkonthun, 2006), *Me . . . Myself* (Pongpat Wachirabunjong, 2007)—and second into the category of independent films. These latter are *Iron Pussy* (Apichatpong Weerasethakul, 2003), *Tropical Malady* (Apichatpong Weerasethakul, 2004), *Rainbow Boys* (Thanyatorn Siwanukrow, 2005), and *Silom Soi 2* (Piya Rangsitienchai, 2006). A new category of mainstream gay movies also appears to be emerging, and the study ends with a discussion of *Bangkok Love Story* (Poj Arnon, 2007) and *The Love of Siam* (Chookiat Sakveerakul, 2007). These last two are the first films produced by a big Thai entertainment company that have gender-normative masculine gay men as main characters. Yet, first it is crucial to begin by understanding the preconditions from which all these movies originate.

Cinematic Environment

In Thailand, a strong concern with positive public representations of Thainess—that is, the defining features of the nation and its people—is deeply rooted. This concern is also reflected in the state's handling of media portrayals of homosexuality and transgenderism. Although *kathoeys* and gays are tolerated by large parts of the society, state censorship is occasionally implemented when they appear in the public arena (Jackson 2002). State intervention became manifest in 2004, when the Ministry of Culture asked TV stations to reduce gay portrayals since it feared that the number of gays was increasing due to their growing media presence. The deputy minister was quoted as saying that these behaviours should be expressed only in private. The issue here was not homosexuality *per se* but rather its public display (Sucheera 2004, Anonymous 2004). This was by no means the first attempt at such censorship (Jackson 2002).

Regarding sexuality, this public-private divide is partly the result of a development that began in the second half of the nineteenth century, when Thailand began to adjust its moral codes to conform to Western understandings to counter European descriptions of Siam as semi-barbarous—imagery that could have been used as a justification for colonial rule (Jackson 2003a). To become a modern nation state, a process of self-civilizing (*siwilai*) was initiated (Thongchai 2000, Harrison and Jackson 2010). Regarding gender roles, this process led to the state promotion of heterosexual relations as "civilized" (Jackson 2003a, paragraph 38). The aim was to alter the public performance of gender to present an image of a modern, civilized Siam to the outside world. In contrast, the state did little to intervene in private sexual practices.

The state has often tried to regulate TV and cinematic representations of Thainess in general and sexuality in particular. The Thai Film Act of 1930 established the legal framework for censorship; it was replaced in 2007 following pressure by filmmakers who came out against the "outdated censorship law" (Kong 2007a). The frequent cutting of scenes that were seen as harmful to social stability—including depictions of naked bodies—fostered the development of a widely apolitical cinematic landscape, thus serving the hegemonic aim of those in power in Thailand. Although Thai cinema had a Golden Age of socially critical movies during a vibrantly democratic period in the mid-1970s, the return to politics of conservative royalists and the military as well as the emergence of a strong capitalist elite after 1976 was paralleled by a profanation and commercialization of the Thai movie scene. Even many Thai New Wave films produced after 1997 are distinguished not by any greater social or political criticism but rather by their stronger visual and narrative styles.

One of the basic questions that analysts of Thai cinema have to consider is, which came first, a conservative and stale cinema or an entertainment-seeking audience indifferent to alternative plots and thought-provoking narrative styles? The latter view is favoured in conservative elite circles, which hold that Thai society is not ready for new artistic styles. Yet, the considerable success of the Thai social-realist films of the 1970s and the obvious potential for innovative, at times pioneering, cinematic approaches among recent Thai New Wave and independent directors suggests that power relations and deliberate considerations at the elite level led to the "stupidity" (*khwam-ngo*) so often observed in today's Thai cinema. Among elite sectors of society, a fear of modern art seems widespread, maybe rightly so since new artistic styles are often intended to provoke a change in mindset, a change that would challenge the feudal remnants that those in power base their rule upon. As one university teacher of performing arts at a Bangkok institution put in an interview:

> Thai art is all about copying the past, and that is so frustrating. They want to prevent intellectual progress. How can modern theatre advance in Thailand if all funds go to *Khon* [classical dance] schools?[3]

Thus, the screening of *Syndromes and a Century* was banned in 2007. It was an art-house movie in which the acclaimed independent director Apichatpong Weerasethakul tells the story of a female and a male physician. Thai authorities objected to, among other things, what they considered the "inappropriate" depiction of doctors drinking and kissing. *Syndromes* followed the style of Apichatpong's earlier movies, based on unpredictable narrative structures, metaphorical details, sudden leaps in time and place, uncommented depictions of everyday Thai life, and often-improvised dialogue, thus demanding a high degree of interpretative effort among audiences (May Adadol and MacDonald 2010). In banning *Syndromes*, the authorities' main objective appears to have been not to uphold the reputation of Thai physicians but rather to prevent the screening of an alternative piece of art. Only months after the banning of Apichatpong's movie, *The Sick Nurses* (2007, Piraphan Laoyont and Thodsapol Siriwiwat) reached the screen. It was a "trashy exploitation flick" that "steals the formula of American and Korean slasher movies, minus their skills and humour", as Kong Rithdee, the *Bangkok Post's* film critic, described it (Kong 2007b). The film's chief evil villain is responsible for a bloodbath and is represented as a stereotyped gay man. Kong critiqued the film as follows:

Sick Nurses wears its misanthropy on its sleeve, but its idiocy
throws not an inkling of political challenge at the rampant rise of
conservatism in this country. . . . If images of doctors drinking liquor
put the profession in a bad light and undermine patients' respect,
what would patients think of seeing a doctor killing, selling corpses
and seducing nurses, as happens here? What's more saddening than
seeing bad exploitation movies is the double standards of the people
who have power. (Kong 2007b)

May Adadol Ingawanij (2008) points to another double standard, namely,
the distinctions Thai censors make between films scheduled for international
and domestic release. Independent Thai films shown abroad are less likely to
be censored by Thai authorities in advance of distribution than if they are to be
released locally. According to May, the underlying elitist rationale is

that Thai viewers are not ready for some films which might nevertheless
be appropriate for international release. The trope of the people being
'not yet ready' has long been part of the elite's defensive barrier against
radical change. . . . What is historically consistent about such claims
is that they create a fiction of a people dependent on elite leadership
amidst a context of the crisis of the latter's authority and furious
discontent from below. (May 2008)

In addition to these ideological feuds, institutional limits to a more
subversive and challenging film industry are set by the local production and
exhibition system, which is dominated by a few companies: Major and EGV
(exhibition), and GMM Tai Hub and Sahamongkol (production, distribution),
the latter being the only relatively progressive mainstream force. First and
foremost, the products of these companies have to be saleable. Hence, commercial
success outweighs artistic or content-related considerations. The absence of a
government funding system means that ambitious filmmakers have to bear the
risks if their movies fail, which is not uncommon in a country whose audiences
have been fed on conservative agendas, are unfamiliar with challenging plots
and styles, and are more accustomed to stereotyped characters following the
tradition of *likay* folk theatre, in which actors are cast for their looks more than
their talent (Lewis 2006, 147). Indie director Apichatpong has criticized the lack
of management, structure, and creative depth within the Thai film industry:

There are many risks here, and it's not worth the size of the market,
which is still small. . . . Most of the films that we [in Thailand] sell are
low-grade films, which create the general view that all our films are
like that. . . . We need . . . something on a larger scale that aids in the
production process. (cited in Thunska 2006)[4]

As Glen Lewis puts it, "Thai movies are often too predictable due to a combination of commercial pressures and over-reliance on tradition" (2006, 147).

Considering this background, it becomes obvious why trashy teen flicks and horror movies dominate the local film industry. Yet, creativity is sometimes boosted by troubled times, as occurred during the Asian financial crisis in 1997, when some directors came up with challenging movies that—oddly enough—were distributed by Tai Entertainment, one of the biggest production companies.[5] In the course of these changes a genre was re-established that had its antecedents in the 1980s and whose success few people had anticipated, namely, *kathoey* movies.

Mainstream *Kathoey* Movies: The First Wave of Thai Queer Cinema

Transgender *kathoeys* occupy a well-established position in the visual media of Thailand and became increasingly common on Thai television from the early 1980s (Jackson 2002, 219). However, more often than not they were, and remain, reduced to stereotypical roles of screaming clowns. Yet, a series of Thai movies in the mid-1980s was the first to treat the subject of transgenderism and homosexuality more sensitively.

Oradol Kaewprasert (2005) has described what she calls the "First Wave of Thai Queer Cinema", referring to three 1980s melodramatic movies: *The Last Song* (*Phleng sut-thai*, Phisan Akraseranee, 1985), its sequel *Tortured Love* (*Rak thoraman*, Phisan Akraseranee, 1987), and *I Am a Man* (*Chan phu-chai na ya*, ML. Bandevanop Devakul, 1987). The political background of semi-authoritarianism provided by General Prem Tinsulanonda, then the prime minister, led to a gradual liberalization that offered space for theatrical and cinematic representations of *kathoeys* (Jackson 2002, 223–24). These movies presented transgenders as suffering from their bad *karma*. Suicidal plots and impossible love counterbalanced TV depictions of *kathoeys* and effeminate gays as lighthearted buffoons (Jackson 2002, 220–225).

In the first and most influential of these movies, *The Last Song*, a male-to-female transgender cabaret performer, Somying, falls in love with a man who leaves her for a biological woman. At the end of the film, Somying, desperate and lonely, enters the stage of the cabaret and, while performing, shoots herself in the head. Oradol (2005) observed that the movies of the first wave of Thai queer cinema courted sympathy from society and did not celebrate queerness or promote rights and identities. However, these movies did bring to the attention of mainstream audiences transgender and homosexual characters who, for once, were more than funny fools.

Mainstream *Kathoey* Movies: The Second Wave of Thai Queer Cinema

In 1996, an underdog group of volleyball players from Lampang Province in Northern Thailand won the Thailand National Games. The fact that the team was made up primarily of transgendered *kathoeys* contributed to the popularity of the victorious "Iron Ladies" (*satri lek*), as the team called itself. However, the Volleyball Association of Thailand prevented the team from taking part in international competitions because it was feared that its members would harm the country's reputation. Four years later, the Iron Ladies made a comeback, this time as characters on screen in an eponymously named film. The movie about their success was the highest-grossing Thai film at that time, with a box-office take of almost 100 million baht.[6] Compared with the 1980s movies that did not promote queer rights and identities, a movie about a group of *kathoeys* joining forces to fight for acceptance in the sporting arena on a national level constituted a new style of *kathoey* films. Towards the end of the movie, during the volleyball finals, the Iron Ladies have to withstand verbal attacks from officials who see their sport as tarnished. The film proceeds to make fun of an obviously behind-the-times sports official when Jung, one of the *kathoey* players, secretly turns on the microphone so the official's voice echoes throughout the stadium as he insults the popular Iron Ladies. In response, the audience begins to shout out the team's name, while the official, now embarrassed, tries to walk away and stumbles over the feet of one of his more liberal colleagues.

Apart from its social criticism, *Iron Ladies* depicts the lives of *kathoeys* as worth living. They support each other, and their identity is strengthened by their group affiliation. Moreover, they have straight friends and parents who are accepting of them. Nonetheless, Buddhist notions of suffering are not absent: The *kathoey* showgirl Pia has her heart broken by Chat, a man who leaves her for a "real" woman in a parallel to the character of Somying in *The Last Song*. But in contrast to the suicidal ending of that 1985 movie, the self-confident Pia moves to China, where she starts a new career.

The focus in *Iron Ladies* on community and companionship follows the Thai cinematic tradition of group-centred plots that is rooted in wider cultural traits within a group-oriented society. Furthermore, the adoption of familiar narrative structures helps to make such movies easily accessible to straight viewers. Lewis notes that the "exotic in this film [*Iron Ladies*] was the subject matter, not its style, which was conventional" (2006, 156). Even filmmakers who are today looking for new ways of approaching homosexual issues beyond the *kathoey* acknowledge the importance of *Iron Ladies*. Vitaya Saeng-Aroon from the independent gay media company Cyberfish Media stated that,

> *Iron Ladies* is a turning point in the history of gay-related movies in
> Thailand locally and internationally. It's the very first movie that
> portrays positive images. (2007, personal correspondence)

International distribution of the movie also made the *Iron Ladies* visible abroad
and attracted audiences in Singapore, Japan, and beyond.

The success of *Iron Ladies* prompted a sequel, *Iron Ladies 2*, by the same
director, Youngyooth Thongkonthun, in 2003. However, with a gross of 70
million baht, it was less successful. In contrast to its prequel, this movie is
entirely fictional and relates the story of what is supposed to have happened
before and after the team's sporting success of 1996. Main issues covered are
envy, friendship, and the search for sexual identity. With many intersecting
story lines and flashbacks, the level of suspense remains low. Yet there are some
interesting scenes regarding the student days of the main characters, when
the *kathoey* friends Jung and Mon meet Norng, who seems to be an average
masculine gay who is still in the closet. When his sexual orientation is revealed
after he falls through the ceiling of the men's shower in a university dormitory
with a camera in his hand, Jung approaches Norng and tells him that everything
about him screams *"kathoey"*. The next scene shows Norng cross-dressed and
on rollerblades on the university campus. This scene illustrates one of the
features of mainstream *kathoey* movies, which generally do not distinguish
between gender-normative homosexuality and transgenderism. In fact, even if
gender-normative gays appear they tend to be portrayed as having an affinity
for feminine accessories, like *Iron Ladies'* Wit, a Sino-Thai team member who
seems to represent a masculine homosexual but nonetheless likes to try on the
jewellery displayed at the shop of his parents.

Iron Ladies' success encouraged other producers. In 2002, *Saving Private
Tootsie* was released. This movie was also inspired by true events and tells
the story of a group of Thai *kathoeys* who, after surviving a plane crash, find
themselves on Burmese soil, where they are soon captured by Tai Yai (Shan)
rebels. The *kathoeys* have to make their way to the Thai frontier with the help of
homophobic Thai soldiers who are sent to rescue them. Their pathetic arrival at
a refugee camp on the Thai side of the border, symbolized by a waving national
flag shot in close up, stresses an underlying nationalist message: Thainess
matters, not gender. The staunch nationalism becomes obvious right at the
beginning of this film, when Cherry, one of the *kathoey* survivors, recollects
that "the plane crash wasn't a big deal, but where it crashed [i.e. in Burma]
concerned me the most". Cherry is the embodiment of a stereotypically tragic
kathoey who has been abandoned by her straight lover. A recurring theme in
three decades of Thai cinema representations of *kathoeys* is the "tragedy" of

being transgendered and the impossibility of finding lasting true love with a man. Yet, the movie assembles different types of *kathoeys* to highlight the diversity of transgenderism. Whereas Cherry and Somying—the latter having already had gender reassignment surgery—are treated more gently by the Thai soldiers who are sent to their rescue, Chicha, an outspoken, plump character, faces many verbal attacks.[7] However, only one of the Thai soldiers, Sergeant Reung, expresses open hatred towards the *kathoeys*. In the end, Somying gives her life to save Reung from Burmese attacks, which leads him to accept his own *kathoey* son and to acknowledge transgender people as equally brave Thais. In the end, Cherry states that "although we were unfortunate to be born with the wrong gender, we're still lucky because we have been born at the right place", namely, Thailand. Starring famous actors such as Sorapong Chatree and the popular homosexual activist Seri Wongmontha, the film made 45 million baht.

Sorapong also starred as a Muay Thai boxing coach in *Beautiful Boxer*, a nicely shot movie that earned just 15 million baht in 2003. Based on a true story about the country boy, *Norng* Tum, who enters a Muay Thai boxing school and saves his championship winnings to undergo a sex-change operation, it again lifts the *kathoey* issue to a national level. As Stéphane Rennesson detailed in the previous chapter, Muay Thai is generally perceived as man's business and as a national form of art and a tradition of self-defence that has protected the nation throughout history. Lewis traces the movie's lack of box office success to the fact that "the transition from ladyboy to Muay Thai boy was just too much for audiences" (2006, 163). However, this does not explain the popularity of the real-life *Norng* Tum. The film's financial failure may have been due more to its unconventional narrative style, which centred on the fate of an individual character rather than following popular group-centred plots. Additionally, director Ekachai Uekrongtham did not come up to the expectations of an audience that had a preconceived, stereotypical picture of *Norng* Tum as a result of his representation in the Thai media. Ekachai admits that he was worried the real *Norng* Tum could be "like she's portrayed in the media . . . a clown, a kickboxer who loves to put on lipstick".[8] But instead of presenting a comical character, he made a movie about a suffering boy who fights not only for his own fulfilment but also to support his poor parents. Hence, it was not the story per se but the unfamiliar way of telling it that hampered its success. If directors choose not to follow conventional cinematic stereotypes of *kathoeys*, and opt instead for a more psychologically tense and personally focused narrative, they take a risk at the box office.

The movies discussed above all depict transgenderism in relation to aspects of the nation. *Kathoeys* demand their share in national sports and want to be accepted by officials and soldiers. This self-confidence, the absence of suicide plots, and the inclusion of nationalist elements that connect the characters to mainstream society distinguish this post-2000 wave of Thai queer cinema from the 1980s first wave. The more recent series of Thai *kathoey* movies is progressive to the extent that it grants *kathoey*s more agency. But this agency is seldom used to challenge underlying power structures, being exercised to become a good member of Thai society. Parallels can be drawn to Western queer cinema, which Grossman (2000, 2) divides into independent films for a limited audience, on the one hand, and "conservative national social propaganda films" on the other.

At the same time, these movies are different from other Asian gay films as described by Chris Berry (2001, 215). He notes that the dominant trope in East Asian gay movies "is the representation of gayness as a family problem" (Berry 2001, 215). Whereas the Confucian requirement to conform to one's expected position in the family is the dominant theme in these movies, Thai *kathoey* films engage the problem of a lack of *official* recognition. Since homosexuality—or at least transgenderism—is tolerated, even if grudgingly, in large parts of Thai society the more urgent problem at the core of many of these movies is that of official suppression. Yet, intolerant parental attitudes do matter when a character is of Sino-Thai background. Wit, the homosexual volleyball player of Chinese origin in *Iron Ladies*, cannot take part in his team's final match when his father recognizes him on TV and forces him to abandon his *kathoey* friends. However, in contrast to East Asian cinema that engages Confucian value systems, in Thai *kathoey* movies queer individualism may be victorious over heteronormative conformity. At the end of *Iron Ladies*, Wit gets into a taxi and leaves his Sino-Thai family behind. The pattern of choosing to follow an independent homosexual lifestyle applies even more to independent gay movies, as we shall see below.

Three other mainstream *kathoey* films are interesting in that they offer different approaches to queer cinema. In 2006, the director of *The Last Song*, Phisan Akraseranee, did a remake of his successful 1985 movie about the *kathoey* revue dancer Somying Daorai. Describing his objective in directing the remake, he remarked:

> The status of transvestites hasn't changed that much from the time of my original film. The point I try to reiterate in this remake remains the same—that these people suffer from prejudice . . . and that their love is always doomed. (Kong 2006a)

The lukewarm reception of the movie, however, was attributed precisely to its outdated depiction of *kathoeys* as helpless victims. History repeats in the remake when Somying's male lover leaves her for her sister because he wants to start a family with a "real" woman, and Somying then kills herself on stage.

The bottom line of the story is summarized in a warning Somying receives from a gay friend, who has been imprisoned for killing his unfaithful male partner: "Whatever will happen [to me], can happen to you, and so be prepared. For people like us, love will never be fulfilling". For Phisan, queerness still has to end in tragedy, and he fails to draw a distinction between *kathoey* and gay lives when he incomprehensibly equates the stereotyped problems of gays (betrayal, as exemplified by Somying's imprisoned gay friend, who caught his philandering partner red-handed) and *kathoeys* (Somying's tragedy of never being a "real" woman). Here, gays and *kathoeys* are bound together in a tragic community of fate. The only progressive feature of the movie was its staging—the frequent and aestheticized portrayal of nude male bodies is unique and may have passed the scissors of censorship due to Phisan's reputation.

In sharp contrast, the comedy *Metrosexual (kaeng chani kap ee-aep*, Youngyooth Thongkonthun) dealt with a very modern phenomenon and was well received at the box office in 2006. *Iron Ladies* director Youngyooth once again proved his sense of the popular *zeitgeist* when he made this film about a "gang" of straight women (Thai gay slang: *chani*) who try to find out if Kong, the fiancé of one of their friends, Pang, is just a "metrosexual" or a "hidden woman" (*ee-aep*), i.e. a closeted gay man. Bee, the gay brother of one of the women, provides them with a checklist of signs to look for in a closeted gay man. Having divorced parents, an oppressive father, or a gay uncle, being an only child or the youngest boy in the family, or having attended an all-boys' school, are said to be possible signs of homosexuality. The underlying irony is laid out by the cast. Bee is played by Michael Shaowanasai, a homosexual artist (see below) who is known for his satirical and socially critical works, whereas the gang of female friends are well-known hosts of a daytime TV talk show. As Youngyooth stated, "People have come up with these theories about how to spot a closet case, but I think there's a sense of paranoia in all of it" (Kong 2006a). In Thailand, where the borrowed English term "metrosexual" became a convenient synonym for "gay", since advertisers and media still shy away from addressing this niche market directly, *Metrosexual* calls on gays not to hide behind this label. Indeed, in the end Kong turns out to be gay, and both he and his former fiancée are saved from the fate of a sham marriage.

The development of the main character in *Me . . . Myself* (2007) is the reverse of that in *Metrosexual*. After being struck by a car, the *kathoey* Tanya suffers from amnesia and forgets her transgender identity. Oom, the woman driver who runs into Tanya, who is not cross-dressed at the time of the accident, takes her victim home. Not remembering his/her past, Tanya now believes him/herself to be a heterosexual man and is henceforth called Tan. Oom and Tan soon fall in love until Tan regains her memory. Her now-platonic affection for Oom nonetheless remains. Whereas the movie was successful enough to be sold to Korea for a remake, it received heavy criticism from Thai gay-rights groups over its "[lack of] knowledge about gays" (Veena 2007). They feared that parents of homosexuals might believe that their children could turn straight if they only had an accident. The Public Health Department reacted and warned parents not to draw wrong conclusions. To its credit, the movie carried discourses about whether gender is socially constructed or biologically determined into larger parts of Thai society.

We have seen above how mainstream *kathoey* cinema has developed over the previous decades. Its success seems to depend on two factors. As argued by Ekachai Uekrongtham, director of *Beautiful Boxer*, the first factor is Buddhism, because "Buddhist beliefs hold that transvestites were born that way as a result of bad karma . . . we feel that it's not something they want to be born with. . . . So we do have more compassion and more tolerance" (BBC, 2004). Hence, those *kathoey* characters who bear their suffering with dignity attract viewers' admiration. In *Iron Ladies*, Pia advises Mon, who is angry with his uncaring father, not to hate him because "hatred only leads to suffering". *Saving Private Tootsie's* Somying ignores all insults from Sergeant Reung and finally sacrifices her life for him. Muay Thai boxer *Norng* Tum is devoted to his loved ones and, like many other *kathoey* characters, has to bear the burden of an unfulfilled love.

Yet movies without comedic *kathoey* characters have had a hard time at the box office, which leads to a second consideration, namely, the cultural valorization of *sanuk*, playfulness, or being unserious. As Suwanna Satha-anand, an ethics professor at Chulalongkorn University in Bangkok, explains, the Thai national obsession with *sanuk* is a means of releasing pressure built up by the preoccupation with avoiding conflict to uphold personal networks. "Without [*sanuk*], we might have long ago gone insane" (cited by Sanitsuda 2001, 42). As playfulness defuses tension, social critique that is expressed in a funny manner is more acceptable than serious accusations. Even more important, outspoken *kathoey* characters become a screen onto which the suppressed feelings of viewers can be projected. Because they are outcasts, loud-mouthed *kathoeys* do not care about social acceptance (Thai: *mai khae sangkhom*). Moreover, conservatives within the state authorities, in the military, and in royalist circles may see these movies as convenient outlets for society to let off steam without threatening existing social conditions; in many recent instances, *kathoeys* are cinematically integrated into the national narrative of group-centrism and sacrifice.

Thus, *kathoeys* are both admired for their courage in enduring suffering and for their ability to express themselves freely. At the same time, the increasing assertiveness of private interests over state considerations through a continuing commodification process has opened a space to represent these transgender characters on screen. While this has not been true for gender-normative homosexuals, a growing number of independent filmmakers have been working to make this second group visible in Thai cinema.

Independent and Art-House Gay Movies

In 2001, Thai businessman Vitaya Saeng-Aroon, together with the American journalist and entrepreneur Paul Bradley, founded Thailand's first openly gay-owned media company, Cyberfish Media. Their aim was "to counter the negative stereotypes of Thai gay people by presenting, realistic, positive images" and to tap an unserved market (personal correspondence, 2007). But why was the market for masculine gays unserved whereas, at the same time, *kathoeys* were trendy? Jackson (1999a, 238) provides an explanation for why evidently gay men are more problematic in a Thai context than effeminate or transgender *kathoeys*. Since *kathoeys* are "generally regarded . . . to be a psychological woman born inside a man's body . . . [the] greater criticism leveled at gay men may derive from the fact that only they are considered to be genuinely homosexual". They are not acting in accordance with the approved image of Thai masculinity and are "more likely to be considered foreign, strange, potentially dangerous, or even criminal, and a perverted form of manhood" (Jackson 1999a, 138). Indeed, until very recently, masculine gays have been portrayed almost exclusively in limited-release independent movies.

Thai gay films have often been straight-to-DVD productions and have been viewed mainly by gay audiences and circulated in independent circles. Sometimes they may get a short theatrical release at Bangkok's art-house cinema, House RCA, run by Sahamongkol Film. Whenever a new gay movie is released, the company can be sure to do a brisk business, as House RCA fills a niche that no other movie theater in Bangkok has yet dared to address (Kong 2007c).

One of the films shown at House RCA was Cyberfish Media's *Rainbow Boys* (2005). Based on the novel of the same name by American author Alex Sanchez, *Rainbow Boys* sold twenty-five hundred tickets over six weeks and was the theatre's fifth-largest grossing movie at that time. The story is about the boys Tat and Nat, who surprisingly meet their fellow student Ek in a gay support group. The story revolves around the blossoming love between Tat and his heartthrob Ek, who has a girlfriend and is confused by his feelings for Tat. The movie is educational in nature, as the producers see "a lack of positive self-images and 'sense of pride'" as the main problems within the Thai gay community, "They have no such concept that they could come out and live a happy life" (personal correspondence, 2007). As Rakkit Rattachumpoth has noted with respect to Thai gay fiction, "[It] often revolves around a romance which ends in tragedy" (1999, xiii). *Rainbow Boys* departed from this narrative pattern.

Silom Soi 2 (2006), a privately produced direct-to-DVD movie, had two public screenings at Bangkok's Century The Movie Plaza, in August 2006. The death of a friend had inspired producer Piyamitr Rangsitienchai to make this film about a gay love that is overshadowed by HIV/AIDS. It centres on Tum, who meets Kaeng at a downtown Bangkok gay hot spot, Silom Soi 2. Before both start a relationship, Kaeng sleeps with a Westerner who infects him with HIV. The movie relates their story until Kaeng's death—the scenes are divided by words in English alphabetical order that hint at their respective content: "P" for "Penis", for instance, when Tum grows impatient with Kaeng, who refuses to have sex with him due to the HIV infection he is hiding, and the letter "X" introduces the scene dealing with Kaeng's death and funeral.

Silom Soi 2 does not simply promote safer sex; it is also a call for gays to cherish love more than sex. Piyamitr states that his film was quite successful in terms of recognition, though some viewers did not understand the alphabetical structure, whereas others expected to see more nude scenes because of the sexy poster that lured them to watch the movie. While the manly actor who played Kaeng was admired, the more effeminate Tum did not arouse much interest. Piyamitr notes that "the gay target [audience] does not appreciate to view more *kathoey* or [people like] Tum", who looks like a "gay queen" (personal correspondence, 2007).

In parallel to these more educational endeavours of directors and producers aiming at local audiences, Apichatpong Weerasethakul, an outstanding homosexual director, has emerged with an international reputation as the most brilliant advocate of current independent Thai cinema. After establishing his own production company in 1999, Apichatpong started producing art movies that are often co-funded by foreign sponsors and lauded at international festivals but little known in Thailand. In 2003, while waiting for the funding for his movie *Tropical Malady* (see below), Apichatpong made a film for his friend, the Thai gay performance artist Michael Shaowanasai, who invented and personifies its main character, a *kathoey* secret agent known as Iron Pussy. *The Adventure of Iron Pussy* was Apichatpong's own interpretation of this already-established performance art character and, with its nostalgic colouring and its sweet musical acts, was an *homage* to the Golden Age of 1960s naive Thai cinema. By order of Thaksin Shinawatra, then the prime minister, and disguised as the housemaid Lamduan, Iron Pussy spies on the wealthy lady Madame Pompadoy and her Indian fiancé. Things get complicated when she falls in love with Pompadoy's son Tang, who is not only involved in criminal practices but is also Iron Pussy's brother. (It transpires that Madame Pompadoy is, indeed, Iron Pussy's mother.) The movie is progressive in that it does not make an issue of the main character's cross-dressing. Iron Pussy is never recognized as a *kathoey* by other characters in the movie but is depicted as a brave woman who is "man enough" to prevail over corruption and to benefit society, a message similar to *Saving Private Tootsie*, while mocking the type of nationalism that pervades that film.

Apichatpong first achieved international success with *Tropical Malady*, which earned him the Jury Prize at the Cannes Film Festival in 2004. In 2010, he won the Palme d'Or award at Cannes for *Uncle Boonmee, Who Can Recall His Past Lives*. Although the beauty and mystery of *Tropical Malady* have been acclaimed by critics, this complex movie has raised many eyebrows. The film is divided into two segments, the first relating the romance between a soldier and a country boy, the second depicting a soldier who is played by the same actor cutting his way through the jungle in search of a vanished boy, who may have turned into a were-tiger (Thai *seua-saming*), a mythical figure of Thai and Cambodian legend. The film depicts the return of man to nature, to the elemental instincts that have been blurred by culture, and exposes social norms that suppress natural drives such as homosexuality. As Apichatpong stated, "[S]ociety says two men do not belong together, but in nature it is more common" (Pfaff 2005). This culture/ nature divide is not only represented in the movie's structural dualism—the first part being played out in a town, the second in a jungle—but also within the sections themselves. Whereas the first part shows the two men gradually forgetting about social norms until, towards the end, they are licking each other's hands like animals, the second part depicts how the soldier enters the jungle in search of the tiger and gradually becomes one with nature. The leeches that suck on him become ever bigger, his radio set breaks down, fireflies turn a tree into a glowing antenna and try to contact the soldier, and a monkey appears and advises him to shoot the tiger "to free him [the tiger] from the ghost world or let him devour you and enter his world". On his knees and licking his hands, the soldier finally confronts the animal. The final scene shows a temple mural of a tiger stretching his tongue towards a kneeling man, symbolizing the soldier about to be swallowed by the tiger. *Tropical Malady* is a movie about cultural suppression and natural liberation—an elaborate message that so far remains unmatched in Thai cinema.[9]

Towards a Future for Thai *Kathoey* and Gay Cinema

> It will take a long time for the authorities to open their minds and stop thinking the entire country needs to be put into a school-children protection framework. (Vitaya 2007, personal correspondence)

Asked about the prospects of Thai queer cinema, Vitaya Saeng-Aroon seems pessimistic, given the censorship that movies such as his *Rainbow Boys* have faced. Though the film was shown uncut at House RCA, the VCD of the film was censored by the Ministry of Culture, which cut five minutes of kissing scenes. These deleted scenes were made available on the Internet (Bkktv.com), which has increasingly become an outlet for Thai filmmakers to present their audiences with scenes they are deprived of by the censorship board. The final VCD contains scenes with blurred-out sections and beeped words.

When, in May 2007, scenes from Apichatpong's film *Syndromes and a Century* were censored, the Ministry of Culture defended its decision as follows:

> [W]e cannot blindly accept everything practised by Western countries. We still have to protect society. Some Thai films, like Saeng Satawat [*Syndromes and a Century*], are very good I'm sure, but Thai people may not yet be ready for it. (Kong 2007d)

In December of the same year, a new Film Act was rushed through the National Legislative Assembly two days before general elections were held. However, the long-awaited new law has been criticized by many experts, as described here:

> [T]he act is one of several authoritarian laws passed at the very last minute to give the military and bureaucracy wide-ranging power to contain, ban and penalise anything or anyone deemed a threat to national security. (May Adadol 2008, 30)

The law replaced the 1930 statute and provided for the introduction of a rating system that governs access to cinemas by age classification and shifts responsibility for overseeing theatre screenings from the police to the Ministry of Culture.[10] Apichatpong called it a "law from hell" (Parinyaporn 2007) since the new Film Act continues to authorize the state to ban movies that "undermine or disrupt social order and moral decency, or that might impact national security or the pride of the nation" (Kong 2008a). Thus, Thailand now has both a rating system and a censorship board in place.

The Act's first "victim" was the indie documentary *This Area Is Under Quarantine* (Thunska Pansittivorakul, 2008) which portrays an erotic encounter between two young men, one a Muslim from southern Thailand and the other a Buddhist from the northeast of the country. This film failed to obtain a permit to be screened at the World Film Festival in Bangkok in 2009 and was eventually banned.[11] And whereas some observers have noted a new openness towards female and heterosexual nudity, the first movie to receive the sternest rating of 20+ was the drama *Mundane History* (Anocha Suwichakornpong, 2009) due to its depiction of a man masturbating in a bathtub (Kong 2010). The limits for more politically themed movies have yet to be tested.

But, with internationally popular filmmakers such as Apichatpong at the forefront, independent Thai producers and directors are finding it easier to circumvent local restrictions by applying for foreign funds and presenting their art at festivals around the world. Hence, in his skeptical assessment of the current Thai movie scene, Kong Rithdee, the *Bangkok Post* critic, pins his hope on creative local players and their global sponsors. "[T]he playing field will be kept ablaze with action by existing forces, namely the steady march of independent filmmakers [and] foreign funding that helps bold Thai films get made" (2008a).

But the situation within Thailand is also changing. As shown above, until recently economic considerations have led to a dualism in Thai queer film. Poj Arnon, director of a number of *kathoey*-themed movies, complains that "[t]here are *gay* movies which are not *kathoey* comedies but our producers are still not interested in making them" (Francis 2005). Yet, there are signs that the gulf between mainstream and independent queer cinema may be bridged in the future. Poj is the first director who has managed to make a gay-themed movie backed by a big Thai studio, Sahamongkol. Given the relative success of indie gay films at Sahamongkol's House RCA Cinema, the movie company may have sensed an opportunity in mainstream cinema as well.

Poj's *Bangkok Love Story* (2007) is about a policeman, It, who falls in love with a hit-man, Mek, who is ordered to kill It but eventually takes him to his rooftop hideout to hide him from his employers. After an extended sex scene, emotional conflicts arise that lead It to return to his fiancée. In a melodramatic finale, Mek's mother—who is suffering from HIV/AIDS, as is Mek's brother Mok, both having been infected by Mek and Mok's stepfather--commits suicide. It is then left blind from a gun battle with Mek's former boss, while Mek is imprisoned and—after many years have passed—Mok commits suicide at a hospice for HIV/AIDS patients. In the final scene Mek is released from prison but is immediately shot down by assassins and is depicted dying in the arms of It, who suddenly and inexplicably regains his eyesight.

The movie sparked criticism upon the release of its trailer in 2006, when the National Police Office feared that the film might damage its image in that It is portrayed as a gay policeman. *Bangkok Love Story* subsequently gathered dust for months. Finally, in September 2007, and after an aggressive advertising campaign, a much-edited version of the film hit the multiplexes—but failed among audiences and critics, with a box office take of only 11 million baht. Kong Rithdee found the movie's homoeroticism "inward-looking and self-serving", a spectacle that "is not designed to earn respect from straight viewers in the same way . . . *Brokeback Mountain* exquisitely shifts the sensitive gender issue into the terrain of universal romance" (2007e). Hence, the advertising campaign remained the most remarkable aspect of the movie. The film was advertised with posters showing Mek thrusting his fingers into the jeans of his lover, It. In his account of what he terms the Thai regime of images, Jackson (2004a, 196–200) pointed out that in 1974 the movie *The Male Prostitutes*, about the then-new phenomenon of men selling themselves to female customers, was banned because an advertising poster for the film showed two nude male bodies. The fact that *Bangkok Love Story's* campaign was allowed to proceed clearly reflects a change of control over representations of exposed male bodies in Thai cinema over the past 30 years.

In researching this chapter I conducted a non-representative survey among thirty-five cinemagoers after a screening of *Bangkok Love Story* at the Grand EGV cinema at Bangkok's Siam Discovery shopping mall in September 2007. The range of respondents, mainly young female and gay/*kathoey* students, reflected what I perceived to be the overall composition of the audience. Whereas 60 percent of the respondents liked the movie and lauded the ambitious cinematography, they were critical of the one-dimensional plot and the crude dialogue. A mainstream market for gay movies exists, but viewers are not satisfied when the depiction of homosexuality becomes an end in itself.

Two months later, in November 2007, Sahamongkol released *The Love of Siam*, directed by Chookiat Sakveerakul, a twenty-six-year-old director. Not shying away from addressing issues of broader significance, such as the tensions between individual aspirations and family conformity in Thai society, the film is built around a story of gay teen love. However, the movie was deliberately advertised as an ordinary teen flick, with billboards depicting two boys and two girls who seem to be engaged in a heterosexual love triangle, or square. Yet, the actual story had the two boys, Mew and Tong, falling in love with each other, leaving the girls frustrated and angry. During an extraordinary running time of 150 minutes, much time is given to character development, and realism is generated by the development of multi-faceted personalities and the setting, which is centred on Siam Square, the social hub of many young, middle-class Bangkok residents.

Critics lauded the movie for its social relevance, the acting skills, and its mature story line with an ambiguous ending. However, given its promotion by newspaper columnists and even the government-owned news agency MCOT, revenue of 40 million baht was still disappointing. Some viewers complained that they had been tricked into seeing a gay movie, whereas others defended its universal relevance, making it one of the most discussed films of the year. The reaction of audiences to the gently staged kissing scene between Mew and Tong reflected this polarization, with some viewers enjoying the romance, others starting to giggle nervously, and yet others displaying outright disgust.[12] Fed up with narrow-minded audiences, director Chookiat reasoned:

> When a movie announces itself to be a gay movie then you can already say the revenue will be gone and the attitude towards such a film will become negative [even] before people come to see it. (Thossaporn 2007)

However, soon after the release of *Love of Siam* a strong fan base emerged. When, in January 2008, an extended director's-cut version was shown at House RCA, tickets sold out immediately as crowds of people, among them many young men, queued up in front of the box office.

Compared with *Bangkok Love Story*, the bigger success of *Love of Siam* can be attributed to two factors. First, the movie was purposely advertised as a teen flick without hinting at its gay content. Second, *Love of Siam* was not hyper-dramatized but had a strong relevance, with gayness being embedded into a broader context as just one of the social issues and facets of love the movie explored.

Despite their differences, the fact that *Bangkok Love Story* and *Love of Siam*, the country's first mainstream gay movies, were both released under military rule may indicate a transformation within the Thai regime of images and its relation to gayness. Jackson has hinted at the possibility of change when the constituting influences of the regime change (2004b, 220–21). Today, openness towards gayness is internationally understood as a sign of liberalism. Accordingly, the constituting influences of the Thai regime regarding homosexuality have changed since the country first responded to Western notions of "civilization" in the nineteenth century.

To legitimize themselves in the wake of international criticism of the military takeover of September 2006, the anti-democratic authorities opened a channel through which to promote an image of Thai liberalism. Hence, those in power began to consider the demands of NGOs lobbying for queer rights, as Douglas Sanders notes in his chapter in this volume, and allowed gay movies to be advertised and shown to wider audiences. As Pasuk Phongpaichit, a political economist at Chulalongkorn University said in a speech at the Foreign Correspondents' Club of Thailand in December 2007, the National Legislative Assembly, the Thai parliament under the military government from October 2006 until December 2007, was carefully selected by the military's Council for National Security. Pasuk noted that, whereas the majority of NLA members were conservatives, some liberals were chosen to deal with social issues, but "the liberal bills cannot outweigh the controversial [conservative] bills".[13] Just as in the nineteenth century, Thailand's elite is struggling to persuade the rest of the world—and an increasingly assertive populace—that the country deserves a place among modern nations in that it is adapting local discourses on gender and sexuality to globalized, and also increasingly local, expectations.

Conclusion

In this chapter I have interpreted some of the diversity within Thai queer cinema in terms of the ways that it reflects local discourses on homosexuality and transgenderism. Mainstream movies most often depict *kathoeys*, as they are culturally and socially less threatening than gay men and are admired for enduring suffering as well as their individualism, therefore making issues of gender and homoeroticism accessible to the general public. On the other hand, independent gay filmmakers are reacting against the marginalization of gender-normative male homosexuals, who are perceived as more foreign than *kathoeys*. Through overseas connections, these filmmakers are introducing new cinematic styles. The movies may also help their gay audiences to gain access to positive self-images in contrast to internalized negative stereotypes.[14] The fact that they are introducing concepts of non-normative male sexuality that do not involve culturally ascribed (cross-)gender behaviours may hint at an opening up to representations of a fuller range of Thai queer life. In fact, the relative success of indie gay movies paved the way for an introduction of gay issues into Thai mainstream cinema. Filmmakers might take further advantage of opening spaces of public representation in the wake of a possible change within the Thai regime of images as related to homosexuality. Recent activities give reason to believe that the next wave of Thai queer cinema may be more than another string of *kathoey* movies.

Figure 5 Cover of the 2005 Thai paperback *Rainbow Boys 3* (translated from Alex Sanchez's 2005 novel *Rainbow Road*) featuring a promotional shot of the three stars of the independent film *Rainbow Boys The Movie* (a.k.a. *Right By Me*, Dir. Thanyatorn Siwanukhroh). As Serhat Ünaldi and Brett Farmer detail here, urban gay youth featured prominently in Thai cinema in the first decade of the twenty-first century. (Source: Cyberfish Media)

Figure 6 The cover of Issue 2 (December 2007 to February 2008) of *PLUTO: People Like Us Travel Orbit*, a bilingual English-Chinese gay travel guide published from Singapore and oriented at the increasingly mobile networks of East and Southeast Asian gay tourists who travel to gay venues, clubs, and dance parties across the region (see Peter Jackson here). The cover of this issue is a promotional still from the 2007 Thai movie, *Bangkok Love Story*, which dealt with a love affair between a Bangkok mafia hit man and the man he is ostensibly hired to murder (see Serhat Ünaldi here). (Source: Neu Ark Multimedia)

4

Loves of Siam

Contemporary Thai Cinema and Vernacular Queerness

Brett Farmer

Under its current entry for "Cinema in Thailand", Wikipedia (2010), the popular, open-content on-line encyclopedia, lists a total of eleven genres that it says are central to the industrial and aesthetic economies of modern Thai film. Of the eleven, the genre with the longest, most detailed sub-entry—and, not incidentally, the only one to have a hyperlinked cross-reference to a separate entry of its own—is "Gay Films". While possibly revealing more about the interests and enthusiasms of Wiki contributors than the actual state of Thai filmmaking, this example nevertheless highlights the extent to which contemporary Thai cinema has invested in, and consequently become popularly associated with, discourses of queer sexuality. From the transgender *kathoey* comedies and the "gay" melodramas of mainstream genre film through the homoerotic thematics of international art-house *auteurs* such as Apichatpong Weerasethakul, and to the iconoclastic sexual avant-gardism of indie filmmakers such as Thunska Pansittivorakul, contemporary Thai cinema is marked by a notable attention to queer issues and themes. It is a striking aspect of contemporary Thai film cultures detailed further by Serhat Ünaldi elsewhere in this volume, and it is noted equally by commentators at home and abroad. Kong Rithdee the resident film critic for the *Bangkok Post* newspaper, comments matter-of-factly that "queer characters have become a mainstay in Thai movies of the past decade" (2006a). Lisa Daniels, an international film-festival director, asserts in the same vein, "There are definitely countries that are producing more queer film and Thailand is one of them" (Hunter 2005).

The use of the term "queer" here is pointed. Despite the singular assurance of Wikipedia's classification of them as "gay", recent Thai films advance a wide-ranging exploration of a variety of non-normative, non-procreative sexualities, some of which approximate, but many of which exceed, Western concepts of gayness. In fact, as many of the essays in this volume attest, the question of whether Thai same-sex erotic practices and cultures can be nominated and understood through non-Thai discursive categories such as "gayness" or "lesbianism" is the focus of intense critical debate. Drawing largely from social constructionist arguments that conceptualizations of the sexual are culturally and historically specific and thus variable, most scholars today stress the need to apprehend Thai—or, for that matter, all non-Western—constructions of the sexual on their own terms rather than through the lens of hegemonic Euro-American sexual discourses (Morris 1994; Jackson and Cook 1999; Jackson and Sullivan 1999; Sinnott 2004). Precisely because the latter *are* hegemonic and thus obtain significant presence and value in global cultural economies, their influence on Thai eroticisms cannot be denied but, even here, how these transnationally circulating sexual concepts are taken up and made meaningful, or not, in the specific contexts of Thai sexual cultures is always and inevitably contingent. In addition, contemporary Thai sexualities are informed not simply by Western discourses but by other transcultural currents as well, especially those that circulate across the dynamic and increasingly influential intra-Asian cultural sphere (Berry et al. 2003; Erni 2005; Wilson 2006). Consequently, conceptualizations of Thai same-sex eroticism, even those that seem broadly congruent to Western notions, sometimes to the point of using the same or similar terms, are never simple importations or identical analogues, but socio-historically specific constructions formed in the complex determinative crucible of contemporary Thai sexual modernities, wherein pre-existing local patterns of sexual organization, which are themselves plural and shifting, intersect the multidirectional trajectories of transcultural exchange.

This chapter is an attempt to contribute to these important discussions through a theoretical and analytic reading of representations of male same-sex eroticism and other modes of queerness in contemporary Thai cinema. It proceeds from the proposition that cinematic expressions of queer desire in recent Thai films possess a distinctive cast that is at once specific and complex, forged in response to shifting discourses of Thai same-sex erotic intimacies as these are conceived and negotiated across the diverse field of modern Thai sexuality and the multiple determinants—social, cultural, and economic; local, regional, and transnational—that govern it. More specifically, the chapter intends to argue for contemporary Thai cinema as an important component of the popular mediated Thai public sphere wherein same-sex eroticisms, and other aspects of Thai sexual modernities, are apprehended and processed in variable ways.

In mounting such an argument, the chapter takes its critical cue from Miriam Hansen's influential account (1999) of popular cinema as a form of "vernacular modernism". A seminal contribution to the broader critical project of complicating and diversifying understandings of modernity and its cultural avatars—as precisely modernities and modernisms in the plural—Hansen's argument is that, for much of its history, cinema has been perceived and enjoyed as "the incarnation of the modern", an aesthetic medium that has not only emblematized contemporaneity but actively articulated what and how it means to be modern and up-to-date for variant mass publics around the world (1999, 68). Film, and by extension other audio-visual media, does this not simply at the level of representation—showing audiences what the modern looks like—but equally at the level of sensory experience: allowing audiences to sense how the modern might feel, providing an aesthetic matrix for the experience of modernity and its various identifications, meanings, desires, and anxieties. By calling this capacity of film "vernacular modernism"—a term that she borrows from architecture, where it has traditionally been used to refer to local adaptations of internationalism and other such modernist building styles—Hansen stresses the localized contingency of cinema's negotiations of modernity. As a mass medium, film addresses its viewers in and through the "language" and styles of the cultural vernacular, offering an accessible idiomatic register—or, more to the point, a range of idiomatic registers—whereby the multiple transformations of modernity can be processed in locally meaningful ways by different audiences.

Hansen develops her theory of vernacular modernism primarily in relation to American cinema, but her argument has been progressively extended to a range of international film practices, from early Shanghai and Japanese film to Indian Hindi or "Bollywood" cinema (Hansen 2000; Zhang 2005; Rangan 2007; Wado-Marciano 2008). As a highly technologized medium and a cultural form dominated from the outset by Western interests and product, cinema developed in these diverse markets as a heady amalgam of contemporaneity, historical change, and exoticism and quickly emerged as a crux for the multiple imperatives of local modernities: how to accommodate and respond to social, industrial, and technological innovation; how to become "modern" without becoming "Western", and how to adapt indigenous popular cultures and knowledges to the "new" realities of urban modernization and global capitalism.

Significantly, much of this work has focused on the role assumed by these competing international film cultures as popular forums for the idiomatic negotiation of sexual modernities. The radical changes in sexual economies and relations wrought by modernization and its attendant forms—urbanism, capitalism, consumerism, transnationalism, and so forth—are often regarded as one of the more spectacular and popularly resonant aspects of modernity, and film, as an aesthetic medium rooted in visual spectacle and sensational appeal, is particularly well suited for the cultural negotiation of such changes (Staiger 1995; Lowy 2007). The theoretical picture of cinema that emerges out of these readings is of a medium that images and, by so doing helps audiences to imagine, the transforming sexual economies of modernity as these are realized in diverse cultural contexts and through diverse aesthetic idioms.

While none of the work to date on vernacular modernism explicitly addresses Thai cinema and much of it, furthermore, is historical in focus, being limited to film cultures of the early to mid-twentieth century, it nevertheless signals a richly suggestive framework within which to consider contemporary Thai film, in general, and its expanding legacy of queer texts and images in particular. To the extent that modernity is an ongoing project, the role of cinema and other mass media as forums for vernacular modernism inevitably continues apace.[1] This is especially pertinent in Thailand, where the increasing scope and speed of modernization, particularly in the latter half of the twentieth century, combined with the expansion of mass media and their penetration of everyday cultural life mean that, if anything, the modernist capacities of cinema have intensified (Hamilton 2002; Lewis 2006). The much-noted renaissance of Thai filmmaking in the 1990s, for example, and the rise of so-called "new Thai cinema" such that, following years of relative decline, the industry experienced a sharp increase in productivity and popularity at home and abroad, has been explicitly linked by numerous commentators to the distinctive conditions of late twentieth-century Thai modernity. The resurgence has been widely understood and explained as a determinate product of the multiple economic and social changes that beset Thailand across the period—including, inter alia, the rapid expansion of the new Thai middle classes, the normalization of spectacular commodity cultures and the associated development of urban consumerist infrastructures, and the steady internationalization of Thai capital and cultural flows (May Adadol and MacDonald 2005; Sudarat 2007). The films of the new Thai cinema have also been routinely apprehended as symptomatic texts that capture and play out the multiple transformative dynamics of the late-modern Thai *zeitgeist* (Lewis 2003; Harrison 2005). Here, much is made of the new Thai cinema's historical rise in the immediate wake of the Asian financial crisis of 1997 and the consequent culture of social anxiety—what Tanabe and Keyes (2002, 5) term "a crisis of modernity"—that ensued, prompting many to define the new Thai cinema as a collective cultural response to, and working through of, this crisis (Lewis 2003; Anchalee and Knee 2006). Furthermore, the realm of the sexual is frequently identified as a key focus and symbolic lodestone for the new Thai cinema's explorations of modern meanings, desires, and anxieties. "Commentaries on Thai men and women as gendered beings and their problematic discourses", writes Pattana Kitiarsa, "feature . . . prominently in the post-1997 films" of the new Thai cinema, serving variably as "visible signs" and allegories of the "upheavals" and changes that have beset "the country's social realities" (2007, 409–410). This lends additional weight to a critical understanding of Thai cinema in terms of vernacular modernism, while also serving to contextualize its investment in textual tropes of queerness.

Housed within and informed by the new Thai cinema's broader provision of an aesthetic matrix for the expression of the multiple meanings of and responses to modernization, the rich constellation of queer images and themes in recent Thai films can be seen to work, at least in part, as a popular articulation and working-through of Thai sexual modernities and their transformative impact on social and cultural life. Peter Jackson (2000, 2003a) observes that the late twentieth and early twenty-first centuries have been a period of profound change for Thai erotic economies. In particular, throughout this period they underwent what he describes as an "explosion" of new sexual discursivity (Jackson 2000), manifest most notably as a significant proliferation of transgender and male and female homoerotic identity categories and a concomitant increase in the public visibility of new gender/sexual cultures. Through its manifold representations of queerness, contemporary Thai film actively engages with this explosion of sexual discursivity, contributing to the articulation of novel and/or re-imagined sexual meanings and possibilities, whether as nostalgic reaffirmation or negotiated revision of existing modes of eroticized being or the adaptive production of new ones. In this sense, the queerness of the new Thai cinema denotes not so much a set of textual representations of predetermined content and value as a processual negotiation of varied possibilities, a translation of the abstract discourses of sexual modernity into accessible and legible form: what might be termed, with a slight reworking of the critical terminology advanced here, *vernacular queerness*.

Thinking of Thai cinematic images of same-sex eroticism in terms of vernacular queerness underscores their interactive "embeddedness" in broader socio-historical contexts. As popular representations of the changing cultures of contemporary Thai genders and eroticisms, these films are not somehow separate from those cultures or mere neutral reflections of them. They are active participants in Thai sexual modernities, part of the broader constellation of discourses, practices, and institutions in and through which those modernities are realized and take effect. They are, in sum, integral components of the dense network of popular cultural and media "public spheres" wherein vital social and political issues—in this case the transformative economies of gender and sexuality—are engaged, debated, and made sense of.[2] As part of the popular mediated public sphere, these films work to express and visualize, both literally and metaphorically, the transformations of sexual modernity and the new possibilities of erotic being they engender. Therein lies their importance and also possibly much of their appeal. Like any such set of large-scale social changes, the transformative processes of sexual modernity can frequently seem monumental and overwhelming, occasioning a variety of negative responses that range from dissociation to phobic disavowal. In and of itself, cinema is not a guarantee against such responses and can even act as a vehicle for their propagation, but the simple process of queer cinematic representation in recent Thai cinema—of giving legible form to the abstract and potentially unreal discourses of erotic queerness, translating them into the accessible vernacular of film—serves importantly to actualize and humanize queerness, defusing much of its unreal alterity and/or, at the very least, offering a cultural space for its public expression and reception.

A critical reading of the new Thai cinema's varied articulations of non-normative desire in terms of vernacular queerness also serves to highlight and uphold the heterogeneity of those articulations, the fact that they possess neither singular form, function, nor effect. As a complex audio-visual medium, film is shaped by multiple dynamics—aesthetic, formal, technological, industrial, commercial, social, political, ideological—and is traversed by competing logics and voices. This multivocality is possibly even more accented in the case of a contemporary film culture such as the new Thai cinema, which must strive to address vastly diverse audiences constituted along local, national, regional, and transnational axes, to say nothing of the myriad intra-social distinctions of age, gender, class, and so forth that frame and regulate the practices and taste economies of contemporary film consumption across its manifold markets. Even within the Thai domestic context, which is, of course, its principal and most important marketplace, contemporary Thai cinema is faced with an exceedingly diverse audience base and must strategize accordingly with an equally diverse set of addresses and appeals. It is a social, industrial, and textual pluralism that is realized in multiple ways. Some films, particularly those produced by the mainstream studio system, which in Thailand as elsewhere, accounts for the vast majority of commercial filmmaking, will pitch for maximal address with multiple points of popular appeal—stars, polygeneric structures, high production values—and familiar, readily legible modes of representation: generic codes, narratives, character types, and popular national mythologies. The long line of populist *kathoey* comedies from *Iron Ladies* (*Satri lek* Yongyoot Thongkongtoon, 2000)[3] to *Sassy Player* (*Taeo te tin rabert* Poj Arnon, 2009)[4] is a clear example of this dynamic. Other films target particular audience segments such as teenagers or women and style their discursive registers accordingly. Recent examples here would include the female-centred comedy, *Metrosexual* (*Kaeng chani kap ee-aep* Yongyoot Thongkongtoon, 2006) or the teen hit, *The Love of Siam* (*Rak haeng Siam* Chookiat Sakveerakul, 2007), discussed in more detail below. Others may aim for even more narrowly defined markets such as subcultural audiences. The advent of digital filmmaking has helped make the latter an ever more significant component of contemporary Thai film cultures and can be evidenced in various manifestations, such as the emergence of "independent" commercial films geared to the developing subcultures of gay, middle-class males in Bangkok and other metropolitan centres. A good example here is Cyberfish Media, a small-scale company that started in 2001 as a publisher of select gay literature but which has recently branched out into film with the release of two, essentially straight-to-DVD titles, *Rainbow Boys: The Movie* (a.k.a. *Right By Me* Thanyatorn Siwanukrow, 2005) and *Club M2* (Nimit Pipithkul, 2007). Another set of examples comes from the vibrant campus-oriented, "indie" short-film scene that, through the influential work of self-styled queer filmmakers such as Thunska Pansittivorakul, Vichart Somkaew, Tanwarin Sukhapisit, Seri Lachonabot, and others, has emerged as an important site of Thai cinematic queerness. Still other films take a very different tack again, prioritizing a broader, transnational dynamic, whether in terms of middle-brow, art house-inflected mainstream films such as *Beautiful Boxer* (Ekachai Uekrongtham, 2003), or the avant-garde, international, *auteurist* cinema of Apichatpong Weerasethakul, or the equally transnational, film-based performance art of Michael Shaowanasai. While it would be difficult to imagine a type of consumer—other than an academic researcher, perhaps—who would engage all of these film forms on an equal footing, enough consumers would and do move across several, to caution against overly hasty or reified conceptions of them as totally disjunctive paradigms. For all their apparent industrial, aesthetic, and social distinctions, these disparate film practices share a common investment in the cinematic operations of vernacular queerness: imagining and giving textual embodiment to the multiple and shifting dynamics of modern Thai homoeroticisms and non-normative gender/sexual cultures and, by so doing, enabling diverse audience constituencies to apprehend and process these cultures.

Is it a Gay Movie or Not? Vernacular Queerness and the Discursive Ambiguities of *The Love of Siam*

The recent and celebrated feature, *The Love of Siam* (*Rak haeng Siam* Chookiat Sakveerakul, 2007), offers a fruitful case study through which to exemplify and consolidate the theoretical claims advanced here for contemporary Thai cinema as a collective site of *vernacular queerness*, the articulation and negotiation of Thai sexual modernities, in general, and Thai queer modernities in particular. Designed and promoted largely as a coming-of-age teen pic pitched to the lucrative juvenile market, *Love of Siam* quickly emerged as what industry pundits term a "crossover hit", a film that finds broad commercial and critical success beyond its expected target audience, earning impressive local box-office takings in excess of 40 million baht in its first month alone and securing widespread critical plaudits, including sweeps at virtually all the national film awards (Kong 2008b). Even more striking was the way *Love of Siam* engendered a devoted, cult-like following; many spectators went back for multiple viewings, and others flocked to a special sell-out season at the trendy RCA House Cinema of an extended, three-hour director's cut of the film hastily organized by Sahamongol Films International, the production company, to cash in on the film's unexpected success (Wise Kwai 2008).

A good deal of the expanded attention accorded *Love of Siam*, and by implication a good deal of its popularity, is directly attributable to the film's central engagement with queerness. Essentially a teen *bildungsroman*-cum-family melodrama, *Love of Siam* takes as its central narrative and affective focus the tale of two young boyhood friends, Mew (Witwisit Hiranyawongkul) and Tong (Mario Maurer), who, after a separation of several years and in the midst of various familial dilemmas, rediscover each other during their senior year at high school and rekindle a relationship that progressively assumes erotic dimensions, serving as a catalyst for emotional growth and resolution in their own lives and those of surrounding characters. It was the latter homosexual aspect of the film—including a frank, extended kissing scene between the young male leads, widely, if erroneously, reported as the first such occasion in a Thai feature film—that garnered most public attention and led to something of a mild controversy with, in the slightly hyperbolic words of one newspaper report, "[m]oviegoers around the country . . . up in arms . . . after discovering that [the film] isn't a conventional boy-meets-girl story, but rather the portrayal of a relationship that develops when one boy falls in love with another" (Vitaya 2007).

The release of *Love of Siam* in mid-November 2007 came as the culmination of an intense publicity campaign of several months' duration, wherein everything from print, electronic, and digital media outlets to city billboards were bombarded with teasers, advertisements, and carefully constructed stories intended to foster interest in and, as much as possible, pre-sell the film. It was the sort of multimedia "blitzkrieg" campaign that has come to be standard practice for many major Thai studio films, especially those pitched towards the crucial youth market, and there was little to indicate that *Love of Siam* would be radically different from other, similarly hyped releases. This was cogently evidenced in the film's principal poster art, with its snapshots of the two teen male protagonists lying supine on fluffy white pillows, gazing dreamily into space and neatly juxtaposed with matching shots of the two young female actors, Kanya Rattanapetch and Aticha Pongsilpipat, who play the relatively minor supporting roles of Donut and Ying. Publicity for *Love of Siam* thus appeared intent on creating an image of generic familiarity for the film, casting it effectively as an entry in the popular cycle of heterosexual teen romances that have been an industrial staple of contemporary Thai film production since the 1980s and that have recently found renewed commercial vigour with a string of major box office hits. These include *Faen chan,* or *My Girl* (Songyos Sugmakanan et al., 2003); *Pheuan sanit,* or *Dear Dakanda* (Komgrit Trimiwol, 2005); *Phror akat plian-plaeng boi,* or *Seasons Change* (Nithiwat Tharatorn, 2006), and *Pit therm yai hua-jai wa-wun,* or *Hormones* (Songyos Sukmaganan, 2008). Characterized, rather disparagingly, by Kong Rithdee as "kiddie love stories" set in "the ersatz world of pop-utopia where happy people prevail" (Kong 2006b), these films are widely noted for their populist combination of highly accessible, formulaic textuality with an ideologically conservative, nostalgic romanticism. Featuring immaculately fresh-faced, peppy casts in heart-warming tales of idealized heterosexual teen courtship, all told with a minimum of fuss and narrative complication, they are, in effect, profoundly "straight" texts in every sense of the term. By explicitly aligning the film with this cycle, pre-release publicity suggested *Love of Siam* would follow suit with a similarly conventional, candy-coated celebration of heterosexual schoolyard romance. Consequently, the film's queer content was not only unanticipated by many viewers but was actively experienced as a form of *genre shock.*

Long understood as systems for the organization of both textual and social meaning in popular cinema, film genres have been suggestively analogized by some critics to Foucauldian categories of discourse, the productive regulation of meaning in accordance with larger systems of cultural knowledge and power relations (Gledhill 1999; Neale 2000). Like discourse, film genres are effectively hierarchical "regimes of truth" governed by sets of common norms and limits and constraints in terms of what is known or unknown, included or excluded, central or marginal. Apropos of the teen romance genre of recent Thai cinema, while it is surely more complex and polysemic than many commentaries allow, its reiterative valorization of heterosexual coupling as textual and ideological ideal, the natural telos of narrative and personal progression, reveals the genre to be explicitly yoked to a discourse of *heteronormativity,* the systemic inscription of heterosexuality as dominant, universalized, and naturalized. By referencing but then refusing the generic promise of heterosexual union, *Love of Siam* effectively disrupts the discursive reproduction of heteronormativity at the heart of the Thai teen-romance film, establishing itself from the outset as a film invested in the problematization of received sexual paradigms and the exploration of new discursive possibilities. That it subsequently forwards the spectacle of homosexual desire in the displaced locus of normalized heterosexual union only compounds further a sense of the film as engaged in profound discursive *qua* genre transgression.

Small wonder that *Love of Siam* should have provoked widespread consternation on its release, with traditional media carrying select stories about audience reaction, both good and bad, to the film and on-line web boards abuzz with active discussion (Vitaya 2007; Nattakorn 2007). Much of this public dialogue was widely couched in terms of spectatorial disorientation, with claims that the film subverted audience expectations through its appropriation and contravention of the generic codes of the teen romance and accusations that the studio strategically sought to create an erroneous impression so as not to alienate unsuspecting viewers and/or to manufacture a media stir (Vitaya 2007). In such a context, issues of interpretability unsurprisingly came to the fore with many viewers struggling to locate the film generically and, by extension, place it within a regulatory framework of meaning. If the film's unexpected narrative detour into same-sex desire ruptured its presumed generic coding of heterosexual teen love story, how was it to be read and made sense of? It was a struggle manifested frequently in the guise of an anxious question, "Is *Love of Siam* a gay movie or not (*pen 'nang gay' reu mai*)?" This implicitly informed many reviews and reports in the traditional media, but the question was much more explicitly posed in on-line contexts such as Pantip.com, the popular Thai-language web board, where multiple threads animatedly debated the point, going so far as to put it to a reader vote. Tellingly, opinions were divided— quite literally in the case of the Pantip.com poll (2008), which ran 60 percent in the affirmative and 40 percent against—and no simple conclusions were reached; most commentaries asserted that the film exceeded unproblematic categorizations of gayness. "To label . . . *The Love of Siam* as simply a gay teen romance is to misjudge its power and intention", claimed one on-line reviewer (Cruz 2008). Another asserted, "It's not a gay movie. It's a teenage love story with a gay theme" (Bkkdreamer 2007). Even the film's director, Chookiat Sakveerakul, waded into the fray, claiming, "The movie is not all about gay characters, we are not focusing on gay issues, we are not saying, 'let's come out of the closet', so obviously, we don't want the movie to have a 'gay' label" (Vitaya 2007; Jureerat 2008). It would be easy, and possibly tempting, to dismiss such comments as blatant disavowals of the film's gay content motivated either by homophobia or, in the case of the film's director, economic opportunism, but to do so would be to reproduce an unhelpful gay essentialism, assuming that "gayness" has an empirical constancy that is manifestly there or not in the film for all to see and/or that possesses a uniform set of signifying effects. Against this, a more analytically profitable approach would be to take such comments at face value, accepting them as genuine, indicatively varied responses to *Love of Siam*'s articulations of same-sex desire, articulations that are not reducible to a single reading but, rather, are open to multiple and competing meanings.

There is a certain evidential logic to Chookiat's claims that *Love of Siam* eludes a gay label for, in many respects, the film plays out a quite explicit struggle concerning the issue of "labelling" or sexual discursivization, with a good deal of the narrative's momentum stemming from Mew and Tong's search to place and make sense of their desires and, by extension, their sexual identities.[5] When the two young men meet again after years of separation, it is obvious to them—and to us—that deep emotions have been stirred, giving rise to an increasingly intense relationship that quickly moves beyond conventional homosociality, but precisely where the relationship is heading or what status it will assume is decidedly less obvious. There is a quietly moving sequence midway through the film that neatly illustrates this mounting sense of ambiguity. Having resumed contact and rekindled their old friendship, the two young men return one evening to Mew's house—where, somewhat implausibly, he has lived alone since the death of his grandmother five years previously—and spend the night together, sharing the same bed in a way that directly mirrors the juvenile "sleep-overs" they had as pre-pubescent boys depicted in the film's prologue. Where the earlier childhood scenes were, however, filmed almost entirely through static long shots, this later scene employs a much more intimate cinematographic style—cutting from an establishing overhead long shot of the two teens lying in bed side-by-side into a rhythmic shot–countershot structure composed of carefully framed close-ups—that effectively emphasizes the boys' growing emotional interdependency. In a poignant exchange, Mew relates to Tong the feelings of deep loneliness that have plagued him since the death of his grandmother and his fear of "living an entire life without loving anyone", prompting Tong to place his arm around Mew and draw him into a comforting embrace. It is a scene that leaves little doubt about the boys' strong love for each other, a love that has continued from childhood, but it also suggests that something in that love has changed, even if what that "something" might be remains strategically undefined and unnamed. It is an unsettling ambiguity made all the more striking by the persistent interlacing throughout the sequence of visual intercuts that show, variously, flashbacks to the death and funeral of Mew's grandmother and scenes of Tong's mother driving the streets of Bangkok in desperate search of her son, as well as shots of Tong on the bus returning home the next morning, gazing vacantly out of the window. Fracturing not only spatial but also—with their fluid movement across diegetic past, present, and future—temporal coherence, these intercuts imbue the scene with a decidedly oneiric quality that further heightens the overall sense of nebulous uncertainty surrounding Mew and Tong's emergent desires.

This ethos of ambiguity equally informs the later, much-vaunted kissing scene, wherein, following a family party at which Mew has premiered his newly penned love song dedicated to Tong, the two share a prolonged kiss on the mouth, watched in shocked disbelief by Tong's mother and, if media reports are to be believed, in equally shocked surprise by Thai film audiences. In some respects, it might seem that the purpose and significance of this scene is a clear, denotative rendering of the boys' desire as finally and incontrovertibly homosexual, and it certainly can be (and has been) taken as such, both extra- and intra-diegetically. In terms of the former, this scene served as principal source and focus of the film's public notoriety and reputation as a "gay film", while in the latter case, several characters, most notably Tong's mother, Sunee (Sinjai Plengbanich), marshal the kiss as indexical evidence with which to read and castigate the boy's desire. Confronting Mew the following day, Sunee reveals that she saw him and Tong at the party and now understands everything (*khao-jai thuk yang laeo*). Yet, despite the professed certitude of her newfound knowledge, Sunee remains curiously unclear in her interpretative rendering of the boys' relationship, skirting around the issue with questions and metaphoric allusions. Not once does she explicitly denominate their desire as gay or homosexual, referring to it, instead, with a string of euphemistic displacements such as "this kind of relationship" (*khwam-samphan baep ni*), "whatever love you have for Tong" (*mai wa Mew ja rak Tong nai thana arai kor tam*), or, more negatively, "this path isn't right" (*thang ni man mai thuk-torng*). In return, Mew responds with equally indecisive circumspection, claiming not once but twice that he and Tong are "just friends" (*rao pen khae pheuan kan*). Thus, while the kissing scene in *Love of Siam* may well be a textual and spectatorial climax wherein the spectre of same-sex eroticism, which hitherto in the narrative has been confined essentially to the shadowy realm of connotation and suggestion, is most fully unleashed and registered in the realm of the visible, the meanings to which that eroticism is conjoined and the values it is ascribed remain, nonetheless, consistently ambiguous.

Within this context, it is significant to note that the word "gay" is uttered only once in *Love of Siam* and, crucially, it occurs in the form of a question. In a later scene, Tong, joining a group of peers for a social drinking session, is confronted by a male friend who, fuelled by alcohol-emboldened curiosity, turns to him and says, "I want to ask you straight out and you tell me, yes or no. Dude, are you gay or not (*meung pen gay reu plao wa*)?" The party falls instantly silent, and all eyes turn to Tong. Reeling back in embarrassed consternation, Tong blurts out, "You guys, this is fucking nonsense (*phuak-meung arai a rai-sara wa*)!" He then rushes out of the room. Ying, a young girl who lives next door to Mew and who has recently come to recognize the erotic nature of the boys' relationship, follows Tong outside to try to comfort him. After an initial burst of accusatory anger, followed by a moment of feeble sexual aggression, Tong breaks down and sobs, "What's wrong with me, Ying? What kind of person am I (*rao pen arai*)?" In many respects, Tong's plaintive cry in this scene explicates the organizational logic of his and Mew's evolving narrative, if not that of the film's hermeneutic economy at large. What am "I" when queerness emerges? What is the "I" of queer desire? How is identity to be defined in the context of same-sex eroticism; and, indeed, is it possible to have same-sex eroticism without identity? That these are precisely the sort of questions central to contemporary economies of Thai sexuality wherein, as outlined earlier, there has been a series of profound changes and a concomitant surge of new sexual discursivity, especially in relation to same-sex eroticisms and identities, indicates the extent to which *Love of Siam* relays and speaks to a much weightier set of social concerns and dynamics than suggested by its guise of a popular teen romance.

Thai reviews of *Love of Siam* seized instantly on the film's expanded socio-cultural resonances. "[T]he movie's carefully observed social nuances," *The Bangkok Post's* film critic wrote, "make it more than a glassy-eyed puppy-love diary, but a portrait of Bangkok lives at their most realistic" (Kong 2007f). "A movie that speaks to the whole nation," declared the Thai-language daily *Krungthep Turakij*, and one of which "all Thais can be proud" (Nantakwang 2007). While Nattakorn (Pleum) Devakula, a politician and media commentator, stated, "The film allows viewers, young and old, to ask themselves important questions about society, relationships, family, love and sex, leading us to understand ourselves in a more self-reflective character-study fashion" (Nantakwang 2007, 15). In this vein, many critics drew attention to the obvious double meanings of the film's title: "Siam" refers literally to Siam Square, a popular haunt of Bangkok teenagers featured widely in the film as a setting for its narrative explorations of teen desire, but it also assumes broader connotations with its allusions to the Thai nation-state. "[C]onsidering the film's scope and ambition," Kong Rithdee wrote in the *Bangkok Post* review cited above, its title should be taken "as a Thai (Siamese) grand narrative on many kinds of love" (2007f). Indeed, Chookiat, the director, claimed that a key objective in making the film was precisely to profile "a range of different kinds of love" and relationships in contemporary Thailand and ended the film, indeed, with the pointedly encompassing closing dedication, "To all the loves that bring us to life" (Nantakwang 2007, 25).

If, among these varied loves of Siam, *Love of Siam* foregrounds queerness, it is important that it does so neither exclusively nor in isolation. Tong and Mew's queer romance and subsequent struggle to find a meaningful place for their (homo)sexual desire may be the film's principal narrative strand, but it is embedded within a network of subplots that profile competing, and mutually imbricated, kinds of love and interpersonal relationships. Chief among these is undoubtedly family. A major subplot of the film focuses on Tong's family and its traumatized disintegration following the loss and presumed death of their eldest daughter, with the father sinking into alcoholic depression and the mother battling to hold things together financially and emotionally. It finds an echoing correlative in a back story of similar familial disruption for Mew, with the death of his grandmother and principal guardian and hence his effective orphaning. By setting Mew and Tong's romance against these twinned melodramatic scenarios of familial disintegration and loss, *Love of Siam* effectively aligns, if not equates, their struggle for queer self-definition and understanding with a search for familial integration.

Such a correlative referral of queerness to a contextual paradigm of family is arguably a widespread feature of Asian cinematic constructions of queer sexuality more generally. In a reading of gay representations in contemporary East Asian films, Chris Berry (2001) notes that a distinguishing mark of these films is that the emergence of homosexual identity is articulated and explored not so much as an issue of *individual* identity as *family* identity. In opposition to orthodox Anglo-American models, wherein gay identity is generally defined as *outside* of the biological family, something one "comes out" of the family into, the prioritization of family in East Asian cultures means that gayness registers and is mapped first and foremost in relation to family, as "a problem within the networks of kinship obligations that constitute the family and bind the individual into it" (Berry 2001, 213).[6] Even though Berry's argument is made in relation to East Asian examples and, Sino-Thai social hegemonies notwithstanding, cannot therefore be automatically transposed into a Thai context, there is a striking similarity between the filmic scenarios he describes and *Love of Siam*, wherein gayness is equally positioned as a "family problem" and worked out accordingly. This is arguably due to the fact that a paradigm of familialism, albeit one articulated differently from the Confucianist traditions of East Asia, is equally crucial to Thai social organization where, embedded in everything from the rich panoply of kinship terms and titles used in everyday Thai-language communication to economic networks of support, it is commonly used as a way of defining and regulating appropriate relations among individuals and between an individual and broader polities. In many respects, family is the *primum mobile* of Thai sociality, the prototype on which all subsequent social identifications and relations are forged. The Thai subject, asserts Niels Mulder, "is first and foremost seen as a member of a family, of a group that spells identity and that defines the relative position and all that follows from it" (1997, 309).

Mulder argues that it is this foundational orientation to familialism that lies behind the classic Thai predilection for rigorously hierarchized collectivism and the valorization of public appearance and harmonious role-playing. The paradigm of family assumes even further intensities in the Thai context given the much-noted centrality of familialism to Thai nationalist discourse and the conceptualization of Thai identity or Thainess (*khwam-pen-thai*) through an imaginary idiom of the national family with the monarch as patrimonial head (Mulder 1997; Reynolds 2002; Loos 2006). Indeed, Thanes Wongyannawa claims that a logic of familialism is so integral to discourses of Thai nationalism that "the Thai nation-state . . . is not so much an imagined community as it is an imagined family" (2008, 29).

To the extent that this discourse of familial Thainess has traditionally been heterosexually coded, non-heterosexual desires or queerness have often been perceived and represented as a failure of, or disruptive challenge to, Thai national identity and cohesion (Morris 1997; Loos 2006). The dilemma of queerness for traditional Thai discourse, then, at least as it is articulated in *Love of Siam*, is essentially one of both familial and national reconciliation, or how to assimilate queerness into the governing paradigms of the Thai (national) family. It is a dilemma starkly explicated by Tong's mother, Sunee, in the scene noted earlier, in which she confronts Mew about his developing relationship with her son. Beseeching him to desist for the sake of Tong's future and general family welfare, Sunee plaintively declares, "You know how our family has suffered. Tong is all we have left, and I don't want to see him taking a path that isn't right (*thang thi man mai thuk-torng*)." She then goes on to explain to a puzzled Mew, "In the future, after Tong has graduated, he should hunt for a job, save money, and look for a good wife, get married and have a warm family (*mi khrorp-khrua thi op-un*) where they can take care of each other in old age. That is life, Mew . . . and I raised Tong so that he would grow up that way (*ni man kheu chiwit na Mew . . . na liang-du khao ma pheua hai khao terp-to pai nai thit-thang nan*)." Metaphorized as divergent paths, queerness and the Thai family are thus represented as mutually exclusive opposites, and the effective task that *Love of Siam* sets itself is to disprove this popular (mis)conception—to show Sunee, and by extension the conservative popular Thai attitude she personifies, that queerness and Thai familialism can, in fact, be reconciled, that one can be the subject of queer desire without forsaking familial *qua* social obligations or disrupting familial *qua* social relations. It seeks to show, in other words, that the queer subject can be successfully integrated into the Thai national family without undue disruption or duress.

At this point, it is worth noting a crucial aspect of the film that has until now been left strategically unaddressed: namely, ethnic difference and the fact that Mew's family is Chinese-Thai, or *luk-jin*, while Tong's family is Catholic, or symbolically marked as *luk-khreung,* or Eurasian. Tong and his family are not depicted as literally *luk-khreung* in the sense of being interracial Eurasians, but their Catholicism, combined with the fact that the actor playing the part of Tong, Mario Maurer, is a well-known *luk-khreung* celebrity, effectively encodes them as such. It is a distinctive feature of the film that is quite heavily pronounced, and it was widely commented upon in almost all local critical receptions; one reviewer quipped that the film's unprecedented focus on a Thai Catholic family possibly made *Love of Siam* "the first Thai Christmas movie" (Wise Kwai 2007). Traditionally excluded, even reviled, as impure hybrids, the figures of the Sino-Thai *luk-jin* and Euro-Thai *luk-khreung* have, since the late twentieth century, undergone radical ideological renovation and reincorporation into the Thai nationalist imagination (Kasian 1997; Tong and Kwok 2001). Indeed, *luk-jin* and *luk-khreung* have emerged as high-profile, valorized figures of the contemporary Thai public sphere where, to borrow Jan R. Weisman's description of *luk-khreung* celebrities, they have been both "fetishised" and "glamourised" as resonant signifiers that "support evolving idea(l)s of Thai modernity" and that help "project a 'modern', 'developed' and 'cosmopolitan' picture of the country" to both local and international audiences alike (Weisman 2001, 232–233). By thus encoding Tong and Mew with competing cultural differences that, like queerness, have also, at one time or other, been regarded as "other" to traditional notions of Thainess but that have, more recently, been culturally assimilated, the film further underscores its liberal, pluralist agenda of (re)incorporating queerness as one difference among many in the ever-diversifying web of contemporary Thai sociality, a difference that ultimately does not make a difference to the familial integrity and harmony of Thainess.

It is perhaps only by understanding *Love of Siam* in these terms that the film's distinctive, and much-debated, ending makes narrative and ideological sense. After Sunee's visit, Mew reluctantly decides to stop seeing Tong, avoiding contact and leaving persistent calls and messages unanswered. Both boys become depressed; Mew drops his friends and a blossoming music career, and Tong feels fractious and despondent. Challenged by her son and others, Sunee starts to rethink her interference. She finally reaches a renewed understanding and acceptance in a gently understated sequence, in which she and Tong are trimming the family Christmas tree. Recognizing that she has failed to support Tong in the realization of who and what he is, Sunee quietly reassures him that she will accept whatever path he decides to choose. It is a choice that is symbolized in the form of a pair of male and female Christmas ornaments—an elf and an angel, respectively—that she holds out for Tong's selection. When Tong unhesitatingly picks up the male figurine and happily places it on the tree, Sunee smiles tearfully to herself in quiet resignation before looking up at her son with a nod of warm, maternal approval. Having made his decision and received parental blessing, the road would now seem clear for Tong to reunite with Mew as a couple, and all the film's generic and textual indicators seem to point towards such a happy "hymeneal" ending, albeit of the queer kind. Tong rushes off to Siam Square, where Mew, who has now also overcome his own emotional hurdles and reconciled with his alienated friends, is performing on stage. Tong arrives just as Mew is singing the uplifting chorus of the love song he wrote for Tong, the two boys grinning intently at each other in the midst of a euphoric, dancing crowd. However, instead of the expected romantic reunion, the two meet backstage, where Tong says gently, "I'm sorry, Mew, but I can't be your boyfriend," adding warmly, "but that doesn't mean I don't love you" (*rao khong khop kap Mew pen faen mai dai tae kor mai dai plae wa mai dai rak Mew*). After presenting Mew with a symbolic gift, the missing nose from a wooden toy he first gave Mew in childhood and which Mew has cherished lovingly through the years as a symbol of their friendship, the boys part; Tong goes back to his family and Mew to his own home, where, before the now-complete wooden toy, he utters a softly voiced, "thank you", tears streaming down his smiling face.

From the perspective of a Western-style identitarian homosexuality, this ending can be hard to understand and even harder to swallow. That Tong would decide not to pursue a relationship with Mew, even after having cleared all apparent obstacles, seems to defy logic, and there is ample evidence in on-line forums of bemused, and sometimes angry, viewers berating the ending as frustrating, even a "cop-out".[7] Read in the context of Thai familialism, however, the ending makes rather more sense. By telling Mew that he loves him but cannot be with him, Tong is not denying his queer desire—indeed, he is explicitly avowing it—but is effectively saying, rather, that he has ultimately decided to put family and his duties as a good Thai son before his sexual and romantic desires. Put another way, Tong opts here for a queerness understood in terms of inclusive familialism, where his role in the collective family is paramount and takes definitional precedence in defining his selfhood, rather than an exclusive individualist gayness, wherein (homo)sexuality becomes the principal axis of subjectivity. As such, Tong's clotural decision allows the film to achieve its desired reconciliation between queerness and Thai familialism, showing that, far from being a dangerous other or external threat, queerness can exist and be happily accommodated within the space of Thai familial and national unity.[8]

The film's failure to furnish the conventionally happy, hymeneal ending of the teen romance is equally consistent with the overall ambiguity of its articulation of queer desire and its concomitant resistance to discursive fixity. The bittersweet openness of the ending may foreclose the spectatorial satisfaction of complete narrative closure and the not-inconsiderable pleasure of a utopian romantic union but, by the same token, it avoids the pitfalls of reification and exclusion that inevitably plague semiotic containment. By refusing to channel Tong and Mew's queerness into the conventionally legible figure of the gay couple, *Love of Siam* leaves that queerness in definitional abeyance, open and fluid, an inessential sphere of possibilities with no singular form or necessary outcome. In this sense, the ambiguity of the ending helps *Love of Siam* perform its operations of *vernacular queerness* more effectively. If, as this chapter has argued, films such as *Love of Siam* function as vital sites for the popular negotiation of modern Thailand's rapidly changing sexual economies, then we can read the insistent indeterminacy with which the film encodes its constructions of queerness as matching the protean flux of those economies. Indeed, it renders such flux present in aesthetic form, while also affording maximum scope for an articulation of their multiple effects in discourse. By keeping open the question of queerness and the eroticized modes of being it engenders, *Love of Siam* enables its diverse Thai audiences to imagine—which is to say, realize—queerness in variable ways. In so doing, it fulfils the promissory function of contemporary Thai cinema as a public sphere of vernacular queerness, wherein Thai audiences can apprehend and process in an accessible and meaningful fashion the transformational maps of Thai erotic modernities and the ever-evolving loves of Siam.

5

Encounters in the Sauna

Exploring Gay Identity and Power Structures in Gay Places in Bangkok[1]

Nikos Dacanay

Introduction

As a young, gay-identified Filipino who first visited Bangkok in 2002, my
initiation into the gay life of the Thai capital came with a visit to the globally
famous sauna, The Babylon.[2] The images that played in my mind at the time
overwhelmed me: the multi-storey building in Mediterranean-style and
incorporating a hotel, gym, pool, restaurant, theme/fantasy rooms; an organized
business operation that employed upward of twenty individuals. I had entered
a highly urbanized Asian metropolis exposed to global cultures that seemed to
have embraced Western-style, gay-themed business establishments in multiple
sites across the city without resistance or hostility from the Thai public or
opposition from the Buddhist clergy. I was struck by the number and variety of
gay saunas across the city, as well as the other visibly vibrant and flourishing
gay businesses that thrived with the support of local patrons and Asian and
Western tourists, offering gay men multiple sites for interaction and networking
and avenues for sexual contact. To someone who had grown up in a relatively
conservative Christian environment in Manila, Bangkok was a gay Mecca.

In the years I spent studying Bangkok gay spaces and the performances
of Thai gay identities, working towards an M.A. thesis, I came to know more
about the lives of Thai gay men and to realize that, for them, Bangkok was not
the gay paradise I thought I saw (see also Jackson 1999a). While conducting my
fieldwork, my interviews with Thai men who frequent gay saunas and other
gay venues revealed how adventures in these places were not as unimpeded as I
had initially thought them to be. My research revealed that my informants spent
considerably more time in the sauna than in any other gay-oriented venue. They
told tales of how they met men in the saunas, the different ways they solicited
sex with other sauna patrons, the various negotiations over sexual acts to be

performed, and the differences between one sauna and another. But while saunas had become places where informants formed networks of friends and acquaintances and organized other gay-oriented activities, they were also places where gay men had experienced rejection and alienation because of their class or ethnic background, body type, or gender behaviour.

After following the activities of my informants closely, it became evident that the gay sauna, and other gay-oriented venues in Bangkok, are highly mediated sites. The movements in and around gay saunas are structured not only by temporal and spatial factors but are also mediated by Thai cultural discourses related to class, ethnicity, gender, and sexuality. However, while their navigation and interaction with men in these places were framed by strong mediating factors, my informants were nonetheless able to find ways to circumvent these structured places and spaces. Within these complex processes, conceptions of the self as gay are performed.

In this chapter I consider the relationship between the structures of power inherent in the movements in gay places and spaces in Bangkok and the performances of gay identity. The constituted images and reputations of The Babylon and Farose, the two gay saunas that are the main focus of this study, point to the power structures operating in these contested and constructed sites. I argue that, for my informants, being gay was fundamentally related to the histories of personal accounts of sexual and non-sexual experiences in and between these places, the voyages and movements becoming, as it were, a ground for performing the gay self.

In this study I caution the reader about the different systems and logics of gender and sexuality in Thailand. In the West, "gay" often carries political connotations, usually implying self-regard or pride in one's sexual and gender orientation. In Thailand, as in other parts of non-Western world, the use of the word "gay" is informed by social and class positionalities and culturally discursive constructs of sex and gender. According to Jackson (1995), some men in Thailand identified themselves as gay as early as 1965. Morris (1997) proposes that this gay identity, including Thai lesbian identity, points to a fundamental shift in cultural paradigms, from the traditional Thai system of three genders to a Western discourse that posits a sexual binary.[3] Because I am conscious that the word "gay" carries Western connotations of sexual-identity politics, which I cannot presume to be present in Thailand, I treat the word as a dynamic, self-ascribed identity that is, to borrow Mark Johnson's thought, "informed by a very different history of gender/sexuality" (Johnson 1997, 14).

Following Cannell, I regard identity in this study as a performative project, as "doing who they are" through the making and remaking of transformative relationships with others (1999, 247). I view identity as distinct from essentialist notions, constituting instead a kind of "cultural performance" in the process of objectification, identification, and embodiment (Johnson 1997, 19). According to Baumann, (1992) identity is performative in the sense that one performs cultural realities such as values, patterns of action, and structures of social relations by "being 'on' or doing something 'for the camera' in the course of ongoing social actions" (1992, 47–48). These cultural realities are themselves discursive by nature, reflecting Western and local values related to gender and sexuality. From this perspective, I consider the project of the gay self as a performance of various cultural discourses, with these performances taking place through a series of fields and locations—gay places and spaces, specifically here the sauna—in a dialectical fashion.

In this study I distinguish between "space" and "place". I take William Leap's definition of place to mean an accessible terrain, and space to mean a constructed, situated, "claimed" terrain (1999, 5). Gay space in this sense is created and owned by actors who transgress the heteronormative operations and functions of localities in the urban geography, carving out queer zones in the heterotopic architectures of the city through moments of rebellion and claiming territories for the expression of various transgressive sexual behaviours. Localities such as public toilets in shopping malls and public parks such as Lumphini and Saranrom function as gay spaces in Bangkok, having been appropriated from their mainstream, heteronormative functions to become recognized locales for male-to-male erotic rendezvous. On the other hand, specific venues in Bangkok are publicly acknowledged as gay places because they are owned, operated, or managed by gay-identified individuals, are advertised in gay media, and house business operations catering exclusively to a gay clientele (e.g. saunas, disco bars, go-go bars, clothing and accessory stores, coffee shops, and restaurants). These gay places are clearly defined and visible landmarks in the urban geography of Bangkok.

Researching sexualized places and claimed spaces that are constantly changing as Bangkok absorbs global tourism, Asian as well as Western, poses considerable methodological challenges. In this research, I have employed ethnographic methods to give emphasis to the personal, subjective stories of actors and to give meanings to their experiences. My focus here is limited to gay forms of homosexuality. It does not consider other identities such as the *kathoey* (male-to-female transgender) or male sex workers. By concentrating my research in the Bangkok metropolis and focusing mainly on gay saunas, I cannot presume to speak for other trends in the development of homosexuality elsewhere in Thailand. It is not my intention to generalize all same-sex sexualities in Thailand, but rather to look at the dynamic process in performing notions of gay identities as gay men in Bangkok move within and among contested fields of urban gay places and spaces.

I spent three years (November 2003 to November 2006) living in Bangkok and following the activities of several gay men as they navigated different gay venues in the city; the fieldwork focused on spaces of erotic possibilities and spheres of gay-related conglomeration that are composed of various establishments such as saunas, disco bars, malls, shopping centres, restaurants, and coffee shops. Field documentation and interviews with nine primary informants and eight minor informants, friends of my primary subjects and owners of and workers in saunas, formed the basis of my research. I carried out six taped, unstructured, and in-depth interviews that ranged from one to two hours and that were conducted in two to three sittings, with a gap of one week between one and the next. I also conducted non-taped and informal interviews in the field with my nine primary informants. All the interviews were conducted with the consent of the interviewees, and notes from these non-taped interviews were consulted as I moved from research to writing. The interview questions were loosely structured and were intended merely as starting points for discussion. I crafted most of the questions according to the direction the discussions took, clarifying and expanding on emerging themes. In this way, I gave my interviewees the agency to shape the conversations and emphasize things relevant to them. The interviews were conducted in Thai using a set of guide questions. Since I have only moderate Thai-language skills, I employed a Thai student from Thammasat University as an assistant and interpreter in conducting the interviews.[4] The tape-recorded interviews were transcribed and then translated into English by my research assistant.

While my broad project considered all of the gay-oriented venues where my informants ventured, I concentrate here only on The Babylon and Farose saunas because they were frequented more often by my informants as compared with other gay spaces. They also pose striking differences in terms of appearance, ambience, location in the city, and clientele, thus providing points of comparison between two gay places with similar business operations but with markedly different local sexual cultures. Gaining access to these and other gay places and spaces was not complicated, because of things shared in common with my informants, such as my age and sexual orientation. But because of my moderate Thai-language skills and the fact that I am not Thai, I was nevertheless "read" as a foreigner, and this may have inhibited more open and liberal responses to the interviews in some situations.

The Gay Geography of Bangkok

Bangkok is one of the major destinations for sexual pleasure and consumption on the global map of tourism and travel (Askew 2002). The dominant stereotype of the city as a global sex capital evolved from the local underworld of prostitution in the nineteenth and early twentieth centuries (see Barmé 2002) to the emergence of a foreign-oriented sex trade in the mid-1960s, facilitated by the US military's "rest and recreation" programme for personnel serving in the Indochina conflict. Subsequently came the economic boom of the 1980s and 1990s, which was marked by commercialization and large-scale investment in sex tourism that was partly aided by the mainstream Thai tourism sector. In the 1980s, Bangkok underwent broader cultural and economic transformations, and the city became the site for the formation of a variety of sexual cultures—lesbian, transsexual, and gay (Askew 2002, 253). The fast-growing Thai economy during this period allowed for the accumulation of material capital in the middle class and the growth of gay businesses. Several types of commercial and non-commercial sex businesses (i.e. saunas, dance clubs, go-go bars, gay magazines, coffee shops, and restaurants) were established.[5] Eventually, gay men were held in regard in Bangkok as trend-setters and fashion experts.

Gay venues are concentrated in several key locations in the city. Silom, which has become a popular red-light district for foreigners, has apportioned Soi 2 ("Laneway 2") exclusively for gay men. Saphan Khwai, which is located in the north of Bangkok, became a local, suburban version of Silom Soi 2. Primarily a residential area with some commercial establishments, it is a densely populated area of the city. Several alleys in Saphan Khwai have gay business establishments in close proximity to each other. In contrast to Silom, which has a more multiracial and international and middle-class demographic profile, the establishments in Saphan Khwai are primarily patronized by younger, local Thai men from lower-class backgrounds.

One of the most notable of gay places that mushroomed in Bangkok as it underwent rapid urbanization was the sauna. Like many of the other gay-oriented business establishments in the city, saunas were originally fashioned after those in Western countries (Jackson 1995).[6] Bangkok's first gay sauna was established in the 1980s and was significant for the fact that it was not located within any of the city's established red-light districts. The gay saunas subsequently established also followed this pattern and were located primarily in private residential neighbourhoods some distance from the sex-tourist areas of Silom and Sukhumvit.[7] Bangkok's gay saunas have at times been raided by the police and become targets of harassment by the government.

For instance, in 2001, a government policy called the Social Order (*jat rabiap sangkhom*) Campaign was imposed, as Doug Sanders delineates elsewhere in this volume. In September of that year, the Farose gay sauna in Saphan Khwai was raided and temporarily closed. However, it defied the initial police ban and soon recommenced operations, subsequently being raided by the police several more times the following year. The Babylon, located in the Sathorn district, was raided in December 2002 as part of the police crackdown during the Social Order Campaign. The local media accompanied the police on these raids, which were reported widely in the press and on television. While the crackdown on gay saunas was seen as a government public-relations campaign and not an isolated incident (heterosexual entertainment venues were also raided) the mediatization of these raids nevertheless created a negative impression of Thai gay men. Despite this, Thai gay men and tourists continued to patronize the saunas.

Over the years, the various gay saunas located across the city came to develop different characteristics and reputations. While they generally provided the same facilities, they were dissimilar in terms of their perceived image or "type". This classification and hierarchy was based on class, ethnicity, and cultural (re)productions of different models of gayness. The different saunas became sites for different typologies of Thai male homosexual desire. The adeptness of Thai gay men in differentiating Bangkok's many saunas from one another was based on their awareness of several criteria, such as the socio-economic backgrounds of patrons, architecture, interior design, entrance fee, and promotional events. For example, my informants stated that those who patronized the GSM Sauna were slightly overweight gay men. The Beach Sauna was popular with adolescent gays, while Cruising II Sauna attracted men of mature age. While The Babylon was said to be populated by "upper class" gay men, Farose was famous as the sauna for "lower class" men.[8]

The differences among saunas were expressed by Ween, a Sino-Thai professional in his mid-twenties. He said that all the saunas were different because each targeted a specific gay sub-population. Ween explained:

> All the saunas are different from the way they look and the kinds of people who go inside. Each sauna has its own character. The Babylon is for rich Thais and foreigners; that's why it's also full of money boys. One thing you have to know about The Babylon is that some of the Thai boys with big muscles and who look rich are only after the foreigners. These guys seem to have a lot of money and they are not working. For all we know their mother may just be someone selling noodle soup in the streets. Most of these guys are not educated, but how come their English is so good? I'm not the only one who thinks like this, but also my ex-boyfriend (who is a foreigner). He went there one time and

many of these Thai boys asked for money from him. They didn't ask for money literally, but one guy invited him to go shopping. The guy said something like, 'Oh, do you want to go shopping tomorrow? I'll go with you.' And do you know what happened after that? The guy wanted my ex-boyfriend to pay for his shopping. They shopped in Siam,[9] in those expensive stores. My friend didn't pay. He just said, 'Bye-bye you money boy. I don't want you.'

Farose Sauna is for those who like to go out at night and spend the whole night out. These guys don't have a place to go to after the gay discos close at 2 am so they go to Farose, because it is open until 6 o'clock in the morning. Farose is so different from The Babylon. Farose is something like a sauna for the lower class.

The differences among gay saunas imply a growing and vibrant market specialization in Bangkok's gay commercial sector. Indeed, gay places have altered the urban architecture of Bangkok. The accommodation of gay culture in the city through the zoning of sexualized sites and the apportioning of specific areas for gay establishments has changed the landscape and experience of the city. One clear example is the case of Silom Soi 2. Whenever the establishments in Silom Soi 2 close at curfew time, a crowd of men gathers at the entrance of this laneway, where most of the restaurants and stalls nearby are still open. The items that are peddled near this Soi, such as "muscle shirts", leather accessories, and popular gay music, cater to gay men. Men in revelry mode outside Soi 2 at two in the morning is a well-known sight in Silom and has defined the experience of the location.

The Built Environments of The Babylon and Farose

The Babylon first opened in 1987 at the corner of Soi Nantha and Sathorn Soi 1, a quiet residential street about two kilometres from the business, entertainment, and red-light district of Silom. Owned by a Sino-Thai man from a rich family that owns the entire soi, the original structure was a purpose-built, three-storey building and was initially intended to serve as a public spa for men.[10] The architecture of the first The Babylon and its environment and activities were captured in detail by Alex Au, a gay Singaporean blogger, who wrote about it in 1995 as follows:

> Babylon—the name suggests it all: freedom, idyllic tranquility, green bucolic surroundings, the cradle of hedonism, playground for the debauched, where the sole aim in life is the fulfillment of carnal desires and the abandonment of all else . . . As you leave the building into the real world, you know you have just left Paradise, and long to return. Babylon is the place where there is no discrimination, everybody's a minority, everybody sympathises, everybody understands. In the

few hours you have been there, you have left the world and all its prejudices, and entered another stage of existence where only pleasure and fulfillment await.[11]

Au details the importance of The Babylon and other Bangkok gay venues for Singaporean gay men in his chapter elsewhere in this volume.

In 2000, the sauna relocated further down Soi Nantha and expanded into the large complex I described in the opening paragraph of this chapter. Around this time, The Babylon was already widely known internationally among gay men, primarily as a cruising place for sex and a recreational place for social gathering. The expansive new compound now consists of a line of apartments, a courtyard, the home of the owner, and a seven-storey building. The first two floors of this building are part of The Babylon sauna complex and are accessible to all sauna patrons. The third floor is made up of massage rooms that are used only if a patron of The Babylon pays for the massage services available at the sauna. The rest of the building is The Babylon Barracks hotel. The Babylon also has several facilities that are connected to the building and that are open to patrons, such as the gym, pool, atrium, and cross bar, which serves as a restaurant and café, as well as a courtyard and a two-storey structure connected to the building by way of the atrium.

When the original The Babylon was built in the late 1980s, there was no gay sauna like it anywhere in the world. Euphemistically known among Thai gay men as the "Miss Universe" of all the saunas in Bangkok, it was the first Thai gay sauna that was said to have emphasized style and form rather than function (Atkins 2005). Touted as being one of the best gay bathhouses in the world by gay almanacs, travel guides, and Internet web sites, the prestige and image of the place is that of a gay complex with a sophisticated design offering international-standard services.[12] The owner of The Babylon chose this name for his sauna because of what he thought were its associations with the biblical Tower of Babel, to denote a conglomeration of different worlds and nationalities.[13] Atkins has made an analogy between the name "Babylon" and the "global" composition of its neighbourhood:[14]

> Soi Nantha itself is a very interesting neighborhood: the Austrian Embassy compound, the Consulate of the Sultanate of Oman sitting behind gilded gates, and the Banyan Tree Hotel. On the other side of the Soi there are new condos. My point is that the whole neighborhood is little islands of race, class, and globalisation all broken into particular areas. And no place is more so a global island than Babylon. (Atkins 2005)

The global flavour of the sauna is extended in its interiors. Themes are taken from different cultures, including traditional Thai architecture, Egyptian statues, and Mediterranean furnishings:

> A second courtyard contains both masculine and feminine symbols: the giant sphinxes that are standing up with their six pack-ed abs. There are concrete penises, very sharply edged to a kind of warrior style masculinity that contrasts with a rounded garden with feminine symbols which are taken from the original Babylon. The third courtyard contains a male-studded frame giving us a sense of Thai military valor. The sense of creating a textured sexuality drives Babylon, including the music, art, objects, media, and other things that are carefully constructed. (Atkins 2005)

According to Holmes (2001), cosmopolitan cities offer sites such as airports and shopping malls that have a "virtual global culture"—a culture constituting a fusion of many different cultures. Because of its foreignness, the experience in these sites is similar to a virtual navigation. This virtual culture is globalized since one's experience of it is similar in every airport and shopping mall around the globe (Auge 1995). The Babylon displays a virtual global culture similar to that of the airport and shopping malls. The hybrid textures and details of The Babylon bring to mind the marriage of different cultures and civilizations, similar to a Disney-like theme park that displaces local practices of urban Bangkok. The feeling that one gets when one enters the enclosed compound is thus similar to that of entering an airport, where objects, artifacts, and services are distinctly foreign. However, while both airports and shopping malls that express the blending of many cultures are globally replicated, The Babylon is not. The Babylon represents the virtual-like experience of the global culture of airports and shopping malls, but it has not been replicated in a gay scene anywhere else in the world. Thus, while the experience of The Babylon includes the foreign, among Thai gay men it is also simultaneously local. The Babylon thus represents and expresses a form of gay "glocality".

The Babylon recreates the heteronormative geography of the city, but this geography is altered and queered as homonormative.[15] The sauna complex recreates the public settings of the gym, swimming pool, fine-dining restaurant, wine bar, and so on that are commonplace settings in the Bangkok metropolis and are understood as heteronormative structures—built around the idea of privileging heterosexuality. However, when one enters The Babylon the senses are heightened by the presence of the male body—whether corporeal, visual, or textual. The place is populated by images of desirable and desiring men, suggesting an attempt to repossess public social space. The sauna is therefore transformed into a gay man's aspirational world where places are organically gay, and where being gay is naturalized. Within the confines of the sauna complex and other zoned sexual terrains of Bangkok, the open pursuit of desiring the same sex is thus normalized.

Like The Babylon, Farose is owned by a Sino-Thai gay businessman. It is situated in a secluded residential area in a row of townhouse apartments in Saphan Khwai, a northern suburban area of Bangkok that is not usually explored by tourists, and where residents are mainly ethnic Thais. Farose opened in 1993 and has since gained popularity within the gay community for its reputation for featuring more unrestrained sexual activities as compared with other saunas.

Farose consists of two apartments connected via a rooftop patio. The interiors of Farose are rather dilapidated, with poorly painted walls, broken mirrors and a neglected shower room. The entrance is via the first apartment, and its ground floor includes the locker area, dry sauna, steam room, shower area, and a mirror room. The second floor has a middle landing with a small gym. Customers who venture beyond this point have to remove their towels, as the second and third floors are "underwear only" zones. The rooftop has several benches with tables shaded by vines. There are food and drinks that are served for free. Not far from where the food and drinks are located there is an open doorway that leads to the second apartment. This is a naked zone and has an attendant that ensures that customers remove their underwear before entering. The rest of the establishment consists of a narrow maze of small rooms. While The Babylon has several wide, semi-private areas where patrons can lounge and relax, Farose is mainly comprised of tightly-packed cubicles. The three floors of the second apartment and the two floors of the first apartment contain rooms with small windows on the doors. Some rooms are bigger than others and do not have doors, allowing men to walk in and out freely. These rooms invite orgies. The basement in the second apartment has a disco and a bar serving free refreshments.

"Upper Class" and "Lower Class" Thai Gays: Gay Places as Contested Domains

The Babylon and Farose are situated within a gay geography of Bangkok in which the terrain is hierarchically marked by different categories wherein activities are organized along class, ethnic, gender, and sexual lines. While The Babylon and Farose serve the same purpose of sexual cruising, they are markedly different in that they host different gay cultures that are embedded in their architectures and the "types" of gay men who patronize each establishment.

The image of The Babylon as a sauna for cosmopolitan gay men in Bangkok is pervasive. Although The Babylon does not screen its patrons or restrict entry to a particular group of gay men, the way it is marketed as a high-class complex suggests that it targets middle- and upper-class local Thai men and foreigners. A large number of The Babylon customers are Caucasian men and middle-class Asian gay tourists from Singapore, Hong Kong, Taiwan, Malaysia, and the Philippines. Most of the Thai customers who patronize it project symbols of wealth. The Thai gay men who go there are generally dressed in fashionable clothes and shoes, have cars, and carry expensive mobile phones. They include "money boys" or "freelancers"—Thai men who work as temporary sexual partners for gay tourists during their stays in Thailand.[16]

The sauna encourages a specific type of gay body aesthetic. The sculptures and columns of The Babylon are prototypes of ancient Egyptian soldiers characterized by muscular body frames, broad shoulders, long and heavy arms, and compact abdominal muscles. The pornographic videos shown in the dry saunas and in the dark rooms feature Western actors who are muscular in build. These images insinuate that the desirable body is one that approximates these images. The male patrons who go to The Babylon are noticeably more muscular and have more gym-toned bodies than those who go to Farose or other gay saunas in Bangkok.

The fashionable ambience of The Babylon caters to gay men who lead what Dennis Altman (2001) refers to as an "international" or consumer-oriented lifestyle. The atmosphere of sophistication that is evident in The Babylon intimates not only a culture of elevated taste but also an equation of homoeroticism with a cosmopolitan lifestyle. Here, cruising for sex is part of other sauna activities such as fine dining and watching a drag performance. The Babylon becomes a part of a set of social activities for a sector of Bangkok's gay men. Thai patrons of The Babylon go to the sauna as part of an itinerary of gay excursions among friends, often preceded by shopping or dining out in a trendy restaurant and followed late at night by visits to the gay disco bars in the Silom area. This is seen in the example of Poon, an insurance agent, and Loon, a dentist, who are both Sino-Thai with above-average incomes. They met each other in a fitness centre where they both work out. Having common friends and recognizing each other in trendy gay venues, they became good friends. A normal weekend for them consisted of dining out with other common friends, a trip to The Babylon until ten in the evening, then followed by a visit to DJ Station, a famous gay disco in Silom Soi 2. According to Poon, he does not normally look for sex in The Babylon. It is just part of a habit among his friends to visit the place during weekends. "If I see a handsome guy and he likes me, then maybe we will have sex," he remarked. Poon added, "But I do not go there for sex alone. I do not need to. I just want to relax and be with my friends. If I want to have sex I can go to other saunas like Sauna Mania, Michelangelo, and Sam Kao (39) Sauna."

In contrast, patrons of Farose do not experience it as part of the gay social activities of the day but rather as a separate world, since it operates late at night, after other gay establishments have closed. As noted above, this sauna is not well maintained and a sense of interior design is wanting. It is in essence a collection of small cubicles. During the day, Farose looks like an abandoned warehouse. The absence of middle-class style and aesthetics directs attention to the exclusive pursuit of sexual pleasure that informs all bodily movements in the sauna. Men of all shapes, sizes, and appearances display their bodies in pursuit of sex with as many men inside the sauna as possible. Because sexual behaviour is isolated from other social settings and becomes the main focal point of interaction, it is performed with "abandon" since its context suggests possibilities otherwise impossible and unavailable (Tattelman 1999). The owner of Farose sauna may have intentionally created the atmosphere of a "raunchy", "working class" environment to mark it distinctively from other gay places in Bangkok.

The different characteristics of The Babylon and Farose, in location, architecture, and clientele, establish a hierarchy among those who patronize these saunas. While a key objective of Thai gay men who go to the two saunas is to have sex, Poon's remarks above notwithstanding, they are placed within a complex set of class, ethnic, and gender/sexual power dynamics that both enable and hinder them from achieving this objective. A level of discrimination exists; patrons of The Babylon regard the patrons of Farose with disdain because of perceived class and ethnic positionalities. To explain this more concretely, I introduce the case of Keen, who cruises for sex in Bangkok gay saunas using a complex system of body movements and actions.

Keen is a twenty-six-year-old ballet performer of Sino-Thai background and is a regular of The Babylon. He projects the "global gay" prototype described by Dennis Altman (1996a): moneyed, urbane, and displaying hyper-masculine, gender-normative behaviour. Like the typical The Babylon patron, Keen is conscious of his physical appearance and invests a significant amount of capital in looking attractive. He does this by going to a fitness centre, having regular consultations with a dermatologist, and wearing fashionable clothes. Keen restricts his choice of saunas, and once at his chosen venue he discriminates his choice of partners. He prefers The Babylon because it is "clean" (*sa-at*) and is a place where "proper" (*riap-roi*), "clean" gay men go. For him, Sino-Thais are the proper and ideal sexual partners because they are "clean and safe". Perhaps not surprisingly, Keen strives to emphasize his Chinese features by taking skin-whitening medicine. He said that he was not attractive during his college years because he was leaner and had darker skin from too much exposure to the sun. Many Caucasian (*farang*) men, however, were attracted to him for his dark features, but he did not pursue them because of the negative image attached to Thai men who seek *farang* as being money boys or prostitutes. As Keen related during an interview,

> I am not very good looking. I look smart. I'm not in the league of those very handsome guys. I'm tall and have slender muscles. When I was a fourth year student in college I was smaller and leaner and had darker skin, and *farang* would stare at me. When I went to Koh Samui the foreigners were eyeing me because I was much leaner then. When I went to DJ Station, Freeman Disco, or the sauna I would get stares from *farang*. But I didn't stare back even if I also liked them. I thought that the *farang* might suspect that I'm a money-boy if I stared back. Today, I think the *farang* do not find me either handsome or ugly, but just fine. I'm talking here of Caucasian foreigners: Americans and Europeans. Chinese and Japanese foreigners like me, I guess. I think Thai gay men prefer their own type. Asian men look like Thais in general—Chinese, Japanese, Singaporeans, Koreans, etc. Japanese men look slightly different. But Chinese, Hong Kong, Singapore men—they're quite close to Thai features. That's why I look for Thai and Chinese. Generally, Thai gay men like Chinese-looking men.

Keen has a longstanding relationship with Noom, a Thai salesman in one of the big department stores in Bangkok. According to Keen, Noom is a "real man" (*phu-chai jing-jing*), but because of a tragic experience with a woman who broke his heart he shifted his interest to relationships with men. This is the reason Noom cannot perform as a *gay queen* (be penetrated in sexual acts), so in their relationship it is always Keen who takes the receptive, or *queen*, role. In the course of their relationship, Keen developed interest in being a *gay king* (the penetrator in sexual acts) and he goes to the sauna so he can play a *gay king* role. When there, he looks for what he calls "small" and "pretty" gay men who will take a receptive role:

> Two years ago I preferred being *gay queen* because Noom had always been *king*. But last year I shifted to being *gay king* after Noom and I started meeting less frequently. I find it now more fulfilling. I don't want somebody to fuck me anymore. This is because there are so many *gay queens* in Thailand, and there are so many small gay men in the sauna. But I'm tall, so being *gay king* is better. When Noom wants to fuck he always does the action, and it's okay. But only with Noom. With other guys, I prefer doing the action.
> I like small and pretty guys. I don't go for big guys. I like guys with lean muscles and a smaller body frame so I can fuck them, since I'm

bigger. I also think there are more smaller guys who get attracted to me than there are big guys. And since there are many small guys around I can choose someone who's really good looking. Don't you ever notice that there are so many *gay queens* in Bangkok? There are just so many of them here, so it's better to become *gay king*, because it's easier to find someone to have sex with.

According to Keen, his muscular build also fits his role as *gay king*. To help him perform a *gay king* role, Keen regularly goes to a fitness centre to develop a more masculine appearance. Inside the sauna, he is noticeably more masculine in behaviour. He chooses men who have smaller body frames so he can play the *king* role with them. When he is not able to find a *gay queen* in the sauna, he becomes a *gay queen* himself.

When he is not in the sauna and in the company of other gay friends, I observed that, like his other friends, Keen often becomes camp or exaggerates effeminacy. This was particularly true whenever I was with Keen and his friends in his house, or when we visited his favourite noodle shop a few kilometres from the gay bar where he and his friends usually go. Keen believes that being gay is a continuous process of development:

> I don't think I can fit into any kind of gay. It's not very definite. I think I'm both *gay king* and *gay queen*. It's conditional. So many things influence me—environment, circumstance, conditions, etc. Who knows, maybe in the future I'll be straight or turn myself into a woman, right? I just go with the flow. I follow whatever may result from all the things that I experience around me. So many things influence me. If I become straight in the future I won't mind. Sex is sex. It's experimental. You just try to experiment with everything and choose what suits you best in life. I used to be a *gay queen*, then a *gay king*, but right now I consider myself simply as gay. I try to experiment whether I will like being this or that.

The attitude of Keen towards his gay life, the feeling that it is a result of his past life, reflects his Buddhist beliefs, especially the idea of impermanence (Pali: *anicca*), wherein the self and its desires are seen as fleeting. It also anchors with the views of Buddhism on homosexuality related to the concept of *karma*. Thais believe that homoerotic desires and transgender behaviour are the results of *karma*, for having committed heterosexual adultery in a previous life. According to Buddhist teachings, *karma* is an "impersonal cosmic law of ethical cause and effect, with moral actions leading to happiness and well-being and immoral actions leading to unhappiness and suffering. Within this schema, homosexuality has been viewed as a form of suffering but not as a sin" (Jackson 1995, 58).

Keen's preference for Sino-Thai partners reveals that the class disjunctures that permeate the differential mobility of Thai gay men among and within different saunas are also racialized. Since Sino-Thais dominate the Thai economy, Sino-Thai gay men are in general economically better off than ethnic Thai gay men and populate the gay-owned and gay-operated cafes, bars, and restaurants in the Silom area. They are patrons and consumers of cosmopolitan lifestyles and regular customers of The Babylon and Chakran, another high-end sauna. According to Girling (1981), the growth of the mostly Sino-Thai middle class in Bangkok since the 1970s has led to their hegemonic hold over Thailand's economy, political processes, and social values. Since Sino-Thai versus Thai ethnic differences are subsumed under socio-economic and class differences, Sino-Thais have come to be looked upon primarily as exemplary models of middle-class success and good taste.

According to Keen, being a *gay queen* or *gay king* refers to both sexual acts and varying degrees of masculinity and femininity. His notions of masculinity and femininity are constructed from various cultural sources. While he subscribes to the Western gay hyper-masculinity that The Babylon projects, he also performs Thai gender role-playing and the relationship between the two genders. Being *gay king* means performing the male role and therefore, by extension, exhibiting Thai expressions of manliness. As *gay king*, Keen chooses a *gay queen* partner— that is, somebody who is penetrated and exhibits more feminine, soft, graceful, and pleasant-looking features.

Because Keen takes the role of *gay queen* whenever he has sex with his longtime boyfriend but prefers to be *gay king* when he goes to the sauna, this shifting of roles in bed means that Keen identifies as neither *gay king* nor *gay queen*, but rather as *gay quing* (sexually versatile), or sometimes simply as gay. He said that gay means acting like an "ordinary man" (*khon thammada*), who alternately takes the *king* (penetrator) or *queen* (receptive) position in the sexual act. For him, there is a certain sense of equality in identifying as gay especially in the sexual act. "If somebody wants to smoke [perform oral sex on] me it's okay, or vice versa. But if somebody doesn't want to smoke me then I won't do it as well. It has to be equal."

The periodic shifts between being *gay queen* at home with his boyfriend and *gay king* at The Babylon are affected by an assessment of his erotic desires and the sexual possibilities in the sauna and other places. Surprisingly, through Keen's gay performance he is also able to sidestep these structures as he strategizes to find a sex partner in the sauna.

The idea that a gay place shapes conceptions of gay identity is not a one-way process, since these places are themselves shaped by gay men. Consider the transformation of The Babylon in the story of Noat. Noat, a Sino-Thai dentist, was a regular client of the original The Babylon and frequented the venue in the 1980s. He eventually befriended the owner. Noat said that The Babylon originally had a Thai-style interior design. After spending some time in London, he returned to Bangkok in 2002. When Noat visited The Babylon he was surprised to see the transformation of the place. It was four times bigger than the original building but had become somewhat less intimate. The interiors now resembled the gay bathhouses in London that had fantasy rooms such as glory holes, poles, and steel-chain curtains. This suggested to him that during the 1990s there had been a sharp increase in the number of foreign patrons, and younger Thai men began to take an interest in looking hyper-masculine. This prompted the owner to change the interiors of The Babylon to reflect a more masculine image.

Strategizing and Negotiating the Performances of Gay

Those who do not fit the model of the ideal gay of The Babylon face discrimination. However, those who are discriminated against employ counter-strategies to acquire a sex partner. We can see this in the case of Ween, who is half Chinese and is slightly overweight. Ween is often rejected in The Babylon. While he thinks that The Babylon is a community of gay men and a place where he can be himself, he still feels alienated in an environment that valorizes muscular men:

> The Babylon is generally a good place to hang out because you can have sex there and you can talk to people who are just like you. You don't need to pretend you're straight. But sometimes I get depressed because I can't find sex. Most of the men want guys with muscles, and I'm fat. Guys do not look at me. I feel terrible and insecure. So when I go home I call my ex-boyfriend and tell him, 'I went to The Babylon and I didn't get any guy. I feel so bad'. I feel better after talking to him. Sometimes we go to Farose when I can't find a sex partner in The Babylon.

Mink, an English teacher who is Sino-Thai and middle class, preferred Farose to The Babylon because his lean features made it difficult for him to meet a sex partner in The Babylon. Ook, a university professor who is also Sino-Thai and middle class, preferred GSM Sauna in Chinatown to The Babylon. GSM, according to him, was where overweight gay men such as Ook tend to go. Noat, a doctor and also Sino-Thai, went to The Babylon late in the evening when most of the clients were beginning to leave. He said that during the last two hours before closing the men in the sauna became less snobbish or selective. Since patrons did not want to waste their entrance fees by leaving The Babylon without meeting someone, they placed fewer restrictions on potential partners as closing time approached. On the other hand, Soom, a Muslim market porter who comes from southern Thailand, preferred Michelangelo Sauna in the afternoon, when there were fewer men and less competition for a sex partner.

My informants Soom, Potae, and Chon, who are all lean and not muscular, were regular Farose patrons. Potae and Chon are Sino-Thai, blue-collar, salaried workers. Unlike many The Babylon patrons, who oscillate socially between the sauna and other gay places, Soom, Chon, and Potae went only to the sauna. With only meagre capital to spend on recreational activities, they thought that going to Farose was more practical than The Babylon because it offered free drinks and food and had longer operating hours. For them, gay men who go to Farose are less pretentious than The Babylon patrons and are more direct (*khon kla*) when it comes to sex than the men who go to The Babylon, whom they viewed as snobbish. Potae said:

> I like Farose because you can be what you want to be inside. In the dancing area you can dance like Tata Young [a famous Thai female pop singer] and become "sexy, naughty, bitchy me"![17] There is no need to pretend to be a real man (*phu-chai jing-jing*) and have big muscles to get sex. Farose is more fun (*sanuk mak-kwa*).

Farose patrons reject the perception of The Babylon sauna patrons as promiscuous. For Mink, even if he has multiple sex partners in Farose he does not present himself as sexually adventurous. On the contrary, he says that, although he often goes to Farose, he only gets one or two partners during each visit and would normally stay inside the cubicle with his chosen partner for the night—until Farose closes. Mink says that he and his boyfriend have stopped having sex because, according to him, his boyfriend has become tired of him, so he goes to the sauna to satisfy his sexual needs and also to look for intimacy. Mink stresses the need for intimacy and affection more than his sexual needs. Because he often feels lonely, he seeks long kisses, hugging, and sleeping together. Mink considers himself a *gay queen* because he is small, and as a *gay queen* he is sometimes forced to submit to his partner's desire to penetrate him because he fears being abandoned or rejected in the sauna. By interpreting his sexual activities as a need for intimacy, Mink weighs the cultural value of love (*khwam-rak*) over lust (*khwam-khrai*). In Buddhist philosophy, the Third Buddhist Precept—to refrain from sexual misconduct—considers both love and lust as worldly attachments, leading to suffering. However, lust is deemed more harmful than love, and because of this is not socially acceptable (Kittiwut et al. 2007, 9). Mink therefore transforms the stereotype image of Farose-goers as promiscuous, low-class Thai gay men into someone who is in search of romantic intimacy as an expression of the loneliness of gay life.

Conclusion

The preceding accounts suggest that movements within and among saunas are mediated by the performance of gay identity based on different cultural discourses of class and ethnicity and notions of gay gender and sexuality. According to Tattelman's account from the United States (2000), the gay bathhouse or sauna homogenizes men of various backgrounds. Since everybody inside the sauna is uniformed by the customary towel wrapped around the waist, issues of class, ethnicity, and sexual orientation are rendered absent and insignificant in the interaction. However, in contrast to this American perspective, what is evident from the accounts of my informants is that the labelling of Bangkok's different gay saunas—based on their reputations and images as being either "dirty" or "clean", as well as the preference for a sexual partner based on his masculinity or femininity—underlie the power structures in this Southeast Asian gay geography and indicate that movements and interactions in gay places are framed under a complex set of mediating factors. Saunas in Bangkok project distinct qualities that impose different models of Thai gayness, and these models impinge on Thai gay subjectivities. The distinctive reputations of The Babylon and Farose in the mapping of gay sexual sites point to the power structures that operate in these contested sites. Gay Bangkok is composed of hierarchies of gay men whose class and ethnicity give them unequal access to, and mobility within, the city's gay saunas.

What is remarkable is that even though the saunas reflect structures of power, created and maintained by the performances of different gay identities, it is also through these performances that these power structures may be overcome. My informants employed strategies, such as staying in dark areas; going to "lower class" saunas; going to the sauna when there are fewer patrons inside and there is less competition for sexual partners; changing sexual roles (*gay king* to *gay queen* and vice versa), and choosing a sauna according to their body types. These saunas have generated diverse cultures, and as gay men strategize to maximize erotic possibilities and pursue their objectives inside these places, they subscribe to or resist these models of gay identity and negotiate their own conceptions of identity. In the process, they perform their gay self. This shows how Thai gay identity may be conceived of as being based on the practice of place.

My ethnographic research in the saunas in The Babylon and Farose reveals gay-identified Thai men as products, and at the same time producers, of homoerotic places in the city. These places configure and reconfigure gay identity as much as they are configured and reconfigured by Thai gays. This account of gay places and the activities of the men who navigate them illustrates how the cultures of these places provide spatial templates for shaping conceptions of gay identities apart from being places for sexual intimacy. The Babylon and Farose consist of images, activities, codes, and rules that govern these spaces. Men who enter these sites are influenced by these images and activities in performing their gay identities. These images and activities constitute cultural discourses. These places constrain and convey rules of how men should behave inside them, directing and imposing ideas about how gay men should behave, desire, love, or have sex. At the same time, the men who go to Bangkok's gay saunas (re)create and (re)constitute these places through the peculiar and often ambivalent ways they are used for pursuing diverse personal objectives. The (re)constructed meanings and associated functions of The Babylon and Farose add to the elements that characterize and locate these sites within the terrain of the gay geography of Bangkok.

Figure 7 Images of young Thai "men who love men" (*chai rak chai*) on the cover of Issue 12 (2008) of the newsletter of the Rainbow Sky Association of Thailand.

Figure 8 A 2006 safe sex postcard oriented at young "men who love men" (*chai rak chai*), produced and distributed by the Rainbow Sky Association of Thailand. The four "usual suspects" pictured hold cards displaying common identity labels among gay and bisexual men in early twenty-first-century Bangkok: "King" (sexually active); "Queen" (sexually receptive); "Bi" (bisexual); "Both" (sexually versatile). (Source: Rainbow Sky Association of Thailand)

6

Cyberspace, Power Structures, and Gay Sexual Health

The Sexuality of Thai Men Who Have Sex with Men (MSM) in the Camfrog On-line Web-cam Chat Rooms

Ronnapoom Samakkeekarom and Pimpawun Boonmongkon

Camfrog: The Sexual Globalization of Thai MSM

> Shocking! Thailand ranks third in the world in the use of sex show program Camfrog, following the US and China. (*Manager Daily*, 14 November 2006, p. 1)

In the era of globalization, the Internet strongly influences the lifestyles and behaviour of Thais in both their working and private lives. In particular, many Thai youths and young adults incorporate these technologies into their lives, behaviours, self-identities, and thinking, so adopting technological innovations to seek time and space to explore their identities and life experiences in virtual domains. One of the technologies they use is Camfrog. This programme fascinates its users, mostly male youths, since it enables the sharing of pictures using a web camera and voice communication in Internet chat rooms. It can be used for simultaneous teleconferencing among several people. It blends speech, images, music (including musical performances by DJs), and views of the actions of other people.

Camfrog has different rooms using different languages, including Thai, English, Italian, German, and sign language for the hearing-impaired.[1] Rooms in each language are further divided into various topic areas. All the rooms used by Thai men who have sex with men, or MSM, have been founded by Thais. However, all users in each room must use the specified language. Many foreign users join rooms such as GAYSpeakGerman, GayforEnglish, or GayFarang.

There are both heterosexual and homosexual/bisexual Camfrog users. However, most users are MSM who use Camfrog as a space to express their identities and desires, to find friends, "become someone", to find sexual partners, to listen to music, to display their bodies, and to find sexual pleasure in different forms. In physical spaces, by contrast, young Thai MSM have limited opportunities for such types of expression (when compared with heterosexuals), because their sexual orientation is judged, interpreted, and controlled through the heteronormative standards of mainstream Thai society, which still regards MSM as sexually abnormal or deviant. This is the main reason Camfrog has become popular among young people, especially MSM. It eliminates spatial barriers and thereby creates virtual spaces that are less controlled, restricted, or judged by external social norms than physical spaces.

Sex is one of the topics on Camfrog, often clearly reflected in the names of the Thai chat rooms, such as Gay Stroke[2] or Gay Zeed-sard,[3] and in the content of conversations in the Camfrog chat rooms. MSM know the rooms in which they can talk about sex or play around for sexual pleasure. This is not different from many other cyberspace media, such as video clips, web boards, or chat rooms using Pirch, which is another on-line chat programme that divides users into different thematically designated rooms.

However, mainstream Thai media have represented Camfrog negatively as a technology that young people use obsessively to view, exhibit, or seek sexual content. It has been presented as a technology leading young people into inappropriate sexual behaviour and to a life of crime involving entrapment and rape. It tends to be described and judged solely according to traditional ethics and normative standards and is often superficially linked to social and behavioural problems, such as pre-marital sex, unplanned pregnancies, unsafe abortions, sexual crime, or even the deterioration of national culture and ethical standards. Rarely, if ever, do the Thai mass media seriously try to analyse and understand the behaviours exhibited on Camfrog, the nature of on-line sexual cultures, or the beliefs of Thai youth regarding gender and sexual identity, all of which influence perceptions and awareness of risks and sexual health among young people who choose cyberspace as a domain for their sexual expression and exploration. The negative representations of Camfrog by the Thai media present an unbalanced picture and are singularly linked to calls to prohibit use of the programme among young people; the Ministry of Information Technology and Communications, the Ministry of Culture, and the Royal Thai Police periodically block the servers of Camfrog chat rooms that involve sexual matters.

Sexual matters among young Thais of all genders and sexual orientations are suppressed, restricted, and excluded by many discourses in Thai society. However, young people are now able to use Internet technologies such as Camfrog to evade social and cultural restrictions to create their own discourses and to share sexual matters with each other. The newspaper quoted at the beginning of this chapter indicates both the significance of Internet technologies to Thai youth and the capacity of new communication technologies to provide them with opportunities to evade barriers imposed by a morally conservative and culturally interventionist state.

Objectives and Methodology of This Study

This study reports the results of a research project based on anthropological concepts and approaches that was conducted to provide an account of the perceptions, explanations, assumptions, belief sets, and meanings related to sexuality and gender among Thai MSM on Camfrog. The chief aims of this project were to document the diversity and complexity of cultures among youth that use Camfrog for sexual purposes; to study the sexuality of MSM and their resistance to and negotiations with the power structures on Camfrog, and, finally, to analyse the perceptions and meanings of actions that constitute risks to and/or promotion of sexual health among MSM Camfrog users. The authors also investigated Camfrog users' points of view about the medium to provide a contrast to the wholesale condemnation of Camfrog users in Thailand's mainstream media. The premises of this research are that the sexualities of people of all genders, orientations, and ages constitute human rights and that they are related to and constituted within the social, political, economic, historical, and individual dimensions of human experiences.

One of the researchers, Ronnapoom Samakkeekarom, is a Thai MSM whose experiences have been formed and constituted within the context of an educated, middle-class background; he had already been a Camfrog member for a period of time prior to carrying out this research study. During the study period, Ronnapoom joined Camfrog rooms to interview MSM users of Camfrog to create networks for data collection and subsequent analysis.

The research methodology involved the observation, collection, and study of data from MSM Camfrog users in four chat rooms: Gay_Zeed-sard, NeoCamBoy, Gay_Thai_View, and GAY_PLAYROOM, which each have different sexual activities. Research was conducted during periods when there were a considerable number of users on-line. The researcher was a participant in these chat rooms and carried out participant observation from 10:00 p.m. to 3:00 a.m. on Fridays, Saturdays, and Sundays, which were the periods when the number of participants and the variety of topics covered were at their highest. The data were collected over a period of approximately six months, from June to December 2007.

The researcher used an ethnographic approach for selecting informants. He became a part of the on-line community by adopting the same identity as the informants and, with their prior consent, selected three informants for interviews and discussion of more in-depth issues than those possible by way of participatory observation alone. The researcher selected only participants who were able and willing to reveal a variety of information on a deeper and more individual level. Following this, the researcher created friendships with the informants by talking and exchanging ideas, life experiences, and sexual experiences with them via mobile phone and in face-to-face interviews. In this process, the researcher informed them of the objectives of the research; the nature of the in-depth interview process; the original Thai-language venue for publishing the research results;[4] the benefits they would receive from the research (they were paid for their time and told that the research might also be beneficial to their communities in an indirect way), and the effects that participating in the research might have on them. (Individual effects were unlikely, but publication of the research report might inadvertently result in temporary closures of chat rooms by state authorities.) This information was provided to help them reach an informed decision as to whether or not they should consent to be a part of the study. Next, the researcher made appointments with each participant to talk about sex in an intimate atmosphere at a place and time of the informant's choosing—as, for example, a restaurant with a private room, or the participant's place of residence.

The researcher collected texts composed of conversations from Camfrog web boards in each chat room where MSM expressed opinions. After each session of participatory observation, the researcher recorded the data in a Microsoft Office Word file. Interview questions were then created based on this data and used as guidelines for informal interviews with the informants. Prior to each conversation, the researcher asked the participant for consent to be audio recorded. After completing each interview, the researcher transcribed it into a text file.

After each interview, the researcher also wrote field notes about new issues that had not yet been raised on web boards in Camfrog chat rooms. The researcher kept all the data confidential and changed the names of the interviewees to preserve their anonymity and that of other people on Camfrog; he shared and analysing the data only with other members of the research team. The researcher conducted textual and discursive analyses to fulfil each research objective. The textual analysis involved identifying both explicit and implied meanings in the text. The discursive analysis went beyond this by identifying discourses underlying the text. After deleting material unrelated to sexuality, the data was then categorized to remove repetition and verified by interviewing the informants. The researchers and advisors brainstormed to generate ideas, alternative opinions, and recommendations for further data collection and analysis. All interviews were conducted in Thai, and the transcript excerpts shown below have been translated from Thai.

The Context of Thai MSM Youth: Not Just a "Trend", a Community

Cyberspace provides a venue for virtual communities in which face-to-face communication does not rely upon physical space. Within this virtual domain, individuals are able to leave aside normative attachments to aspects of individual identity, such as sex, class, or ethnicity. In the cyberworld, one can be anyone or anything one chooses to be. One can delete one's old self and create a new, virtual self, take on a name that no one knows, or even assume a mask behind which no one can see. Furthermore, cyberspace is not only an abstract space but also a social event or culture, structurally embedded with values, power systems, rules, and forms of hierarchy. Cyberspace is organized in terms of notions of femininity and masculinity, dominance and passivity. It is a cultural medium that creates both socio-political and socio-economic relations among individuals (Armitage and Roberts 2002).

Correspondingly, on Camfrog, individuals can create new personas, names, and sexual identities, or adopt user names that do not match their genders. Camfrog has chat rooms for discussing general topics, open to all members, and adults-only chat rooms in which members discuss mostly sexual topics. One can type on-line messages in the chat rooms, chat in private with particular members in the instant-messaging rooms, or enter rooms where MSM DJs play music, talk with, and control/direct other members by speaking into a microphone, all as detailed below.

According to the data collected, there were more than four hundred adults-only chat rooms on Camfrog and more than three thousand users each day, counting rooms in all available languages. While there were a variety of stated sexual orientations among the members, more than two hundred of the rooms were clearly intended for adult MSM, with more than a thousand users each day. These included both Thai and foreign users, as indicated by user counters on the web site. The number of members in each room varied according to the activities available. There were more users in the rooms that had sexual shows (e.g. shows exhibiting the bodies of DJs and the genitals of the members, showing acts of masturbation or sexual intercourse) than in those that had only music and dance. Sexual activities took place primarily in rooms with a high volume of users, which, in turn, attracted other users to join. Users also recommended these rooms to people of a similar sexuality.

Informants who had been using Camfrog for long periods of time since it was introduced in Thailand in 2006 stated that in the beginning, Camfrog had not been popular among MSM. There had not been many Camfrog chat rooms until mainstream media disseminated negative news and information about the programme, which was at first related mostly to heterosexual issues. Censored pictures from Camfrog published in the mass media stimulated public curiosity and incited a desire among more people to "check it out". As a result, at the time this study was conducted, there were more than a hundred thousand users each night, counting all rooms in all languages. This overall influx of people into the chat rooms increased the number of MSM chat rooms.

This study found that almost all members in MSM chat rooms were eighteen to thirty-five years old and identified themselves as gay. A minority identified as *sao praphet-sorng*, literally a "second category of girls", i.e. transgendered or cross-dressing males. Most members were students and middle-class professionals who had relatively independent lifestyles and were free during the evenings or late nights. Most MSM users logged onto Camfrog between 7:00 p.m. and 2:00 a.m. on Fridays, Saturdays, and Sundays, or during public holidays. 95 percent of these users logged on in the privacy of their own homes, where they could express themselves and their sexual identities as they desired, while three percent went on-line at an Internet café.[5] When the study was conducted, some Thai Internet cafés gave their clients a degree of privacy by providing more personal Internet zones partitioned into small rooms, which enabled Camfrog users at these public venues to use the physical space of the café in quite personal ways. The remaining two percent of users logged onto Camfrog at their workplaces or at schools during the daytime hours.

There were two main ways MSM users first became acquainted with Camfrog. The first was their friends' recommendations that Camfrog was better than either Pirch (on which one could get to know people via text messages only) or Windows Live Messenger (MSN), on which one could see the people with whom one was talking but only via a single camera. On Camfrog, by contrast, one could see the various people with whom one was talking via many cameras. Many therefore believed that Camfrog saved time and enabled the simultaneous creation of multiple relationships. DJ Phu, a twenty-six-year-old employee in the private sector, said:

> My friends told me there was a new fun program. After that, I installed and used it like MSN, in which two people can talk and see each other's faces. But via Camfrog, we can see all the people via a web cam. Having microphones, we can talk with one another although we're far away from each other.

The second way users got acquainted with Camfrog involved the television and newspaper reports that there were sexy shows by young people on the programme, which made some people curious to try it out.

The wide variety of primarily sexual activities and topics available in Camfrog's MSM chat rooms was reflected in the presence of following five types of users:

(1) First-time MSM users who wanted to know, try, and use Camfrog: If they liked it, members of this group would continue using it; if they did not (perhaps because such public activities did not suit their more private lifestyles), they would stop using it.

(2) MSM who wanted to listen to the music and programmes presented by the on-line DJs. (Camfrog members could request songs and participate in other activities, quite like listeners of radio programmes.)

(3) DJs who were all MSM themselves: There were not many in this group, but they were very important in the chat rooms because they were the only people who could speak using a microphone. (Others would communicate by typing instant messages.) They could give orders and instructions and persuade and control other users to follow the rules and regulations of each chat room. Each DJ had to establish his own identity to attract and impress other members. Most of these DJs created their on-line identities by telling jokes and sexual stories, or exhibiting dances, facial expressions, and gestures. Similar to radio DJs, they had to make their chat rooms popular to increase the volume of listeners/viewers in their chat room.

(4) MSM who sought friends, sexual partners, and sexual encounters. Most MSM Camfrog users in the adult chat rooms used them as virtual spaces for creating relationships or finding new friends and sexual partners. They did this in a number of ways—for example, by presenting social or sexual personas that could not be expressed in non-virtual life due to their jobs, ages, sexualities, gender roles or other reasons, or by engaging in sexual behaviour through words, conversations, body images, gestures, clothes, or ornaments. If the people contacted became interested, they would then take the relationship further by talking with each other on the phone to get to know each other better. Finally, they would make an appointment to see each other in a physical space such as a department store, apartment, or hotel. This would transform the virtual space of Camfrog chat rooms into a physical space, as presented through the messages on the web board. The following are examples of users specifying their locations with the intention of meeting someone near their physical location:

JeJe_123:	From the Thai Chamber of Commerce University. I want to make friends with someone.
lovejang02:	Anyone from Tha Nam Non?[6]
M_love_Yo:	From Ram 65 16/173/55.[7] I want to meet sincere people.

> **b_tirk:**   Does anyone live in Chiang Mai? I'll go there
> tomorrow.
> **kenjihatyai2007:** From Hat Yai. I want to make friends with someone.

(5) MSM who showed photos of their naked bodies or body parts considered sexy (e.g. chest, buttocks, and genitals); performed sexy dances wearing nothing but underpants, or performed solo or group masturbation or engaged outright in sexual intercourse. The findings suggest that Camfrog was used for expressing gender and sexual identities through body shows, masturbation, or sexual intercourse by single persons, pairs, and groups. This took place with the motivation that users could become "stars" or targets for the gaze of other users. These on-line displays could result from a user's own desires or from the admiration, request, from persuasion by other members who had already given a show or by the DJs. DJs would encourage shows by making references to ideas of Thai masculinity—for example, that "men never lose anything" (*phu-chai mai mi arai sia-hai*) by engaging in such activities because Thai society approves of male sexualities more than those of other genders. For example, DJ Wincy, a thirty-year-old civil servant, stated:

> I tell all Camfrog users that they have a right to reveal themselves. I
> use psychology to ask them if they dare to reveal themselves and that if
> they are fully manly, they must show [their bodies].

DJs and other members would encourage shows also by asking users to be "nice" and "good" members; by complimenting their bodies, genitals, and faces as good-looking (*du di*), sexy (*seksi*), cute (*na-rak*), admirable (*na-chom-cheun*), or attractive (*na-deung-dut*), and through direct challenges for them to be as daring as other members. If users felt embarrassed or were afraid of exposing themselves, they could perform without showing their faces.

Apart from words, symbols were also very important for constructing the context of desire, for increasing the attractiveness of MSM on Camfrog (common criteria for attractiveness are noted below), or for showing the kinds of sexual images described above. These symbols included pictures of flowers, thumbs-up signs, clapping hands denoting praise or persuasion, and assigning a certain colour to the performers, meaning that they were considered prominent, attractive, and interesting members.

The names of the chat rooms provided the first clue to the on-line identities of MSM in each area they had joined, because most chat rooms' names characterized the self, gender, and sexual identities of their users, drawing on terms generally understood within the context of the Thai MSM sexual culture. They were not all in slang, but most began with or contained the word "gay". Most MSM chat-room names were related to sex because adult Camfrog rooms were used primarily for sexual purposes. The names of the rooms sometimes represented activities taking place in them, and most were catchy, often mixing Thai and English. The names of rooms such as Gay Stroke, Gay Chak Wao,[8] and Gay Ma Du K[9] indicate that these rooms were for masturbation or sex shows. The names of rooms such as Gay Baby Boy, Gay Na-rak,[10] Gay Krapok,[11] Gay Y 2 K,[12] and Gay Kradae[13] were simply catchy words, while Gay Krung Thep,[14] Gay Chiang Mai,[15] and Gay Isan[16] denoted the geographical location of their members.

Bell has stated:

> [R]ituals are repetitive practices that determine privileging actions, as well as classifying and differentiating them from other types of actions. Rituals are the essence of a culture's expressions of difference, creativity, and privilege, as well as of differences between sacred and non-sacred, and serve as a means of authorisation through their enactment. Furthermore, rituals are practices for negotiating with and establishing an understanding of power, rightfulness, self, and society. (1992, 74)

In these terms, these chat rooms' names can be considered as parts of rituals through which MSM reveal and introduce their sexual and gender identities to their communities,[17] resulting in the construction of their identities in cyberspace (an abstract space nonetheless controlled by norms or sexual standards similar to a physical space, only to a lesser extent).

Furthermore, the chat-room names served a screening purpose for the people who would use them. Generally, those who were not interested or did not want to give a show or to disclose their status as MSM in these rooms would not join them. Some women and non-MSM men, however, did join these spaces out of curiosity. Nonetheless, because a basic rule of Camfrog was the requirement to engage in conversations via web cam, women were generally excluded from the MSM spaces. (If a DJ spotted a female user in an MSM chat room, he would probably ban that user.) Most non-MSM men, on the other hand, would leave the rooms soon after entering, since activities taking place in the rooms were specifically intended for MSM.

Thai MSM on Camfrog: Concepts of Sexuality, Power Structures, and Sexual Health

While Camfrog is a virtual space created by cybertechnology, users can nonetheless see one another via web cam and can create real relationships through chatting and viewing each other's bodies or sexual activities. In this space, people can express their sexualities quite freely; they are controlled only minimally by the rules that guide behaviour in the outside world. As seen in this study, MSM used the area for revealing their gender and sexual identities and for responding to their sexual desires through shared rituals and practices.

This matches the ideas of Zygmunt Bauman and Howard Rheingold (Lyon 2002, 25–26) that although cyberspace is a product of electronic communication, the relations that take place in this virtual space are real. Freedom emerges in cyberspace because of its capacity to transcend temporal differences, life backgrounds, and physical limitations. Cyberspace thus creates communication that extends beyond physical boundaries and temporal experiences and in this liberated form of communication new identities can emerge. A number of feminists thus consider that cyberspace provides women with a sanctuary for their existences, perspectives, and worldviews that contrasts with the material/ temporal realities that largely control dominant patriarchal cultures.

In this study, it was also found that many MSM used Camfrog to find temporary sexual partners who were particularly able to respond to their specific sexual desires. In such cases, both parties disclosed their faces and social and/or sexual identities via Camfrog, followed by an appointment in physical space. Some sought long-term relationships. In this respect, they focused on responding to emotional affection as well as sexual desire and would type conversations on the web board to indicate the preferable characteristics of their prospective partners. Furthermore, it was found that all MSM and DJs of all sexual identities could express themselves freely and openly on Camfrog, as seen in the sample conversations detailed above.

Criteria of Physical Attractiveness among Thai MSM on Camfrog

The analysis suggested that the concept of sexual pleasure of MSM was primarily centred on the desirability of a physically attractive and sexy body and/or face, defined as having the following characteristics: a good-looking face (*na-ta di*), smooth skin (*kliang klao*), "white" skin (*phiw khao*), no pimples or blemishes (*mai mi siw fa*), not being bald (*hua mai lan*), being muscular (*mi klam*), a good physique (*hun di*), no abdominal fat (*na-thorng mai mi khai-man*), pink nipples (*hua-nom si-chomphu*), and no plastic surgery (*mai tham salayakam*).

Genitals were one of the most important body parts for the gaze of MSM users of Camfrog, because they could show theirs to other members (even more easily than their faces because one cannot be identified by one's genitals). Most MSM expressed their sexual desires and their sexual pleasure by masturbating in view of other users. Sexual organs are used for attracting and creating sexual desire in other MSM. In the views of the MSM surveyed, an ideal penis should be big, long, clean, and not too dark. This is not different from heterosexual men's common view that a man should have a big, long penis. Furthermore, buttocks can also be sexually attractive to MSM, since most MSM have anal sex. Ideal buttocks were said to be neither too big nor too small; muscular and tight; have no wrinkles, and not have too much hair. Importantly, a body that can attract other MSM in the chat rooms must be naked, and its owner has to be daring enough to show it to other members in response to their own desires, their partners' desires, or in accordance with the rituals of the Camfrog chat rooms—that is, in response to other MSM members' demands.

Therefore, the bodies of MSM are not only physiological bodies but also social bodies, reflecting their location (urban or rural), status, role, and social class. For example, a muscular, nicely figured, and white-skinned body was seen as a representation of an urban, highly educated, healthy man as well as a sexy body. In turn, this influenced the construction of sexual desire, behaviour, gender, and sexual identities of MSM, as presented through conversations in the Camfrog chat rooms.

Chatting about Sexual Pleasure from Orgasm and Ejaculation

The analysis suggested that MSM sexualities mediated by Camfrog were focused on the achievement of orgasm and ejaculation by both parties while in visual and auditory communication. On Camfrog, the DJs and members in each chat room could respond to their sexual arousal and pleasure through masturbation and sexual relations. Furthermore, sexual gratification, excitement, or arousal through sexual expression on Camfrog came from performing shows and other activities for other people, even when they were in public physical spaces such as Internet cafés. Compliments and encouragement from other members also increased their sexual pleasure and gratification, as presented in the following conversation:

concor13:	Take it out and wank to make it come.
Hikaruz:	Horny . . . I haven't come for many days.
BENEFIT_BOYS:	The sperm burst right in the middle of the hole.
Cutedoctor:	Wow, [it] spurts!
Infiniteboiz:	It came out like volcano eruption! Superb! Very thrilling!
DJ:	Assumboy, please show the evidence after it's done.

This study also found that Camfrog members placed special emphasis and value on attaining frequent and extended orgasms in each period of on-line sexual activity. In a genital show, for example, the penis should be erect for a long period of time. Masturbation should last for a long time before orgasm or ejaculation is achieved, and performers could masturbate more than once each time they were on-line. In the case of sexual intercourse, the performers should perform a long act comprising multiple rounds, as reflected in the following conversation:

> **69bomby69:**   Excellent round! 69bomby69, great, second round!
> **ASUJI_KIGN:**   How many rounds already?
> **DEENPAE:**   It'll be the third round, Ek.
> **Jack2007Jack:** The DJ's really tough.

Gender Identity and Sexual Identity on MSM Camfrog

It was found that each MSM was limited in his ability to define and express identities within a given time period and context. The gender identities that the MSM expressed were defined in terms of a relatively simple "feminine" versus "masculine" binary, demonstrated by their expressions, speech, clothing, and actions. Similarly, the MSM were also limited in their definition and expression of their sexual preference within the period and context, since the gay sexualities revealed by MSM on Camfrog were essentially either "active" or "passive" only. There were not many MSM who expressed both masculine and feminine gendering, or both active and passive sexual preferences, or who alternated between these binary genderings and sexual preferences in different temporal or relational contexts—that is, in different log-in periods, or with partners varying in terms of experience, age, or social class.

Since Camfrog was used for responding to sexual desires and for finding sexual partners, the MSM found it necessary to continue performing or exhibiting the same actions to reveal their gender and sexual identities to other members. Similarly, they continued to talk or conduct their relationships with the partners they preferred through quite limited language references, such as "feminine gays" (*gay sao*), "masculine gays" (*gay maen*), and "active gays" (*gay ruk*) or "passive gays" (*gay rap*). It seemed necessary for Camfrog members to present an "expected persona". In other words, they had to reveal their gender identity and sexual preference clearly, unambiguously, and in accordance with their prior expressions to fulfil their own expectations and those of other members.

However, the gender identities and sexualities of the MSM were not always stereotypical, in that the so-called feminine gays did not necessarily have a preference for passive sexual behaviour, and the so-called masculine gays did not necessarily exhibit a preference for active sexual behaviour. This is no different from physical spaces in which gender identities are not necessarily in accordance with sexual preferences or behaviours. In line with Butler's argument (2000) that identities are constructed and not static, types of gender and sexual identities cannot be precisely identified because they are composed of various dynamic elements. Individual identities are not fixed but are constructed through repetitive and continuing expression and depend on the circumstances. Therefore, gender and sexual identities do not necessarily "match" each other. This is not to imply that gender and sexual identities on Camfrog have neither fluidity nor coherence. In the personal conversations between MSM preferring each other, we can see diversity, fluidity, and changes in gender and sexual identities.

Power Structures on MSM Camfrog

Based on the textual and discursive analysis of the conversations in the MSM chat rooms, as well as information from users, Camfrog also exhibited a power structure composed of a complex network of relationships within cyberspace. Sassen (2002, 109–119) has argued that while cyberspace can reproduce the masculine culture and patriarchal power hierarchies of mainstream society, it also enables women to negotiate with that power to create other realities. In a similar vein, Camfrog also exhibited a mix of enforced conformity to and transgression of mainstream gender and sexual expectations. There were definite power structures involved in Camfrog, with the following three levels of hierarchy:

(1) *Room/Server Owners.* This group influenced the setting, shaping, or reshaping of Camfrog chat rooms, and their positions of authority placed them high in the Camfrog power structure. It was the room/server owners who gave names to the various chat rooms which, as noted above, always had specific meanings and catchy connotations that conveyed the predominant activities taking place in the rooms. Furthermore, the room owners could reward members by giving various symbolic appellations to them (e.g. the colours blue, green, and grey denoted different levels of "stardom" or outstanding participation). Some symbols expressed not privilege but punishment, as room owners also had the power to expel members or even suspend access to their rooms from certain IP addresses[18] altogether.

Such inequitable power structures could result in a scenario in which any member who was also a sexual partner or boyfriend of the room owner would have certain privileges and therefore gain a greater sense of power and pride. Accordingly, the owners of chat rooms who distributed these privileges had the highest frequency of sexual relationships and the highest number of sexual partners in the rooms. To become the owner of a Camfrog chat room, one had to purchase a license and on-line time from the company that owned the server of Camfrog in Thailand.

Capitalism also influences Camfrog. The chat rooms on Camfrog needed income to pay for the rent of the Internet system and server—even virtual space requires real funding. The owner of each room was responsible for finding financial support, mostly from MSM-oriented venues and services (e.g. gay pubs, bars, saunas, spas, and restaurants). In the chat rooms there were messages that encouraged the members to use the services of such venues, often accompanied with special discounts or promotions. There might also be real-world meetings among Camfrog users in locations and businesses giving support to the chat rooms as a form of compensation. This would seem to make the virtual world turn into a real space, where seeking friends and sexual relations could occur more easily and rapidly. Camfrog members could join it for free.

(2) *DJs.* Following the owners of chat rooms, DJs had the most power, and they could strongly influence the number of members who visited each chat room. If there was a high volume of users or visitors each day, the business of the gay venues that advertised on Camfrog would be more profitable. As stated above, DJs often designed an on-line identity to generate interest among users through a particular expression of gender and sexuality, which might be something completely different from their identities in the real world. As DJ Tan, a twenty-seven-year-old employee in the private sector, said:

> I'm a girlish DJ. I say rude words and speak very loud. This is not my nature, though. I'm a top but the audiences thought that I was a bottom because of my feminine actions. I've got to make them adore me. If I presented them with a boring program, they would soon leave the rooms. They seek happiness and relaxation, not stress. They don't want to listen to serious things.

The DJs also had the power to stimulate, warn, prohibit, punish, or even ban members who did not conform to the rules of the rooms or did something possibly illegal (which could lead to the closure of the chat room by the police or the Ministry of Information Technology and Communications), such as posting announcements about commercial sex services or drugs, messages that might be considered slanderous towards the monarchy or the royal family, and deceptive or risky behaviour such as unsafe or unprotected sex. DJs could also stimulate desire among members to perform or exhibit sexual activities in response to the sexual desires of other members. Such encouragement commonly involved three tactics:

(a) The DJ might compliment a performer on his attractiveness (as defined above).

(b) If any member refused to give a performance, the DJ would plead with him by referring to the unfulfilled desires of all the room members, the importance of behaving well as a "useful" member, and the privileges he would gain from the show by receiving "colours" and other status symbols. If the member still refused to perform or if he argued that he might be affected negatively by, for example, public dissemination of his video clip, the DJ would negotiate with and persuade him further, explaining that all members were men and that doing a show would not bring the member any adverse consequences, that doing so was not unethical, and that the member would not need to show his face if he was afraid of adverse consequences.

(c) If the previous tactics did not work, the DJ could use his power to ban the non-compliant member from the chat room altogether. Or, short of such drastic action, the DJ himself might sometimes show his own body to create and promote the desire to perform, and to improve the atmosphere, but not too often, as members might then find this boring. DJ Wincy, the thirty-year-old civil servant quoted above, explained the matter as follows:

> All members must not only be part of the audience but also performers. Yesterday, I asked which members wanted to see a show by a boy and all of them voted for him . . . Then, the boy stood up. He was very handsome and gave a perfect show. Another boy was a freshman. Other members urged him to show but he didn't dare to. He gave me a *wai*[19] for forgiving him, which made me laugh. But later, he had sex with me in real life. It was surprising. I didn't think he would be so daring. He came to my room. He kissed me and gave a show via web cam. He touched my thing and gave me oral sex. For those who frequent the chat room but never give a show in exchange, I'll expel or ban them. They shouldn't be selfish.

Like the owners, DJs who distributed privileges had a high frequency of sexual encounters and a high number of sexual partners from the chat rooms, as stated by DJ Wincy:

> Being a DJ eases access to pricks. This is my target. This is our kingdom. I become a star and they are too. The stars have fucked me. We all know each other. There are no secrets. But if I find my true love, I'll have only him.

(3) *Users/Members/Performers.* This group constituted the bottom rung of the MSM Camfrog power hierarchy. However, among them, they had their own sets of power relations. Performers had more power than members who never gave a show, because the former revealed their bravery, expressed their identities clearly, and responded to the sexual desires of others (which made

them popular). But if a non-performing player had an attractive body and was the target of DJs, owners, or other users for on-line or real-life sex, he would receive more power and privileges, which provided access to more partners for both on-line and real-life sex. The users or members in general rooms who did not want to show their bodies and faces had the least power. Most of them were passive audience members. They might choose to have personal conversations but not to engage in collective activities.

Thus, power structures on MSM Camfrog were linked directly to the roles, duties, and status of members and participants. The people with the greatest power were the MSM room owners and DJs. This constituted a structural power that MSM assumed over their gender and sexual identities, and they usually exercised this power in active negotiation with their own sexual desires and those of other room members.

Autonomy, Negotiation, and Resistance on MSM Camfrog

Nonetheless, power in Camfrog did not always operate from the top down. On Camfrog, MSM members could also seek autonomy from, negotiate with, or resist the sources of power outlined above. The users within this category had sets of explanations and defined activities on Camfrog for receiving, resisting, and negotiating with the power exercised by other people by means of request, admiration, pleading, forcing, punishing, or banning to encourage a show or sexual activities. A user might contend that he already had a boyfriend and therefore did not want to do a performance or find a new sexual partner. Or a member might contend that he had neither a nicely shaped body nor the large, long penis that other members expect to see. These members would not care if they were punished or banned for refusing to follow directions because their intentions or agendas were not primarily sexual, as Wat, a twenty-four-year-old student, said:

> I've come here to find friends, not sex. If they ask me to give a sex show, I'll go away or to other rooms. In the general rooms, there are many friends to talk with.

The players often asked the DJs to participate in the body shows or sexual activities and negotiated safe-sex activities (e.g. using condoms and lubricant) with other members. And so, although the predominant power structures in MSM Camfrog were indeed based on the beliefs, constructs, and negotiations intended to encourage body shows and sexual activities or to stimulate sexual desire, the power and discourses of autonomy, negotiation, and resistance existed as well. There were some MSM who did not care about creating an atmosphere of sexual arousal through body shows or sexual activities in the chat rooms but nevertheless decided to give a show to avoid reproach. This was a means of compromising with the admiration, stimulation, or requests from other members, or persuasion from the DJs, to maintain one's status as a room member. Ar, a twenty-two-year-old employee in the private sector, said:

> In fact, I didn't want to give shows but was annoyed by those using IM[20] to encourage me and the DJs. I was bored with them. Therefore, I gave them shows. If I hadn't shown, I'd have been banned. After ejaculation, I didn't talk with anyone. It's like masturbation. I am also happy.

MSM Camfrog: A Virtual Space for Sexual Expression in the Context of Sexual Health Risks and Sexual Health Promotion

There have been government measures in Thailand, such as the Computer Crime Act, that penalize users and owners of on-line spaces with content that is deemed likely to undermine the state, violate individual rights, or show obscenity and immorality. While these measures have at times been invoked to seek to control the sexualities of young people in virtual spaces such as Camfrog, empirical data from this study show that Camfrog is still used as a space for expressing diverse gender and sexual identities and for the promotion of same-sex sexual desire and arousal.

While MSM Camfrog does not exist in physical space, the relationships among MSM on it are real. Accordingly, the status and quality of the sexual health of MSM who use Camfrog is a very real concern. The MSM interviewed for this study were asked to consider whether or how Camfrog and the activities conveyed through it created a context of risk and/or benefit to their sexual health. It was found that whether Camfrog constituted risks or benefits to sexual health was based upon various individual factors such as age, class, personal experience, gender, and sexual identity, as well as collective factors among the MSM Camfrog community—for example, common experiences and backgrounds, the viewpoints or behaviours of DJs, who can influence the ways of using Camfrog, and the predominant sexual values and culture of each chat room. Camfrog can promote sexual health among members of the MSM user community who share common lifestyles, backgrounds, and access to Internet technology. Camfrog is a medium for the expression of self and sexual identity, for seeking friends, advisors, or simply someone with whom one can share experiences and who can give one encouragement. Furthermore, it is a safe and secure space for expressing and responding to the sexuality of MSM, which is not the case with physical spaces such as public parks, pubs, bars, and saunas, all of which involve risks such as criminal victimization, the risk of being identified, and transmission of HIV and other sexually transmitted infections. MSM users also regarded the technology as safe, user-friendly, and globally accessible.

Body shows or masturbation performances are expressions of safe sex, occurring with mutual desire and consent. However, almost all the MSM considered that relationships originating on Camfrog were not permanent. Furthermore, as they did not know anything about the sexual experiences of their prospective partners, they had to use condoms and lubricants every time they had sex with a temporary partner they met via Camfrog. As DJ Tan, who was quoted above, stated:

> I don't know with whom they've had sex or if they have any diseases. I must protect myself. They safest way is wearing a condom. But if we have a long relationship and love each other, we may not wear a condom.

Nonetheless, MSM Camfrog can pose risks for the sexual health of MSM in some ways. For example, addiction to Camfrog may affect the health and work of MSM. Most MSM interviewed stated that they took little rest, became unhealthy, and had acne, which they attributed to taking so little rest that they had no time to clean their faces (an important negative consequence, considering the common attractiveness criteria for sexual partners). Some had fainted while using Camfrog because they had not eaten or had rested too little. Furthermore, at times there was pressure from other users on Camfrog to use drugs to make users alert so that they could chat longer and engage in longer, more intense, and more frequent sexual acts. Sometimes there was deceit and theft during dates arranged via Camfrog.

The study also revealed that while all MSM seeking sexual partners used condoms with their Camfrog partners, they did so primarily out of concern for HIV/AIDS, and not to prevent the transmission of other sexually related diseases (e.g. genital warts, Hepatitis B, syphilis, or gonorrhea). They tended to reason that while these other diseases can prove inconvenient and complicated to treat, they are nevertheless curable, while HIV/AIDS was seen as a deadly disease.

Moreover, while protecting themselves by wearing a condom when having sex with a Camfrog partner, MSM users of Camfrog did not do so with their long-term lovers (*khu-rak*), since the word "lover" suggested a deeper, closer, and happier relationship that the presence of a condom would seem to invalidate. The practice of sex without a condom with a permanent sexual partner or boyfriend as an expression of trust and love is not limited to the MSM community. The same happens among Thai heterosexuals, who also tend to believe that sexually transmitted diseases can be contracted only from temporary sexual partners.

Camfrog provides a virtual space for MSM in the context of Thai society as it is becoming ever more globalized. In this space, MSM members can create and build community by expressing themselves quite freely in terms of gender, sexual identity, and sexual activities. On Camfrog, interactions among MSM generate and build thought and belief sets about sexuality, perceptions, and awareness of sexual health, as well as personal and shared sexual experiences. These interactions significantly influence the awareness of both risks to and promotion of sexual health among the MSM Camfrog community. Importantly, since adult Camfrog rooms are commonly used for sexual enjoyment and relaxation alone, spending time to educate or raise users' awareness and knowledge about health risks might be impractical or of no interest to the user, DJs, and owners, unless an innovative format can be devised that users find interesting. DJs' involvement is necessary because they are the focal point of each chat room.

The thought sets and beliefs concerning sexuality, perceptions of sexual health, and experiences are embodied within the self-awareness of each MSM. Therefore, active promotional campaigns, education in matters of sexually related diseases, and continuing surveillance of risks and promotion of sexual health among MSM on Camfrog must be implemented individually and personally to provide interventions that are experienced as personally meaningful and relevant.

However, common sexual experiences transmitted through the Camfrog MSM community also constitute a kind of content through which knowledge and awareness can be communicated. Therefore, active promotional campaigns, disease-prevention education, and surveillance of risks and promotion of sexual health among MSM on Camfrog must also be implemented at the community level as an essential component of Camfrog's content.

This work should not be undertaken with strategies intended to close or eliminate Camfrog. The findings of this study suggest that thought and belief sets concerning sexuality, perceptions, and awareness of sexual health and sexual experiences are the essential factors leading either to risks or to the promotion of sexual health. These thought and belief sets are not a product of Camfrog. Rather, they are a product of human experience. Camfrog is but a medium. If it were closed or eliminated, similar alternative spaces would be created in its stead.

Conclusion: Cyberspace, Power Structures, and the Sexual Health of Thai MSM

This study has revealed Camfrog as an alternative space through which Thai MSM express their gender and sexual identities, participate in activities, and respond to their sexual needs. Camfrog is different from physical spaces used for sex by MSM (e.g. public parks, public toilets at petrol stations, saunas, spas, bars, and pubs). It is a virtual space for meetings and interactions without physical boundaries or limitations. Camfrog is highly personal and draws on the imaginations and experiences of its users. Moreover, on Camfrog, there is a potentially unlimited number of communities, networks, and chat rooms. MSM Camfrog thus does not need to depend on, interfere with, or overlap with the spaces of heterosexuals, such as public parks. Because community networks in virtual space can spread rapidly and widely, spatial and temporal differences almost never constitute obstacles to its activities.

As seen above, power on Camfrog does not operate from the top down only. In the interactions among MSM on Camfrog, there are examples of power manifested through resistance, negotiation, and autonomy, or power from other sources. On the one hand, Camfrog can be used an effective medium for the dissemination of information to promote the sexual health of MSM. On the other hand, participation in this virtual domain can also pose risks to sexual health. Whether it is beneficial or harmful to its users depends largely on the thoughts, beliefs, or discourses on HIV/AIDS and other diseases that are prevalent within the Camfrog MSM community.

Closing down Camfrog, as some Thai government agencies have sought to do, would not solve the problems facing Thai MSM; it would merely destroy a virtual space that is beneficial to diverse groups of people. Instead of closing down Camfrog, the opportunities offered by this medium need to be taken advantage of. Innovative health-promotion approaches are needed, targeting both individuals and entire chat-room communities, using the influence of Camfrog DJs to educate users about safer sexual activities and the promotion of users' sexual health.

II

Queer Bangkok
in Twenty-First-Century
Global and Regional Flows

7

The Romance of the Amazing Scalpel
"Race", Labour, and Affect in Thai Gender Reassignment Clinics

Aren Z. Aizura

We All Pay the Same Price

The clinic is a pink and white four-storey villa on the main highway through Chonburi, a provincial city on the eastern gulf coast of Thailand, one hour's drive from Bangkok.[1] A cosmetic-surgery clinic for trans people seeking surgical feminization, it is one of the town's most impressive buildings.[2] The highway is a smog-filled, eight-lane span crossable only by way of a pedestrian overpass. In this chaotic landscape, the clinic radiates an unlikely serenity. Inside, patients relax in the air conditioning and check their e-mail on the Wi-Fi network. After undergoing facial feminization surgery, breast augmentation, or, the most complex procedure, genital vaginoplasty, at a private hospital in Chonburi, patients use this clinic not only for consultations with nurses and the surgeon, but also as a lounge or a salon. A number of Thai attendants wait on the patients. Some are nurses, some are administrative assistants, and some are present to fulfil requests for cushions, water, or entertainment, or to provide for less tangible needs such as reassurance or affection.

The non-Thai trans women I spoke with who obtained surgery at this particular clinic described it as a very welcoming place.[3] Although the surgeon's technique is said to be outstanding, patients reported that they do not pay for his surgical skill in creating sensate vaginas and clitorises as much as for the entire "care package". This care package comprises full service from the moment one is met at Bangkok airport through lengthy hospital and hotel stays. It ends when a patient gets on a plane to return home, wherever that may be. The service, numerous patients told me, is second to none—even by the high, tourist-targeted medical standards of Thailand. "We provide the Rolls-Royce treatment here," a clinic manager told me.[4]

This clinic is one of seven or eight gender reassignment clinics in Thailand that service an overwhelmingly foreign clientele. Over the past ten years, gender reassignment surgery, or GRS, has become a very profitable procedure for Thai reconstructive surgeons.[5] Thailand is now known by many as one of the premier sites worldwide to obtain vaginoplasty and other cosmetic surgeries; indeed, many surgeons advertise that Bangkok is the "Mecca" of transsexual body modification.[6] While at least one surgeon in Bangkok specializes in masculinizing surgeries for female-to-male transsexuals or trans men, most surgeons performing gender reassignment surgeries in Thailand cater to trans women—that is, persons assigned male gender at birth who now live as women. These clinics see hundreds of patients per year, most from overseas.[7] Most clinics, such as the Preecha Aesthetic Institute at Piyawate Hospital in Bangkok, are housed within private hospitals with similarly large proportions of non-Thai patients. These clinics provide one of a range of medical services offered to foreign visitors to Thailand, now an international centre for "medical travel", or "medical tourism". They constitute a destination for many people globally who cannot, or who choose not to, access gender reassignment surgeries close to where they reside.

To gain a reputation for managing surgery candidates well involves careful attention to patient care. During major surgery, a process that involves a considerable and prolonged experience of pain, the practice of care demands, above all, attention to a patient's comfort. To offer comfort, of course, is distinct from the state of being "comfortable": One does not guarantee the other. Neither is comfort merely a state that pertains to the corporeal. It registers an affective disposition, and so does its opposite, discomfort. Comfort eases one's passage as one moves through the world. However, if there is difficulty in moving, one may experience discomfort. "If whiteness allows bodies to move with comfort through space," Sara Ahmed writes, "and to inhabit the world as if it were home, then these bodies take up more space. Such physical motility becomes the grounds for social mobility" (2000, 136).

To attend critically to the minute differentiations between comfort and discomfort within the gender clinic I describe above, then, might unfold into more than the mere narration of individual affects. Not all of the trans women I interviewed professed to feel comfortable there. Som, for example, told of difficulty with the aftercare procedures associated with her vaginoplasty, and also of feeling that she could not expect the same service as would be proffered to non-Thai, or white, patients. Som is Thai and grew up in the poor rural north of Thailand. She moved from her village as a teenager, first to Chiang Mai to study and then to Bangkok for work.[8] She met an Australian who became her boyfriend on www.thailadyboy.com, a *kathoey* dating site, and he encouraged her to migrate to Australia to live with him. He also paid for her gender reassignment surgeries at the clinic described above. During our interview, she initially said that her experience of surgery had been excellent. During recovery, she said, she felt like a "princess". Later, we began to discuss the fact that 95 percent of her surgeon's patients are non-Thai, the majority of them affluent American, British, or European trans women. Thailand is famous for its large population of *sao praphet sorng* ("second type of women"), or *kathoey*, male-to-female gender-variant people.[9] It seemed remarkable that non-Thais constituted the overwhelming majority of patients undergoing GRS at the most well-known clinics. As Som commented on this, she revised her previous narrative about the level of care at the clinic she had attended:

A. A: *When I talked to Dr ——, he said that most of his patients are* farangs [foreigners], *some from Japan, some from Europe, America, Australia. But not many Thais.*

Som: Because he is very expensive! He put his prices up!

A. A.:   *Many of them put their prices up, I heard. Also Dr ——?*

Som: Dr ——, I didn't like. He doesn't even care about the Thais.

A. A.:   *What surgeons do Thai* kathoey *or ladyboys go to?*

Som: Well, they can do [surgery] in a public hospital, which is quite a reasonable price, and the result might not be . . . not so good. And sometimes I hear from Thai ladyboys and some people, they said that in photos, it looks weird, it's not the same as . . . [Gesturing to herself]

A. A.:   *Not the same as your surgery?*

Som: No. It looked terrible. Indeed.

A. A.:   *What do you think about this, that the best [clinics] seem to be for* farangs [foreigners], *and some surgeons don't seem to care about Thais?*

Som: Dr ——'s staff [at the clinic] too. When I come to meet them, they will be very nice to foreigners. But they forget about Thais . . . Because they think foreigners have lots of money, more than Thai. But we all pay the same price! So, we should deserve to have the same service. But we don't have the right to say that.[10]

Another patient, Emma, is Vietnamese and had been living in Australia for twelve years when she had gender reassignment surgery in Bangkok in 2006. She travelled to Thailand from Australia and stayed in one of Bangkok's premier medical-tourism hospitals, having surgery with the one of most well-known surgeons practicing GRS in Bangkok. Emma was travelling without a support person. By the time I met her, during her recovery from surgery, she had decided that coming to Thailand was a bad idea. She said she would advise trans people in Australia to obtain surgery with Australian surgeons:

> Dr —— is very busy and it's very difficult to get him to come to see me.
> I am very annoyed. Also, the nurses do not come to see me. I ring and it
> takes half an hour for them to come . . . I didn't bring anyone with me to
> take care of me after the operation. They told me on the phone that the
> nurses would take care of me, but where are the nurses?[11]

To place these comments in context, the majority of Australian trans women involved in my project were scathing about Australian surgeons' technique. Most agreed that the hospital care available in Thailand far surpassed that available even in Australian private hospitals. Karen, a white trans woman living in Brisbane, Australia, who obtained GRS in an equally well-resourced hospital in Phuket, commented that the hospital felt more like a hotel. "[There were] heaps of nurses, everybody always had lots of time . . . You could ask for something and five minutes later it was in the room."[12] Som's and Emma's stories did not match the overwhelmingly positive narratives I heard from Americans, Britons, and Australians who attended the same clinics at the same time and underwent the same procedures and who were apparently paying for the same service.

Ahmed appends the lines cited above on comfort and whiteness with a cautionary caveat. "This extension of white motility should not be confused with freedom. To move easily is not [necessarily] to move freely" (2000, 136). It is clear that even white-skinned or affluent gender-variant subjects are not guaranteed freedom. Across the globe, gender reassignment technologies such as hormones and surgery are notoriously difficult for gender-variant people to access. With few exceptions, most governments refuse to cover gender reassignment under public health funding (Lombardi 2007; Namaste 2000). Private health insurance corporations are equally reluctant to cover what is regarded as "elective" treatment (Butler 2006; Gorton 2006). If the provision of gender reassignment surgery began in Thailand as a market serving the large number of local *kathoeys*, over the past ten years it has transformed into a niche medical-tourism market targeted to well-off citizens of affluent nations. Yet the fact that gender reassignment surgery is big business in Thailand does not account for why, in a clinic that is reputed to provide the best care and clearly has the capacity to do so, Som felt that the staff cared more about foreigners than Thais. Neither does it account for why Emma articulated that her needs were not valued. It is dangerous to generalize a distinct frame of experience from two personal accounts, and this is not my intention. Nevertheless, these stories highlight a number of critical questions. Even when gender reassignment technologies are freely available to anyone who can meet the financial cost, which gender-variant bodies carry more value than others? Within the growing globalization of biomedicine along neoliberal lines, which racialized subjects constitute the ideal to whom the labours of care and respect are made available, and which subjects fall outside of that sphere of care and respect?

In the first part of this chapter, I argue that Thai gender reassignment surgery must be theorized as a market, embedded in the historical and economic context of its local development. Next, I investigate how Thai tourist-marketing strategies are always already inflected by a Euro-American, orientalist discourse, wherein Thailand is imagined as the ultimate space of exotic transformation and the fulfilment of desire across multiple sites. In marketing tourism, this becomes a self-orientalizing strategy. Discussing the strategies GRS clinics use to market their services, I suggest that a similar dynamic is at play. I then turn to non-Thai trans women's accounts of GRS in Thailand to highlight the pervasive sense that being present in Thailand somehow facilitates the experience of psychic transformation towards femininity for non-Thai trans women. I ask, What about this sense of transformation specifically comes to bear for *non-Thai* trans women? Finally, I argue that to answer the question of the value of racialized bodies sufficiently, we need to understand the affective labours expended at Thai gender reassignment clinics. The care, the nurturing, and the transmission of affect to non-Thai trans women patients fulfils a medical function *and* facilitates the self-transformation of those patients into more feminine-"feeling" subjects. Affect can be defined as "bodily capacities to affect and be affected or the augmentation or diminution of a body's capacity to act, engage, and to connect" (Clough 2007, 2). Affective labour here registers as both "emotional" work (Hochschild 2003) and as a form of biopolitical production, wherein particular practices reproduce the discursive effects of particular forms of subjectivity.

Before moving on, a few words are in order grounding this chapter geographically and in relationship to queer and gender-variant travel criticism. As the chapters in this volume attest, Thailand is currently undergoing a boom in urban queer sexual cultures in the context of a continuing market in queer tourism. Scholarship on the transnational gendered or sexual dimensions of Thai tourism and migration most often explores tourist involvement in the Thai sex-work economy (McCamish 1999). Aside from some mainstream media coverage, Thailand's gender reassignment tourist market has received little critical attention. Although gender-variant tourism needs to be understood as a distinct (if related) geographical and political circuit, queer tourism offers some useful conceptual tools. Queer tourism, Jasbir Puar notes (2002), is the most visible form of sexual or gendered transnational circulation. However, Puar cautions that queer tourism discourses most often privilege white, middle-class, and affluent queer-tourist practices while relegating the spectre of the (non-white) other to the status of the desired object, encouraging and reproducing "colonial constructions of tourism as a travel adventure into uncharted territory laden with the possibility of taboo sexual encounters, illicit seductions, and dangerous liaisons" (2002, 113). This reminder provokes us to remain alert to the (neo)colonial constructions floating beneath many tourist discourses.

Theorizing trans or gender-variant tourist circuits must take into account the fact that within Euro-American gender-variant discourses, the trope of a "journey" is almost ubiquitous as a metaphor to narrate transsexual transformation from man into woman or vice versa (Prosser 1999; King 2003) in autobiographies, films (such as *Transamerica*, 2005, directed by Duncan Tucker), and novels. According to Prosser, the "desire to perceive a progressive pattern of becoming underlies the pervasive metaphors of journeying or voyaging in [transsexual] autobiographies" (1999, 91). The trans journey metaphor often encodes within it dominant understandings of East, West, home, and elsewhere. In tracing those encodings, we need to draw attention to how flows of global capital intersect with the broad range of gender reassignment technologies (O'Brien 2003). But just as global capital flows in inconsistent transnational trajectories, gender reassignment practices and technologies are equally diverse, inconsistent, and geographically dispersed. Deciphering the complexities of how neoliberal capitalism intersects with gender- variant practices and identities cannot proceed effectively without analysis of the geocultural trajectories of those practices.

These critical frameworks informed my research methods. During clinic observation sessions in Thailand, I would often speak with the patients present as well as surgeons and staff. This enlarged the field of GRS candidate interviewee subjects to include people from many different regions globally. I also investigated access to surgical modification for Thais—particularly *kathoeys*, but also *toms*, or trans masculine people.[13] Surgeons performing GRS for a Thai clientele do not tend to advertise as widely on-line or in English, and possibilities for Thais to afford gender reassignment surgery are limited. It is crucial to bring the reader's awareness of these inequities into contact with an analysis of the "Rolls-Royce treatment" in the most luxurious clinics. While Rolls-Royce clinics are a small niche within a much larger local market, their operation nonetheless still warrants analysis.

Gender Reassignment Technologies and Medical Tourism in Thailand

Within the context of Euro-American theorizations of trans body modification, it is impossible to imagine surgical procedures taking place entirely outside the history of the medicalization of gender variance as gender dysphoria or gender identity disorder. It is equally impossible to imagine surgeries not mediated by psychiatric frameworks governing the categories of gender identity "disorders", which, in turn, have determined who is eligible for diagnosis with gender identity disorder and thus who may access surgeries. Across Europe, North America, Australia, and New Zealand (and increasingly in other regions), most surgeons require surgical candidates to conform to the World Professional Association for Transgender Health (WPATH) Standards of Care. WPATH began as the Harry Benjamin International Gender Dysphoria Association and is a transnational organization of medical "experts" on gender identity, including psychiatrists, endocrinologists, surgeons, and others; until recently there were very few trans participants. Periodically, WPATH releases a Standards of Care document, which provides the most widely accepted regulating criteria for what are termed "gender identity disorders" (WPATH 2006). These criteria recognize desires for gendered body modification under the rubric of transsexuality, where genital surgery is assumed to be desired by most candidates. The mechanisms for assessing an individual's suitability for gender transition include psychiatric assessment and the fulfilment of a "Real Life Experience" in the gender one wishes to be recognized as.[14]

Access to gender reassignment surgeries in Thailand differs from this broad Euro-American context of medicalization in a number of ways. Despite a history of Thai scholars importing Euro-American psychological arguments against homosexuality and gender variance and deploying them in local research (Jackson 1997a; Jackson and Sullivan 1999, 10–11), gender reassignment is not regarded by most Thai specialists as necessarily requiring psychiatric evaluation. Neither are *kathoey* or *tom* desires for GRS universally understood within a medicalized discourse of transsexuality. *Kathoey* as a category is far more fluid and covers a wider range of cross-gender practices than the English-language category "transsexual". *Kathoey* is sometimes understood as a "third sex" and has been used in the past to refer to effeminate homosexual men as well as those assigned male at birth who feel like, or want to be, women (Jackson 1997b, 170). *Kathoeys*, or *sao praphet sorng*, are not defined within Thai culture by their desires to have gender reassignment surgery, but rather by their feminine behaviour. Many begin taking feminizing hormones in adolescence and, by adulthood, may have been living as feminine persons for years. In this cultural context, psychiatric evaluation is regarded as unnecessary. "Patients in Thailand see the plastic surgeon first, not the psychiatrist, because to them, they are normal people," Dr. Preecha Tiewtranon, the surgeon whose clinic is noted above, explained in a 2006 interview. He added, "[They say], 'Psychiatrists are for insane crazy people. I am not insane!'"[15] The state-subsidized GRS programme at Chulalongkorn University Hospital in Bangkok requires Thai GRS candidates to be assessed for gender identity disorder, but this particular programme operates on only around thirty patients per year. However, anecdotally it seems that only around 30 percent of *kathoey* desire vaginoplasty.[16] In a study conducted by Nantiya Sukontapatipark on *kathoey/sao praphet sorng* subjectivity, only eight of twenty informants had had genital reassignment surgery (Nantiya 2005, 99). In fact, *kathoey* are far more likely to seek "aesthetic" surgical procedures such as rhinoplasty, breast augmentation, eyelid surgery, and silicon injections before full genital reassignment. "Improving" physical appearance through aesthetic surgery is seen as fashionable and desirable for *kathoey* generally.

Non-medicalization, and the greater emphasis placed on *kathoey* beauty, rather than the importance of "female" genitals, have both helped transform gender reassignment surgery services in Thailand into a large, unregulated, and highly commodified industry. This industry operates within an equally sprawling, unregulated, and commodified local cosmetic-surgery industry. For this reason, and to contextualize this local industry in relation to the more recent development of a tourist-oriented gender reassignment surgery market, I want briefly to outline the history of gender reassignment surgery in Thailand. According to Nantiya, surgical gender reassignment was first performed in Thailand in 1972, on one individual moving from female to male and one individual moving from male to female. Prior to 1972, individual requests for gender reassignment surgery were assessed by a state committee that had apparently refused all applications (Nantiya 2005, 65). After 1972, candidates were assessed by psychiatrists. Although surgery was practised in state-run hospitals, candidates for surgery had to pay for it themselves. In the late 1970s and early 1980s, surgeons began to practise gender reassignment in private practice and state-run psychiatric assessment programmes. Of these, only the programme at Chulalongkorn University Hospital remains in operation.

In the late 1970s, Dr. Preecha Tiewtranon, who was then established as a reconstructive-surgery specialist in Bangkok, trained himself in vaginoplasty technique after a number of *kathoeys* asked him to perform surgical revisions on neo-vaginas that were, in his term, "mutilations".[17] Dr. Preecha trained younger surgeons in this technique, many of whom subsequently established private clinics. As well, what are known as "shophouses" sprang up. Shophouses are cheaper private clinics run by surgeons, who will often rent rooms in private hospitals to perform surgery. Nantiya's Thai informants generally preferred to obtain surgery in shophouses. Informants "considered that the surgeons' shop houses had more facilities than the hospitals, especially the state hospital" (2005, 99).

In the mid-1990s, non-Thais began travelling to Thailand in larger numbers to seek GRS. A Thai surgeon quoted by Nantiya attributes this to the large number of *kathoeys* who obtained GRS and then migrated to Europe and North America.

Others observe that the explosion of (largely English-language) Internet trans culture in the mid-1990s enabled Thai surgeons to advertise more broadly and led to a sharp increase in the number of non-Thais seeking GRS there. Non-Thai trans women began to travel in Thailand in large numbers to obtain GRS. A small number of surgeons gained a reputation outside Thailand and began to attract a large non-Thai customer base. For example, Dr. Suporn Watanyasakul performed twenty to thirty GRS procedures in 1996, mainly on Thai patients. By 2006, he had expanded his operation and was operating on around 220 patients per year.[18] These patients were almost exclusively non-Thai, coming from Europe, North America, and other locales outside Asia. The explosion of popularity of Thai gender reassignment surgeons among non-Thais has pushed up prices for gender reassignment surgery and enabled its rebranding as a luxury service rather than a budget option. One clinic catering mainly to non-Thais raised the price for vaginoplasty from US$2,000 in 2001 to US$15,000 in 2006.[19] Other surgeons followed suit. While even US$2,000 is expensive by Thai standards, the higher prices mean that only very affluent Thais can now afford surgeries with the five or six surgeons with international reputations. Clinic web sites now constitute the main marketing tool to gain non-Thai customers and offer comprehensive information, usually in English, about every aspect of a GRS trip. In seeking recognition as an elite and globally competitive cohort of biomedical specialists, Thai gender reassignment surgeons must also present an image indicating that they comply with internationally recognized standards. Most surgeons who cater to a non-Thai customer base also now require patients to supply evidence of psychiatric assessment and a "Real Life Experience" in line with the WPATH Standards of Care.

The availability of gender reassignment surgery in Thailand also needs to be framed within the context of medical tourism. Medical tourism, sometimes known as health tourism or medical travel, is the most popular term to describe the growing trend among citizens from affluent nations to travel to less-wealthy nations to access cheaper health services of all kinds. The slogan "first world medical treatment at third world prices"[20] encapsulates how medical tourism packages the lower global value of non-"North" currencies, services, and human labour as a commodity. In Thailand, medical tourism has exploded since the year 2000, facilitated by successive governments eager to find a new source of international revenue in the wake of the 1997 Asian economic crisis. By one estimate, the country currently hosts 400,000 medical tourists every year (Bookman and Bookman 2007, 3). On a different estimate, more than a million foreign visitors received medical treatment in Thailand in 1996 (Wilson, forthcoming).[21] As Wilson points out, expatriate demand for a high standard of medical care in Bangkok meant that the biomedical infrastructure already existed in Thailand prior to the development of a specific medical tourism market (Wilson, forthcoming). The development of Thai gender reassignment technologies as a market also predates the larger medical tourism industry by a number of years.

Touristic Orientalism and Feminine Transformations

I turn now from a historical and economic context of GRS and medical tourism to consider some of the specific discourses pervading Thai tourist-marketing strategies, GRS marketing strategies in particular. Although one could argue that gender reassignment surgery candidates visiting Thailand for medical reasons are not tourists, the trans women I interviewed certainly participated in tourist activities. As a popular late twentieth-century tourist destination, Thailand had accrued a particularly dense field of the "conflicted and compulsively repetitious stereotypy" that constitutes Orientalist discourse (Morris 1997, 61). Thailand often figures in this discourse as a space of magic, exotic transformation, and the fulfilment of (Western) desire. Rosalind Morris points to the fantasy of Thailand as a "place of beautiful order and orderly beauty" and simultaneously a place wherein anything goes, whose spaces and people are "responsive to all desires" (1997, 61). This fantasy is always racialized and gendered, often iconized in the image of the responsive Thai woman and, according to Morris, the *kathoey*.[22] Here we witness the production of "ideal" feminine gender through an exoticization of otherness that simultaneously facilitates a moment of self-transformation for the Euro-American subject. Hamilton remarks that this "libidinization" of Thailand is so familiar that it repeats itself in *farang* discourse everywhere (1997, 145).

Thai tourist marketing strategies reflect this libidinization, even in nonsexual arenas, where the promise to the tourist focuses on health. A Tourism Authority of Thailand article promoting health tourism expounds upon Thailand's "traditional" assets thus:

> The Kingdom's legendary tradition of superior service and gracious hospitality is working its magic in a new sector. Timeless Thai values and traditions are very much alive in places where it is least expected—in hospitals and clinics around the country. Patients are welcomed as 'guests' and made to feel at home in unfamiliar surroundings. The reception is gracious and courteous. Medical staff consistently provide superior service, often surpassing expectations.
>
> Spa operators likewise report that guests are charmed by the traditional 'wai'—a courteous greeting gesture that conveys profound respect, infinite warmth, hospitality and friendliness. The 'wai' is

perceived by visitors to be uniquely and distinctively Thai. The magic
is taking hold.[23]

Infinite warmth, magic, grace, and courtesy: All are stereotypically
feminine traits. Even if Thai workers meant to embody such attributes are not
female and the intended visiting recipients of Thai warmth or grace are not
male, this language instantiates a sexualized and racialized economy within
the touristic exchange. It comprises part of a strategy I call self-orientalizing,
following Aihwa Ong. For Ong, self-orientalization accounts for the fact that
"Asian voices are unavoidably inflected by orientalist essentialism that infiltrate
all kinds of public exchanges about culture" (1999, 81). Self-orientalization
involves the performance of the stereotype of an ethnicity or a nationality to
be recognized by the cultural edifice in which the stereotype originates. By
framing the Thai medical-tourism experience as particularly beneficial because
of Thai rituals and traditions, the marketing language narrates the stereotype
of a Thailand freed from the realities of Bangkok smog, traffic, and political
instability.[24] Numerous instances of this strategy can be found in generalized
tourist marketing, but, as the example above illustrates, it is particularly
apparent in health and medical tourism.

Marketing strategies used by Thai gender reassignment clinics follow a
similar pattern. When I was interviewing surgeons in Thailand, I found that
most were keen to emphasize Thailand's liberal attitudes towards gender
variance in comparison with the West. When asked what makes Thailand such
a popular place for GRS, for example, Dr. Preecha said, "Thailand is a very open
and tolerant society . . . There is no Thai law against the operation."[25] Dr. Sanguan
Kunaporn, a surgeon who runs Phuket Plastic Surgery and, with Dr. Suporn, is
considered by many non-Thai trans women as among the best, explained to
me that gender reassignment is a successful industry in Thailand because of
surgical technique and the competitive price. He added:

> [Also] the hospitality of the people, not only the staff in the hospital
> but also the Thai people. Very friendly and welcoming! Compromise,
> high tolerance. I found that a lot of patients of mine say that this is the
> place they would like to live, if they could choose this. Not only in
> the hospital, but also in the country. They feel safe here when they're
> walking, or shopping.[26]

We might, however, take these positive interpretations with a grain of
salt. Most of the *kathoeys* and *sao praphet sorng* I have spoken with in Thailand
describe the difficulties of gender-variant daily life in detail. In fact, many see the
"West" as having a far more liberal and "open-minded" culture than Thailand.
Homosexual and gender-variant people are not overtly discriminated against

in Thai law, and *kathoey* are certainly more visible in Thailand than in North America, Europe, Australia, or New Zealand. Although it may be true that young gender-variant Thais are accepted by family and society without the violence, disavowal, and shame that characterize transphobic Euro-American responses to gender variance, stigma still attaches gender variance in many parts of Thai society. Forms of discrimination against gender-variant and people attracted to same-sex relations do exist (Jackson 1999a, 2003a). In the same manner that ordinary tourists are encouraged to understand Thai culture generally as timelessly friendly and responsive, Dr. Sanguan's discursive production of Thai culture as universally tolerant of gender-variant subjects seems intended to resonate with potential clients—who are coded implicitly as non-Thai.

A brief survey of graphic representations on GRS clinic web sites offers other examples of self-orientalization in the context of marketing. As noted above, web sites, along with word-of-mouth, constitute the main marketing strategy for Thai GRS surgeons. Here, an explicit connection is made between the "traditional" beauty of feminine Thai bodies and the promises of self-transformation through feminizing surgical procedures. The Phuket Plastic Surgery Clinic web site banner features the face of a smiling, beautiful Thai woman on a background of white orchids, along with a slide show of landscape photographs.[27] The section of Hygeia Beauty's web site concerned with GRS features three glamour shots of equally beautiful women who might be read as *kathoey*, all with long, coiffed hair, evening dresses, and flawless makeup in the style of the "feminine realness" genre of *kathoey* beauty pageants.[28] That the images of bodies represented here are non-trans women or *kathoeys* is not as relevant as how they might be read by prospective customers. The images associate ultra-femininity, the destination (Thailand), and surgical transformation in a promise to the non-Thai browsing trans woman that having GRS in Thailand will not only facilitate her transformation into full womanhood but will also transform her into a *more beautiful* woman.

It is salient to note here that what is now regarded as "traditional" feminine beauty in Thailand emerged relatively recently in historical terms and is a modern discourse and performance that originated more in Thai responses to nineteenth- and twentieth-century Euro-American beauty standards and practices than in any "ancient" local Thai culture (Jackson 2003a, Van Esterik 1996). Recalling Annette Hamilton's remarks on the libidinization of Thailand as it is represented by Thai women characters in English-language expatriate novels, we could read the laughing Thai women on clinic web sites as standing in metonymically for Thailand, as both objects of desire for non-Thai trans women and the potential vehicle of their own somatic self-transformation. The key difference is between desire and identification. In the novels Hamilton critiques, the exchange is a heterosexual relationship. Here, the exchange is about the non-Thai subject's own feminization—both somatically and, perhaps, psychically.

In exploring how non-Thai trans women relate to marketing discourses associating Thailand metonymically with feminine beauty, I found that the association between travelling to Thailand and self-transformation was reflected back by many non-Thai trans women themselves. Although most were self-conscious of the urbanized modernity of much of Thailand's actual geography, many talked about their experiences in Thailand as radically distinct from their daily lives at home. Karen, the Australian trans woman referred to above, described travelling to Thailand as "a magical experience". Other participants commented that, aside from the novel techniques of Thai surgeons, having GRS in Thailand, this "magical" place, was precisely what marked their surgical experiences as a special rite of passage. When I asked her to identify what made getting GRS in Thailand different from having it in Australia, Gemma, a trans woman living in inner-city Sydney, asserted that Thai surgeons were more technically skilled in gender reassignment surgery than Australian surgeons. When I asked her how she felt overall about travelling to Thailand for GRS, she added:

> It's something kind of tangible and symbolic, to take a journey [to have gender reassignment surgery] . . . Do things and see people in a situation outside your normal circumstances . . . Psychologically it makes quite a difference to go through a process like that and be outside yourself a bit and come home in a different circumstance, having passed a landmark. With a lot of people who have been over [to Thailand] and have had that same experience, you really notice the feeling that they've done a concrete, tangible thing, you know, and been through quite a symbolic journey . . .[29]

Melanie, a trans woman from the American Midwest, expressed her feelings about how travelling to Thailand had changed her thus:

> [Thailand] imprints on you very deeply . . . It's such a change you know. People come here and it's such a changing experience. And you go outside [the hotel] and it's very urban and you're in a different environment. But still, I don't know, it kinda charms you in a way.[30]

When I asked her to expand on what precisely had charmed her, or imprinted on her so deeply, she said:

> It's the people . . . There's just a level of kindness and friendliness that I haven't observed really anywhere else . . . And [Thai] people, they just, people brighten up, and they wanna help.[31]

It is a convention of the "classical" Western transsexual narrative that genital surgery is the most significant marker of gendered transition: the dramatic final step, what really makes one a woman (or a man, in the case of trans men who obtain genital surgery). The normative psychiatric definition of what a transsexual is depends on the existence of the desire to possess the genitals of the "other" sex. The "traditional" transsexual narrative that emerged in the second half of the twentieth century classically features a case history involving cross-gender behaviours exhibited in early childhood to the desire to live life as a "real" man or woman in adulthood (Spade 2006, Stone 1992). Genital surgical transformation features within that narrative as the desire that confirms one is "truly" transsexual. It is clear that as many ideas about forms of hormonal and surgical transformation exist as there are gender-variant individuals, but the traditional transsexual narrative still dominates many Euro-American gender-variant communities and social and scientific theorizations.[32]

As I noted above, the geographical "journey" is almost ubiquitous as a metaphor within English-language trans narratives to relate the transsexual transformation from man into woman or vice versa (Prosser 1999, King 2003). The trans women involved in my project seemed to associate the imagined cultural and spatial milieu of Thailand with femininity (implicitly encoding the "West" as the masculine part of a heteronormative East/West dyad). Thus, Thailand is understood as having a transformative power specific to trans (feminine) embodiment. This, in turn, hinges on the perceived transformative power of travelling in general: the alchemical, or magical, properties of journeying to an exotic location. Thus, the imagined geography of Thailand combines a set of orientalizing discourses that permit surgical candidates to imagine themselves as becoming more feminine in that space.

A photomontage produced by one of Dr. Suporn's patients illustrates precisely this metonymic association of popular Thai iconographies, GRS and psychic feminization.[33] Created by a trans woman called Rebecca on an America Online home page, the photomontage accompanies her account of two trips to Thailand for gender reassignment surgery. The page's text reads:

> I had SRS with Dr. Suporn Watanyusakul on January 11, 2005. I had the most wonderful time in Thailand and made friends with some of the most amazing people . . . If you go to Chonburi leave your inhibitions and worries at the gate. Lose yourself in Thai culture. Enjoy every moment of your experience whether you're heading over for SRS, FFS, AM or just visiting! Thailand is a wonderful place.[34]

The montage presents glamour shots of Rebecca after her GRS and facial feminization surgery, known as FFS, spliced with symbols emblematic of stereotypical "Thai culture". Vividly coloured shots of orchids, Thailand's most popular botanical commodity, surround the centre of the montage, where Rebecca poses with a fan and a spray of cherry blossom in her hair, in a dress that gestures towards a cheongsam or a kimono. Surprisingly, the outfit looks nothing like Thai "traditional" costume or a tourist interpretation thereof; perhaps this underscores the slippage between the imagined aesthetic of Thailand itself and that of a more generic "Asia". Accompanying an account of Rebecca's experience having surgery in Thailand, the montage associates her journey with her feminization. The incoherently "Asian" iconography is the vehicle through which Rebecca makes explicit the message that she is now a true woman. It also serves to confirm her sense of the power of the exotic to supplement her white-skinned femininity.

To draw attention to the mélange of significations at work in Rebecca's photomontage is not to dismiss her experience of surgery, or of travelling in Thailand, or to dismiss the aesthetic Rebecca deploys to communicate the importance of her trip. Neither do I intend to discount the personal significance of my informants' experiences. Their affective experiences of connection with Thailand are as valid as the felt sense of connection I experience as a traveller to Thailand as a tourist and researcher, and to other locations that are not my "home". Yet to acknowledge the depth, or "truth" of an affective experience is not to naturalize it as an existing outside discourse, quarantined from critical consideration. To return this discussion to questions about the value of particular racialized bodies within the setting of the gender reassignment surgery clinic, I want to suggest here that a form of subjectivation in which one can metonymically associate travelling to Thailand for GRS with the power to supplement one's femininity already assumes that subject is non-Thai, non-*kathoey* and non-Asian. To imagine Thailand in such precise ways places one within a specifically Euro-American, Orientalist discourse. A sometime resident of Bangkok such as Som, who books into a private hospital and an expensive hotel mostly frequented by non-Thais, would almost certainly experience a very different set of expectations, desires, and affective associations about GRS than that reflected in Rebecca, Gemma, and Melanie's accounts. Crucially, Thai culture, landscape, and traditional forms of sociability were not coded as exotic for Som. The marketing discourses that targeted specifically non-Thai, or Euro-American clients, were not developed with her in mind.

Affective Labour in the Clinic

Thus far, my argument has been limited to the sphere of symbolic representation: web-site images and photomontages. To relate this to material practices, and to ground my analysis in a critique of economies of feminized and racialized transnational labour, I turn to an analysis of encounters between Thai staff and non-Thai patients in the clinic featured at the beginning of this chapter. As I noted above, many of the clinic's staff are young Thai women (and occasionally *kathoeys*) who fulfil patients' needs. During a visit to this clinic, the British patient-liaison manager and two or three staff members arranged a lunch for me. During lunch I made inquiries about their working conditions, as most of the staff seemed to be on call twenty-four hours a day. The consensus from those assembled was that every clinic employee is expected to be friendly, hospitable, and available whenever a patient expresses a need, no matter how trivial and no matter what the time of day. The Thai financial administrator (who is also the surgeon's wife) described the working atmosphere as "a big family".[35] She also stressed that being employed at the clinic involved hard work and that if an employee did not respect the system, he or she would not last long.

The patient-care manager was a young Thai woman, Mai, who happened to embody precisely the polite, attractive, and courteous standard of so-called traditional Thai femininity. Mai informed me that because the clinic was so busy, she did not take vacations. Sometimes, she said, she was invited to accompany patients on sightseeing trips within Thailand as a guide and assistant, and this gave her a break. Because Mai spoke the most fluent English of all the personal caregivers, patients seemed to approach her most often. Throughout the afternoon, her mobile phone rang constantly with calls from patients. Many of Mai's labours seemed to be mediatory. This involved literal Thai–English interpretation between patients and staff members, as well as the task of "translating" Thailand itself for the benefit of the patients as a kind of tour guide: cultural practices, the layout of the town, where to find the best restaurants, and so on.

Since patients at the clinic usually spend at least a month convalescing after surgery, entertainment activities are very popular. These include trips to the local cinema, or to nearby Pattaya to watch *kathoey* cabaret shows and to shop. A Thai massage specialist is employed by the clinic, just as many Thai hotels and guesthouses employ in-house masseurs. Other activities involve learning about feminine skills: the clinic runs small classes on Thai cookery and makeup application. Patients can arrange manicures, pedicures, and hair appointments. To note only these scheduled activities, however, neglects the constant hum of sociality taking place in the clinic, at the hotel, and in the hospital, all of which involved the Thai attendants aiding the mostly non-Thai, Anglo-European trans women patients in whatever they desired to do. This might include playing with each other's hair, or doing each other's nails, or engaging in chitchat. Mai and other employees were not expected merely to behave in a caring way; it seemed that they were also expected (and saw it as their duty) to make friends and to behave as women friends do.

These tasks can be identified as affective labour. As I indicated above, affective labour can be defined as work that blurs the line between a purely commercial transaction and an exchange of feeling. It involves practices of care, the exchange of affect, and work that forms relationships of some kind. Affective labour, or emotional labour, as Arlie Hochschild theorizes it (2003, 138) constitutes part of what has been called the feminization of labour (Cheah 2007, 94); its presence as a micro-political practice is intimately related to broader shifts within globalization, migration, and the gendered division of labour. Mai and her fellow workers are part of the global population of "third world women workers" (Mohanty 1997), or, within Cheah's theorization of the new international division of reproductive labour, "foreign domestic workers" (2007, 94).

Thailand's service industry, on which tourism so heavily relies, is powered mainly by young women who migrate from rural areas and who perform various forms of service that blur the boundaries between commercial and non-commercial labours (Wilson 2004: 84). While these workers are not strictly "foreign domestic workers", since they may not migrate transnationally, rural-to-urban migration may be just as significant as transnational migration in marking these workers as "other" to the metropolitan elites of Bangkok, while also providing the means with which rural migrants can aspire to be modern and socially mobile themselves. For these subjects, domestic work, service-industry work in tourism or hospitality, including sex work, are key industries (along with textiles and other manufacturing activities). As Ara Wilson points out, affective labour is a hallmark of many different service industries in Thailand. She additionally points out that forms of caregiving are naturalized within these economies as traditional Thai behaviours, which conceals their function as commodities:

> [T]he modes of hospitable engagement found in medical tourism—or sex tourism—are often attributed to Thai culture. The labor involved in gracious caretaking is naturalized in this cultural attribution. Without denying the possibility that structures of feeling or the effects of social hierarchies might produce patterned modes of comportment and interaction, it remains worth considering their commodification. (Wilson, forthcoming)

One of the most important affective labours expected of the Suporn Clinic staff was to model femininity itself for the benefit of the patients as a kind of pedagogical practice. The Thai workers were not present just to care for the trans women patients. Through repetition of gendered behaviours, they performed a particular, racialized feminine gender that supplemented the patients' sense of themselves as female. This performative gender modelling may or may not be conscious and certainly is not surprising, given the context. It is also reflective of the generalized orientalization of Thai femininity within tourist cultures. Simultaneously, there is something specific to the production of gender-variant subjectivity happening here. It becomes clearer if we imagine affective labour as biopolitical production: practices that produce and reproduce particular forms of subjectivity. Sandro Mezzadra locates affective labour within theorizations of postfordism undertaken by Paolo Virno (2004), among others:

> Virno stresses the fact that subjectivity itself—with its most intimate qualities: language, affects, desires, and so on—is 'put to value' in contemporary capitalism . . . [T]his happens not only with particular jobs or in particular 'sectors' (e.g. in the sector of services), being rather a general characteristic of contemporary living labor . . . [T]he concept of 'biopolitics' itself should be accordingly reworked. (Mezzadra 2005, 2)

This reading of Virno by Mezzadra reworks biopolitics in a different direction to Foucault's deployment of the concept to speak about the regulation of populations, as opposed to individuals (Foucault 1995 and 2007). It also steers away from a practical definition of affective labour as work that involves the creation of relationship. Mezzadra also argues that affective labour plays a role in differentiating subjectivities from each other:

> In a situation in which the boundary between friendship and business is itself being blurred . . . specific problems arise, which can nurture specific disturbances. (Mezzadra 2005, 1)

This is what I gesture towards when I ask, "What forms of labour are being performed in a gender clinic in Thailand to produce a particular *non-Thai* trans-feminine subjectivity?" As I have argued throughout this chapter, such a biopolitical production of trans-feminine subjectivity is made possible through the cultural specificities of Thai gender norms. Further, it is an intersubjective process that occurs principally between Thai women, or their images, and non-Thai trans women. Patients attend makeup classes to distract themselves from discomfort and to pass the time, which flows excruciatingly slowly during convalescence. The always already racialized, commodified circulation of feminine-gendered practices unfolds as an unobtrusive excess to the main concern of gender reassignment surgeries. But it is central to the "care package" offered by the clinic.

It is possible to read this scene in a number of ways. We could regard this intersubjective process as a moment of solidarity between equally disenfranchised feminine-identifying subjects under global capitalism. We might also think of it as a moment in which individuals mutually benefit from an economic and social exchange, freely exchanging money for the feeling of being cared for, and wages for acts of caring. Alternatively, we might regard it as a moment in which affective and biopolitical pedagogies producing an idealized, imagined femininity conceal the economic dimensions of the exchange. It is difficult to ignore the fact that the trans women who purchase the surgical product and its attendant services are by and large affluent, by Thai standards, and white. They have privileged access to consumption practices in ways that their Thai caregivers might only aspire to.

I want to steer away, however, from presenting this as a situation in which "first world" trans people exploit "third world" caregivers. Economically, the clinic owners benefit most from this exchange. For their part, the Thai workers at various clinics (and in health tourism more generally) might regard this kind of work as of higher status than other forms of caregiving work, since it is highly paid by Thai standards. Despite the romanticized vision of Thailand evinced by many of the non-Thai trans women I spoke with, they were also grateful to find treatment in a space in which their needs were met and where they were valued as human beings, unlike hospitals in the United States, Europe, and Australia. Additionally, we cannot point to Euro-American gender-variant cultures as commodified without acknowledging that more localized *kathoey* practices of embodied transformation rely just as much on the commodification of gender-variant subjectivity as the gender clinic catering to non-Thai tourists described in the introduction to this chapter. However, recalling Som's and Emma's experiences of not feeling cared for, it seems evident that the intersubjective practices of affective labour supplementing patients' sense of themselves as women within the space of gender reassignment clinics relies on a form of racialization which, no matter how pervasive elsewhere, differentiates between the bodies of more and less valuable, more and less ideal, trans subjects.

On Gender-Variant, Cross-Border Solidarity

This chapter began by proposing that gender reassignment clinics in Thailand deploy self-orientalizing images to market surgical services to non-Thai tourists. I then argued that a corollary of this process is that some non-Thai trans women who obtain surgery in Thailand narrate their experiences in terms of a magical, transformative (and finally orientalizing) journey, which has everything to do with their sense of being gendered subjects. Finally, I discussed the affective and micro-political practices within the gender reassignment clinic scene that facilitate the reproduction of that Orientalist narrative. In making this argument,

I drew attention to the commodification of gender reassignment surgery as a tourist industry in Thailand, consistent with its commodification elsewhere, but configured in ways specific to the history of Thai gender reassignment surgery and dominant perspectives on gender variance. Most important, I suggested that the biopolitical production of trans subjectivities in this transnational context relies not only on commodification and forms of labour, or on the reproduction of gender norms, or on racialization, but also on simultaneous racialization, gendering and political economy. Each works through, and is inseparable, from the other.

When I asked in my introduction how particular gender-variant bodies circulate within the transnational commodified gender reassignment surgery market, I was thinking already in the context of the low value ascribed to gender-variant bodies within Euro-American surgical cultures. Access to surgical procedures is often dichotomized between what one wishes for and what one bears because it is the only option available. Under these circumstances, it is necessary to place the micro-politics of gender reassignment surgery in Thailand within the context of ongoing political struggles for trans and gender-variant self-determination. It is essential to engage with the power structures that have made gender reassignment surgery into a commodity globally. One of the most important of these is the privatization of health care globally. It is equally as important to target the widely held assumption that gender reassignment surgeries are a "choice" trans people make, and the opposite but equally as pervasive assumption that one cannot be a "real" man or woman, or person, without surgery to make one's genitals congruous with the gender one identifies with. Ideally, gender reassignment technologies would be state-subsidized. But this would not solve the problem that some nations can afford state-funded health care and some cannot. This is the context of global neoliberalism, in which every subjectivity or practice provides another way to extract surplus value. Under these conditions, work within national boundaries is insufficient. More gender-variant, cross-border solidarity work is needed to trace, and cut across, these productive, exploitative flows of transnational capital.

8

Bangkok's Beautiful Men
Images of Thai Liberality in an Indonesian Gay Novel

Ben Murtagh[1]

Introduction

This chapter focuses on the Indonesian novel *Lelaki terindah* (The most beautiful man) by Andrei Aksana (2004a).[2] A discussion of this novel has come to be included in this book not just because of its gay theme, but also because of its predominantly Thai setting. A significant section of the novel is set in the Thai capital, and the representation of Bangkok, and in particular its queer spaces, will be a central focus of the chapter.

Lelaki terindah is part of a noticeable recent growth in Indonesian writing on same-sex relationships. The novel seems to have been at the forefront of the current upsurge in published fiction on this theme and, apart from its remarkable sales, there was a significant and quite long-lasting interest in the novel on the Internet.[3] It appears that the book attracted a degree of attention on the web far in excess of other recent writing portraying *gay* or *lesbi* characters in Indonesian fiction.[4]

A key theme of *Lelaki terindah* is an idealized relationship between two *gay* men. Attention should be directed specifically to Tom Boellstorff's argument (2005) that, in New Order Indonesia under former President Suharto, it was through marriage and having children that *gay* Indonesians showed their proper citizenship in the modern Indonesian nation. While recognizing that there was a minority of *gay* men who chose not to marry, for most *gay* men the failure to enter into heterosexual marriage was seen as a failure of self and citizenship. As Boellstorff remarks, "*gay* or *lesbi* love does not get you national belonging: heteronormativity lies at the heart of national love" (2005, 107). Boellstorff's (2005, 20) fieldwork centred on the period 1997–98, immediately prior to the fall of the Suharto regime, and it is pertinent to question to what extent the collapse of Suharto's New Order regime and its family ideologies may have affected the ways in which *gay* men lived and imagined their lives in the subsequent ten years. As we will see, the idealized *gay* relationship presented in the novel under scrutiny is far from typical in view of Boellstorff's findings, and it is significant that the flourishing *gay* relationships described in the novel unfold in what its author represents as the progressive and gay city of Bangkok, away from the restrictions of Indonesia.

Notions of a global gay identity and of a supposed one-way flow of influence from the global North to the South have been supplanted by arguments that the particular national or regional manifestations of queer identities should be understood both in terms of the effect of transnational flows and also in terms of local specificities.[5] One question that will be raised in this chapter concerns what the novel discussed here tells us about Indonesian understandings of *gay* sexuality, both at home and in Thailand. Linked to this is the picture as fostered by some Indonesian *gay* men of Thailand as a utopia, or "gay paradise". Dennis Altman has highlighted middle-class gay men in Southeast Asia who make frequent reference to gay bars in Paris and San Francisco and to American gay writers, and he has suggested that for those Southeast Asians who take on gay identities there is an aspiration to be part of global culture (2001, 93). For a small number of *gay* Indonesian men, global travel, including several trips a year to Southeast Asian cities such as Singapore, Kuala Lumpur, and Bangkok, and, more rarely, trips further afield to Europe, Australia, or the United States, have become a reality. For these men, global gay culture can be witnessed firsthand. Nonetheless, for the majority of Indonesian *gay* men, including many from the middle class, while perhaps imagining themselves increasingly to be part of a global culture, foreign travel remains a dream. Thus, as Fran Martin has commented, while not denying the importance of transnational aspects of culture, "connections to non-local scenes are for most people only ever experienced from within particular and limited local contexts" (2003, 30). Especially in Indonesia, where foreign travel remains the preserve of a wealthy minority, any connection with non-local cultures will, for the majority, be through the mass media, including, for a growing number, through the Internet.[6] A certain section of the population will also gain access to other gay cultures through literature and film. With regard to the incorporation of ideas from other non-local cultures, Homi Bhabha's arguments on mimicry—"almost but not quite" (2004, 121–31)—inform us that an inevitable slippage will occur in the meaning of the original sign. Thus, new localized meanings and attachments will be put onto ideas taken from other cultures.

Before turning specifically to the burgeoning corpus of texts that portray non-heteronormative Indonesian sexualities, we should briefly note that since the fall of Suharto's New Order, which lasted from 1965 to 1998, there has been an evident increase in the number of Indonesian books focusing on sex across the board. As Michael Garcia noted (2004), when it comes to contemporary Indonesian publishing, "sex sells". For anyone who visits his or her local branch of Gramedia, the largest chain of bookstores in Indonesia, the truth that sex sells—or at least the suggestions of it—will become immediately apparent. Alongside works by those authors already mentioned, browsers will also come across a large number of books with often fairly racy covers that are aimed at both the teenage and adult markets. Perusing the bookshelves one might come across books intended for teenagers such as *Pacarku Ibu kosku* (My lover is the matron of my college halls) by Wiwik Karyono (2004), or the phenomenally popular *Jakarta undercover: sex 'n the city* by Moammar Emka (2002).[7] Thus, while more research is needed on this topic, and it is not the aim of this chapter to address this phenomenon, it is clear that there is a flourishing market for books linked by the common theme of much more overtly sexual content.

Indonesian Queer Literature

Since the 1970s, there has seen a steady trickle of literary writing in Indonesian that has dealt with issues of homosexuality (Mujiarso 2006, 8). Nonetheless, it has until very recently remained an uncommon topic in Indonesia. As Boellstorff points out with regard to the mass media, it was only from the mid-1990s that there emerged a notable, albeit small, presence of *gay* and *lesbi* voices, "with a substantial increase after 2002" (2005, 75). Boellstorff argues that these voices are particularly evident on the new private television channels, on radio, and in magazines, though this visibility remains fragmentary and is still far from being a daily occurrence (2005, 77). A number of literary publications have taken male-male love as their main theme in recent years,[8] including *Ini dia, Hidup* (This is it, Life) by Ezinky (2004) and *Kau bunuh aku dengan cinta* (You are killing me with love) by Andy Lotex (2004). There have also been increasing numbers of short stories exploring various aspects of non-heteronormative sexuality, culminating in *Rahasia bulan* (Secrets of the moon), a collection that the editor, Is Mujiarso, notes as having "gay, lesbian, bisexual and transgender themes" (2006, 7). As the editor of that collection points out, none of the sixteen authors contributing to the collection—who include Andrei Aksana—is publicly identified as *gay*.[9] Finally, it is well to remember that this literary output is not necessarily representative of Indonesian *gay* culture, but concerns, rather, how *gay* culture is represented in Indonesia.[10]

Andrei Aksana: The Distribution and Reception of His Works

Central to the ever-growing presence of *gay* and *lesbi* characters in Indonesian literature is the popular author Andrei Aksana.[11] *Lelaki terindah* is his fourth novel.[12] He has also published a colourful guide intended for budding young authors in search of fame, entitled, *Be a writer, Be a celebrity* (2006b).[13]

Aksana's published output is notable for its distinctive packaging, which is a factor that cannot be ignored when considering his sales figures. The author works full-time as a marketing director for a company that handles Indonesian franchises of international retail outlets (Body Shop, a cosmetics chain known for its ethically produced products). This is a background that is perhaps an additional clue to his publishing success. The books have eye-catching covers: The cover of *Lelaki terindah* features a naked male torso with rippling "six-pack". But so, too, each book published since his 2003 novel, *Abadilah cinta*, has been accompanied by a compact disc containing a song specifically written to accompany the novel. The song written to accompany *Lelaki terindah* was, according to the author, inspired by the sounds of the Chao Phraya River, with the strings of the harp reminiscent of the sound of Bangkok's major waterway (Interview with Aksana, 10 December 2006). Aksana himself sings these tracks; hence, his promotional material describes him as "the singing author". The products are enhanced by colour images of the author, some quite sexy, others more dreamy. The inside back cover of his 2004 novel, *Cinta 24 jam,* contains a detachable bookmark with a number of colour images of the author; another of his novels has a photograph of the author as an insert. Thus, it is an entire package that is being sold and, as Aksana himself says, the reader is able not only to read the author's words but also to visualize him and to hear his voice (Interview, 10 December 2006).

Lelaki terindah has received a fair amount of criticism, most notably from Joko Anwar, the Indonesian film director and screenwriter (2004), who describes it as campy, corny, melodramatic, and self-indulgent, and also from John Badalu (2005), organizer of Jakarta's queer film festival. While the author himself states that with *Lelaki terindah* he was trying to bridge the gap between high and popular literature (Interview, 10 December 2006), most critics would probably see Aksana's work as having little literary merit. But it is nonetheless evident from a number of Internet chat sites and notice boards that the novel has a considerable following. Furthermore, the book is admired and recommended for the very characteristics that Joko Anwar criticizes, namely, the romantic nature of the relationship between the novel's central characters and its use of emotive language and metaphor.[14] While the use of clichéd imagery and a repetitive literary style may rankle with literary critics, it is a novel that seems to appeal to a large number of Indonesians, and, given its subject matter and setting, one that may well inform many Indonesians' perception of Bangkok as a supposed gay paradise.

Concerning his readership, on Internet discussion boards there appear to be more male than female contributors, though in an interview the author said that correspondence is shared equally. Despite his considerable output, most of the letters and e-mails Aksana receives are about *Lelaki terindah*. At promotional events and book signings, the author states that women in the fifteen-to-thirty age bracket are in the majority, though many young men tend to lurk in the background, approaching him only after a given event draws to a close (interview, 10 December 2006).

The last few pages of the later printings of his books also include quotations from readers who have presumably e-mailed or written in. Accompanied by pictures of the fans, the quotations—some in English, others in Indonesian—give clues to the types of readers with whom the publisher wishes to associate Aksana's books. *Lelaki terindah*, for example, includes quotations from readers among whose occupations are research project officers, marketing staff, bankers, students, and accounting executives. Men and women are represented equally, and the pictures suggest a readership spanning in age the late teens to the early thirties. For example MaYa, a housewife and entrepreneur, remarks, "It made me cry, it's really great. I like its poetry and the song." Fuad, a marketer, comments in English, "Finally Indonesia has a great author! I never read Indonesian novel [*sic*]. But your book really opened my eyes. I love *Lelaki terindah*." Heru, a customer service manager, rejected the criticisms some sections of the press made concerning Aksana. "Lots of people think that Andrei is an arrogant and picky person," Heru wrote, "but if they can get to know him more closely, all that perception is ABSOLUTELY WRONG. He is someone who has a really good imagination and also his ideas are brilliant" (emphasis in original).

Lelaki terindah: A Synopsis

The plot of the novel is fairly simple. The narrator, who presents himself as the author, meets Rafky, a twenty-seven-year-old, extremely handsome, and athletic office worker, out of the blue at Jakarta airport. Rafky begs him to write a love story, which will be beautiful and meaningful, the story of his total love for another man, the most beautiful man (Aksana 2004a, 16). At first the narrator is shocked and refuses to write about "this forbidden love, a love like a virus which can never be cured" (Aksana 2004a, 16). However, he soon becomes entranced by the mysterious Rafky and agrees to write the story of "Rafky, Valent and . . . I" (Aksana 2004a, 21). The novel takes the structure of a *cerita berbingkai* (framed story), and after the first twenty pages is structured as a retelling of Rafky's story to the narrator. Thus, after the opening section, in which we learn how the anonymous narrator came to write the story of the love between Rafky and Valent, the narrator then retells the story of the two men's love affair as it was told to him. This narrative is interrupted by occasional interludes, in which the narrator expresses his difficulties in writing the story—such is its emotional intensity and the difficulty of the subject matter. One section in the middle of the novel, which recounts Valent and Rafky's exploration of the gay scene in Bangkok, is mirrored by passages that tell of the journey by Rafky and the anonymous author to Bangkok as they retrace the steps taken by the two lovers.

The novel within the novel begins with Rafky flying to Bangkok. By chance he sits next to Valent, and the two men are inextricably drawn to each other. Valent falls asleep on Rafky's shoulder, and on reaching their destination Valent asks Rafky if he wants to share his pre-booked hotel room. The two men make various trips to the attractions of Bangkok. They are inseparable. Valent is clearly attracted to Rafky. Then one day, after too much exercise, Valent falls ill and we discover that he is diabetic. Rafky nurses him back to health. The friendship becomes ever closer, until one night they become lovers. The next morning Rafky is horrified and leaves, saying that Valent has ensnared him. However, as he travels on the Bangkok metro sky train he admits to himself that the events of the previous night had been a source of mutual pleasure, and so returns to Valent. They then move to a different hotel, J House, on Soi Pratuchai off Surawong Road, in the middle of one of the main concentrations of gay bars in Bangkok. Rafky is again horrified by the burgeoning awareness of his sexuality, and decides to go to a bar, where he hires a female sex worker. However, he is unable to become sexually aroused by her body. Again he returns to Valent, and they get on better than ever, visiting the well-known gay nightclub DJ Station.

Eventually they return to Jakarta, where they have to face their respective girlfriends, whom they are each due to marry. Rafky breaks off with his girlfriend, and tells her that he is in love with a man. She is horrified, refuses to accept his sexuality, and tells his parents of his secret. They are at first dismayed that their son is not *normal*, but eventually come around to affirm their love of him. For Valent, the reverse occurs. When he tells his girlfriend of his love for a man she is initially hysterical but then accepting. However, his mother, who had come to love Rafky as an ideal role model for her son, refuses to let her son out of the house and continues to plan his imminent wedding. Eventually this takes its toll, and Valent has a diabetic relapse and ends up in the hospital. His mother remains hostile to Rafky. It seems that Valent is getting better, so the mother leaves his bedside to go home to send out the wedding invitations.

The next morning Valent's mother, his ex-girlfriend, and Rafky all arrive at the hospital. Valent's mother makes a terrible fuss, saying that Rafky should go away, but then we discover that Valent has died overnight, and finally Valent's mother is regretful.

We then return, in the final pages, to the voice of the anonymous narrator/author. As the novel has progressed it has become clear that Rafky and the narrator have become increasingly close, even going to Bangkok together to revisit the places that Rafky and Valent had been to, including DJ Station. While purportedly for the author's better understanding of the time Valent and Rafky had spent together, these interludes are also used to show the emergence of a new understanding of male-male love, and also of the narrator's growing feelings towards Rafky. Before the final scene of Valent's death, the story is broken by the narrator's deliberations, as he is reluctant to finish writing the story, for to finish the book would mean the end of the narrator's proximity to Rafky. The narrator muses:

> I do not want to lose Rafky . . . To lose a man who is so good. A man
> who is so intelligent. A man who is so good looking.
> The most beautiful man in my life. (Aksana 2004a, 202)

Finally, in the last short section, entitled "The 2nd ending (and it should be the ending)"[15] the two visit Valent's grave and Rafky asks the narrator to stay with him. However, the narrator is torn by a variety of emotions. He has clearly become infatuated with Rafky but feels that Rafky should keep Valent as the first and final love in his life (2004a, 214). Instead, the narrator walks away from Rafky terrified that if he were to turn back he would be at Rafky's side forever. And so the novel ends with a somewhat enigmatic conclusion, in which the narrator is unable to commit to Rafky, "not because I did not want to, but because I was unable to" (Aksana 2004a, 214).

Thus the novel closes as a requiem for a love and a relationship between two men that was depicted through its interior qualities as being perfect. For, as is common in modern Indonesian literature, one of the protagonists has to die at the end. The perfect relationship is not allowed to survive. Neither is the future potential of the relationship between the narrator and Rafky given a chance to flourish. The narrator wants to commit to Rafky, but he is not able to. In contrast to the freedom of expression and individuality embraced by the characters when they are in Bangkok, back in Indonesia love and desire are thwarted by societal and familial pressures.

Gay Indonesia Through a Thai Lens

In this section I would like to focus on two particular aspects of the novel that might be useful in furthering an understanding of representations of Indonesian queer subjectivities. First, I will discuss the contrasting imaginings of Bangkok and Jakarta in the novel. Second, I will consider the author's portrayal of the two *gay* characters with regard to their physical appearance, the reasons given to explain their homosexuality, and also the depictions of intimacy in the novel.

The image of Bangkok and comparison with Jakarta

Aksana (Interview, 10 December 2006) has stated that his aim in writing this novel extended beyond the simple desire to write the story of a love affair between two men. Rather, he wished to demonstrate the difficulty for Indonesians of expressing themselves in their homeland and that true and honest expressions are possible only overseas. Hence, rather than opt for the most obvious destination for Indonesian gay men, Bali, the author chose a setting beyond the Indonesian nation-state. Clearly, Bangkok is used very much as a contrast to the imprisoning nature of Jakarta. In the Thai capital the two men are free to make their own decisions, free of their families and the norms of Indonesian society. When Valent later explains why the relationship will not work in Jakarta, he says it is not only because of his mother, but also because of society, norms of behaviour, and the law. This disaffection with the Indonesian state is heightened as a result of his non-normative sexuality, and the contrasting appeal of Thailand for these marginalized Indonesians is all the stronger. The extent to which Aksana has succeeded in his stated aim is debatable, but he does tell us much about the Indonesian imagining of Thailand as something of a gay paradise. This idea is clearly not unique to Aksana's writings. Almost anticipating Aksana's novel, the Thai critic Rakkit Rattachumpoth has stated:

> Gay male holiday makers from both Western and Asian countries may feel that when they are here in Thailand they are free to be openly gay without being subject to the heavy criticism that is common in their home countries. (1999, ix)

As Rakkit goes on to argue, the reality for sexual minorities in Thailand is, in fact, radically different from this image.[16] Nonetheless, this stereotypical idea of Bangkok as an ideal gay destination is a persistent one, as is evidenced by a variety of Southeast Asian gay web sites.[17] It would be a mistake to assume that the potential audience for even such gay sites as *Utopia Asia* is exclusively Western, for it is clear that Thailand is also recognized as something of a gay beacon by other Southeast Asians. On a 2007 podcast on the Singapore-based *Queercast* web site,[18] Nick D, one of the two podcasters, describes his recent first trip to Bangkok, which he labels "the land of the banging cock" as the "compulsory gay men's destination". When asked what he did there, he said that he had visited the usual destinations, such as Jatujak Market, DJ Station, and The Babylon gay sauna.[19] It is also worth noting that a popular *gay* men's cruising and meeting spot in Surabaya in eastern Java is known as Pattaya, named after the Thai beach resort "that is rumoured to be full of gay men" (Boellstorff 2005, 13). Boellstorff notes that most places for *gay* men to meet in Surabaya are named after locales outside of Indonesia, citing Texas and Kalifor (i.e. California) as examples[20] (Boellstorff 2005, 24). Thailand is certainly seen as something of a gay paradise by a number of men Indonesian *gay* men I have spoken with, including some who have been there. The references to the United States in the locations mentioned above probably suggest an imagination of the West generally as a place of gay freedom rather than something specific about the United Sates, given many Indonesians' far-from-precise and often-confused knowledge of the geography of Western Europe and North America. Nonetheless, these names are also suggestive of the idea held by many Indonesian *gay* men that they are "linked to a global network" (Boellstorff 2007, 96).

Aksana states that he purposely chose Bangkok as the location of the novel in preference to London, Paris, Amsterdam, or San Francisco, cities with which he is also familiar, as he wanted to highlight a contrast between Jakarta and another Southeast Asian city (Interview, 10 December 2006). However, for many Indonesians Bangkok is also the Asian city that is most associated with a gay lifestyle. Thus, not only is Bangkok a place where Rafky and Valent are free of family; it is also described as a place where men walk hand-in-hand and where Rafky and Valent are not stared at in the street. In contrast, there are frequent references to Jakarta as a place of imprisonment, where the couple feel like escaped criminals and are forced to maintain their relationship in silence behind closed doors.

Aksana's portrayal of Bangkok has been described negatively by John Badalu (2005) as reading like something out of a *Lonely Planet* guidebook. Indeed the author himself reports that readers have used it as a guide to the city (Interview, 10 December 2006). Whatever the merits of his literary approach, it is surely interesting to look more closely at where the two Indonesian lovers are shown as visiting. The section entitled *"and love has just begun"* does, indeed, read something like a guidebook, being divided into short sections, often of less than a page in length, each with a specific Thai location or event as a heading. Thus, we are taken to a variety of sites and events: "Ayutthaya, the first capital of Thailand"; "Thon Buri, the original city of Bangkok"; "Loy Krathong festival"; "The Golden Mount, temple with 320 steps"; "Grand Palace, palace of the monarchy until King Rama VII"; "Mo Chit, Northeastern Bus Terminal"; "Tha Phra Chan, old harbour"; "Saladaeng—BTS Sky Train Station"; "Rama VI Statue, Lumphini Park". In addition to describing the burgeoning friendship between the two men as they travel around these sites, the reader is also given details about the attractions themselves. For example, we are told the following about the Golden Mount:

> Wat Saket Temple is on the side of a man-made hill that is called The Golden Mount, on Rattanakosin Island. With a height of 78 meters it was the highest point in Bangkok until 1960. On the western side of the temple there are 320 steps that climb up to the top of the hill. (Aksana 2004a, 52)

Interspersed among the historic sites are details of the perceived modernity of Bangkok, a city where, at least in the novel, traffic flows freely and the population moves round by sky trains, accessed via magnetic-card reading machines. In the minds of the Indonesian reader, this, of course, stands in contrast to the chaos of Jakarta, a city that the narrator says never engenders a feeling of longing to return (Aksana 2004a, 136). We also find conversations that criticize stagnation, corruption, and exploitation in Jakarta. In particular, material goods are said to cost more in Jakarta than in Bangkok, despite lower labour costs, inducing Indonesians to travel abroad to buy quality products.

With each day that passes in the Thai capital, Valent and Rafky become more relaxed, coming to prefer riding the bus and the train to a pre-arranged limousine. Just as they relax into their surroundings as the Thai capital allows— indeed, almost encourages—the love between the two men begins to flourish. For example, in Lumphini Park, while Rafky is exercising Valent enjoys watching fit, shirtless young men lifting weights. The narrator states that such is the desire to show off one's body that it is pondered that maybe, if allowed, they would actually prefer to be exercising naked. While Valent is clearly entranced by the muscular beauty of these young men, the spectacle serves only to heighten his fascination for Rafky, "the most beautiful among all the beautiful men" (Aksana 2004a, 71). Bangkok is also represented as a city so accustomed to gay couples that when Rafky and Valent change hotels, and ask a taxi driver to take them to a cheap and simple guesthouse, they are knowingly taken to J House, at 38 Soi Pratuchai, Surawong Road, a guesthouse in close proximity to a male go-go bar,

> which every night served up a show of naked male dancers. Several fit men with hard muscular bodies started to group together outside the bar, each radiating their charm in order to attract the attention of the tourists passing to and fro. (Aksana 2004a, 106)

When, immediately after that description, Rafky notes that the taxi driver had made a clever choice of guesthouse, he substantiates this statement by pointing to the cleanliness of the room, but at the same time his gaze has been fixed on the go-go bar outside, and we see a growing confidence and eagerness to be proximate to the visible and disinhibiting gay scene. The conversation between Rafky and Valent then continues in an increasingly emboldened way, with Valent quipping that they may have been mistaken for a honeymooning couple and with the exhibitionist Rafky revelling in the fact that there was no partition wall between the bedroom and shower.

The two are clearly now shown to be in the centre of gay Bangkok. Coming out of a Family Mart convenience store, they walk along a narrow road, lined with gay bars. The road is busy with people passing by, "particularly men. Men who like men. A strategic place to see and be seen. While sitting outside a bar they could see whoever passes by. And send each other a signal if mutually attracted" (Aksana 2004a, 109). Of course, Rafky attracts the attention of a foreign tourist as they pass by. The tourist winks and invites him to join him by patting the empty seat beside him. Valent is seemingly oblivious to this, and when Rafky points out the attention he is receiving from the white man, he jokes that maybe he has been mistaken for a go-go boy, and they go on to quip that Valent would not give up Rafky for any amount of money. While the scene is obviously intended as an opportunity to show the mutual love and loyalty between the two Indonesian lovers, at the same time it seems to carry a presumption that many sexual relationships in Bangkok will inevitably have a financial basis, particularly those between Thais and Westerners.

The culmination of the trip to Bangkok for both Rafky and Valent, and also for Rafky and the narrator as they retrace the journey taken by Rafky and the now-deceased Valent, is a visit to the nightclub DJ Station. It is Valent who brings Rafky there, on the pretext that the club is famous worldwide and, while he has been to Bangkok before, he has never been brave enough to go there alone.[21] The two are amazed by the sights in the club, enjoying being part of a gay scene that includes Westerners and Asians, and white, brown, and black skins. Wherever Rafky turns his gaze, there are handsome men with bodies so sexy that they are a delight to look at, whatever they are wearing. It is here that Rafky and Valent feel themselves to be part of a wider gay culture, part of an international scene. This new gay world is a confusing one, however, particularly for Rafky, who cannot understand the presence of women in the club. Valent laughs as he tells him not to be surprised as they are, in fact, men. Rafky's response confirms every cliché that exists regarding Thailand:

> 'Wow . . . ,' cried Rafky in astonishment. 'Thailand really is the land of
> dreams, isn't it? Everything that one looks for is here. Everything that
> is false appears genuine.' (Aksana 2004a, 132)

However, it is not just their naïvety that prevents them from fully embracing this supposed site of global gay identity. While they are content to dance on the ground floor, Rafky is nervous about ascending to the upper levels of the club. The ground floor, a place to dance and to make dates is enough of a novelty for Rafky. The second floor is described as the place to continue to after finding a date and also as a place to watch those on the dance floor. However, when Valent describes the third floor as a place "for those who can no longer contain themselves—they can do whatever they like there" (Aksana 2004a, 131), Rafky resists by replying that he does not want to see such "vulgar sexual activity" (*kencan yang vulgar*). We might interpret this as Rafky's inhibition regarding open displays of sexual activity, or maybe it is the unexpressed fear that Valent had perhaps already visited this location on a previous occasion, for immediately Valent again has to qualify his knowledge with the explanation that this is what he has heard and he has never experienced it personally. Either way, there is an unmistakable ambivalence—a desire to experience, yet also a nervousness, and even a moral condemnation of what might be seen.

Just as Valent introduces Rafky to the nightclub, so, later, on Rafky introduces the narrator to the club. Such is the effect of Bangkok on the innocent Indonesian that the initiate has subsequently become the initiator. The narrator uses a style more akin to investigative journalism in describing his first foray into the famous club, including details of the queue for entry and the need to show identity cards so as to prevent those under the age of eighteen from gaining admittance. The narrator's initial reaction to the club is one of bewilderment and dislocation:

> I wiped my eyes, which were smarting from the attack of cigarette
> smoke. 'What is this place?' I asked confused. I tried to accustom myself
> to the noisy boisterous environment, but failed. I was increasingly
> overwhelmed, feeling isolated. (Aksana 2004a, 127)

One might be forgiven for finding the reaction a little extreme, for smoky, noisy clubs are not unique to Bangkok: Jakarta certainly has several that could compete on this level. However, it is not just the noise; it is the sight of the all-male crowd that shocks, and yet also appears to excite—the imagination of the narrator. A full-page description of the scene follows, replete with handsome and muscular bodies, tight-fitting shirts, exhibitionist young men with tight jeans with the top button left undone, before the narrator tells us of his nausea at the scene, which Rafky helpfully tries to cure by giving him a vodka-strawberry cocktail—another first for the author, as he had never previously drunk alcohol. Thus, it is in Bangkok that the narrator is exposed to a completely new side of life. Just as he is intoxicated by the alcohol, so, too, is he intoxicated by the male bodies. In his drunkenness they return to the hotel, and as he is supported by Rafky, a support he clearly enjoys, his ambivalence is further evident when he explains the fact that nobody is concerned at the sight of the two of them, walking together, as it is normal in the area to see men on the street walking hand-in-hand, embracing and kissing, "vulgarly demonstrating their love" (Aksana 2004a, 134). Thus, Bangkok is the city in which the relationship between the narrator and Rafky becomes intimate, even erotic. When the narrator, drunk and still confused regarding his own sexual desires, is escorted back to the hotel and put to bed by Rafky, he feels protected and safe. And when Rafky goes back to his own room, he feels a sense of loss, and all he can do is scrape at the wall that separates him from his desired companion.

Beautiful Men and Reasons to be *Gay*

One of Joko Anwar's criticisms of this novel is its apparently clichéd representation of *gay* men (Anwar, 2004). Certainly the development of the two central characters is superficial, but what is more interesting for the purposes of this chapter are the qualities that the author bestows on his *gay* characters and also their backgrounds, which might also be seen as drawing on quite familiar stereotypes.

The image of Valent is particularly intriguing, for he is almost androgynous in his appearance. There is something about him that captivates Rafky at first sight, and, while he seemed somewhat weak, his physical proportions are described as being ideal (*ideal*). In one particular passage the syntactic structures used to develop the physical perfection of Valent echo descriptions of idealized beauty from traditional Malay texts:

> The profile of his face was perfect. Like a painting by a maestro of a past century. His aquiline nose was a flawless marble sculpture. His chin was beautifully tapered, with a central dimple like an ocean abyss. His eyelids resembled crescent moons, which even when closed were able to light up the night. Adorned by curled eyelashes, like the flowing fronds of casuarina trees caressed by the wind.
> He was not handsome.
> He was beautiful . . .
> He was a heavenly nymph who gave colour to the spring . . .
> . . . Man. And woman. Masculine. But also tender. (Aksana 2004a, 37)

This feature-by-feature description is highly reminiscent of traditional conventions, in which the various parts of the body are named and likened to parts of a flower, fruit, or even to an animal. It was the comprehensive totality of ideals that was deemed important as a means of reflecting physical beauty, and the above example is further evidence of the continued use of these conventions by modern authors, albeit in a modified form. Jackson (1999a) observes that classical Thai literature follows very similar conventions in descriptions of idealized forms of male beauty.

Rafky's physical appearance could not be more different from Valent. He is an extremely fit young man who, while growing up, has become used to attracting the stares of both women and men. Handsome and athletic, he attends the gym to maintain his health and the beauty of his body. In the hotel room, Valent sneaks a look at Rafky in his thin, tight, sleeveless shirt and his tight boxers, which draw attention to his defined and muscular body. While both Rafky and Valent are described as "the most beautiful man", it is clear that Rafky's description is nearest to the image of the muscular male torso on the book's front cover.

Just as Valent's appearance is somewhat androgynous, so his behaviour has been affected by a lack of masculine influence. As an only child, he had been brought up by a domineering mother, his father having died when he was young. Thus, it is explained, he never had a man's warmth or love, as any young boy needs once he reaches a certain age, a mother no longer being sufficient. Indeed, it is the smothering nature of his mother that has caused him to be so weak. As he grew into adolescence he had felt as if he had been caged inside the body of a boy. Brought up in a world surrounded by women, he longed for the warmth of men in his life. Finally, due to pressure from his mother to marry and produce a grandchild, he had "officially killed the abnormal feelings inside" (Aksana 2004a, 57) by becoming engaged to a colleague. Thus, Aksana draws a picture that is at odds with the situation described by Boellstorff's findings that many *gay* men look forward to marriage as "a source of meaning and pleasure", not just because it will allow them to please their parents and raise children, but also because it will give a sense of national belonging (Boellstorff 2005, 111).[22] While we are told little about Valent's past sexual history, we do know that he has visited Bangkok several times, and he often seems to know more about gay life in the city than he lets on. Certainly, he is not troubled by his emerging feelings for Rafky, but rather embraces the opportunity to develop the relationship. Valent's turmoil as an adult lies in his attempt to reconcile his own sexuality with his mother's ambitions for him.

It is interesting to note the similarities between Valent's portrayal and the character of Reuben, who plays a minor part in Aksana's earlier novel

Abadilah cinta (Let Love Be Eternal, 2003).[23] Unlike his elder brother, Reuben had never liked to play outside as a child, hating the rough-and-tumble play of his brother. Rather than be soiled by the dirt of the backyard, he preferred to stay inside playing, drawing and cooking with his somewhat dominating mother. His mother, never having had daughters, treated her third son as a little girl. In Reuben's childhood ambition to play Arjuna, a character always played by females on the Indonesian stage (Aksana, 2003a, 110–111), there are further points of comparison with the androgynous appearance of Valent. So, too, we are reminded of Valent when Reuben tells his brother that his lover—who is twice his age—is like a father figure (*figur ayah*) and that he has at last found the father's warmth (*kehangatan ayah*) that he had always sought.

With Valent and Reuben, a clear link is made between their effeminacy as children, the role of the domineering mother, the absent or aloof father, and their homosexuality. The lack of a father's warmth, or any father figure at all in Valent's case, is hinted at as the reason for both Valent's and Reuben's subsequent erotic attraction to men. Explanations for Rafky's same-sex attraction are more ambiguous. Until meeting his present girlfriend, he had flitted from girl to girl. To all intents and purposes he is perfect—indeed, that was how he had been brought up to be; there could be no defect, he had to be the best. It is only on meeting Valent that he feels able to begin to show his weaknesses and confusion. Nonetheless, facing up to his same-sex desire is a difficult process for Rafky, hence his numerous arguments with Valent, and the various instances wherein he affirms his *normal*ness and denies his *gay*ness. Ironically, it is only with his return to Jakarta and the acceptance he receives from his parents that he seems to come to terms with his sexuality, to the extent that with the death of Valent he is spurred to ask the narrator to write the story of his life and eventually to invite the narrator to stay with him.

According to Aksana, one criticism of his novel is the over-sentimentalization of the relationship and the absence of actual sex. Indeed, Aksana suggests (Interview, 10 December 2006) that his short story *Menanti pelangi* (Waiting for a Rainbow) (2006c) is a response to such criticism and shows that he could address the steamier side of *gay* life. Certainly that story, which relates the sexual exploits of a young man in a variety of locations including a lift, the toilets in a shopping mall, and the changing rooms of a swimming pool, engages with an imagining of a raunchier and more controversial aspect of *gay* sexual behaviour. Nonetheless, even in that story, it is true love that is sought, and the tale comes to a close with the realization that "love matters" (Aksana 2006c, 220). Indeed, the sexual act with the protagonist's newfound love is described in terms more reminiscent of a newly married couple as they check into the hotel and are finally entwined on the bed. It is romanticism and the celebration of love that prevails. For Aksana, it is a monogamous, committed relationship between two beautiful people that is idealized.

Conclusion

For some, Aksana's willingness to recast same-sex couples with similar ideals and intentions as heterosexual couples may be a disappointment. But it seems that it is his preference for romanticism over the "vulgarity of the sexual act"— to use the words of both Rafky and the narrator—that has perhaps made him so popular among many Indonesians. What is more, the criticism of Aksana for his melodramatic style in this book seems unjust, given the nature of his other writings, many of which fall into the same romantic genre. It may be appropriate to criticize the genre as a whole—and there is a raft of authors contributing to this corpus of works, the overwhelming majority of whom take *normal* relationships as their focus. However, one only need to look at the large number of blogs and discussion boards about *Lelaki terindah* (see note 14 above) to notice that the one aspect that is focused upon is the perceived beauty of Aksana's language and the romantic nature of the text. Indeed, another approach to this novel would be to recognize that Aksana has succeeded in adding a *gay* novel to a genre, albeit a sentimental melodramatic one, which had previously been an almost exclusively heteronormative domain.

In *Lelaki terindah* we have a situation quite removed from that described by Boellstorff (2005) regarding the dominant desire to marry heterosexually. For the characters in the novel it is impossible to consider carrying on their relationship while at the same time marrying. What Aksana presents to his readers is perhaps better understood as an ideal that draws on both modern heterosexual ideas of romantic relationships and also perceived notions of Thai understandings of modern gay relationships. Thus, we see the couple coming to recognize themselves as *gay* in a sense that seems more connected with Western meanings of the word than with the Indonesian term that Boellstorff has described. This is not to deny the validity of Boellstorff's research. Rather, it is to argue that the representation of the *gay* couple in this novel may have more to do with an idealized imagination of the *gay* subject position than it has with any attempt to depict a broad Indonesian reality. Nonetheless, one point that still requires further research, as should be evident in an analysis of this novel, is that there seems to be a significant class dimension to *gay* Indonesian's subjectivities, and perhaps there is something distinctive about the situation among the *gay* Jakarta elite. It should also be questioned the extent to which this novel may reflect something of a general change in the attitude of *gay* Indonesians towards marriage since the fall of the Suharto government in 1998 and the ensuing emphasis on honesty to which many *gay* men refer. Certainly, my conversations with a number of *gay* men in Surabaya and Jakarta in 2007 and 2008 would suggest that the desire to marry is not as strong as Boellstorff found in the late 1990s.

In particular, it is notable that Aksana himself has specifically situated his novel in Bangkok to make the point that Jakarta constrains and saps the identities and aspirations of all its inhabitants. He purposefully embraces the idea of a Bangkok in which gay men from all nationalities and all skin colours can come together. While the attitude of the Indonesian visitors to the Thai capital is at times ambivalent, it is nonetheless a city in which they flourish and develop as individuals. It is in Thailand where, temporarily free of the shackles of the Indonesian state, these young men are able to imagine themselves as members of a global gay culture. The importance of Thailand in the Indonesian *gay* imaginary is brought to the fore and serves to underline the need for deeper understanding of the cultural flows within Southeast Asia and their effect upon emerging gay cultures. The question that should be asked, but which cannot be answered at this point, is what influence such depictions of *gay* relationships, which have certainly been well received by sections of the Indonesian community, will have on attitudes to same-sex relationships in Indonesia, at least in the main cities, in the years to come.

Finally, despite the clichés and the criticisms in some reviews of the book, this novel, whatever its literary merit, remains an interesting and an important one. It criticizes Indonesian society for its rejection of love between men, a love that is painted in a positive, if somewhat superficial, way. The fixation on exterior beauty, which is perhaps matched by a lack of psychological development of the characters, is the dominant theme. The narrator's attraction to Rafky, despite his apparent heterosexuality, might simply be seen as a result of the bewitching nature of Rafky's good looks. But, in effect, the novel's ending serves as an acknowledgement that sexuality is more complex and more ambiguous than mainstream Indonesian society is ready to accept. The narrator does not turn back to this most beautiful man at the end, not because he does not want to, but because he is unable to. Is this because he is unable to face up to his attraction to someone of the same gender? Maybe. But it seems more likely that it is an inability to face the verdict of a society that had effectively killed Valent that causes him to turn away.

9

Speaking of Bangkok
Thailand in the History of Gay Singapore

Alex Au

Prefatory Note

Alex Au Waipang has been a gay activist in Singapore since 1993, when he began working with the then newly formed People Like Us, a gay and lesbian rights group with which he is still associated. Using business to push the envelope for gay issues in Singapore, he was also the main shareholder in a gay sauna that operated in the city-state from 2000 to 2005. Among Singaporeans in general, however, Au is best-known for Yawning Bread (www.yawningbread.org), a web site that has been on-line since 1996 and that has a reputation for fiercely independent commentary on social, political, and gay issues. For some two decades, Au has observed the gradual evolution of gay life and the gay scene in Singapore, occasionally as the centre of public attention himself. Over these same two decades, Au has also been in love with Thailand—for a few years, literally, with a Thai boyfriend—and has also become familiar with the evolution of the Thai gay scene through frequent visits since the late 1980s. In this chapter, Au reflects on the role that Bangkok's gay scene has played in the emergence of gay identity, community, and gay politics in Singapore. All informants' names have been changed at their request.

"To speak of Bangkok was to speak of being gay," Stanley, a lawyer and frequent traveller to Bangkok, said. Those were the times, in the 1990s, when many felt it was impossible to be gay in Singapore. Self-preservation dictated a habit of closeted silence among Singaporean gay men, imposed more rigorously every time a fresh report appeared in the city-state's newspapers that homosexual men had been arrested and sentenced to imprisonment, or subjected, even, to flogging. Until 2008, Section 377 of the Singaporean Penal Code prescribed a sentence of up to life imprisonment for "carnal intercourse against the order of nature". Even today, Section 377A of the revised Penal

Code criminalizes "gross indecency" between two males, a term that covers a wide range of erotic acts, even if they are consensual and conducted in private. Section 377A provides for up to two years' imprisonment. With these and other politically convenient laws, the government went about its task in the 1980s and early 1990s of trying to eliminate homosexual behaviour in public. Until 1994, the police regularly sent decoys into parks and back alleys to entrap men cruising for sex. The names, occupations, and even faces of those charged were splashed in the local newspapers. The Sunday night gay disco—it moved from place to place through the years—was frequently raided. In one well-recorded instance in May 1993, many partygoers who could not produce identification were hauled off to spend the night in a police lockup and had to call their families to the police station to bail them out. Since Singaporean law does not require its citizens to carry identification at all times, such detention amounted to unlawful harassment. This, however, was just one of many similar cases of the institutional homophobia that was the constant backdrop of Singaporean gay men's lives in the second half of the twentieth century.

Cruising and even mixing with other gay men in a known gay bar was an activity fraught with danger. Large numbers of Singaporeans with homosexual inclinations stayed away from the city's few gay venues, especially if they had good jobs that they would never want to risk. Probably even larger numbers denied to themselves that they were homosexual or bisexual. Between a social climate of disapproval and silence on the one hand, and, on the other, government censorship that filtered out any positive representation of homosexuality from abroad in the local press, Singaporean gay-identity formation was stillborn.

Yet, by the 1990s, Singapore was already a middle-income country, with the prime minister at the time, Goh Chok Tong, painting a vision of Singapore attaining a "Swiss standard of living" within ten years. Increasing numbers of Singaporeans had the wherewithal to travel abroad; however, a complex set of factors went into their choices of destinations. Going to the West brought status, but it was also more costly. For those who were already gay-identified and whose idea of erotic beauty was based on the Caucasian model, the allure of San Francisco, Amsterdam, and Sydney was irresistible.

The majority of Singaporeans, however, were either only vaguely aware of the reputations of Western gay capitals or could not afford to travel so far afield, except perhaps on a packaged tour whose tightly scheduled programme was unlikely to provide enough time for a personal agenda to explore local gay scenes. For most, regional travel within Asia was a more practical option, in which case, Thailand stood out as one of the most popular and inexpensive destinations. Accommodation, shopping, and eating out in Bangkok were relatively cheap by Singaporean standards. In addition, a liberal air-services agreement between

Singapore and Thailand meant that there were quite a number of airlines serving the route with highly competitive airfares. The Singapore–Thailand air-services agreement meant that is was usually cheaper to fly two hours to Bangkok than half an hour to Kuala Lumpur in neighbouring Malaysia. Bangkok was near enough for large numbers of Singaporeans to scoot over for "quickie" weekend holidays. Gradually, from the mid-1980s and through the 1990s, Singaporeans discovered the gay saunas, pubs, man-to-man massage parlours, and go-go boy bars of Bangkok and the nearby seaside resort of Pattaya. In Thailand they could do everything they wanted but dared not do in Singapore.

An interesting question is: Were these travellers to Bangkok gay before they discovered the scene in Thailand, or did they become gay as a consequence of the experience? The latter view was asserted by Woon, a university lecturer in information technology now in his forties, to whom this author spoke when gathering information for this chapter. Woon said, "For me and many people, you don't fully realize you're gay until you've experienced the sex." His point was that one could be latently homosexual, but so long as one was celibate in Singapore, afraid of exposure and arrest, how would one know one's own sexual orientation? Many might even have denied that they were homosexual. As Stanley, the lawyer quoted at the start of this chapter, remarked: "Out of social expectations, you have a girlfriend and you even have sex with her, and so you think you're straight." A weekend in Bangkok could well turn such perspectives upside down. "But when you've had your first love affair, fling, or just a one-night stand with another guy, you realize it feels completely different," Stanley said. He explained further, "How do you deny to yourself after that, even if you do not breathe a word about it to another soul, that maybe, just maybe, you're homosexual? How do you not want to go back to Bangkok for more?"

For a while, in the early 1990s, not breathing a word to another soul about such sexual explorations and self-revelations in Thailand remained possible. After all, many closeted gay Singaporeans often sneaked off to Bangkok alone and, while there, typically enjoyed mostly the company of Thais and other non-Singaporean gay tourists. Anonymity was important, since in Singapore careers and family life could be put at risk with the mere rumour of homosexuality.

Those who were even more concerned about staying under the radar could avoid Bangkok's gay discos, saunas, pubs, and restaurants and instead avail themselves of male commercial sex workers in the go-go bars and massage parlours. It is the nature of commercial sex to be discrete; no real names or telephone numbers are expected to be exchanged, unlike the case with a new love one has met in a gay sauna or dance club.

An intriguing suggestion that another informant, Cyrus, made was that Singaporeans flocked to Bangkok's commercial sex venues not only because they were discrete and (at least to middle-class Singaporeans) affordable, but also because there was subconsciously the compensating pleasure of mastery. Whereas these same persons felt like powerless victims of a relentlessly homophobic state in Singapore, even though they often held professional, executive positions in government or business, as a buyer of sex in Thailand there was a sense of attaining control over one's sex life. Economic dominance, at least temporarily, was sexually and personally liberating. This might be an interesting question for researchers to follow up on, namely, the relationship between commodified sexual relations and the emergence of a personal sense of homosexual autonomy.

Yet, as more and more Singaporeans made their way to Bangkok, anonymity became harder and harder to sustain. Stanley recalled a 1995 incident in Telephone Bar, a well-known gay pub in Bangkok's "gay soi" of Silom Soi 4, when he bumped into a former colleague, albeit one whom he had long suspected to be gay. "Fortunately, he had left the firm by then," Stanley said. "If I had had to face him at work the following week, I'm not sure I would have known how to deal with it." Woon came face-to-face with his boss in the Dream Boy go-go bar, while Chow, a naval officer, encountered his own brother in the dark recesses of Obelisk, a Bangkok gay sauna popular with Asian men from across the region until its closure in 1997. The instinctive response on these occasions was for both sides to pretend such meetings had never happened.

Yet, by around 1995, from this author's memory of conversations with friends, an elliptical way of speaking had developed among the more travelled gay Singaporeans. They were beginning to acknowledge the reality that Bangkok was a canvas upon which colour was being added to their gay lives. "How is it," the author overheard someone ribbing a mutual friend many years ago, "that in the last two years I have seen you just once in Singapore—at a Christmas party—but three times on Silom Road in Bangkok?" Various "white lies" about one's frequent weekends in Bangkok came to acquire loaded meanings. "I tell my mother I go to Bangkok to pray at the temples. But she doesn't know I worship the reclining Buddha." Here the reference, though it may be offensive to some Buddhists, is to the bed and the supine position. Or, "I like Bangkok for its shopping," said with a wink, and the listener or listeners would understand what the speaker was shopping for.

The many ways to speak of Bangkok thus became healthy outlets for expressing and affirming one's orientation and homosexual desires. And with that, a new phenomenon arose. What began as a shadowy world of sex tourism— and here the term is used broadly to mean much more than commercial sex adventures and includes all holidays with sexual intentions, such as those that include afternoons spent in saunas—became a platform for a shared identity.

The lonely furtiveness of cruising in Singapore, or the self-imposed isolation of not cruising and avoiding all gay places totally, was gradually superseded by a camaraderie of shared escape. And that was on top of growing numbers who, through fulfilment of sometimes-unsuspected desire, found themselves acknowledging a homosexual orientation they otherwise might not have recognized in themselves.

The ways by which Singaporeans interacted with Thai men were manifold. They were certainly, by the late 1990s, a visible presence at DJ Station, a popular dance club on Silom Soi 2. "Every time I go there, I never fail to see another Singaporean I know," Ian, a self-described "disco queen", said. By 2 a.m., as the party at the disco wound down for the night before the legally imposed closing time, many would have paired off with new friends and be making their way back to their hotels for more intimate relations. Then there were those who had steady Thai boyfriends; many of these ones set about buying an apartment in Bangkok, or learning the language, or both. The number of gay Singaporeans who can speak some Thai is quite remarkable for the city-state's small population.

Others preferred anonymous sex and the sauna scene, spending many lazy hours cruising the corridors of the world-famous Babylon sauna. For many years, Lee, a shipping officer, could be seen there every fourth weekend. The Babylon's rooftop (at its original location) was the setting for one chance encounter the author had, in 1996 or 1997, with Edmond, a twenty-year-old at the time who used to drift in and out of the gay-support groups that the author ran in Singapore. Edmond had relocated himself to Bangkok and had found a new vocation as a callboy. He could command a premium compared with Thai callboys, he said, because he was fluent in English. (Five years later, Edmond was back in Singapore running his own photography business. One can speculate about how he raised the needed capital.)

It was unlikely that Singaporean tourists would have wanted to avail themselves of a Singaporean callboy while in Bangkok—the risks of exposure would be too great, though it might have been considered kinky. But avail themselves of Thai go-go boys from the various bars in the vicinity of Surawong Road they most certainly did. The number of times the author came across Singaporean friends in these bars are countless; likewise, at massage venues such as Albury or Hero. It is noteworthy that Banana Club, a gay club in the same vicinity as these two massage venues, has had a Singaporean manager for at least a decade.

One way or another, sex in Bangkok went into making today's gay community in Singapore. This might not be a history that many would wish to boast of, but it stands to reason, for the defining characteristic of homosexuality is the direction of the romantic and erotic, and unless this is realized through personal experience, how would most people who are homosexual know it? And then, unless these shared desires are expressed through conversation, how would a common identity—being gay—emerge?

That having been said, the local evolution of the Singapore gay scene itself across this period should not be ignored. Through the 1990s, gay themes gained prominence in Singapore theatre, and the 1992 liberalization of film censorship allowed a number of gay-affirmative films to be screened. Augmented by their novelty factor, films such as *The Wedding Banquet* (1993, directed by Ang Lee), *Philadelphia* (1993, directed by Jonathan Demme), and *The Sum of Us* (1994, directed by Geoff Burton and Kevin Dowling) created a buzz in the nascent gay community. Nor were English-language films the only ones. *Farewell My Concubine* (1993, directed by Chen Kaige) and *Happy Together* (1997, directed by Wong Kar Wai) depicted homosexual longing in Chinese contexts, helping to indigenize such feelings among the ethnic Chinese, who form the majority of Singaporeans.

Police entrapment more or less ceased after 1994, when the Chief Justice found it "somewhat disquieting" that a man who had been entrapped had been charged, under Section 354 of the Penal Code, with outraging the modesty of a police officer to whom "it must have been plain," said the Chief Justice, that homosexual activity was to be expected. This was the case of *Public Prosecutor vs. Tan Boon Hock* (Appeal MA 493/93/01). A few months earlier, a public outcry had erupted when the authorities and state-controlled media came down hard on Josef Ng, a performance artist, when he protested police entrapment in one of his works—an outcry that led, the author heard from unofficial sources, to a re-examination of policy. However, it was not obvious to the general public that police operations against the gay community had ceased until at least a decade later. The gay community's memory and fear of police raids would persist for a very long time.

From the mid-1990s on, more and more pubs and karaoke bars opened in Singapore to serve gay men. For a long time before that, the only bar that was gay on all nights of the week was Vincent's, located on one of the upper floors of a shopping centre along Orchard Road, the main downtown shopping street. Even the Sunday night gay disco was an itinerant event that leased a straight dance club one night a week from an owner who was prepared to make better use of an otherwise slow evening, when few heterosexuals went out to party. Other bars that figured in Singapore's gay history in the 1980s, such as Niche, Shadows, and Marmota, did not operate as exclusively gay venues. And in any event, none of these was still operating in the 1990s, partly the result of licensing difficulties and repeated police visits.

It is worth noting that the first gay karaoke bar to open in Singapore with the dramatic expansion of the gay scene around 1995 was called Babylon, the same name as Bangkok's leading gay sauna. The owners knew that the name would connote a gay space to the Singapore market, a judgment that testifies to how widespread the Thai holiday experience had become. This was no isolated example. Within a year or two, a pub opened on Singapore's Tras Street called Why Not, which was also the name of a small gay go-go bar on the upper floor of a shophouse on Bangkok's Thaniya Road from the late 1980s to the early 1990s. In the 1990s, a little business opened in Orchard Plaza called Barbiery Massage, later renamed Jupiter Massage—both names the same as those of two of the more popular Bangkok go-go bars. Barbiery in Bangkok closed about ten years ago, but Jupiter is still doing well. The massage shop in Singapore, however, did not last long and had disappeared by 2000 or 2001.

In 1997, Max Lim opened Spartacus, the first gay sauna in Singapore. For some years prior to this, Lim had organized gay parties at various hired venues. As a project involving considerably greater investment than one-off events such as gay parties, opening this sauna was a brave venture at a time when it was still not clear that police raids on gay venues had become a thing of the past. That uncertainty necessarily dictated a minimal investment, and so the sauna's facilities were rather basic, with little more than a gym, a steam room, an aerobics room, and a rooftop terrace. Signs saying "No obscene acts allowed" were put up to provide some legal defence for the owners. This notwithstanding, from day one of its opening, gay Singaporeans knew what this sauna was for, a result of their "Thai education", and took to it like fish to water. Spartacus, however, did not last long. It closed in 1999 for business reasons. Max Lim would go on to open another sauna, Stroke, in March 2000, with similarly limited facilities. In July of that year, the author and his business partners opened Rairua, which consciously borrowed a few more ideas from Bangkok's saunas, including a jacuzzi and private cabins with lockable doors. Each cabin had a mattress, freely available condoms and lubricant dispensers, which at the time was a revolutionary innovation for Singapore. Freely distributing condoms tested official comfort with the idea of gay sex. Having cabins with lockable doors tested a stated rule for the design of massage parlours in Singapore (massage parlours being in police eyes the nearest equivalent to gay saunas, there being no rules for gay saunas since such things had never been contemplated by the country's authorities). These tests were passed two months later, when the police made an inspection. They ignored the condoms but noticed the locks. In the end, they decided that since the venue was not really a massage parlour, there was nothing illegal about lockable doors. Thereafter, there was an explosion of gay saunas in Singapore, with Blue Heaven, One Seven, Towel Club, The Box, and Raw (successor to Stroke) following in quick succession.

There is one feature of Singapore's gay saunas that was influenced by Bangkok and Hong Kong saunas; the use of the private rooms is always free of charge. This is unlike the common practice in American bathhouses, where private rooms incur an additional charge above the entry fee. One Seven was the only sauna that experimented with paid rooms, but the idea never took off. Customer resistance was strong, probably the result of expectations traceable to the Bangkok experience. By way of comparison, the author has noticed that the gay bathhouses he has visited in Manila offer paid private rooms, suggesting an American influence.

Bangkok gay saunas would later return a compliment to Singapore, in the form of all-nude nights. Rairua was the first to introduce such a concept, in late 2000, a few months after its opening, designating Friday evenings for such a thrill. They were formally branded "Freedom Fridays", but the name never quite gained traction. Instead, among patrons it was popularly known as "Skin Night", taking off from the advertising tagline: "Tonight, don't wear towels, only wear your skin." Today, numerous Bangkok saunas have nude nights regularly on their calendar. Sauna Mania, on Bangkok's Soi Phiphat 2, was noted in December 2008 to have named its weekly events "Skin Nights".

Gay circuit parties were another phenomenon that sprang up at the turn of the century. For four years, from 2001 to 2005, the region's premier gay-circuit party, organized by fridae.com and its affiliates, was held in Singapore. Fridae.com is one of two successful Singapore-based gay portals, the other being SgBoy.com, now renamed Trevvy.com. In 2004, fridae's three-day Nation Party held at Singapore's Sentosa Island resort was reported to have attracted about eight thousand participants, the most successful of three such gay events on the local annual calendar, the other two being called Squirt and Snowball. Clearly, the development of the gay scene in Singapore had come a long way and had acquired a dynamic of its own.

However, trouble was to come. Unlike pubs and saunas, or even gay-male massage places in Singapore, which generally maintained a low profile, by attracting huge crowds and making inroads into the media, circuit parties such as Nation, Squirt, and Snowball drew the attention of the government. In December 2004, Snowball was banned, as was Nation in 2005. Fridae moved the Nation party to Phuket in 2006, once again indicating how Thailand had come to be seen as a natural alternative to Singapore's gay scene. After two years however, Fridae decided that for a number of reasons, Phuket could never attract the same crowd as Singapore, and it discontinued its Nation parties.

It is necessary to come back for a moment to Vincent's, for this bar represented a period in Singapore's gay history that is now largely forgotten. Throughout its existence, from the 1980s until around 2003, when it finally closed, Vincent's was the kind of place where "Asians"—a term that connotes a Westerner's perspective on Singaporean people—would go to hook up with white tourists and expatriates. It just was not the done thing at that time for a Singaporean to cruise another Singaporean at Vincent's. This was not a matter of convention; rather, there was no demand for local sexual partners. Through the 1970s and 1980s, large numbers of homosexually inclined Singaporeans idealized the Westerner for a love partner. To them, it was the Caucasian male form that embodied beauty, and white flesh that oozed the erotic. Singaporeans consumed images of male desirability imported from America and Europe in which non-Caucasian races were either invisible or asexual.

Yet, by the time the new generation of gay bars and saunas opened in the latter part of the 1990s, their clientele was predominantly local. Where did this ready market come from? Obviously, it would have included Singaporeans who previously had cruised at great risk to themselves in the city-state's parks and back alleys, and those who had danced at the weekly disco on Sunday nights half-expecting a police raid. But it also included those who had been initiated into gay life in Bangkok and who had hitherto shunned the gay scene in Singapore until they had become more self-assured. It could therefore be argued that Bangkok was an incubator for Singapore's contemporary gay scene.

More interestingly, another argument could also be made, namely, that the Thai experience redirected Singapore gay men's desire from the white male to their own kind or, at least broadly, the East Asian and Southeast Asian kind. Cruising the corridors of Bangkok's gay saunas with heightened expectation of erotic encounters among Asian bodies (mostly Thai, but also gay tourists from Hong Kong, Taiwan, Korea, Japan, and Malaysia), gazing on young, almost naked, Thai men dancing on a go-go stage, and ultimately shuddering in orgasm enfolded in the arms of another Asian man, imprinted the desirability of Asian male flesh on a new generation of Singaporeans. Love and beauty were translated from the foreign into the indigenous.

Ten years before, gay sex in Singapore often took the form of competition for the rare, visiting Caucasian, and identity was typically shaped to fit Western preconceptions of the soft, demure, and accommodating Asian "wife". But by the turn of the millennium, a new cohort of gay men desired sex with a fellow Singaporean and saw a fellow Asian as friend and potential lover. As elaborated below, this re-orientation of desire towards "one's own kind" has political implications. Without it, the leading motive of Singapore's gay men would be to escape the homophobic confines of the city-state and seek lovers from abroad. The relationships that the first generations of Singaporean gay men formed were not just infused with a racialized hierarchy and dependency; they were also aimed at emigration. There would be little interest in staying and fighting for one's rights at home in Singapore in such a situation. The re-orientation to see fellow Asian–Singaporeans as objects of desire was not only a great boost to one's sense of self-worth; relationships also became less hierarchical and more domestic, as well as egalitarian. And these local, egalitarian relationships, in turn, formed the necessary bases for domestic political consciousness. One's fellow gay Singaporean was no longer a competitor for the heart of a white male saviour, but a compatriot in a common cause.

To this emerging sense of community must be added another important ingredient that would give the gay community in twenty-first-century Singapore its contemporary character—the language of rights. This came largely from Singaporeans who had studied or worked in the West. As Singapore's middle class grew, more and more families could afford to send sons and daughters to universities in the United States, Europe, Britain, or Australia. In these locations, the gay ones were exposed to the ideas and methods of Western gay-liberation movements, which are based on a discourse of rights and justice, and they would bring these ideas home when they returned after completing their studies.

At the same time, Singapore's aggressive adoption of Internet technology meant that others, sitting at their computers at home, were also absorbing the same ideas. Since 1996, when the government enunciated its "light touch" policy, there has been no restriction on access to gay-related material on the Internet, with the exception of a few extremely pornographic sites. Nevertheless, even adding those returning home from abroad fired up with politicized demands to those who became radicalized by way of web-surfing, there were never many politically active gay Singaporeans—in keeping with the long-observed fact that political awareness is a rare attribute among Singaporeans of all genders and sexualities.

As a small minority of an already-small minority, politically aware gay men and their lesbian associates could easily be ignored by society, let alone by the government of an autocratic state. It is hard to imagine that they would ever have the numbers, by themselves, to make much of an impact. But they were fortunate that by the time the language of gay rights was articulated, from the late 1990s on, Singapore had a gay community in place. These eager (or idealistic) individuals found themselves, if not quite with a ready constituency, at least with a sympathetic audience. Most gay individuals' interests might have been primarily personal—career, love, sex, entertainment—but it was not a huge leap to identify with the political aspirations sketched out by the small number of activists: decriminalization, non-discrimination, and rolling back censorship, among others. The People Like Us organization has been the lightning rod for many of these issues, making public demands for registration as a society under Singapore law (denied in 1997 and again in 2004) and speaking out against various bans it encountered when it tried to organize public forums, art exhibitions, and outdoor events. Formed in 1993, it has been such a fixture that its initials, "PLU", have gained widespread currency throughout Singapore, Malaysia, Indonesia and even non-English-speaking Thailand as shorthand for "gay".

Yet, People Like Us has never had a large following. Many Singaporeans still consider such overtly political organizing a rather dangerous activity. Despite this, it is notable that the gay issue figures in this society's political debates quite regularly, which suggests that gay arguments resonate with enough people for them to be raised again and again. A burst of debate in the press followed the government's ban on the Snowball and Nation dance parties; two months' media attention had followed a 2003 comment by a minister that the government was not averse to employing openly gay civil servants; gay blogs continually highlight attempts by censors to strip local television of gay content; and a gay boycott of Singapore's leading bank, DBS, led to it withdraw its support for the Singapore arm of Focus on the Family, an American evangelical group with an anti-gay agenda. In 2007, amidst a few hundred suggested revisions to the Penal Code, one revision that the government did not moot dominated debate above all the others: the repeal of Section 377A. In the end, after nine months of heated debate, grassroots agitation failed to move the government to repeal this residue of nineteenth-century British colonial law. But the experience nonetheless showed how the call for repeal had by then gained support from large sections of Singapore's heterosexual community.

This reflected a significant shift in social attitudes towards homosexuality, particularly among those under thirty years of age. For example, a 2006 opinion survey conducted by students of Singapore Polytechnic, under the direction of Kwa Lay Ping, a lecturer from the college's School of Business, found that 50 percent of Singaporeans aged fifteen to twenty-nine—considered homosexuality "acceptable". (Forty-two percent disagreed and eight percent said "don't know".) This study, which polled eight hundred respondents, was featured on Channel NewsAsia, a Singapore-based TV news channel, on 17 January 2007. What would have generated this shift in social attitudes? Many studies in the West have demonstrated that having a member of the family or a close friend who is gay is the factor most closely correlated with gay-accepting attitudes. Indeed, there has been a steady coming-out of gay Singaporeans, particularly younger adults, through the last decade. As one young interviewee said to Channel NewsAsia on the 17 January 2007 programme, "In fact, if you ask any youth, he'll say that he knows at least one homosexual friend."

The story of gay Singapore in 2010 has come a long way from Bangkok in the 1980s and 1990s. While the relations of cause and effect are necessarily speculative, it is hard to imagine that the kind of mass holidaying experienced by gay Singaporeans in Bangkok from the early 1990s had no role in shaping self-perception and the resultant socialization. To summarize, my argument here is that what first began as escape from the harsh barrenness of gay life in twentieth-century Singapore became shared experience that, in turn, catalysed a local sense of homosexual community. The social confidence that this sense of community generated contributed to self-esteem, which propelled self-outing. As visibility increased, and with the language of rights added, the gay community began to have an impact on the broader Singapore society. Perhaps it is not as dramatic as the apocryphal chaos theory suggesting that a butterfly over Africa flapping its wings may eventually causing a hurricane over Florida, but somewhere in the story of gay Singapore would have been that moment when a first-time visitor to Bangkok arrived at the door of The Babylon gay sauna, hesitated a moment, and with a heady mix of trepidation and eager anticipation, pushed it open and walked through, never to look back.

III

LGBT Activism, Rights, and Autonomy in Thailand

10

Capitalism, LGBT Activism, and Queer Autonomy in Thailand

Peter A. Jackson

Ambivalent Queer Perspectives on Capitalism and Globalization

Queer studies in the West have had an ambivalent relationship to both capitalism and globalization. Alternative accounts variously emphasize the moments of subjection and exploitation on the one hand, and of autonomy on the other, in the intermeshing of queer gender and sexual cultures with globalizing capitalism. Citing Bernstein and Schaffner, Jeffrey Weeks summarizes these tensions when he observes:

> While the spread of global capitalism has exacerbated social inequalities, fragmented families, and severed individuals from traditional social ties, it has also given rise to transnational feminist activism, a burgeoning lesbian-gay-bisexual-transgender-queer (LGBTQ) movement, a renewed commitment to international human rights, and myriad forms of eroticism and community. (Bernstein and Schaffner 2005, xi, cited by Weeks 2007, 199)

The studies brought together in Arnaldo Cruz-Malavé and Martin F. Manalansan's edited collection *Queer globalizations* (2002) reflect these tensions in Western queer studies; some contributors see the market as a source of queer subjection and others argue that it provides the basis for movements to enhance queer autonomy in an overwhelmingly heteronormative world. As editors, Cruz-Malavé and Manalansan negotiate these tensions when, in introducing the collection they state:

> Queerness is now global. Whether in advertising, film, performance art, the Internet, or the political discourses of human rights in emerging democracies, images of queer sexualities and cultures now circulate around the globe . . . In a world where what used to be considered

>the 'private' is ever more commodified and marketed, queerness has become both an object of consumption, an object in which nonqueers invest their passions and purchasing power, and an object through which queers constitute their identities in our contemporary consumer-oriented globalized world. (2002, 1)

Early accounts of cultural globalization by queer studies analysts tended to emphasize two main points, namely, that it was a process of Westernizing cultural homogenization and that subjection to globalizing market processes involves a loss of autonomy. These intersecting views are reflected in Chela Sandoval's succinct claim, "At the turn of the twenty-first century the zones are clear: postmodern globalization is a neocolonizing force" (2002, 26). More recent studies, including the chapters in this book, challenge the presumption that cultural globalization necessarily entails a neocolonizing Americanization or homogenization of the world's queer cultures. Cruz-Malavé and Manalansan (2002, 6) themselves reject the view that globalization equates with cultural homogenization, pointing out that the rise of intra-Asian and other regional gay networks reflects the fact that globalizing processes emerge as much from the non-West as from the West.

As reflected in the chapters here, over the past decade queer Bangkok has arguably been much more influenced by, and become a source of influences for, gay Asia than the gay West. Stuart Koe, co-founder of the Singapore-based gay and lesbian web portal fridae.com, believes that in the 2000s gay America is no longer as important for gay Asians as it was in the 1980s and 1990s, contending that gay Asia is now "feeding off itself" and is increasingly decoupling from Western queer cultures (Interview, 25 February 2008). Dédé Oetomo, founder of Indonesia's first gay NGO, Gaya Nusantara, argues that Sydney's Gay and Lesbian Mardi Gras is a significantly more important cultural influence for gay Indonesians than either the United States or Europe (Interview, 25 February 2008).

However, the studies here provide a less clear-cut answer to the question of whether the market provides more avenues for queer autonomy and institutionalizing LGBT rights or whether it operates as a system of subordination and exploitation. Thailand's communities of gay men, lesbians, and *kathoeys* each have somewhat different relations to the market, and their lives and distinctive cultures are not affected in uniform ways by the commodification inherent in capitalism. This diversity and the absence of uniformity among Thai gay, lesbian, and *kathoey* cultures is indeed a general feature of their respective relations to Western queer cultures, not only of their relations to global markets and transnational processes (see Jackson 2004c).

Overall, Thai gay and *kathoey* cultures are more highly commodified than *tom-dee* lesbian culture and, at the risk of overgeneralization, it is perhaps the case that Thai gay men are more anxious about their cultural-financial status as consumers than they are concerned about their role as homosexual citizens. Interestingly, as both Megan Sinnott and Douglas Sanders note in this volume, Thai lesbians have been at the forefront of the Thai LGBT rights movement. While increasing numbers of Thai gay men have succeeded in creating a diverse range of commercial niches for themselves, Thai lesbians, suffering from the lower-than-average purchasing power and the cultural restrictions imposed on all Thai women, have made the politicized public space of rights and citizenship much more their domain of action.

At the same time that capitalism provides avenues of opportunity for some Thai gay men, it also erects barriers of exclusion for others. As a highly commodified identity with a middle-class caché, Thai gay identity comes literally with a price tag, often excluding men with lower incomes from participating fully in this market-based zone of sexual autonomy. In the early 1990s, one working-class welder from a rural background in northern Thailand whom I interviewed in Bangkok made the bitterly ironic remark, "I'm too poor to be gay." This man was in his early thirties and was certain of his homosexual identity. He was dating a younger man from northeast Thailand who was working as a waiter in a Bangkok restaurant and whom he had met at a cruising spot in a Bangkok park. What he meant was that he could not afford the consumerist lifestyle that, by the 1990s, had come to mark representations of "gayness" (*khwam-pen-gay*) in Thailand. In brief, one needs money to afford the gay lifestyle, and poverty is a barrier to full participation in this market-based identity and culture, which are to a significant extent based on consumption.

Transgender *kathoeys* also have an ambivalent relationship to the market. On the one hand, as Stéphane Rennesson observes in his chapter, the commodification of feminine beauty in Thailand, in the form of mass-mediatized transgender/transsexual beauty contests, provides a platform from which *kathoeys* can challenge disparaging stereotypes and stake a claim for cultural and social recognition. On the other hand, Aren Aizura points out that the internationalization of Thailand's cosmetic-surgery industry has inflated the prices of gender reassignment surgery and related technologies of physiological feminization, making it increasingly difficult for Thai *kathoeys* to afford the self-transforming medical interventions that permit them to perform successfully on the national stage of feminine beauty.

Queer Consumers or LGBT Citizens?

Being a consumer cannot be equated with being a citizen, and market rights to consume cannot be taken as guaranteeing political rights. In reviewing the 2007 book *Consumed: How markets corrupt children, infantilise adults, and swallow citizens whole*, by Benjamin Barber, who is well-known for his 1996 study, *Jihad vs McWorld*, Barry Schwarz distinguishes the commercial freedom of consumers from the political freedom of citizens:

> We respond to dissatisfaction in the market with exit: We leave a store (or website) and go to another. We respond to dissatisfaction in the state with voice: We march, we write letters to the editor, we work in political campaigns . . . It's a serious mistake . . . to confuse the two. And it's an equally serious mistake to assume the success of one implies the success of the other: [Barber states] 'The victory of consumers is not synonymous with the victory of citizens. McWorld can prevail and liberty can still lose.' (Schwarz 2007, 10)

It would seem to follow that there must be two forms of analysis of the possibilities for queer autonomy and rights under capitalism. On the one hand, we need to study the market-based aspects of autonomy gained by queer purchasing power, but, on the other hand, we equally need to consider the extent to which market-based societies provide opportunities for institutionalizing queer rights in law. Market-based queer cultures can find niches even in the absence of institutional rights, by working within and around restrictive legal and bureaucratic systems, by evading state power ("flying under the radar", as it is put by queer Singaporeans), or by paying the police and other homophobic authorities to look the other way, as was often the case in Thailand in the twentieth century.

Western gay/lesbian and queer studies, often operating under the residual impact of Marxism and, more recently, of post-Marxist anti-globalization analyses, have at times placed too much emphasis on the exploitative dimension of capitalism. Drawing upon the experiences of the modern West, such analyses do not give sufficient attention to the extent to which capitalism can become a vehicle for enhancing queer autonomy in politically authoritarian Asian states that are nonetheless committed to market-based economies. In their different ways, twenty-first-century China, Singapore, and Thailand each provides an instance of the importance of the market for queer autonomy in authoritarian, market-based economies. Despite the intense political controls exercised by China's Communist Party, the decades of one-party rule by Singapore's People's Action Party, and the abolition and subsequent rewriting of the country's constitution by the Thai military after the September 2006 coup, all three countries have nonetheless permitted spaces for booming queer commercial scenes. (See Alex Au here on Singapore, and Leung [2008], Ho [2010], and Ching [2010] on China and Hong Kong.) In the early twenty-first century, anti-democratic political authoritarianism takes diverse forms in different Asian societies, but is not necessarily homophobic or anti-gay. On the contrary, in Thailand military governments have at times provided more spaces for queer autonomy than democratically elected governments that have followed populist moral agendas.

The studies here provide standpoints from which to question the Eurocentric assumptions that, in the 1990s, marked both neoliberal and neo-Marxist accounts of cultural globalization. In addition to providing evidence for a critique of the neoliberal, McDonaldization view of global queering as emerging from the export of Western cultural models (see Wilson 2006), they also lead us to question the neo-Marxist view that the spread of capitalism necessarily entails the imposition of an alienating, foreign-controlled regime of economic exploitation. In contrast to both these positions, the chapters in this book present pictures of Thai queer cultures as emerging within the economic matrices of both local and emerging intra-Asian regional markets. In contrast to the Eurocentrism inherent in both Western neoliberal and neo-Marxist frameworks, Thailand's commercial queer scenes are here seen through the lens of local agency as indigenous phenomena, not as the outcome of either Western hegemony, exploitation by foreign capital, or the imposition of alien cultural forms.

The moment of autonomy was in fact foregrounded in one of the earliest and consistently most influential accounts of the relationship between capitalism and queer cultures and communities. According to John D'Emilio, it was American capitalism's replacement of both the self-sufficient rural household and slave production with wage labour that "gave individuals a relative autonomy, which was the necessary material condition for the making of lesbianism and gayness" (1993, 467). He identified the free-labour system as a key factor that allowed, "large numbers of men and women in the late twentieth century to call themselves gay, to see themselves as part of a community of similar men and women, and to organize politically on the basis of that identity" (1993, 468). D'Emilio's analysis was first presented in the early 1980s, before the emergence of queer studies in the 1990s. However, his argument can be reformulated in the idiom of queer studies as the proposition that *a body of capital precedes the emergence of modern queer bodies*. D'Emilio's analysis is relevant beyond the gay and lesbian histories of the United States and is echoed in a wide range of subsequent studies. In seeking to explain global queering, Dennis Altman has stated that "there is a clear connection between the expansion of consumer society and the growth of overt lesbian/gay worlds" (1996b), and Chris Berry has argued:

> Behind the adoption and adaptation of lesbian and gay sexual identities
> into Asian metropolitan cultures lies the global spread of postmodern
> consumer capitalism and the construction of identity not around
> national production but multiple niche markets. (1994, 11)

Peter Drucker (2000) has also drawn on D'Emilio to argue for the primary role
of the market and capitalist urbanization in the global rise of new queer cultures
and identities: "Involvement in a market economy and a certain minimum
income level seem essential in allowing people to become part of lesbian/gay
communities in the Third World" (2000, 17).

Ann Pellegrini has sought to disentangle the ambiguities in the relationships
between capitalism and the expansion of autonomous social, cultural, and
political spaces for queer existence. She looks for relationships between the
economic transformation from industrial capitalism to post-industrial or
commodity capitalism on the one hand, and the cultural transformation from
homosexuality as a minority identity to an alternative lifestyle on the other. She
opens her study with the following questions:

> [W]hat is the relationship between [queer] legal and social rights, on the
> one hand, and economic recognition and consumptuary opportunities,
> on the other[?] . . . [W]hat is the relationship between being addressed
> as consuming subjects . . . and becoming full social subjects, subjects,
> that is, of rights? (Pellegrini 2002, 134–135)

While the causal linkages require further explication, the chapters here
nevertheless show that the two processes—of queers emerging as both publicly
acknowledged consuming subjects and as the subjects of legal rights—took
place in tandem in early twenty-first-century Thailand. In concluding her study,
Pellegrini disagrees with the view that the commodification of gay cultures
equates with depoliticization:

> [I]t seems to me that commodification is not the end of politics, need
> not amount to depoliticization, but may actually constitute the starting
> point for contemporary lesbian and gay politics in the United States.
> Rather than nostalgically yearning for lesbian and gay identities
> unmarked by commodity capitalism, what if we acknowledged that
> lesbian and gay identities have always been in some way marked by
> capitalism, so too have heterosexual identities . . .
> [T]here is nothing new about the intimacy of capital and community
> formation, to the relay capital-identity-community, we might then
> reply, 'So what?' This is not the end of politics, gay, queer, or otherwise,
> but among its operating conditions and constraints. (2002, 141)

Cruz-Malavé and Manalansan arrive at a similar conclusion, namely,
that the current conditions of market-based globalization are not only a site of

dispossession but "also a creative site for queer agency and empowerment" (2002, 2). Despite its tendency to reduce the social and political significance of queer sexualities and cultures to commodities in the marketplace, capitalism "has also provided the struggle for queer rights with an expanded terrain for intervention" (Cruz-Malavé and Manalansan 2002, 2). This relation was exemplified in 2007 in Bangkok. As Douglas Sanders details in his chapter, in that year Bangkok's Novotel Hotel management offered a public apology to a prominent *kathoey* businessperson who had been denied entry to the hotel's popular discotheque because her feminine gender presentation did not match the male gender specified on her official identity card. This apology was offered after the NGO Bangkok Rainbow initiated an international Internet campaign calling for a boycott of the Novotel hotel chain because of its discriminatory policy. In this case, the right to unfettered access to consume entertainment in an up-market venue was linked directly to the broader issue of rights for transgender persons.

Tourist Zones as Spaces of Thai Queer Autonomy

Literature on international tourism in developing countries such as Thailand often focuses on its destructive impact on the local culture and physical environment and the subjection of tourism-industry workers to the dictates of foreign tourists. It is rarely mentioned, however, that some Thais may choose to work in tourist zones such as Pattaya because they offer spaces of relative autonomy from the restrictive cultural norms that obtain in the rest of the country. Timo Ojanen reports that the transgender manager of an NGO in Pattaya dealing in transgender health and rights issues "considered Pattaya to be a territory of freedom" (2009, 22) because it is home to one the biggest communities of transgenders and transsexuals in the country, who provide mutual support and help for each other. Many Thai gays, lesbians, and *kathoeys* find their own society highly restrictive, with tourist zones such as Pattaya and Phuket, which Thai authorities permit to cater for and pander to foreign tastes and cultural expectations, offering an escape from the heteronormative expectations that dominate much of the rest of the country. The "traditional Thai culture" packaged and sold to tourists may not always be experienced by Thais as a source of exotic beauty, but rather as an oppressive expression of state control over everyday life. As historian Kasian Tejapira observes:

> The current rapid . . . changes in Thai identity have been brought about by two major forces. First, there is the pervasive process of economic and cultural globalization. On the other hand, there is the attempt of the Thai state to hold on to its cultural and political hegemony; to

control the signification of Thainess amidst the flux of globalization and commodification. Under the pretext of conserving Thainess, the state tries to maintain and reassert its official nationalist authority over an increasingly fluid and complex society and culture. (2001, 164–165)

Designated tourist zones, which contain potentially disruptive foreign cultural influences within highly delimited geographical spaces, may provide Thai queers with places in which they can leave behind Thai heteronormative expectations without leaving Thailand. Rather than being "Westernized" by participating in these zones of commodified cultural escapism, Thai queers may find the space and opportunity to experiment in new ways of being Thai. The development of Pattaya and Phuket as containment zones for international tourism means they have emerged as spaces in which broader Thai cultural norms may be transgressed, not only by foreign tourists but also by both Thais.

Research on male sex workers in Thailand (e.g. Storer 1999a) has pointed out that, as in other countries, many men engaging in sex work are not homosexual. However, some male sex workers are gay and may not enter sex work merely because they have no other option to make money. For a young man from a poor background who is aware of his homosexual interests, but whose opportunities are limited by poverty and a poor education, sex work may provide a way to participate in the bourgeois Thai gay world—albeit as a service-provider rather than as a consumer. Research on male sex work too often focuses on the element of exploitation while overlooking the capacity of prostitution to provide an avenue for achieving a degree of sexual autonomy, that is, of being able to live a gay lifestyle and participate in the gay scene (*sangkhom gay*). Some poor gay men and *kathoeys* may choose to pay the price of being stigmatized by engaging in sex work to be able to live some form of the idealized Thai gay/*kathoey* lifestyle.

Buying Spaces for Queer Autonomy in Thailand

Witchayanee Ocha provides insight into Thai cultural attitudes in which personal wealth can be used to "buy" a space for queer sexual autonomy within a heteronormative culture wherein family ties remain central to queer identity and sense of self-worth. As part of her doctoral research on Thai transgender sex workers, Witchayanee interviewed a *kathoey* sex worker in Pattaya, Ton, aged twenty-eight:

> Ton lived in extremely poor conditions before migrating to Bangkok to work in the sex industry. His family noticed his physical change because of the hormones (he was having injections of oestrogen and anti-androgens) but his father did not complain. Ton said, 'He shut his mouth up after I gave him money.' (2008, 95)

Witchayanee's study points to the way that Thai queers may "buy" the right to sexual and gender autonomy within their families by providing financial support. Here a *kathoey's* participation in sex work, which, as Sam Winter observes in this volume, is an occupation forced upon many Thai transgenders and transsexuals as a result of discrimination in the job market, nonetheless provided her with the means to evade conforming to heteronormative expectations to live as a man and marry while still fulfilling filial expectations to care for aging parents. Having an independent source of income is therefore important for many Thai queers in enabling them to buy a space to be different within their families. This is not only true for queers from poorer backgrounds such as Ton; it is equally so for middle-class gay men and lesbians who, in taking care of nephews, nieces, and aging parents, demonstrate filial responsibility that, in turn, confers a degree of sexual autonomy that permits them to lead a gay or lesbian life.

It is perhaps for these reasons that Thai queers appear less anxious about the market than many Western observers of global queering. In Asian societies with highly restrictive and gender conformist cultures, often monitored and policed by state bureaucracies, such as Thailand's Ministry of Culture, the market can provide a zone of relative autonomy from the heteronormative demands of both the state and family. Viewed from the perspective of the queer cultures and communities now maturing on the western shores of the Pacific Ocean, capitalism is more likely to be seen as a force of queer autonomy than of subjection, and of local cultural differentiation rather than Westernizing homogenization.

As Yao Souchou, a Singaporean scholar, observes, the "nation states of Southeast Asia—of both the socialist and liberal democratic kinds—are endowed with awesome coercive power to impose their iron will on their societies" (2001, 4–5). In this context, Kasian argues that commodified popular culture in Thailand, of which Thai queer cultures can be classed as one rapidly growing sector, should be seen as an escape from the "desolate semiotics" (cited by Yao 2001, 19) of the notion of Thainess defined by the Thai state. For Kasian, consumerist consumption provides a means of "cultural liberation from the nationalist regimes of the past and present, be [they] radical leftist or right-wing authoritarian" (2001, 153), and he concludes:

> The liberating force of consumption and brand names leads to the next logical step: the liberation of identity from the national as defined by the state . . . The manifold freedom from the barriers imposed by national or ethnic self-identity simultaneously allows Thai consumers the possibility of consuming commodities, not for their utility value, but as cultural signs of desired identity. (2001, 156)

Despite the severe economic setback of the 1997 Asian economic crisis, in Thailand post-Cold War neoliberalism provided the means for initially bourgeois LGBT cultures—formed during the country's earlier Fordist phase of capitalist development—to expand to beyond their middle-class origins and become a new way of life for increasing numbers of working-class Thais. Indeed, as I detail in my earlier chapter here, one striking outcome of early twenty-first-century globalization for Thailand's queer cultures has been its provision of the means for gayness and other identities to become affordable by the working classes. The market is indeed a zone of both queer autonomy and subordination, providing a means to resist and establish freedom from heteronormative state cultural controls and family expectations at the same time that it subordinates queer people to the vagaries of unpredictable market forces. Nonetheless, the market has provided a space upon which queer rights are being built. In the twentieth century, Thai queers "enjoyed" a begrudging cultural tolerance that was rare in most developing countries, but they were nonetheless minoritized and discriminated against as laughing-stocks who had no guaranteed rights. At the end of the first decade of the twenty-first century, we see the beginnings of acceptance as they are taken seriously as consuming subjects by marketing agencies and as citizens deserving of legally enshrined rights by the bureaucracy and increasing numbers of politicians. It would be surprising if these parallel developments were not different faces of the same processes of social, economic, and cultural transformation brought about by Thailand's further integration into both regional and global networks.

The Language of Rights, Deviance, and Pleasure

Organizational Responses to Discourses of Same-Sex Sexuality and Transgenderism in Thailand

Megan Sinnott

Introduction[1]

When describing a cultural or societal pattern of beliefs, it is tempting to slip into a singular narrative. Ascribing a set of attitudes or beliefs to a cultural area reinforces the idea of a discrete, almost organism-like entity that has unity, coherence, and defined borders such that the cultural entity can be compared with other, similarly discrete entities. This model, popular in early anthropology in the form of structural-functional or cultural-personality approaches, has been largely nuanced, if not replaced, with more discursive approaches, influenced by Foucauldian discourse analysis, often combined with a focus on Marxist conceptions of hegemony (e.g. Ortner 1989; Roseberry 1989; Stoler 2002; Williams 1977).[2] These complementary approaches have yielded analysis and appreciation of the fluidity of boundaries and borders in the construction of cultural entities. Studies of the multiple and shifting meanings of sexuality and gender have also been an important dimension of recent Thai studies (e.g. Jackson 1997a, 1997b, 2004d, 2006; Loos 2006; Terdsak 2002; Wilson 2004) and queer anthropology more generally (Blackwood 1998, 2007; Boellstorff 2005, 2007; Leap and Boellstorff 2004; Manalansan 1997, 2003; Wekker 2006). This chapter builds on these approaches by exploring the shifting and contextual discourses of sexuality and gender within two Thai organizations, Anjaree and Lesla, that are devoted to lesbian/gay/bisexual/transgender, or LGBT, communities but have particular emphasis on female same-sex sexuality. Here I contrast the distinctive approaches to sexual and gender rights of these two organizations.

Anjaree, Thailand's longest-standing LGBT rights organization, has been the most consistent in engaging directly with rights-based discourses. While the members and organizers of Anjaree are women, the organization is geared towards challenging and changing normative attitudes towards same-sex sexuality and transgenderism more broadly. An important agenda for Anjaree is the contestation of Thai academic and psychiatric discourses that have consistently deployed Western narratives of sexual pathology. In contrast, Lesla, formerly Thailand's largest organization of women in same-sex relationships, but which ended its activities in 2008 due to the political situation in the country, was more focused on entertainment and community formation. Lesla was essentially a commercial and social organization that drew from much the same membership base as Anjaree, but it focused more on the development of community and the celebration of eroticized gendered identities. These two organizations demonstrate the complex and varied approaches to activism on sexuality and gender in the Thai context.

I use the term "LGBT" to frame these organizations to recognize their transnational linkages and their appropriations of the language of LGBT rights-based movements. However, the term itself is not particularly salient in the Thai cultural context, and based on my research in Thailand I postulate that it would not be recognizable to many Thais themselves. In other words, it should not be taken to be a locally significant category of identity or politics outside of these organizations. These organizations reproduce and challenge existing local narratives of sexuality and gender, themselves complex, overlapping, and varied, to influence and redirect dominant meaning systems.

Defining the unit of analysis for this study is problematic and reveals the instability and multiplicity of meaning systems that I focus on here. I explore the production of discourses on sexuality and gender within the geographic entity of the Thai nation-state and within the Thai language. However, this geographic and linguistic framework downplays the cultural and linguistic distinctiveness within various sub-regions of Thailand and imposes a false sense of cultural homogeneity within the country. The geographic boundaries of the nation-state also impose false cleavages of difference between "Thai" belief and behaviour patterns and those found in neighbouring countries such as Laos, Burma, and Cambodia. However, a reasonable claim can be made for the integrity of the study's framework as "Thai discourses on sexuality" in that these are discourses that exist on a national level, and are systematized through the mass media, academic institutions, and government policies. To capture a more "folk" sense of sexuality and gender, I rely on interviews, conducted from 1992 to 2003 and in the summer of 2005, mostly with people living in Bangkok and the surrounding provinces. Many of these individuals were migrants from rural areas within Thailand. The two organizations I discuss, Anjaree and Lesla, have each participated in these larger-level discourses, but importantly have attempted to make critical and distinctive interventions. Information on these organizations comes from interviews with leaders and members, from participation in group activities, from organizational literature such as newsletters and brochures, and from media coverage of the organizations.

Anjaree

Anjaree is a feminist-lesbian organization in Thailand established in 1986 by women's rights and feminist activists who participated in the development of women's non-governmental organizations in the 1980s. The 1980s in Thailand saw a strong growth of NGOs focused on a variety of social issues, including women's/feminist NGOs such as the Foundation for Women (*Mulanithi Phu-ying*) and Friends of Women Foundation (*Klum Pheuan Ying*).[3] The original founders of Anjaree worked with or within these organizations and decided to form an organization dedicated specifically to the issues of "women who love women" (*ying rak ying*). Anjaree operated an office, produced a newsletter until 2002, and more recently managed a web site (www.anjaree.net). For much of its history, it has had a paid staff member and has been supported through grants from international funding agencies such as Astraea[4] and through national funding sources, including the Hotline Project of the Aids Project in the Thai Ministry of Public Health. At the time of writing (2010), Anjaree was in a period of transition as it applied for "foundation" status from the Thai government, and it focused primarily on lobbying for legislative and policy changes. During much of its earlier existence, activities included monthly social meetings for members, occasional field trips to tourist sites, and workshops that were often co-sponsored by academic institutions and individuals. Recently, key organizers, including Anjana Suvarnananda, who has served as the public face of the organization since its inception, have become established within local human-rights movements and institutions (National Human Rights Commission of Thailand 2007). Doug Sanders details Anjaree's involvement with the National Human Rights Commission of Thailand elsewhere in this volume.

Anjaree's central platform has been to advocate wider public understanding of same-sex sexuality based on the transnational language of human rights. The key leaders of Anjaree have strong backgrounds in feminist activism, and many are linked to academic institutions or have advanced university degrees. The organizers have important relationships with national, regional, and transnational women's/feminist NGOs. These linkages are evident in Anjaree's participation in events such as the 1995 Beijing Conference on Women, which was attended by several Anjaree members/organizers with Anjaree's sponsorship. Anjaree organizers also organized and hosted the first Asian Lesbian Network meeting in 1990, which served as a networking tool for activists and individuals throughout Asia working on issues of "women who love women" (Anjaree, 1995). Anjaree developed an international reputation among transnational LGBT rights organizations, evident in 1995, when Anjaree was awarded the international Philip de Souza award, an international human rights award for gay and lesbian groups. An Anjaree representative travelled to Brazil to receive the award, which was covered in the international LGBT press. Anjaree is essentially a political organization that is geared towards challenging negative attitudes towards same-sex sexuality, both among its target group of women and on a state and institutional level. Anjaree has campaigned for its members and target group—women who are, have been, or want to be in same-sex relationships—to rethink categories of identity and normative discourses that pathologize, trivialize, or negate same-sex love. Anjaree also has operated on a more institutional level to challenge formal edicts and institutional positions that perpetuate or initiate negative attitudes towards LGBT people as well as exclusionary policies of the state. Each of these levels of activism will be discussed below. I turn first to Anjaree's interactions with its constituency, "women who love women".

Anjaree's Terms

"Tom" and *"dee"* are the most common terms of reference in contemporary Thailand for women who are involved in same-sex relationships. The term *"tom"* is derived from the English word "tomboy" and refers to a masculine-identified female, who, as an extension of his/her gender identity, has an attraction to feminine women. *"Dee"*, derived from the English term "lady", refers to the feminine partners of *toms*. *"Dee"* is a looser term of reference, and many women involved with *toms* refer to themselves, and are referred to by others, as simply "women" (*phu-ying*) or "ordinary women" (*phu-ying thammada*). Female same-sex relations are understood primarily as a pairing of male and female elements such that for a relationship to be understood as sexual it must by definition imply some masculine versus feminine gender distinction between the partners. Common Thai perceptions of same-sex sexuality as a whole frame it as a function of an individual who is "misgendered" (*phit-phet*), that is, a womanly man (*kathoey*) or a manly woman (*tom*), and who is regarded to be "naturally" attracted to the opposite gender. That is, a *kathoey* will be sexually attracted to a masculine man, while a *tom* will find a feminine woman attractive. Because of this presumed homology between misgendering and same-sex sexuality, the gender-normative partners of *kathoeys* or *toms* are often not understood as "homosexual", although local understandings of the categories of gay and *dee* have worked to somewhat destabilize this understanding without replacing it.

The term "gay" is popular among many men who love men (*chai rak chai*), as well as *kathoey*. "Gay" has been adopted as an identity label by normatively masculine-identified Thai men who have sexual and emotional interest in other masculine-identified men as a way to differentiate themselves from the gender-transgressive (or transgendered) *kathoey* (see Jackson 1997b, 2004a). The term distances these men from Thai conceptions of same-sex sexuality in which males with an exclusive sexual interest in other males are linked to femininity and misgendering. However, the foreign connotations of the term are appealing to these men as well as to *kathoey*, and the term has been used interchangeably with *kathoey* within the Thai media. Thus, the term "gay" introduces the concept of a type of sexuality in place of discourses that privilege transgenderism as the defining quality of same-sex sex.[5] Likewise, the category *"dee"* is based on a woman's sexual-object choice, not her misgendering. However, *"dee"* is a loose term, and unlike "gay" is not a firmly established identity. Many of the women who may at times refer to themselves as *dee*, or be called *dee* by others, do not distinguish themselves from women in general. *Dee* is more of a situational and emerging category of identity that has not replaced the basic understanding of sexual desire as an extension of gender identity. The ability of *dee* to avoid pathologizing inferences of misgendering or homosexuality is probably a source of the term's appeal. Indeed, very few academic studies on homosexuality even include *dee* as one of the categories of analysis, although gay, *kathoey* and *tom* are routinely analysed in this context.

Many individuals within Anjaree's target group identify as either *tom* or *dee,* but in contrast Anjaree has promoted a gender-neutral identity category of *ying rak ying,* commonly translated as "women who love women". *Ying rak ying* is an alternative to *tom* and *dee* and focuses on the shared femaleness of the couple rather than the gender distinction that defines *tom-dee* couples. Mathana Chetamee, an early Anjaree activist, used the expression *ying rak ying* in her M.A. thesis in anthropology at Thammasat University in Bangkok (1995) as the defining analytical construct. This term has since become the standard within the growing field of Thai academic work on female same-sex sexuality (e.g. Sulaiporn 2002; Sumalee 2006; Saithid 2006). Anjaree introduced the term in its first publication, *Anjareesarn*, in 1993, although it was probably in use among Anjaree members earlier. While the term has only a limited resonance as an identity label for many women-loving women outside of Anjaree, or even for rank-and-file Anjaree members, it is a significant intervention into the previously overwhelmingly negative and pathologizing discourse of Thai academic work on same-sex sexuality, which will be discussed below.

Anjaree's deployment of the term *"ying rak ying"* has had two audiences. The first is an "internal" audience of women involved in same-sex relationships, most of whom are familiar with *tom-dee* discourses and many of whom self-identify according to these categories. The discourses of Anjaree's leaders are rooted in a feminist perspective that is suspicious of gender binaries and identifies their potential for imposing oppressive gender norms. A persistent message of Anjaree's publications, group meetings, and social events aimed at their constituency has been to question the necessity of rigid gender-based categories of *tom* and *dee* and to promote a gender-neutral category of *ying rak ying* that stresses sexual *choice* and sexual *rights*. This message of sexuality as an issue of human rights and individual choice has been the main thrust of Anjaree's media campaigns in which Anjaree spokespeople have provided interviews to friendly media members, and of Anjaree's academic interventions.

One of the advantages of *ying rak ying* as a central identity category is that it resonates with transnational LGBT discourses and movements that revolve around themes of "sexual orientation" (*phet-withi*). The value of this transnationally salient concept is that it both adds prestige and validation to Anjaree's efforts to confront local anti-LGBT positions, and allows Anjaree to enter transnational conversations about LGBT rights and community. The term *ying rak ying* relies on a concept of sexual orientation and privileges the shared sexed body within relationships, and the common use of the concept downplays gender-defined categories, such as *tom-dee*, as derivative or pre-liberated identity categories. Indeed, my own attempts to provide a culturally neutral analytical category for this study—"same-sex sexuality"—reproduces this privileging of the sameness of the sexed body within *tom-dee* couples. Anjaree and others have also started using the term "same-sex love" (*rak phet diao-kan*) instead of the pathological-sounding term "homosexuality" (*rak-ruam-phet*). According to Anjaree organizers, *rak-ruam-phet*, or "homosexuality", can also be read in Thai as "to love to have sex", which, they suggest, reinforces negative stereotypes of promiscuity among lesbians and gays. More important, the term "homosexuality" is consistently used within anti-LGBT academic and state narratives and reproduces the pathologizing origin of the term in the West.[6]

One of the most important ways that Anjaree has communicated the alternative discourse of *ying rak ying* has been through its newsletters/magazines *Anjareesarn* and *AN*, the latter being an offshoot publication also edited by an Anjaree editorial team. These were published somewhat intermittently from 1994 to 2002. A key feature of the magazines was the inclusion of advice columns in which members wrote letters asking for advice from an anonymous columnist. For example, one reader wrote:

> I am 36 years old. I was once married and I'm now divorced. During the past couple of years, many men have tried to heal my heart, but

believe it or not, there is only one person that makes me get aroused, who is one of my colleagues, a woman. She has a very good personality (*nisai di*), she is kind, polite, and has short hair. The problem is I'm not sure if she is actually a *tom* or not. I have seen her ex (they have already broken up). She also looks like a *tom* but a little bit tougher. To conclude, we have had meals together many times. We have made eye contact (with meaning) many times, but the relationship hasn't gone any further. I'm not sure if it is because she is not a *tom*, so she doesn't dare to open up first (there were two times she wore skirts to have meals with me). For me, I have long hair but I like to dress casually, in the "style" of a working woman . . . but she knows that I had a husband. I want to ask for advice. If she is actually a *dee*, should I change myself to be a *tom*? How to start to be a *tom*? This is in order to move our relationship forward.

The answer was as follows:

Your letter is really cute (*na-rak mak*). It tells me about your sincerity towards that person. It is a very big issue for a person to try to change themself for the sake of the person they love. But sometimes the love that requires that you trade being yourself may have a long-term impact if you don't know each other that well. From your question you understand that that person might be a *dee*, and you understand that the relationships of women who love women (*ying rak ying*) have only one form, which is if one is a *tom* then the other must be a *dee*. The meaning of *tom-dee* that I gather from your letter mainly refers to the way we dress or personality (including character traits). For example, a *tom* (should) have short hair, wear trousers, dress toughly (*thamat-thamaeng*), be brave, etc. *Dees* should have long hair, dress prettily, wear skirts, be sweet or tender, etc. But do you know there are many couples of women who love women (*ying rak ying*) in the world who love each other without the restriction that they can only be *tom* and *dee*? People who have short hair do not always need to pair with people who have long hair, like you told me . . . Is it possible perhaps she doesn't stick with any model? She might just like to have short hair or accidentally sometimes has a manly (*hao hao*) personality. Maybe she doesn't define herself to be anything but a "woman." Therefore, my advice here is you don't have to "try to be a *tom*" as long as you and she haven't opened up to a "role" . . . Is it necessary that love has to be divided and defined by rules? (*Anjareesarn*, August 1998, 3(23): 19–20)

Anjaree thus prompted readers to rethink the necessity of *tom-dee* classifications within relationships between women, introducing the novel idea, for Thais, that sexuality and romance do not necessitate gender distinctions of masculine and feminine pairings. Anjaree has made consistent efforts to introduce *ying rak ying* as a locally palatable expression of sexual orientation in place of the rigid gender dualism that dominates female same-sex cultures in Thailand. Anjaree publications included news stories on international LGBT rights and lesbian-positive culture from other parts of the world in an effort to introduce Thai readers to a feminist lesbian understanding of sexual choice.

Significantly, Anjaree's *ying rak ying* terminology has not succeeded in replacing or disrupting the gendered *tom-dee* discourses or patterns of self-reference, which remain largely positive and dynamic categories for many Thai women who love women. For example, *Tom Act*, a new and flashy commercial fashion magazine first released in December 2007, is devoted to *tom-dee* commodified culture. The magazine produces high-fashion Western-styled imagery (including some images of very Caucasian-looking women) with highly gender-dichotomous imagery of Thai *tom-dee*.

Lesla, a dynamic Internet club discussed below, was also clearly focused on self-identified *tom-dee* communities. However, Anjaree has been more successful in challenging the dominance of Western-derived terms of pathology that have been incorporated into Thai academic and medical discourses. "Sexual deviance" (*biang-ben thang-phet*) and the sexological-sounding term *rak-ruam-phet*, an approximation of "homosexuality", have long dominated the Thai academic approach to same-sex sexuality and transgenderism, and it is to these discourses that I now briefly turn.

Academic Narratives

Research on same-sex sexuality among Thai academics until relatively recently was concentrated within the field of clinical psychology (see Jackson 1997b, Sinnott 2004). The overall themes of these studies was that same-sex sexuality is a "problem" that needs to be solved, is ultimately caused by a failure of socialization within the family, and is isomorphic with misgendering or being transgendered. These studies of homosexuality have, in fact, focused on those who can be classified as *kathoey*, that is, feminine-identified transgendered males whose sexual partners are normatively masculine men. The lack of emphasis on *tom-dee* or female same-sex sexuality within these studies is significant and indicates an important feature of female same-sex sexuality within the Thai context, namely, that women engaged in same-sex relationships, or masculine-identified females, are often framed within a narrative of innocent, almost childlike love and are not problematized as strongly as males engaged in same-sex relationships. Improper heterosexual activity is regarded as a more significant category of deviance for women, I argue, and a great deal of invective is aimed at female sex workers or women who are understood as promiscuous and not properly feminine, or not "proper women" (*kunla-satri*). The pathologizing discourse of Thai sexologists has predominantly been aimed at males who are seen to be improperly masculine, i.e. *kathoey*, who are typically framed as males who have a feminine/female interior subjectivity and who have been improperly socialized into women's social roles. However, the categories of "homosexuality" (*rak-ruam-phet*) and "gender deviance" (*biang-ben thang-phet*) that are central to these studies merge both male and female transgenderism and same-sex sexuality into one conceptual unit, even as the researchers place more emphasis on the gender "deviance" of males. As a side note, it is then somewhat ironic that the most consistent public challenge to these pathologizing discourses that focus on male homoeroticism has come from Anjaree, an organization that focuses primarily on "women who love women", rather than from any of the more numerous organizations whose constituencies are "men who love men". (See Doug Sanders in this volume for summary accounts of Thai gay NGOs.)

The mainstream pathologizing discourse on same-sex sexuality that dominated the Thai academy until the turn of the twenty-first century is reflected in a set of twelve M.A.-level theses that were produced between 1989 and 1991 on the subject of "sexual behaviors and attitudes of adolescent students" in each of the twelve regional educational districts within Thailand. These studies, most of which were conducted under the supervision of the same team of faculty members of the Clinical Psychology Faculty at Mahidol University in Bangkok, repeated and reproduced a standard set of assumptions and conclusions regarding the "causes" of same-sex sexuality among both men and women. The framework of these theses was clearly an ideological attempt to "prove" the applicability of a Western sexological model to an analysis of Thai same-sex sexual practices and transgenderism. As will be seen below, the authors of the studies, or perhaps more accurately the academic team supervising these graduate students, were aware that the pathologizing theories of homosexuality they cited were outdated and had been discarded by international and Western institutions. The data produced through these studies were contradictory and did not support the premises of the research students/faculty; nonetheless, the pathologizing assumptions adduced were not challenged or discarded.

These works reproduced older Western sexological categories, themes, and approaches to the study and understanding of same-sex sexuality into Thai academic discourse. According to Peter Jackson (1997b), the sexological discourses of these studies are continuations of themes within Thai academia since the 1950s, themselves based on sexological publication from the United States dating from the 1930s and 1940s.[7] The assumption of these studies within clinical psychology was that same-sex sexuality was "caused" by improper socialization and family relationships. Earlier Thai studies (e.g. Paga 1973; Pattaya 1984) are cited repeatedly in later texts, produced in the 1980s and 1990s, such as these twelve M.A. theses, resulting in a repetition such that the literature review sections of almost all these studies contain nearly the same information and the same rote premises. Western sexological approaches that pathologized same-sex sexuality were clearly influential within the field of clinical psychology in Thailand, but it is probable that only a few of these authors actually read the English-language texts, and most authors relied on summaries of these texts provided in earlier theses.

As already noted, by the time that the series of twelve Mahidol University theses were written it was already known in the Thai academy that the pathologizing theories referred to in these earlier Thai works had been discarded in the West. For example, the thesis by Oranong Kittikalayawong (1991) is rife with pathologizing discourses such as a presumed link between same-sex sexuality and poor parenting, crime, and social decay. However, under a section titled "Diagnosis", Oranong explains that the American Psychiatric Association in 1974 changed the classification of homosexuality from a "personality disorder" and

> announced that homosexuality was removed from the list of 'psychological abnormalities' (*khwam-phit-pokati thang-phet*) and gave it a new name of "sexual orientation disturbances" [no Thai word given as translation] . . . but not long after there was a change in the name which was 'dyshomophilia', 'homosexual conflict disorder' and in the end the word ego-dystonic homosexuality' was used. (1991, 36)

Oranong faithfully reported the shifting English-language terminologies as the APA responded to critics in the 1970s who claimed the association promoted homophobia by removing homosexuality from the diagnostic manual of disorders. However, she failed to acknowledge the underlying rejection of classifying same-sex sexuality as a psychological disorder, which was the significance of APA's change, and instead misrepresented the change as merely an issue of renaming a type of disorder.

In Oranong's discussion of the shifting APA terms, she reported that a distinction was made between people who have a problem with their sexual orientation on the one hand, and, on the other, people who are happy with their sexual orientation but who have social problems because of feelings of shame and anxiety. Yet this distinction is not pursued and does not disturb the search for psychological dysfunction as the "cause" of homosexuality, which was the primary topic of the study (Oranong 1991, 37). The result is a demonstration that the author and her supervising academic department are up-do-date in the latest American psychological terminology, aware of Western literature on these changes, and the study is therefore consistent with international standards. However, the ideological nature of these theses required that the theories be again reproduced and "supported" by evidence that ironically almost always contradicted the presumptions of the study.

For example, Tasanee Thanaprachoom (1989), who wrote one of the twelve Mahidol University theses on sexual behaviour and attitudes among Thai students, provided a routine summary of the premises that guided these studies. Tasanee explained that the earlier psychology theses of Paga Sattayatam (1973) and Pattaya Yaisoon (1984) supported the general conclusions of Western psychological approaches to the "causes" of homosexuality, namely:

> The father has a weak character, is not strong (*khem-khaeng*), is not brave (*kla-han*) and rarely joins family activities, does not support the sons to have various activities, and expresses flat affect when the sons play with their mother. Other than this, it was found that the father was dictatorial and was not friendly, which causes the sons to be afraid, shy, and unable to express themselves. The father does not have the character to be open to compromise, has a tendency towards depression and cannot get along with others. The socialisation of the father has two characteristics, which are either frequent socialising or rarely any socialising. The fathers of these male homosexuals have less success than the fathers of non-homosexuals. The sons express negative attitudes towards their father more than the non-homosexual sons. (1989, 19)

Interestingly, despite the above, Tasanee finds from her data, "Male students who have homosexual behaviour choose to describe both parents in similar ways, which is that both father and mother are leaders, warm, respectable, charming" (1989, 72), and, "Other than that, it was found that the characteristics of the parents did not have a relationship to the son's homosexual behaviour" (1989, 72). When discussing female students, Tasanee also found it difficult to find a difference in girls' relationships to their fathers. In her conclusion she refers to her own data chart and states, "A difference was found in this research regarding the characteristics of fathers who are harsh (*khaeng-kradang*). It can be explained that fathers who are harsh cause there to be a lack of warmth toward children which can cause children [daughters] to be close to their mothers, which should be a good thing since it will cause them to model themselves after their mother" (1989, 117). Note that the author equates same-sex sexuality with transgenderism here, and incorrect gender role modelling as the cause of presumed transgenderism is the key premise of these studies. However, under the chart that she refers to, she concludes, "It was found that there was no difference in the relationship between the student and her father for both the heterosexual (*rak-tang-phet*) and the homosexual (*rak-ruam-phet*) students" (1989, 87). Tasanee further argued that the main difference between these two groups was that "homosexual" girls were closer to their brothers and sisters but that many factors must be taken into account, including the role of fathers (1989, 117). The evidence provided by Tasanee is representative of the almost ludicrous intellectual gymnastics required to pathologize the subjects of these studies to affirm the model of sexual pathology supported by the faculty and institution supporting the study. The research subjects inevitably provided information about their families that was too varied and complex to produce the types of simple conclusions required by the researchers' premises. Nevertheless, these studies, and studies by similarly aligned scholars in the field of psychology, were often routinely used by the Thai press throughout the 1990s to provide "authoritative" information on same-sex sexuality. Since the 1970s, prominent scholars have served as public intellectuals whose opinions have considerable clout in national policy debates.

Since the 1990s, Anjaree's campaigns geared towards shifting attitudes among scholars have been closely linked to activism against governmental institutions and official government policy that reflect the views summarized above. Most prominent scholars are part of the highly centralized state educational system and are thus members of the civil service. Anjaree's successful challenge of a December 1996 ban against "homosexual" or "sexually deviant students" at the Bangkok campus of the Ratchabhat Institute, a government-run teacher-training college (see Jackson 1997b, 84–85; Morris 1997), is an important example of this linkage and one that I have discussed in-depth elsewhere (Sinnott 2000; 2004, 194–203). Briefly, conflicting and poorly defined terms used to define the targets of the ban illustrated the influence of these Thai sexological discourses, such as referring to the targets of the ban as "sexually deviant" (*biang-ben thang-phet*) students, while specifically targeting *kathoeys*, or male-to-female transgendered people. The discourse of deviance conflicted with other popular discourses of the period, such as the language of "rights" and LGBT identity, which ultimately led an embarrassed Ministry of Education to rescind of the ban.

Important shifts in academic discourse on same-sex sexuality/transgenderism have come with a new generation of scholars producing research outside of the clinical-psychology model. These scholars have worked in fields such as anthropology, sociology, and history (e.g. Mathana 1995; Sulaiporn 2002; Prempreeda 2003; Terdsak 2002; Sumalee 2006; Nantiya 2005). Many of the authors of these texts have been advised by progressive faculty members and are themselves aware of, sympathetic to, or members of, the NGOs discussed here. Anjaree has not only confronted the pathologizing model of an earlier generation of academics by critiquing it from the outside; it has also penetrated the Thai academy, as some of the important members and organizers of Anjaree have earned graduate degrees by conducting research on same-sex sexuality and transgenderism. All the more recent academic work on same-sex sexuality/ transgenderism by Thai students that I have been able to find, such as the studies listed above, has been guided by LGBT-friendly premises and language. Timo Ojanen (2009) has come to a similar conclusion in his study of the recent literature. In addition, most of the higher-quality Thai newspapers, such as the Thai-language *Matichon* and *Phujatkan* and the English-language *Bangkok Post* and *The Nation*, now routinely use the LGBT-friendly language promoted by Anjaree, such as "same-sex love" (*rak phet diao-kan*) in place of the previously dominant categories of "homosexuality" (*rak-ruam-phet*) or "sexual deviance" (*biang-ben thang-phet*).

An example of a successful challenge to the pathologizing model can be found in Anjaree's longest-standing and ultimately successful campaign challenging the Thai Ministry of Health to remove homosexuality from its list of mental illnesses. In June 1995, Anjaree invited Bianca Cody Murphy, an American psychologist, a professor of psychology at Wheaton College in Massachusetts, and the chair of the American Psychological Association's Committee on Women in Psychology, to talk about current understandings of same-sex sexuality within American and international academic communities. The talk was held at Thammasat University and was co-sponsored by Thammasat's Women's Studies Program. Members of the media were invited to attend, and one of the Anjaree organizers provided interpretation into Thai. The talk was covered by several newspapers, including *Matichon*, a broadsheet Thai-language newspaper. Kittikorn Mitharaphat, a psychologist sympathetic to Anjaree, was quoted in an essay titled "Perspectives of Psychologists" affirming the position that leading psychological organizations had changed their position on homosexuality and no longer classified it as an illness. To "balance" Kittikorn's position, the newspaper also interviewed Wanlop Piyamanotham, a well-known anti-gay psychologist. Wanlop said that it was very dangerous for Anjaree to reveal itself in public because people would then learn that there are many lesbians in society:

> Anjaree has opened up to the public for the primary reason of making more lesbians because Anjaree thinks it is a normal thing, and they are without shame. This will make our society something to be laughed at, as being all lesbians . . . Whoever is lesbian should be quiet about it. It is not necessary to announce it. You do not have to make the whole country follow suit. You should not make it a bigger trend than it already is. I do not agree with activities that have Westerners (*farang*) come and explain about lesbians to Thai people. You do not need to have Westerners to be behind-the-scenes supporters for things that they do or say is the right thing. The media should be quiet. They do not need to talk about this,

and make people think this is something they should be interested in.
(*Matichon Weekly*, 8 August 1995, pp. 76–78)

The need for silence on a subject to save face has been identified as an important dimension of Thai patterns of discourse by Peter Jackson (2004a), who has built on the work of Rosalind Morris (2004) and Penny Van Esterik (2000). Jackson argues that concern with surface is a central component of Thai modes of representation. Jackson uses the term the "Thai regime of images" to describe the cultural practice in which surface calm is required in public representations. In contrast to Western modes of representation in which a private truth must be in accordance with public representation, Thai representational systems value the "smooth surface", or respectable presentation in public spaces. In this representational system, private truths are not to be projected onto the public stage, and the obvious discrepancy that results is not a conceptual problem in the way it is in the Foucauldian description of Western systems of representation. This insight is useful in understanding the strategic choices made by the organizations discussed here and why Anjaree, in particular, places emphases on public declarations and challenging official positions.

One of the most successful strategies of Anjaree, as well as another prominent LGBT rights organization, the Rainbow Sky Association of Thailand—Fasiroong in Thai—has been to mobilize the discourse of modernity and international standards to persuade Thai politicians and policymakers that their position on same-sex sexuality and transgenderism is outdated and even embarrassing. This strategy was used successfully to alter the Mental Health Department's position on homosexuality. In 2002, seven years after the public talk by Bianca Cody Murphy, detailed above, and the widespread press it received, the Mental Health Department within the Ministry of Public Health announced the elimination of homosexuality from its list of diseases. Phermsak Lilakul reported in the English-language newspaper *The Nation* that the official endorsement of removing homosexuality from the list of psychological disorders was related to the need to be up-to-date. "But Dr Prawate Tantipiwatanasakul, a director of the Department of Mental Health, admitted that his office's endorsement lags behind academic consensus by more than 30 years," the report read (Phermsak, 2002).

Lesla

The organization Lesla represented a significant shift from the feminist/ women's NGO movement of the 1990s. In 2000, Mantana Adisayatepakul, an entrepreneur, formed a small social group for *toms* and *dees*, which rapidly grew to an extensive social network based on its Internet club.[8] The membership of Lesla and Anjaree overlapped to some degree; Lesla being more popular with younger, middle-class women who had access to, and interest in, Bangkok commercial entertainment venues. Anjaree's focus on gender-neutral terms such as *ying rak ying* alienated some *toms*, particularly older ones with a well-established sense of *tom* identity, and often a longstanding network of *tom* friends.[9] Organizers from Lesla and Anjaree often knew each other, and each group allowed the other to distribute materials at each other's functions. Lesla's web site directed readers interested in rights issues and current events to Anjaree's web site. While the membership of each group was aware of each other's existence, and many *toms* and *dees* at some point attended functions sponsored by each organization, the perspectives and orientations of Anjaree and Lesla diverged enough that each had its own distinct realms of action. Anjaree members also accessed Lesla's web board, and the term *ying rak ying* was introduced to Lesla web-board readers in this way, yet the term itself did not catch on as a category of self-reference within the group. Lesla, which at the time of this writing has apparently shut down in consequence of the political instability that followed the military coup of 2006, had a style that was distinctly market-oriented, with a flashy web site and the short-lived production of a Lesla magazine. The web site included images of Western lesbian films and pop-culture phenomena. It is important to note that Anjaree also deployed images of Western lesbian pop culture, such as pictures of k.d. lang, the well-known Canadian lesbian singer. However, Anjaree has contextualized these images within a discourse of a global standard of human rights that includes sexual rights and LGBT rights. Anjaree has operated in terms of a feminist political agenda, while Lesla astutely tapped into the social needs and aspirations of many urban women.

Most Lesla members are or were literate, urban, middle-class women who have access to Internet technology and the Bangkok nightlife. The most significant Lesla project was its organization of regular parties in Bangkok clubs and restaurants. Originally the group held these monthly, attracting four hundred to five hundred women by my own observation and the reports of organizers. The organizers reported more than eight hundred women attending some events, recorded through the sale of entry tickets. As noted, these parties were initially held each month, but Lesla, until recently, had had regular Friday night parties at an established club in Bangkok. In October 2000, Lesla produced its first monthly magazine, distributed via its new paid-membership system. Lesla's membership skyrocketed to more than six hundred within the one year of its existence and quickly surpassed Anjaree's membership. While Anjaree attempted to introduce a sense of politics to sexual identities, Lesla was unapologetically a social organization for *tom-dee*. However, Lesla, like Anjaree, also provided a forum for the open discussion of the strict gender roles of *tom* and *dee*. Lesla did not reject *tom* and *dee* roles or the possibility of female masculinity—one of the articles in Lesla's magazine, *LeslaZine*, included instructions for breast-binding, a practice that would be consistent with *tom* masculinity[10]—but through Internet discussions gave its members an opportunity to reflect on their beliefs that *toms* and *dees* are fundamentally different.

New terms began to emerge on Lesla's web board in the mid-2000s. These terms are part of the self-naming process that, in essence, is also at the core of Anjaree's activism. Some of the most popular terms introduced have been *les king* and *les queen*, playing on the Thai gay male appropriation of the terms "*king*" and "*queen*" to index a gendered reading of sexual behaviour, comparable to "top" and "bottom". (Of course, there is contestation over the meaning of these terms as well.) Interestingly, this play with English words uses terms that do not derive directly from a Western context, but instead are a product of local Thai gay male culture (see Jackson 2004c).

The terms "*les king*" and "*les queen*" incorporate the root "les" from "lesbian", which has historically been a highly stigmatized term with which few Thai women would identify.[11] *Toms* and *dees* explained in interviews that the term "lesbian" implied for them a feminine woman who performed sex with other feminine women, usually for the sexual satisfaction of a male viewer—a concept that clearly had no appeal among the masculine-identified *toms* or their feminine partners. The term "lesbian" was associated closely with Western heterosexual male pornography and was therefore understood as referring to salacious voyeurism and excessive sexual expression. The appeal of the terms "*tom*" and "*dee*" for many women is that these notions highlight gender identity, even gender conformity, rather than sexuality per se. Sexual relationships between *toms* and *dees* are typically coded as an expression of gender opposition. The term "lesbian" implied a gender similarity (between two feminine women) and sexual reciprocity between these female partners, which violated *tom* notions of female masculinity. *Tom* masculinity depends largely on the premise that a *tom* performs sexually for his *dee* as an expression of being the active sexual agent (*fai ruk*). In contrast, a *dee*, who is considered feminine and therefore sexually passive (*fai rap*) in accord with Thai norms of appropriate female behaviour, is not supposed to reciprocate sexually for her *tom*. While actual sexual behaviour does not necessarily mirror social norms, the public suggestion that a *tom* allows a *dee* to perform sexually for her, which is implied by calling a *tom* a "lesbian", can be taken as a serious insult (see Sinnott 2004, 147–150).

Below is a web discussion among Lesla members over the definition of the neologisms *les king* and *les queen* that took place over the course of 2004 (accessed on Lesla.com on 15 July 2005). Peter Jackson (in a personal communication) suggests that the term "*les*" is more palatable to Thai women because this abbreviation softens the word "lesbian" and downplays its sexual associations. One of the appeals of *"tom"* and *"dee"* as identity categories is that they do not directly reference sexuality in the way that terms such as "gay", "homosexual", or "lesbian" do. Many of the *toms* and *dees* I interviewed stressed the emotional aspects of their relationship and avoided directly linking their relationships or identity to sexual desire, and in this way positioned their relationships within normative frameworks for appropriate female demeanour, a discursive technique that will be evident in the web-board passage translated below. The sexual nature of *tom* and *dee* relationships is coded within the often-heard descriptions of *toms* as sexually active and *dees* as sexually passive. It is important to understand that sexuality within Thai discourse in general is typically understood in terms of a masculine "active" partner who performs sexually for a feminine "passive" partner. The term *"les"* confounds these gendered sexual roles by implying, in many *tom* and *dee* perspectives, an almost perverse sexual and gender *sameness* shared by the members of the couple. This rupture is only partially mitigated by the gendering of the term *"les"* by adding the Thai gay male slang expressions *"king"* and *"queen"* to the term. Also, the term *"les"* is at times conflated with *"dee"* in that they are both understood as feminine categories; it is the ambiguity of the sexual role of this ostensibly feminine category that prompted the extended discussion on the Lesla web board, as follows:

> **Writer 1.** I have only had *tom* lovers. One day I decided that I wanted to meet a *les* . . . but I'm not sure if I should because I don't know if someone who is a *les*, when you are having sex [*mi arai kan*] . . . I have to do it for her too, right? That is, I'm not very good at being the active party [*fai kratham*]. Are there *les* that are the active party only so that I don't have to mess [*yung*] with her?
>
> **Writer 2.** Oh, before when you had a *faen* [lover], did you do it for her or not? Usually *toms* do it for *les* or *dees*, right?
>
> **Writer 3.** I don't think you understood what she wrote. She clearly said she had never done anything before for her girlfriend who was a *tom*, otherwise would she be looking for a *les* who does it for her only?
>
> **Writer 4.** A *les king*, you see, only does it, so that you don't have to do it for her.
>
> **Writer 5.** How is a *les* different from a *dee*?
>
> **Writer 6.** Are you a *les king* or *les queen*? I'm a *les king*.
>
> **Writer 7.** I don't know, *les* or *tom*, but if I'm going to be a *les*, I'll be a *les king*. But I'm a friend, we can talk and discuss experiences, but anyway, please tell me the difference between a *tom* and *les*.

Writer 8.   I'll answer you. A *les* is like a woman in general, different from a woman like a *dee* is. A *les* is different from a *dee* in that a *dee* likes a *tom* who looks manly. A *les* likes a woman, not a *tom*. Is that clear enough?

Writer 9.   I'm a *les queen*. Now I want to have friends the same as me to talk to, to get advice from.

Writer 10.   I'm a *les king*. I don't show it [*sadaeng ork*], but I'm a *king* just because of sex, that's all. I want to meet a *les queen*.

Writer 11.   Let me explain it. A les king dresses like a woman but is the active partner [fai ruk], a les queen dresses like a woman but is the passive partner [*fai rap*]. A *tom* dresses like a man and is active; a *dee* dresses like a woman and is passive. A *les queen* likes a *les king* but why doesn't she like a *tom*? From looking on the outside how can you tell who is *king* or *queen*? How much like a woman does a *les queen* have to dress so you can tell the difference between her and a *les king*? So, for a *tom* to partner with a *dee* is clear. Will a *tom* like a *les queen* or not, or will a *dee* like a *les king* or not? Why do we need four categories? I think a *les king* and *queen* are hard to distinguish. I understand that a *les king*, having to dress that way, might be because of society.

The Lesla members engaged in the above on-line discussion were exploring the ways that a familiar gender-binary (*tom-dee*) can operate within a more sexualized binary (*les king*, *les queen*) that homes in on the specifics of sexual behaviour as a determining feature in an identity category. The heightened focus on sexual behaviour as an articulated element of identity draws from familiar Thai gay terminology. These terms were popular on the web site and also among women at an organizational meeting I attended in July 2005 at the Rainbow Sky Association of Thailand. Young women, mostly in their twenties, introduced themselves to me as *les queen* and *les king* in the group context in a playful manner. However, the tone in the web board discussion above indicates some ambivalence towards the categories. The categories *"tom"* and *"dee"* have emerged as the terms of choice in the new high-fashion magazine aimed at *toms* and *dees* called *Tom Act*. The magazine is devoted almost entirely to narratives of *tom* and *dee*, combined with a highfashion, transnational aesthetic, such as using models who look European, Eurasian (Thai: *luk-khreung*), or East Asian. The term *"ying rak ying"* has been used in this magazine on occasion, and "lesbian" is used in reference to foreign celebrities such as Ellen Degeneres, but overwhelmingly the narrative of the magazine revolves around *tom* and *dee* imagery and terminology.

The discussion regarding *les queen* and *les king* detailed above is typical of the types of conversations conducted on the Lesla web boards. The Internet has provided a forum for women to exchange views and explore new ways of thinking about themselves. Discussions within a group of women regarding sexuality and gender were difficult when tried in person. I had difficulty introducing topics such as the relation between someone's identity as a *tom* or *dee* and their sexual pleasure, or sexual roles they take with their partners, when conducting my fieldwork research. I also witnessed Anjaree members struggle with these group discussions in their meetings and social events. It is impossible to know whether these new terms will be of lasting significance or whether they may fade with the introduction of yet newer categories and terminologies. The significance of these discussions lay more in the direction that organizations such as Lesla are taking by combining commercialism, social activity, and style. Lesla, with its largely commercial and social focus, has stimulated the production of spaces where these interactions can take place, and in so doing has complemented Anjaree's more policy-oriented activism and academic approach to intervening in larger discursive frameworks that pathologize same-sex sexuality and transgenderism.

Conclusion

It is tempting to look at these shifting narratives as a form of advancement or progress towards LGBT equality. In particular, positive changes might be seen as reflected in the relative success that Anjaree has had in challenging official anti-LGBT (or *gay, kathoey, tom, dee,* etc.) discourses, or the production of *tom-dee* Internet clubs, such as Lesla, or commercially successful publications such as *Tom Act*. While I find it difficult to dismiss this notion of progress out of hand, I find it useful to situate these discursive shifts within larger frameworks. I have selected three strands of discourse concerning sexuality and gender—those produced through Anjaree, twentieth-century academic texts, and Lesla. They all recognize a dominant construct of sexuality defined by gender dualism. While the academic texts inserted these assumptions into the pathologizing language of twentieth-century Western sexology, Anjaree has challenged these concepts among its own members. Anjaree, aware of academic and sexological theories, uses transnational discourses of human rights and sexual rights to challenge and confront the negative sexological approaches. Anjaree's use of the term *"ying rak ying"* has been transformative within Thai academic circles and the educated press and media, but, somewhat paradoxically, this has had little impact on the groups of women identifying as *tom* or *dee*. In contrast, Lesla has provided spaces for the gender dualism of *tom* and *dee* to be explored, celebrated, and elaborated through their social events and publications, and to be discussed and even challenged in their web discussions. Lesla, while drawing upon transnational media images, such as Western lesbian films, has not promoted *ying rak ying* as an identity category or emphasized transnational discourses of sexual rights and sexual identity. Lesla provided a space for members themselves to introduce and toy with terms and concepts such as *les king* and *les queen* that adapt familiar Thai gay male language to the context of Lesla members, many of whom engaged in some appropriation of *tom* and *dee* categories. The range of narratives regarding same-sex sexuality introduced here draw upon a diverse range of transnational sources, including Western sexology, human-rights language, and popular culture. The multiplicity of narratives is clear, as is the multiplicity of forms of transnational narratives and their creative appropriations into the Thai context.

Figure 9   Images of young Thai "women who love women" (*ying rak ying*) on the cover of a 2008 "Lady Version" of the newsletter of the Rainbow Sky Association of Thailand, the country's largest LGBT community organization (see Meagan Sinnott, Chapter 11).

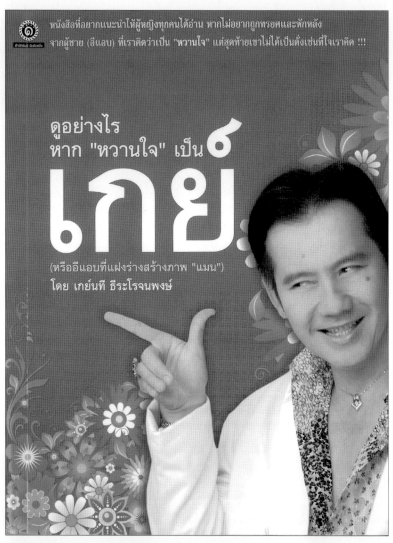

หนังสือที่อยากแนะนำให้ผู้หญิงทุกคนได้อ่าน หากไม่อยากถูกทรยศและหักหลัง
จากผู้ชาย (อีแอบ) ที่เราคิดว่าเป็น "หวานใจ" แต่สุดท้ายเขาไม่ได้เป็นดั่งเช่นที่ใจเราคิด !!!

ดูอย่างไร
หาก "หวานใจ" เป็น
เกย์
(หรืออีแอบที่แฝงร่างสร้างภาพ "แมน")
โดย เกย์นที ธีระโรจนพงษ์

Figure 10　Cover of 2009 Thai paperback, *How to tell if your sweetheart is gay (or just a closet queen in the guise of a 'man')* by Natee Teerarojjanapongs (pictured on the book cover). As discussed here by Douglas Sanders in Chapter 12, Natee is a prominent gay rights activist who founded Thailand's first gay NGO in the early 1990s. (Source: Happy Books Publishing Limited)

'หนังสืออ่านสนุกที่ชวนให้คุณลุกออกจากที่ซ่อน'

เลิกแอบเสียที

วิทยา แสงอรุณ

จากคอลัมน์ฮิตในเซ็กชั่น Metro Life หนังสือพิมพ์ผู้จัดการรายวัน

Figure 11 Cover of the 2007 Thai paperback, *Stop being closeted: A fun book to get you out of your hiding place,* by Vitaya Saeng-Aroon, co-founder of Cyberfish Media, Thailand's first gay multimedia organization. As Peter Jackson (Chapter 10) and Doug Sanders (Chapter 12) note here, since the early 2000s, increasing numbers of Thai gay men and transsexuals have come out to make highly public calls for social acceptance and LGBT rights. (Source: mars publishing)

สิทธิมนุษยชน
ของบุคคลที่มีความหลากหลายทางเพศ

Human Rights of Lesbians,

Gays, Bisexuals, Transgender

and intersex People

สมาคมฟ้าสีรุ้งแห่งประเทศไทย
Rainbow Sky Association of Thailand

Figure 12 Cover of a 2007 paperback on LGBTI rights in Thailand, jointly published by the National Human Rights Commission of Thailand (NHRCT) and the Rainbow Sky Association of Thailand. As Doug Sanders (Chapter 12) details here, in 2007 the NHRCT joined forces with a coalition of Thai lesbian, gay and transgender community organizations to lobby for recognition of queer rights in Thailand's revised national constitution. (Source: Rainbow Sky Association of Thailand)

12

The Rainbow Lobby

The Sexual Diversity Network
and the Military-Installed Government in Thailand

Douglas Sanders

A Thai Paradox?

Twenty years ago, observers described a Thai paradox. Thailand, it seemed, had a relaxed attitude towards homosexuality. There were no anti-homosexual laws. Gay host bars, discos, saunas, and massage parlours functioned openly. Gay bars paid off the police to operate, just as straight bars did. Transgender *kathoeys* were visible and were understood to be part of Thai society. There was no apparent ban on homosexuals taking government jobs or serving in the military. In the 1980s, a long-serving, unmarried prime minister was said to be gay, and no one seemed to worry about that. Over time, he became an honoured elder statesman and advisor to the king. There were (and are) no vocal, religiously based opponents of lesbian and gay rights in Thailand, unlike in Malaysia, Singapore, Hong Kong, South Korea, and Taiwan. When Major General Chamlong Srimuang, a puritanical Buddhist, was governor/mayor of Bangkok in the 1980s, there were no campaigns against either gay or straight bars. In 2001, when then Minister of the Interior Purachai Piamsombun initiated his Social Order Campaign, gay venues were not picked out for any special surveillance, and there was no campaign against prostitution itself, whether heterosexual or homosexual.[1]

Yet Thai homosexuals were not "out" to their families, friends, or co-workers. Issues of sexual diversity were not discussed within the family. *Kathoeys* were either glamorous showgirls, sales clerks, sex workers, or objects of ridicule and humour. And there were hardly any lesbian or gay non-governmental organizations or "out" activists. Apart from a couple of flamboyantly camp hairdressers and actors, there were no "out" celebrities or politicians.[2] To non-Thais, this mix of social tolerance and trenchant perpetuation of the Thai closet was paradoxical.

Yet, perhaps it was not so paradoxical. Activism is only likely as a response to external pressure or new opportunities. It was the increased sexual repression in the West in the post-World War II years that triggered a lesbian and gay minority rights movement. In contrast, state hostility was low or manageable in Thailand, and opportunities for any further amelioration of official policies seemed nonexistent. The problems for Thai homosexuals were with family acceptance and interpersonal relations, not with the police, religion, or the government. Would there then be a way out of this "closet", which was the prevailing reality in Thailand for gender-normative gay men and lesbian women?

A basic role of the state is to bring the various groups in society into a productive interaction with each other. The need for the Thai state to reach out to homosexuals first became clear with the spread of HIV/AIDS. In much of the world, state actions and social prejudices had prevented homosexuals from forming organizations and developing community leadership. But to control the spread of HIV/AIDS, it was necessary to organize homosexuals, and not just those who adopted a "gay" identity but also a broader, newly named category of "MSM", men who have sex with men. The late 1980s saw the beginnings of Thai state support for gay-run HIV/AIDS programmes, which were necessary since existing health programmes lacked the ability to reach the MSM populations.

In this chapter we see how the initiatives of an autonomous national human-rights commission in Thailand have been a factor as the state has begun to play a more active role in recognizing and organizing the country's various LGBT communities to promote their social and economic participation in society. The promotion of human rights is one mechanism to overcome social prejudices, and the discourse of "human rights" (*sitthi manutsayachon*) has been mobilized in Thailand as a modernizing discourse to promote progressive social change.

Broader socio-economic change has been under way in Thailand for some time. For a decade prior to the 1997 Asian economic crisis, the kingdom had one of the world's highest rates of economic growth. Beginning in the 1980s, the commercial gay scene expanded dramatically in Bangkok, with new bars, restaurants, and saunas. Small, pioneering gay and lesbian organizations began in the late 1980s, prompted by feminist activism and by the HIV/AIDS crisis. Only the gay-run HIV/AIDS organizations managed to secure ongoing funding, staff, and offices. Given the largely unorganized nature of the LGBT communities in Thailand, as compared to most Western countries, it was striking that, in 2007, a coalition of lesbian, gay, bisexual, and transgendered individuals and organizations became involved in public meetings and campaigns focused on the drafting of both a new national constitution and legislation to allow transsexual *kathoeys* to be identified in their post-operative sex. This coalition was called the Sexual Diversity Network (SDN, or *khreua-khai khwam-lak-lai thang-phet*), and its degree of public activism was a new phenomenon in Thailand.

The SDN emerged during the life of a military-installed government. A bloodless military coup had deposed the elected prime minister, Thaksin Shinawatra, in September 2006. In the eyes of the country's establishment Thaksin had become too powerful. His party had gained a majority in the Thai parliament—after years of weak, fractious coalition governments. With his political base in the populous northeast and north he had eclipsed the authority of the established central Thailand elites and the Bangkok middle class. He was also accused of corruption, of undermining independent constitutional agencies, and of promoting his family's business interests while in office. After the September 2006 coup, the military established a Constitutional Drafting Assembly, tasked with revising the 1997 constitution. A new document was approved in a public referendum in August 2007, and a democratic election was held on 23 December 2007, ending the life of the interim, military-appointed government, or National Legislative Assembly, which had been active in 2007 in passing a number of bills.

It is paradoxical that a military coup ushered in a year-long period in 2007 during which LGBT organizations came to participate in major public issues. This opening to civil society groupings was a legitimizing strategy on the part of the interim government. In this chapter I suggest the factors that made the emergence of the Sexual Diversity Network possible in 2007. I first set the scene with: (1) a description of the 1997 constitution (the subject of the 2007 amendments); (2) an assessment of the LGBT organizations and personalities active in 2007; (3) a look at the National Human Rights Commission, and (4) references to the sexuality issues that were current in 2007.

As a retired Canadian law professor resident in Thailand, I was able to attend many of the SDN meetings that took place in 2007 as an activist and scholar known to many of the spokespeople. I prepared two background papers, requested by participants, which were used in lobbying. These were compilations of practices in other legal systems on equality rights for LGBT people and on the recognition of a changed-sex category for transgendered individuals. These papers were written in English and translated into Thai. I have no fluency in Thai and depended on others for translation and assistance. I am very grateful for their help. It is important, in my view, that this story of Thai LGBT activism be recorded in some detail. Some of the activists referred to in this chapter normally use nicknames, and I use these familiar nicknames in those cases. Others used pseudonyms, as was common in earlier stages of LGBT activism in the West, and in these cases I respect their desire for personal anonymity.

However, the full names are provided for activists who are consistently "out" to the Thai media.

The 1997 Constitution

A movement for political reform emerged in Thailand in the difficult years after the military coup of 1991 (see Connors 2007, 162). A Constitutional Drafting Assembly was created, from which politicians were barred. While the government of the day openly criticized parts of the draft and wanted to change the constitutional procedure, there was strong support for the new constitution from the King and from popular organizations. A very specific series of political events had led to the drafting and final adoption, without changes, of what came to be called by some the "people's constitution", a naming that, it was hoped, would give the document a status above the many previous constitutions that had come and gone in the context of Thailand's many military coups. In a major innovation, the provisions of the 1997 constitution could be enforced by the courts against government actions and against legislative enactments. There were also significant human-rights provisions, as has become virtually mandatory in any new or revised constitution in any part of the world. These included:

> Section 4.   The human dignity, rights and liberty of the people shall be protected.
>
> Section 30. All persons are equal before the law and shall enjoy equal protection under the law.
>> Women and men shall enjoy equal rights.
>> Unjust discrimination against a person on the grounds of the difference in origin, race, language, sex, age and physical or health conditions, personal status, economic or social standing, religious belief, education or constitutionally political view, shall not be permitted.
>
> Section 31. A person shall enjoy the right and liberty to his or her life and person.

In an interview, Naiyana Suphapung, an activist lawyer at the time, said that the women's network she was involved with as part of the public activism around the drafting of the 1997 constitution had avoided proposing that LGBT issues be included in the constitution out of concern that such a move would create resistance to the reforms on women's rights they sought.[3]

The LGBT Players in 2007

The lesbian organizations: Anjaree and Sapaan

In Thailand, lesbian organizations have often been more prominent than gay male groups. The lesbian group Anjaree became the most active and vocal LGBT organization in Thailand after its founding in 1986. Anjaree engaged in its first public campaign in 1996. In December of that year the Ratchabhat Institutes, a national system of teacher-training colleges, announced a ban on effeminate male students that was phrased in terms of opposing "gender/sex deviance" (*khwam-biang-ben thang-phet*). This ban constituted an express official discriminatory policy that Thai activists could challenge. Anjaree led the fight. The organization brought together prominent scholars and medical professionals to speak at a public forum. Thailand's English-language newspapers supported the campaign. After public controversy, the ban was rescinded. A Ratchabhat official said that the policy had been misunderstood, giving a garbled explanation for its withdrawal: It was intended to apply only to perverts, not inverts, a spokesperson said (Sinnott 2004, 194). Rakkit Rattachumpoth, a former journalist, has commented on the Anjaree victory as follows:

> Feminist-inspired lesbians have been politically active in Bangkok, and they played an impressive role during the Ratchabhat controversy in publicly countering the discriminatory ban against homosexual students and appearing before a parliamentary committee which inquired into the ban. (1999, xi)

Anjana Suvarnananda, or Tang, was a member of Anjaree and became a spokesperson the Thai media regularly turned to for an informed viewpoint on gay and lesbian life. She is an attractive figure and speaks excellent English. When Anjana subsequently left Thailand for a job with a foundation in the United States and later to study in the Netherlands, Chanthalak Raksayu, or Lek, who had been with Anjaree from before the Ratchabhat campaign, became the head of the organization. Anjaree had another media success with a public, day-long seminar in 2002 publicizing a written statement from the Ministry of Public Health that homosexuality was no longer officially considered a pathological condition. But after that 2002 event, Anjaree faded from public view for a number of years. Anjana returned to Thailand in 2006 and revived the Anjaree name for a couple of years. In the interim, Chanthalak had created a new lesbian organization, Sapaan, which published a newsletter/magazine, as Anjaree had earlier, and developed a newsy web site. Chanthalak came to work closely with the National Human Rights Commission, which was established under the 1997 Constitution.

The HIV/AIDS organizations: Fraternity for AIDS Cessation in Thailand (FACT), Rainbow Sky Association of Thailand (RSAT), M-Plus, SWING (Service Workers IN Group)

The first modern, visible gay-rights organization in Thailand was the Fraternity for AIDS Cessation in Thailand, or FACT, founded in 1989 by Natee Teerarojjanapongs, who had lived and studied in the United States in the early 1980s. In many Asian countries AIDS led to the establishment of health-focused, gay-run activist organizations, usually with some foreign funding. In Thailand, the health ministry was also supportive. FACT became famous for its White Line Dancers, who performed HIV/AIDS education shows in Bangkok gay host bars for male sex workers. In the 1990s, the HIV education and prevention role of FACT was eclipsed by government programmes when Dr. Mechai Viravaidya, head of the national family planning organization and famous for promoting condom use, became the cabinet minister responsible for HIV/AIDS prevention. FACT became inactive by the mid-1990s, but Natee has continued to appear regularly as a public figure, author, and gay spokesperson. He is often quoted as speaking for the Gay Political Group, which is, perhaps, a loose network. In the past decade, newer, largely gay-run health organizations have also become active in Thailand on HIV issues, notably the Rainbow Sky Association of Thailand, M-Plus, and SWING. In effect, they are the heirs of FACT and all have offices and staff. Another NGO, Bangkok Rainbow, has a constituency based in the gay middle class. It screens gay movies, holds parties, does some HIV/AIDS work, and, for a couple of years, organized media awards for gay-friendly mainstream press and television. It is much less visible than Rainbow Sky. A Pattaya-based organization, Sisters, seems the only organization of *kathoeys*.

Other civil society organizations

Notably missing from visible, public support for LGBT rights in 2007 were generally focused progressive or human-rights organizations. Anjana Suvarnananda of Anjaree commented on this absence as follows:

> Progressives mostly work on economic justice and social justice. They have not seen sexuality as part of the movement. They don't take up some of the women's issues, or child rights or LGBT issues. Most of them fight for community rights . . . On the other hand, the LGBT community does not see itself as part of a broader social justice movement. Many LGBT don't connect their issues with other forms of oppression . . . so we stay separated on how we approach our struggles and there is not enough dialogue between groups. LGBT groups are also under-resourced and there is no capacity to work with other groups and be part of the broader movement.[4]

Amnesty International documents supporting LGBT rights were used in the lobbying in 2007, but, somewhat oddly, Amnesty International Thailand was silent on the issue of promoting rights for gays, lesbians, and *kathoeys*.

The National Human Rights Commission of Thailand

The "people's constitution" of 1997 created a number of independent organizations as checks on the power of elected governments. One of these was the National Human Rights Commission. The process of drafting legislation to establish the commission was highly charged, and after bitter fights, legislation was enacted that established a highly independent commission with a broad mandate but with no enforcement powers (Klein 2002, 25). This followed the international model set out in the United Nation's "Paris Principles" for national institutions on human rights.

Commissioners were selected in 2001, but the timing was bad. Thaksin Shinawatra's new Thai Rak Thai party had won 248 of the 500 seats in the House of Representatives in the 2001 national election. Thai Rak Thai formed a government, in coalition with some old-style politicians. Thaksin was the first elected prime minister in Thai history to serve a full four-year term, and in the 2005 election his party won an absolute majority of 377 seats and governed alone—Thailand's first single-party government. Thaksin was a rich businessman, intent on change but with no particular interest in human rights. The first chairman of the National Human Rights Commission had a personal focus on countering the negative impacts of development projects on rural populations, a concern that was in conflict with Thaksin's goal of strong economic growth. The Commission took stands that were highly critical of the Thaksin government (Connors 2007, 257), and the government ignored it. In July 2007, the NHRC's chairman, Saneh Chamarik, was asked what had been the major problems faced by the Commission. He replied as follows:

> Government negligence in not taking into consideration our reports and recommendations is the biggest problem. We investigated over 3,000 cases, but the Thaksin government took only one for consideration, the Thai-Malaysian gas pipeline, and sent it to parliament. It was very discouraging during our first three years in office as the government did not even inform us if they received our reports. Only in the last three years did they bother to tell us that the document had reached the prime minister's office.[5]

The role of NHRC Commissioner Naiyana Suphapung

Central to the story of the LGBT lobbying in 2007 is the role of one commissioner, Naiyana Suphapung, who, from her appointment in 2001, spoke out in support of gay and lesbian issues.[6] Naiyana, as a lawyer, had previously worked for twenty years with women's NGOs, mainly the Friends of Women Foundation. In an interview, she recalled that twenty-five years earlier the women heading the small women's NGOs in Thailand avoided lesbian issues. However, over that period she frequently met visiting feminists from the West, a number of whom were openly lesbian. A controversy over the role of male lawyers and advisers occurred within the Friends of Women Foundation, resulting in Anjana Suvarnananda leaving the organization and founding the lesbian NGO Anjaree in the 1980s. It was only then that Naiyana learned that Anjana was a lesbian. In the following years, Naiyana came to know many more Thai lesbians. In her private law practice, supplementing her NGO work, she often handled family law disputes involving a wife who had come to identify herself as lesbian.[7]

With this background, as an NHRC commissioner Naiyana immediately identified sexual orientation as raising human rights issues. She spoke at a seminar on violence against homosexual women in November 2001, along with a representative of Anjaree and scholars from Mahidol and Thammasat universities.[8] In December 2001, she was quoted in a full-page background article on lesbians in the *Bangkok Post:*

> Sexual orientation is a human rights issue . . . The right to love and to develop a relationship with another human being, regardless of their sexuality for example, is a basic human right.[9]

Article 30 of the 1997 Constitution ensured equal rights to citizens regardless of sex, race, age, physical ability, and religion. Naiyana told the *Bangkok Post* that this article of the constitution also protected homosexuals.[10] Naiyana gave credit to Chanthalak, of Sapaan, and Miew, of the Rainbow Sky Association of Thailand, for working with the NHRC from its early days, and the Commission formally recognized their respective lesbian and gay organizations as human rights NGOs. The NHRC hosted an anniversary party for Rainbow Sky at its offices in 2007, and the NHRC poster for International Women's Day in 2007 featured three women, including a smiling Chanthalak from Sapaan in the centre. The Commission named Chanthalak one of three "Women's Human Rights Defenders 2007".

On 28 January 2007, the Commission made its premises available for the annual board meeting of the Bangkok Pride organization.[11] Around thirty-five individuals were present. Commissioner Naiyana opened the meeting, saying the Commission was happy to be collaborating with the various organizations involved. She referred to certain issues that were current at the time: the military treatment of *kathoeys*; possible discrimination against homosexuals in providing life insurance, and compulsory blood tests. She referred to the Commission as a new institution that was still trying to find its role in dealing with human-rights issues. She said that a year earlier the Commission had still not felt very comfortable in dealing with LGBT issues, but in 2007 there was less discomfort when such issues arose. She looked ahead to dealing with such issues in the drafting of the new constitution required by the military-appointed government. And she said that dealing with LGBT issues had given Thailand's National Human Rights Commission a lead role in its relations with similar commissions in the region, noting specifically those in Malaysia and Indonesia.[12]

The National Human Rights Commission Workshop on Sexual Rights

On 6 April 2007, the National Human Rights Commission held a one-day workshop on sexual rights. Around two hundred representatives from LGBT and HIV/AIDS organizations from various parts of the country were brought together with NHRC funding. A senior female commissioner, Ambhorn Meesook, gave an opening talk. She had been a teacher and became involved in issues relating to sexuality, mental health, and women's issues. She said the first purpose of sexual relations was reproduction, and that many sexual issues were hard to talk about. If those of the older generation were confused about how to deal with such issues, it was not surprising if young people were also confused. While her comments were an odd opening to the workshop, her presence and welcome legitimated the event. Naiyana was making sure that she was not the only NHRC commissioner publicly supporting LGBT issues. Dr. Kritaya Archavanitkul, from the Institute for Population and Social Research at Mahidol University, then assumed the chair. She held up a booklet published by the NHRC on women's reproductive rights and stated that the goal of the workshop was to produce a similar publication on sexuality rights.

In the morning programme of the workshop, three scholars spoke. One, Dr. Vitit Muntarbhorn of the Faculty of Law at Chulalongkorn University, is an internationally recognized expert on human rights who has played a number of roles at the United Nations, including Special Rapporteur on the Rights of the Child. He noted that eighty countries still had criminal laws against homosexual acts and that while many doctors still saw homosexuality and transgenderism as mental- health issues, the World Health Organization had, in fact, declared fifteen years earlier that no mental illness was involved. He referred to the Yogyakarta Principles, drafted the previous November by a group of United

Nations experts, scholars, and NGO activists in a meeting that he had co-chaired in Indonesia. The Yogyakarta Principles applied internationally recognized human rights norms to the situation of LGBTI individuals. But, he added, there was no consensus at the United Nations on these matters. In the latter part of the morning there were presentations by a number of community groups dealing with various issues, including HIV/AIDS, the disabled, Muslims, and children.

What emerged concretely from the NHRC workshop and subsequent activities was the Sexual Diversity Network, which brought together various organizations and individuals in a loose coalition. Later in 2007, a two hundred-page book, *Human rights of lesbians, gays, bisexuals, transgender and intersex people*, was published under the name of the National Human Rights Commission and the Rainbow Sky Association of Thailand.

The Sex/Sexuality Issues Current in 2007

The LGBT activism detailed took place during a period in which a number of public issues and debates concerned with sex, sexual orientation, and gender identity were taking place. I note here some of these major issues.

The military draft

While homosexual orientation has not been a basis for exclusion or expulsion from compulsory military service in Thailand, *kathoeys* were exempted on the basis that they suffered from a "mental disease" or a "permanent mental disorder". This language appeared on their military-service documents, which are routinely required to be shown to potential employers. The NHRC worked on the issue of overturning this pathologizing terminology in collaboration with Sapaan, Rainbow Sky, Bangkok Rainbow, and also the military. As a result, the Thai military ceased using discriminatory phraseology in its military-service exemption documents in April 2006. It announced a new policy, which was reported as follows:

> The military would respect the human dignity of transvestites by running physical check-ups on them in specially provided rooms and not requiring them to expose their bare breasts in public. However, only those who had had breast enlargements or sex change operations, not those who simply looked or acted like women, would be exempted [from military service].[13]

In November 2006, a twenty-two-year-old transgender, living as a woman, with breast enhancement but no genital surgery, sought to have her two-year-old military-service exemption document changed to omit the wording relating to "mental disorder". The case was supported by the NHRC, the Lawyers Council of Thailand, the Rainbow Sky Association of Thailand, and Sapaan. The matter went to the administrative court but was not resolved during 2007.

Rape law

Thailand's rape law was rewritten under the military-appointed interim government in 2007. While the lead issue was the recognition of rape within marriage, the revision extended the definition of rape to include male and transgender victims. Both Natee Teerarojjanapongs and Anjana Suvarnananda publicly campaigned for this change.

The Novotel Hotel discrimination case

On 22 June 2007, a nightclub in the Novotel Hotel in the Siam Square shopping area in Bangkok barred Sutthirat Simsiriwong from entering after checking her identity card, which listed her sex as "male". Sutthirat is a *kathoey* and at the time was the local brand manager for a French cosmetic firm. She filed a human-rights complaint with Naiyana Suphapung, who said the NHRC would investigate the case.

Bangkok Rainbow launched a sophisticated media campaign against Novotel, calling for a gay boycott of all Accor chain hotels, of which Novotel is one section. A campaign logo, with the slogan "Novotel/No Homo" and a "no entry" design, was reprinted in *The Nation* newspaper, which gave the story front-page coverage for two consecutive days, 28 and 29 June 2007.[14] Novotel Bangkok initially tried to downplay the incident, saying that barring *kathoeys* was against hotel policy. But on 6 July, in the presence of media, the manager of the hotel, Gerald Hougardy, publicly apologized to Sutthirat. Sutthirat accepted the apology and said she would ask her supporters to end calls for the boycott of Accor hotels.

In addition to the sexuality-related issues summarized above, a number of other human-rights issues were also given wide coverage in the media in 2006 and 2007. For example, a bill on employment non-discrimination and accessibility for people with disabilities sailed through military-appointed National Legislative Assembly. This followed Thailand's signing of a U.N. convention on people with disabilities in 2006. The interim government also decided to sign the United Nations *Convention against Torture*. *The Nation* editorialized on this decision, saying:

> [I]t has become obvious that the [military-installed] Surayud government wants to leave behind a legacy as an administration that respected human rights and promoted democracy.[15]

Revising the 1997 Constitution

I now turn to the central concern of this chapter, the Sexual Diversity Network's efforts to lobby the government in mid-2007.

The political opening

The military leaders who staged the coup in September 2006 believed that the existing "people's" constitution had allowed Prime Minister Thaksin to consolidate excessive powers. Revising the 1997 constitution was a basic goal of the military-installed government to prevent a similar situation from developing again. The task of drafting the revisions was assigned to a new Constitutional Drafting Assembly. The amendments would be approved or rejected in a national referendum. Public hearings were convened to provide forums for community input. This created a significant political opening for public involvement in revising the constitution similar to the consultative process involved in the drafting of the 1997 constitution itself.

The organized LGBT lobby

As noted above, the Sexual Diversity Network originated from initiatives of the NHRC, specifically: (a) its sponsorship, recognition, and patronage of particular leaders and organizations,[16] and (b) its work in bringing together diverse LGBT groups and activists from all parts of the country, most notably at the workshop on sexual rights in April 2007 summarized above. Commissioner Naiyana had clearly foreseen a role for LGBT issues and organizations in the work of revising the constitution, mentioning this as early as January 2007 at the Bangkok Pride board meeting. She played a double role of facilitating the creation of the Sexual Diversity Network and suggesting its lobbying agenda. In this, Naiyana had the support of other members of the National Human Rights Commission. The Commission was committed to playing an active role in the public consultations concerning constitutional revision, if, for no other reason, to attempt to gain some creditability and recognition after having been ignored by the Thaksin government from 2001 to 2006. Lobbying on LGBT issues became a joint project of the Commission and the SDN.

Constitutional Drafting Assembly

After the September 2006 coup, the military set up a process to select one hundred representative members for the Constitutional Drafting Assembly. Twenty-five members of the CDA were then selected to serve on a drafting committee, along with ten non-voting experts, and their draft amendments to the 1997 constitution were then debated by the full quorum of CDA members.

The CDA arranged hearings in various provinces as part of its deliberations, but LGBT representatives were not included in these meetings.[17] At the same time, the National Human Rights Commission also organized public forums on constitutional reform in various parts of the country, and Naiyana insisted that LGBT representatives be heard at each of these meetings. On 11 May 2007, the NHRC presented its recommendations to the CDA, which included a proposed amendment to Section 30 of the 1997 constitution to include the words: "Men, women, and people of sexual diversities shall enjoy equal rights." Anjana Suvarnananda identified "sexual diversities" (*khwam-lak-lai thang-phet*) as a Thai expression coined and used by the LGBT movement in the previous few years. While in English the wording "diverse sexualities" would have been more correct, the translation follows Thai-language word order. Anjana circulated an explanation of these developments to an e-mail list:

> Since the NHRC presented these recommendations, Anjaree group has been working on mobilising LGBT groups to give support and to spread the information to the public. Together with other LGBT groups, in the name of the Network of LGBT, Anjaree group also made recommendations to the Constitution Drafting Assembly (CDA) to include this issue in the debate agenda. We have also managed to get some members of the CDA to sponsor this recommendation. In an effort to advocate for the inclusion of this clause, Anjaree group organised another seminar with the National Human Rights Commission and other LGBT groups on 25 May 2007 (please see the news from *Bangkok Post* dated 26 May 2007 as attached).[18]

At the 25 May event at the NHRC offices mentioned by Anjana, Miss Tiffany 2007, winner of the famous annual transgender beauty contest, presented flowers to Commissioner Ambhorn Meesook on behalf of the LGBT communities to show thanks and respect. Ambhorn said the Commission supported an amendment to insure the gay community equal rights. Miew, from the Rainbow Sky Association of Thailand, said the new wording would require the rape law to be extended to deal with the rape of males and that it would permit same-sex marriage and in this way extend inheritance rights. He added that discrimination in employment would also become illegal. Sanitsuda Ekachai, a respected human rights journalist, wrote in the *Bangkok Post*:

> Sawing Tan-oot, a member of the National Legislative Assembly (NLA) and the Constitution Drafting Assembly, will propose the clause on gay

rights be included in the draft [constitutional] charter. But many NLA members still do not understand the concepts of gender and diverse sexuality, he said.[19]

Alisa Phanthusak was a key CDA member supporting these issues. She is the manager of Tiffany's Show in Pattaya, the oldest of the large transvestite cabaret theatres that cater to the tourist market. Alisa was nominated by the business sector in Chonburi Province, which includes the Pattaya beach resort, to be one of that province's representatives on the CDA. Tiffany's had been started by gay men, then bought by her father, who was no longer active in running the business. Alisa was very familiar with homosexuals and had hired Dr. Seri Wongmontha, a pioneering gay activist, as a consultant on marketing, public relations, and the organizing of the annual Miss Tiffany transgender beauty pageant and the Miss International Queen contest.[20]

The Debates in the Constitutional Drafting Assembly

On 11 June 2007, the Constitutional Drafting Assembly debated the "sexual diversities" amendment of Article 30 for two and a half hours. The debate was broadcast live on Thai television. In the end, the amendment was defeated by 54 votes to 23. Anjana Suvarnananda noted,

> Some assemblymen said the word 'sexual diversities' is not precise enough and [not] immediately understood. Another assemblyman expressed the prejudice more liberally by saying that protecting these [LGBT] people will make Thai society weak. There were many positive opinions expressed by several assemblymen and women who stood up to debate to propose changing of the draft for LGBT protection. Among these positive presentations, there were many great explanations and reasonings that help clarify who LGBT people are and what misunderstanding and discrimination we are facing. The issue of being m3entally ill was mentioned but also explanation to correct the misunderstanding was offered. Many assemblymen read from the text we presented including information about WHO [World Health Organization] position on homosexuality as not-illness, the information about various countries national law that render protection, Amnesty International document on human rights of LGBT (ACT 79/001/2004) although in English and the latest Yogyakarta Principles. We wish we had a Thai version of this AI text.[21]

Alisa Phanthusak realized that she now had to take an initiative. To raise the issue again required the signatures of one-third of the CDA members, and she lobbied strenuously to get enough signatures to reopen the issue. The issue was reopened later in June with a proposal to refer to "sexual identity" (*attalak thang-phet*) rather than "sexual diversities". The Novotel Hotel discrimination case described above was in the Thai-language and English-language newspapers the same day, and many CDA members had copies with them. The media publicity on that issue made it easier to get the signatures necessary to get the "sexual identity" proposal on the floor. A vote occurred on the "sexual identity" proposal, and the revised language was approved.

29 June 2007 turned out to be a crucial day for two issues: the "sexual identity" amendment and also the issue of whether Buddhism should be recognized as the official state religion. Some Buddhist monks had organized highly visible actions on this second issue. The constitution specifies that the King must be Buddhist and that the state should promote Buddhism, but it goes no further. When the CDA rejected the formal recognition of Buddhism as the "national religion" (*sasana prajam chat*), monks outside the hall overturned a giant monk's bowl, a symbolic affront to the legislators by indicating a refusal to allow them to make merit by contributing alms food to monks. In Thai the expression *khwam bat*, "to overturn a monk's alms bowl", also means "to boycott".

After the rejection of the state-religion proposal, surprisingly, the "sexual identity" issue came back on the floor. A CDA member argued that the "sexual identity" amendment was the same as the "diverse sexualities" amendment and that the matter could not be voted on a second time. Kaloon Siam, a former senator, pushed for a final vote. While it was said that the objection was procedural, some NLA members said they did not want to be seen as voting in favour of homosexuals and against Buddhism and on the same day. On a second vote, twenty-nine to twenty-nine, the "sexual identity" amendment was defeated. Apparently self-conscious about the negative vote, there was a promise to publish an explanation indicating the legislators' intent on the issue. It was said that this memo of intent could be used in court. Some CDA members insisted that the intention of the CDA was to protect homosexuals and that this intention would be clear in the memo of intent. Other CDA members, however, clearly had no such intention. Explanatory comments were prepared for each of the decisions of the CDA and subsequently published together in a book.

The Constitutional Drafting Assembly Intentions Document

The Constitutional Drafting Assembly subsequently issued a document, "Intentions of the Constitution of the Kingdom of Thailand", dealing with Clause 3 of Article 30, the provision on equality that had been the subject of the "diverse sexualities" and "sexual identity" amendments. The key term in the document is *"phet"*, a Thai word that variously denotes "sex", "gender", and "sexuality". In the list of prohibited grounds of discrimination in Article 30 (3), *phet* is included, and in this context is normally translated into English as "sex".

The relevant section of the "intentions" document concerned with the meaning of *"phet"* in the context of Article 30 (3) is as follows:

> The state has the responsibility to eliminate obstacles and to promote the conditions in which individuals are able to use their rights and freedoms in the same way as other individuals, without discrimination, which accords with the fundamental principle of human dignity.
>
> Differences in *phet*, in addition to meaning the differences between men and women, also denote the differences between individuals in sexual identity or gender or sexual diversity, which may be different from the *phet* in which the person was born. Consequently, the above are not specifically provided for in section 30 because the word *phet* already denotes the above meanings and the individuals within the above categories should not be discriminated against.[22]

This interpretation of Article 30 (3) supported what Naiyana Suphapung had said the article meant in her speeches beginning in 2001. Now there was a formal statement of the reasoning. LGBT people were protected by Article 30 (3) of the national constitution because the meaning of the term *"phet"* cannot be interpreted as simply meaning physical sex. It is much broader.

In 1994, in *Toonen vs. Australia*, the United Nations Human Rights Committee, interpreting the wording of the *International Covenant on Civil and Political Rights*, which Thailand has signed, ruled that discrimination on the basis of "sexual orientation" is a form of discrimination on the basis of "sex". Sexual-orientation discrimination is, in that way, covered by the equality/non-discrimination clause in the Covenant. The members of the CDA possibly knew this, for one of the documents they had from the Sexual Diversity Network was a description of provisions in international law and other national constitutions (written by the present author). That document began by describing the ruling in the *Toonen* case, noting that it was binding on Thailand. In the document setting out the "intentions" of the CDA in its decisions on Article 30 (3) the same analysis is adopted and stated expansively. The wording would clearly cover transgendered individuals as well as homosexuals. Some members of the CDA said that the end result had been a victory for the Sexual Diversity Network— less than what the SDN had sought (for the two proposed changes in wording had not been adopted) but a victory nonetheless. With the official "intentions" document we saw, for the first time their reasoning, which brought LGBT people within Article 30 (3) of the Thai constitution.

In August 2007, a national referendum approved the altered constitution. Elections were scheduled for December of that year. The existing members of the NHRC continued in office, awaiting implementation of the new constitutional rules for the Commission. The military-installed National Legislative Assembly continued to function until the election, and a second issue engaged the Sexual Diversity Network.

Female Titles for *Kathoeys*

In the second half of 2007, legislation was introduced to allow married women to use a "title" that did not indicate their marital status. In Thailand, there are no men's titles that distinguish between married and unmarried men, the term *"nai"* (Mr.) being used for all adult males. However, unmarried adult women were required to use the title *"nang-sao"* (Miss) on official documents and identity cards, while married women were required to use the title *"nang"* (Mrs.). With the opening up of this issue of official personal titles for women, a context was created in which *kathoeys* could argue for changes in their personal-identity documents, in this case from "Mr." (*nai*) to "Miss" (*nang-sao*).[23]

A preliminary meeting of about forty people to discuss a lobbying strategy took place at the offices of the National Human Rights Commission on 21 August 2007. Most of the participants were *kathoeys*, but there were also a number of individuals from LGBT organizations, including Bangkok Rainbow, the Rainbow Sky Association of Thailand, and Sapaan. The most prominent of the *kathoeys* in running of the meeting was from the Venus Flytrap pop music group, who co-chaired along with Chanthalak, from the Sapaan NGO. *Norng* Tum, Thailand's most famous m-t-f transsexual of *Beautiful Boxer* film fame was there. (See the chapter by Stéphane Rennesson in this volume.) A number of *kathoeys* told stories of the problems they had faced because their identity documents did not correspond to their feminine appearance.

Naiyana Suphapung advised the group to proceed in a step-by-step, incremental manner. This seemed to suggest limiting the request for a change in title to post-operative transsexuals, i.e. those who that had completed genital reconstruction surgery, not simply breast enhancement and hormonal treatment. Legislation in the United Kingdom and Germany goes further in allowing some change of documentation for individuals diagnosed as transsexuals who have not had genital surgery but who live everyday lives in their chosen sex on a permanent basis. Throughout the three weeks of meetings that followed, there never seemed to be a set of specific proposals from the individuals involved in the Sexual Diversity Network. Yes, it was agreed, a title change should be allowed. But should it be limited to post-operative transsexuals? Would it include changing the birth certificate? Could educational and medical records be altered? Was there a need for some document to indicate there had been a sex change (so innocent straight men would not be deceived)? None of these questions was clearly resolved. At a second planning meeting at NHRC offices, Naiyana referred to the fact that sex reassignment surgery was not covered under the Thai government's free health-care system. She thought this was one reason not to require surgery as a condition for title change. She also said that the debate had implications for the law on marriage, and she supported a *kathoey's* right to marry a man legally.

On 14 September 2007, a formal parliamentary subcommittee hearing on the female-titles issue was held at the Vieng Tai Hotel in Bangkok. The draft female- titles law had to be made final by 20 September. It would then be studied by the government for thirty days and come back to the NLA for a vote on 20 October. Any delay would mean that the legislation would miss the current legislative session—and the life of the military-appointed government. During the discussion period, the meeting was chaired by a member of the NLA along with Sutthirat Simsiriwong (the *kathoey* who had been discriminated against in the Novotel Hotel incident detailed above), and the 2007 winner of the well-known Miss Alcazar transgender beauty pageant, which is held annually in Pattaya. They had also played the role of co-chairs in previous consultative meetings. Commissioner Naiyana Suphapung said she hoped that the session would confirm that there are not just men and women in Thai society but many kinds of groups. It was transgender groups that really needed the change in the law, she said, and it should be a choice as to whether to have sex-reassignment surgery. This suggested that the law should not require genital surgery before allowing a change in title. She did not want to see a distinction drawn between non-operative and post-operative individuals. Naiyana also noted the greater invisibility of female-to-male transgendered individuals in Thai society compared with male-to-female transgenders and said that this other, less-visible group of transgendered people may also want a legal change of title, from "*nang-sao*" (Miss) to "*nai*" (Mr.).

Natee Teerarojjanapongs, the founder of FACT and rights campaigner, also supported making a change of title available to pre-operative or non-operative transsexuals. He argued that both groups faced the same problems in getting jobs, in foreign travel, and in having a legally and socially recognized status that fit with their feelings. A *kathoey* estimated that there were one thousand *kathoeys* in Pattaya, of whom only ten percent had undergone surgery. This was one of a number of references to transsexuals who had completed genital surgery as being in a minority situation.

Juree Vichid-Vadakarn, who chaired the session, ended it with cautionary comments that not everything can be achieved at the same time. The draft bill forwarded by the National Legislative Assembly to the Interior Ministry on 24

October 2007, did have provisions for post-operative transsexuals to change their titles, but some NLA members publicly voiced concerns and opposed that decision.[24] In the end, the bill returned to the NLA without those provisions, and it was enacted as such. It came into force on 4 June 2009, and married women, divorcees, and widows can now decide whether they want to be addressed formally as either "Miss" or "Mrs.". A reason was publicly given for deferring consideration of title changes for *kathoeys*, as explained in *The Nation:*

> 'Some contents of the draft bill have been found to affect other acts, for instance the Civil Registration Act. We have to discuss the effects on other acts to adjust appropriate details in the draft before we submit it to the new government for consideration,' Suchit [Tripitak, deputy director-general of the Office of Women's Affairs and Family Development] said.[25]

Abhisit Vejjajiva, then the leader of the Democrat Party and later to become prime minister, said that the issue of *kathoey* titles needed more consideration. He did not support immediate change.

After the December 2007 National Election

The national election in December 2007 was a victory for the supporters of Thaksin Shinawatra, the former prime minister. Their party gained the most seats and formed a government in coalition with smaller parties. The following year was a period of considerable instability, with massive anti-government demonstrations by the anti-Thaksin Peoples Alliance for Democracy, including, most dramatically, the occupation and closure of the two Bangkok airports for more than a week. The Constitutional Court ousted two pro-Thaksin prime ministers, dissolving their parties for corruption and banning many politicians from political office for five years. The originally pro-Thaksin "Newin faction" of politicians shifted position and aligned itself with the opposition Democrat Party, allowing it to form a government in late 2008 and leading to Abhisit Vejjajiva's premiership. This prompted large demonstrations by the pro-Thaksin "red shirts", including the blocking of an summit of the Association of Southeast Asian Nations, in Pattaya in April 2009, and stopping traffic at key points in Bangkok during the Thai new year Songkran holiday.

During this period, there was constant public discussion of again revising the constitution. For pro-Thaksin figures, the 2007 constitutional amendments had been made by an illegitimate government and were aimed against their leader and their party. When the Democrat Party formed a government, it said it supported some further constitutional revision, but no agreement was reached between the government coalition and opposition parties. The government dropped its support for the process in early 2010, after internal disagreement within the opposition camp had become clear. While the issue of titles for *kathoeys* was understood as unfinished business, there seemed no chance that the government would take it up anytime soon. The two political openings for LGBT lobbying in 2007 had passed.

As a result of government inaction in 2007 and 2008, the first group of commissioners appointed to the National Human Rights Commission gained an extended mandate, beyond their official six-year terms. A series of additional meetings with LGBT activists took place at the NHRC in 2008 on blood donation and military issues, and the launching of the Thai translation of the Yogyakarta Principles. The Commission brought about eighty LGBT activists from various parts of the country together on 19 March 2008, to help in the drafting of a final report summarizing the commission's work on LGBT issues since 2001. Commissioner Naiyana chaired the meeting, describing it as insuring there was a record of the Commission's work on these issues. The chairman of the Commission, Professor Saneh Chamarik, gave opening remarks. Saneh's presence demonstrated unequivocally that Naiyana had official support from the Commission as a whole in this work, even though Saneh had not been present at any of the other meetings described in this chapter.

The 2007 revisions to the constitution made some changes to the National Human Rights Commission. It reduced the number of commissioners from eleven to seven, and the selection process, which had guaranteed the independence of commissioners, was changed to give majority control to nominees of judges and government departments. The first set of commissioners had been praised for their representative diversity.[26] The new process produced a much different result, and there were protests over the new commissioners who were selected, as noted by Thongbai Thongpao, a former senator, in his *Bangkok Post* column:

> As for the seven candidates themselves, Section 256 of the charter requires that they must have 'apparent knowledge and experience in the protection of the rights and liberties of the people'. Some of the candidates clearly do not possess this qualification. Section 256 also requires that there be participation in the NHRC of representatives from private organisations in the field of human rights, which none of the seven candidates are . . . The sad part is that there was no lack of constitutionally qualified people to choose from. Many of the original 133 applicants for the Commission do have active roles in human rights, as labour leaders, women's rights defenders, leaders of private human rights organisations, etc.[27]

Protests over the new NHRC appointees came from local groups and from the Asian Human Rights Commission, an NGO based in Hong Kong, as well as Human Rights Watch, based in New York.[28] Nonetheless, the seven new appointees were approved by the Senate on 1 May 2009. It thus appeared that the body, which had been so vital to the LGBT lobbying of 2007, had been tamed. The new chairperson, Amara Pongsapich, gave an interview to the *Bangkok Post* in July 2009, confirming a new direction or style and referring to criticisms of the previous Commission. She said the fact that the Commission was now mainly composed of former bureaucrats would "change the image of the NHRC from an anti-government or NGO-like body to a softer accommodative mechanism".[29] At the same time, she said that the Commission would have to network with grassroots organizations.

After the December 2007 election, the loose Sexual Diversity Network was no longer very visible. A "Human Rights Day for Sexual Diversity" was held on 29 November 2008, in a small plaza in the heart of the main shopping area of Bangkok. Sponsors were Central World (whose giant mall was a couple of blocks away), the NHRC, the Global Fund for Women, the human-rights programme at Mahidol University, and the Southeast Asian Consortium on Gender, Sexuality and Health, funded by the Rockefeller Foundation. The day-long event included speakers, panels, and cabaret entertainment. The Thai-language translation of the Yogyakarta Principles was distributed. The events ended with the participants walking through the shopping crowds to the nearby plaza of the newly opened Bangkok Art and Culture Centre, carrying rainbow-coloured umbrellas. Gay businesses were not involved. A smaller workshop event was held the following year, again in the name of the Sexual Diversity Network.

The Significance of the Events of 2007 and 2008

The context for the LGBT lobbying in Bangkok in 2007 was unique. NHRC commissioner Naiyana Suphapung was an essential figure, able to support LGBT organizing and put the NHRC publicly behind LGBT rights. When she became a commissioner in 2001 there was no functioning LGBT network in Thailand. With her support, a working relationship among the various LGBT NGOs and individual activists came into being, laying the groundwork for the lobbying in 2007.

There had been a major issue of legitimacy for the military-installed government in 2006–07, and the Constitutional Drafting Assembly was very worried that its revised constitution might be rejected in the promised referendum. Many in the CDA were unfamiliar and uneasy with LGBT issues; however, good lobbying meant that speakers supporting inclusion of LGBT rights in the constitution were active and well-informed. In the end, the supporters of the proposed amendments could not overcome the apprehensions of other CDA members, but it was close. LGBT rights won on one vote—only to be quickly reversed in a tie vote—with the consolation prize of a positive "explanation" of legislative intent to ban discrimination against gays, lesbians, transgenders, and transsexuals.

When the titles legislation emerged as a proposal on women's equality rights, the issue of titles for transsexuals was successfully linked to it. There were two sub-committee meetings at which *kathoeys* represented themselves on the national political scene as self-confident and talented people who deserved recognition as serious individuals. This was in sharp contrast to the clownish images that appear regularly on television and in Thai movies. (See Serhat Ünaldi and Brett Farmer's chapters here.) The *kathoey* lobby suffered from the lack of a precise proposal. The lobbyists never answered the question of whether the reform should be limited to post-operative individuals or whether some indication of transsexual status should occur in personal documentation (if only, it seemed, to protect "innocent" heterosexual men). In the rush of legislative action in the second half of 2007, the titles bill was passed without any provisions for transsexuals. But the issue is unfinished business that may well come back onto the political agenda. Even conservative jurisdictions such as Indonesia, Japan, Korea, and Singapore allow the change of personal documents.

Thailand's commitment to human rights is weak. It has signed a number of important United Nations human-rights treaties, though it has played only a cautious and limited role at the UN. While it has abstained on every country-specific human rights resolution at the UN since 2000,[30] it has nonetheless supported the creation of a human-rights mechanism at the ASEAN level. It has usually followed the ASEAN pattern of not criticizing human rights issues in neighbouring countries such as Myanmar. It has no overtly anti-homosexual laws, but it has made absolutely no legal accommodation for *kathoeys*. It lacks a general anti-discrimination law and has not implemented by legislation even the constitutional ban on discrimination on the basis of sex. The apparent emasculation of the Human Rights Commission in the spring of 2009 seems the clearest indication of the limited support for human rights on the part of both the government and the opposition. It would seem that the openings of 2007 are unlikely to be repeated soon.

Transpeople (*Khon kham-phet*) in Thailand
Transprejudice, Exclusion, and the Presumption of Mental Illness[1]

Sam Winter

All Asian countries, Daniel concedes, are culturally very rich, and each has its very own unique attractions. **But Thailand has to be the most openly accepting of them all.** Which other culture throws open its arms and embraces every kind of person, not just letting them be but letting them be on their own terms? The acceptance here is complete and unconditional. 'I mean just look at the *katoey*s (also known as ladyboys),' says Daniel. 'So many of them, everywhere, this place is so open, it's just impossible to find anywhere else.' The level of freedom and right of existence is just incredible.

> —Aparna Raut Desai, writing for the web publication
> Global Gayz.com; emphasis in original[2]

My father hated my behavior very much; he was ashamed. He beat me until I was 14 years old. The final time my father beat me he yelled at me, 'What are you?' I told him, 'You can beat me until I die but I will always be like this. I cannot be a man.'

> —Mumu, cafeteria worker and transwoman in Chiang Mai,
> cited in Costa and Matzner (2007, 113)

Introduction

Gender identity variance (a person's identification as belonging to a gender other than that into which he or she was allocated at birth) appears to be a cross-cultural and trans-historical aspect of human diversity; people of gender variant identity have been present in many societies across many historical periods. In the past, such people were often mistakenly labelled as "hermaphrodites", even when their physiologies were indubitably male or female. In recent decades, gender-variant people in the West have come to be called transsexual, sometimes transgender, often more informally as "transpeople".

There is no commonly accepted Thai equivalent for the English term "transpeople". Indeed, a single word, *"phet"*, denotes both "sex" and "gender", undermining attempts to translate English terms such as "transgender" and "transsexual". To make matters worse, Thai terms such as *"kathoey"* and *"tom"*, commonly used to describe Thai transpeople, are over-inclusive, often being used to describe gender-variant and sexual minority groups more generally. *"Kathoey"* has historically been used for those who, in the West, would identify as transpeople, as well as for men who would identify as gay. It is also used to describe men deemed effeminate. The term *"tom"* (from "tomboy") is a female equivalent, not only describing transmen but also lesbians and other women deemed to have masculine qualities. It is worth noting that both these terms often offend the individuals to whom they refer, at least when used by outsiders. In other contexts, these terms are under-inclusive, referring to birth-assigned males and females respectively (but not to both). This sex specificity also applies to other, more trans-specific terms such as *"phu-ying praphet sorng"* ("second kind of woman"). Moreover, it is noteworthy that the term *"phu-chai praphet sorng"* ("second kind of man") for masculine women, as a possible parallel to the expression *"phu-ying praphet sorng"* for feminine males, is entirely absent from common Thai usage.

In their struggle for rights, Thai transpeople face the challenge of constructing an affirming vocabulary of gender identity variance that recognizes the identities of all transpeople (*both* transmen *and* transwomen), yet also distinguishes transpeople from other queer groups in Thailand. A promising candidate is the neologism *"khon kham-phet"*, translated either as "person who crosses sex/gender" or, as its originator, Prempreeda Pramoj Na Ayutthaya, intended, as a "person who goes beyond gender". As Peter Jackson notes in this volume, *"khon kham-phet"* was coined to try to capture the sense of gender and sexual fluidity reflected in contemporary Western understandings of "queer". Drawing on this terminology, transwomen could be described as *phu-ying kham-phet*.[3] By extension, transmen could be described as *phu-chai kham-phet*. However, Thais do not use this latter term, perhaps reflecting the lower level of cultural awareness of transmen in Thailand as compared with transwomen. The reader should note that both these usages ignore the birth-assigned gender of the persons concerned, instead emphasizing the person's actual gender identity. *"Khon kham-phet"* enjoys increasing use.[4]

In many societies today, transpeople are the victims of stigma, leading to prejudice. This prejudice, a cocktail of negative attitudes and irrational beliefs that together reinforce the stigma and underpin discriminatory and oppressive behaviour, is often called "transphobia", corresponding to "homophobia" in regard to gays and lesbians. In truth, "phobia" (fear) is but one element in this cocktail, and Mark King et al. (2009) have recently pointed out that a more accurate term may be "transprejudice".

Transprejudice engenders discrimination because it delegitimizes, undercutting transpeople's claims to a quality of life corresponding to that of other people in their societies. In turn, discriminatory behaviour leads to the exclusion of transpeople from economic and social activity, driving them to the margins of society. Worldwide, transpeople living in transprejudiced societies encounter discrimination in the family, in places of worship, in education and the workplace, in the provision of health services, and in housing. The end result is social and economic marginalization—indeed, exclusion. Many governments and their agencies fail to protect transpeople against discrimination. At worst, they are active offenders, sometimes perpetrating egregious abuses. When a government neglects to protect a discriminated group, or actively perpetrates discrimination, then discrimination can be viewed as systematic, and one can speak only of oppression.[5]

What then, about Thailand? Thailand is home to a large and vibrant community of *khon kham-phet.* As many as six in every thousand individuals assigned male at birth may later present as transwomen or *phu-ying kham-phet* (Winter 2002a).[6] As is evident in the first of the two quotations at the start of this chapter, Thai society has a reputation for being tolerant, even accepting, towards *khon kham-phet*, consistent with its reputation in regard to its treatment of homosexuality.[7] Indeed, evidence suggests that indigenous cultural traditions have allowed a social space for gender-diverse Thais.[8] Compared with some other religions, Thai Theravada Buddhism is relatively non-judgmental on matters of sexual and gender diversity, at least outside the monkhood. While some Buddhist scriptures disparage *khon kham-phet* (see Jackson 1998), at least one senior Buddhist scholar recently pleaded for tolerance towards such individuals. Moreover, while it is commonly believed that heterosexual adultery can lead to a person being *khon kham-phet* in the next life (Jackson 1998), there appears to be no corresponding belief that living as a *khon kham-phet* in this life generates similarly bad karma. Thai Buddhism therefore appears to take a relatively neutral stance on gender identity variance. No religious sanctions are imposed.

Comparative historical and ethnographic research suggests that cultural space for gender diversity was once common across much of Southeast Asia. Peletz (2006) has written about the "gender pluralism" evident across much of the region, and which ensured social inclusion for those we would nowadays call transpeople. Peletz argues that in more modern times this pluralism has declined, noting a "widespread but regionally variable delegitimization and stigmatization of transgendered practices" (2006, 310). However, Peletz may be misreading the nature of what has happened. For example, Jackson, in referring to *khon kham-phet* working in the Thai beauty sector, has observed that there are probably more working in this sector nowadays than ever. The implication is that as one set of roles waned others flourished, and Jackson notes that the cultural space of gender variance in Thailand has likely shifted from the field of religion (described by Peletz) to the modern rituals of femininity and beauty.[9]

The limits of Thai acceptance of *khon kham-phet* are now well documented in research reports compiled by academics, service providers, and social activists.[10] Jackson (1999a), blowing the whistle on the "myth of a Thai 'Gay' Paradise", describes the situation as "tolerant but unaccepting". As will become evident, the situation of *khon kham-phet* is somewhat similar.

Cameron describes the subtleties of social exclusion in Thai society for *khon kham-phet*, as well as a variety of other marginalized groups:

> Those who break or defy social mores in Thailand are not directly challenged but rather they are ignored and rejected from society. Social alienation in Thailand is often a very subtle, but an extremely painful and debilitating, force for those who experience it. The visibility in society of . . . transgender people does not mean acceptance. Along with many men who are open about having sex with men, they are highly stigmatised and socially sanctioned members of Thai society. (2006, 6)

In some ways, transphobia seems less pronounced for *khon kham-phet* as compared with some other places worldwide. The worst excesses of transphobia seem absent. True, there are cases of fathers assaulting their gender-variant sons to coerce them into gender conformity, and of straight men sexually assaulting and raping young *phu-ying kham-phet*.[11] On the other hand, it appears that fewer *khon kham-phet* are murdered than in places such as the United States and the Indian subcontinent. Violence aside, I argue in this chapter that some of the most fundamental rights of Thailand's *khon kham-phet* are denied on a daily basis. A recent publication commissioned by UNAIDS is instructive in this regard (Caceres et al., 2008). After researching the legal frameworks within which GLBT individuals live in low- and middle-income countries worldwide, the authors categorized each country on a five-point scale running from "highly repressive" at one end to "protective with recognition measures" at the other. Thailand made it only half way along the continuum, to the "neutral" category. On one hand, Thai *khon kham-phet* are not criminalized, unlike in neighbouring Malaysia, for example, where cross-dressing is banned (see Teh 2002). On the other hand, there is no protection against the subtle forms of sexual oppression that pervade Thai culture, nor is there any legal recognition of the gender status in which *khon kham-phet* live, or of their intimate relationships (most commonly in mixed-gender couples regarded in law as same-sex). Recently, *khon kham-phet* have shown an unwillingness to continue passive acceptance of this minoritized position, beginning instead to organize themselves to fight for rights, and working with activists in the broad GLBT community to do so (see Douglas Sanders' chapter in this volume).

Before going on I need to clarify two of this chapter's limitations. First, though I will be addressing legal matters, I count myself as only a reasonably informed commentator; I have no training in law. Second, all my research in Thailand concerns *phu-ying kham-phet*, a more socially visible group than transmen, and, in my view, a group that possibly suffers more discrimination, too.

Constitution and Covenants

Thailand's national constitution guarantees basic rights, human dignity, and equality under the law in accordance with democratic rule under the king and in accordance with international obligations.[12] The most notable obligations are the International Covenant on Economic, Social, and Cultural Rights, or ICESCR, and the International Covenant on Civil and Political Rights, or ICCPR. Together, these two covenants seek to guarantee rights not only for the majority in a society, but also for the less privileged and for minorities. Article 2 in each treaty makes this explicit, stating that the rights listed should extend to all in a society, "without distinction of any kind, such as race, colour, sex, language, religion, political or other opinion, national or social origin, property, birth or any other status". The "any other status" provision is key here. In the view of many working in the field of human rights, "any other status" should include sexuality and gender identity.[13]

Note that, in acceding to these two treaties (in contrast to simply signing them), Thailand has undertaken to be legally bound by their terms. It presumably places on the country a particular responsibility to promote and protect the rights specified in these treaties.

What are these rights? Writing in an international context, Caceres et al. (2008, 13) list a range of eighteen rights commonly cited in regard to the LGBT community. It might be argued that *khon kham-phet* experience violations of many rights on the list. The most commonly and comprehensively violated may be the following: the right to work (ICESCR Article 6), the right to marry and to found a family (ICCPR Article 23, paragraph 2), and the right to privacy (ICCPR Article 17, paragraph 1).

Transprejudice

Except where it is an unintended effect of inept legislation or bureaucracy, discrimination is an expression of prejudice; it is thought as expressed in action. What evidence is there, then, for prejudice against *khon kham-phet* in Thai society? In 2002 and 2003, together with Thai colleagues Nongnuch Rojanalert of Silpakorn University (Nakhon Pathom campus) and Kulthida Maneerat of Chulalongkorn University, Bangkok, I researched the attitudes and beliefs of 216 university undergraduates in those two universities regarding *phu-ying kham-phet*. The research was part of a larger study involving undergraduates in seven nations.[14] Prejudice was evident. Half of the Thai students believed that *phu-ying kham-phet* were "somewhat unnatural" (*mi khwam-phit thammachat yu bang*). Nearly half (49 percent) could "not accept" (*mai yorm-rap*) their son becoming a *phu-ying kham-phet*, while around a third (31 percent) could not accept their sons having a *phu-ying kham-phet* as a girlfriend. In view of such prejudice, it was not surprising that discriminatory beliefs were in evidence. More than a quarter (twenty-eight percent) believed that *phu-ying kham-phet* should not be allowed to marry men. Around one in six (16 percent) could not accept being taught by a *phu-ying kham-phet* lecturer. Around one in eight (13 percent) believed that *phu-ying kham-phet* should not be allowed to work with children. These were the views of a young, highly educated, urbanized sample. We can only speculate as to the views of older and less-educated people, perhaps in the provinces. In many cultures such groups may be less open-minded, although in Thailand, and in regard to *khon kham-phet*, that cannot necessarily be assumed.[15] Not surprisingly, in a separate study conducted in 2002 we found that 17 percent of *phu-ying kham-phet* believed that Thai society rejected (i.e. was actively negative towards) people like them (Winter 2006a). The second quotation at the start of this chapter spotlights what this can mean in reality.

Khon kham-phet clearly have a special type of problem here. Gays and lesbians who make public their sexuality find such "indiscretion" strongly disapproved of. Many therefore choose, and manage, to keep their sexuality a relatively private affair. Transpeople find discretion much more difficult. Gender identity variance is about who you are and how you present yourself. Transpeople, by their very nature, run the risk of being "outed". They do so by simply being who they are: adopting an appearance and demeanour inconsistent with their natal sex.[16]

There are many transpeople worldwide, of course, who manage to get through most, if not all, social situations without anybody guessing that they are transgender. In Thailand there are many *phu-ying kham-phet* who manage to "pass" in various social situations as natal females. But I suggest that even for these individuals Thai society contrives to hold them at arm's length, at worst pushing them out towards the social and economic margins.[17]

The Mechanics of Marginalization

Privacy issues

Many of the *khon kham-phet's* problems regarding discrimination are linked to the personal documentation she carries. Regardless of how long she has identified as female and lived in a female role, and no matter the extent to which she now appears female and successfully "passes" as female, the Thai *phu-ying kham-phet* carries a male identity card and national health card, and if she travels abroad, a passport identifying her as male. The transman is in a similar situation. Of all documentation carried about the person, the identity card is particularly important in Thailand. It facilitates activities at the interface with business (e.g. opening a bank account), bureaucracy (e.g. registering for an educational course or medical care), and law enforcement (e.g. when asked for identification by a police officer). Whenever *khon kham-phet* need to show their identity cards, their status as transpeople is communicated: They are "outed".

In the light of the requirement that the ICCPR places upon the Thai government to protect its citizens' rights to privacy (including those of *khon kham-phet*), there would appear to be cause for concern. While Asian societies such as Hong Kong, Taiwan and mainland China, as well as Japan, South Korea, Singapore, Iran and Kyrgyzstan all offer transpeople the opportunity to change some of their personal documentation (at least after sex-reassignment surgery), similar inclusiveness in Thai society remains a comparatively distant goal.

For the *phu-ying kham-phet*, the identity card is not the only threat to privacy. All birth-assigned Thai men who have not undergone reserve-officer training at secondary school are liable to be called for military service at age twenty. For many *phu-ying kham-phet*, the immediate consequence is that upon being called up they have to undergo a physical examination, often with other recruits in their locality, and (in some documented cases) in full public view (see Jenkins et al. 2005)—so much for privacy.

Those *phu-ying kham-phet* who are conscripted and whose gender transition is relatively limited are often assigned non-combat duties, and are even allowed to wear makeup and modified uniforms during their period of military service. In contrast, those with breasts or who have undergone sex-reassignment surgery are discharged from military duties. But this is where another problem of privacy arises. Until recently, discharge papers (called *Sor. Dor. 43* in Thai) have been issued indicating the individual concerned suffers from "a disease causing permanent psychological damage". Throughout her later working life, whenever she applies for a job a *phu-ying kham-phet* may be required to show the *Sor. Dor. 43* document to her potential employer and is outed as "permanently psychologically damaged". After extensive lobbying by Thai LGBT groups, and to the relief of *phu-ying kham-phet* nationwide, the military authorities recently indicated that these *Sor. Dor. 43* documents will no longer carry the offending phrase.[18]

Employment issues

With identity cards that "out" them (and military-discharge papers marking *phu-ying kham-phet* as "psychologically damaged"), it is not surprising that jobs commensurate with education and abilities are often elusive. A common refrain I have heard from *phu-ying kham-phet* is: "We just can't get good jobs." The following case provides some indication of what challenges can confront them:

> I try waitress, bartender, any position that I can do. They telephone me for interview but after that it is silent. I do not know what to do later. I get older per day. When I get enough old they will not hire me. I do not know what will happen when I get old and no job. I feel depressed. So sorry to say.

The above quotation is from a short-message text sent to me on 15 October 2008, by Weewee, a twenty-eight-year-old university graduate and *phu-ying kham-phet*. By the time she sent this message she had already experienced a twelve-month period of almost continuous unemployment, despite many applications for jobs in the tourism, catering, and clerical sectors. Over the five weeks following this SMS, she attempted to earn money making snacks with her sister and selling them on the street. She was moved on by police and then, as a last resort, began working in a Patpong sex bar, where she was attacked by another bar worker. The night of the fight she went back to her room, took an overdose of prescription drugs, and slashed her arms and legs eighty-eight times, necessitating her admission to hospital. Within a week of discharge, and returning to the same life situation, she took another overdose and was hospitalized again.

The Thai government has also practised employment discrimination. Daily instances go unreported, but a particularly egregious case in 1996 attracted wide media coverage, when the Department of Education attempted to ban *phu-ying kham-phet* from training as teachers. Though the department backed down under opposition to the move, the effect was to send a message to training institutions.[19] Interestingly, no report of the affair indicates that the proposed ban extended to transmen.

The effect of employment discrimination is pernicious. Some *phu-ying kham-phet* do not go to university because they feel their education there would be wasted. Those that do often find that they can get a job only in a back office, kept from contact with clients and customers. Two research studies of mine give an impression of the employment situation. In one study of 198 *phu-ying kham-phet* (Winter 2006c), of whom 153 had jobs of some sort, the major occupation sectors represented were cabarets for tourists (acting-dancing and makeup, costume design, and wardrobe work), beauty salons, and sex-work bars (dancer-hostesses). A few reported casual work in restaurants and cafes, shops, and stalls. There were few "middle-class professionals". This was despite the many university graduates in the sample. Instead, the overwhelming impression was of "ghetto" employment, that is, employment in a narrow range of jobs where the more formal type of job interview might not be involved and, therefore, towards which *khon kham-phet* are nudged. Only a few worked outside the "ghetto" at travel and tour agencies and in offices and chain stores. One owned a small restaurant. Another reported work as a teacher.

It is often difficult to demonstrate that employment discrimination has taken place. Some employers may reject job applications from *khon kham-phet* because of their own prejudice. Others may do so because of anxiety about how customers, clients, or workmates will react to a *khon kham-phet* as a colleague. Still others, one imagines, might use concern for people's sensibilities to conceal their own prejudices. Of course, the genuine reasons for the refusal to employ are seldom given. Nevertheless, sufficient evidence exists in Thailand to confirm that employment discrimination poses a very real problem for *khon kham-phet* and that it is a form of discrimination against which they have no effective legal protection. Thailand's failure to enact effective anti-discrimination legislation in regard to employment undoubtedly undermines its inclusiveness. While legislation is not a sufficient pre-condition for equal opportunity (effective enforcement is also necessary) it would be an important first step, one that would be in line with human-rights obligations associated with Thailand's accession to the ICESCR.

Legal status, marriage, and family issues

I wrote above of the privacy problems that arise out of the *khon kham-phet's* inability to change the gender marked on the identity documentation he/she carries—documents that are intended to smooth interactions with businesses, bureaucracies, and law-enforcement agencies but which, in fact, undermine any gender privacy he or she has in those situations. A further problem arises in connection with his or her birth certificate, the document that designates the individual's actual legal status as a man or woman. Increasingly worldwide, transpeople are able to change their legal gender status.[20] The right to do so is an important one, enabling heterosexual marriage and all its benefits, including parenting and adoption. Where it is available, this right usually extended only to those who have undergone sex-reassignment (i.e. genital) surgery. In a few countries it is extended even to those who have not.[21] In Thailand it is denied to all. The *phu-ying kham-phet* therefore not only carries male documentation about her person; she is also legally male, and she remains so regardless of how long she has identified or lived as female, how much she has changed her body, or how well she "passes" as female in front of strangers. The same is true for transmen.

The absence of opportunity to change legal status has a dramatic effect on the lives of *khon kham-phet*. First, as Cameron observes, *phu-ying kham-phet*, "regardless of how they identify, travel as a man, are hospitalised as men, jailed as men, and drafted into the military as *men*" (2006, 29; emphasis in original). The law on rape, which held that only legally recognized women could be victims of rape, has also posed a problem.[22] A recent legislative change, the result of determined lobbying by the Rainbow Sky Association of Thailand, a prominent non-governmental organization, has finally rendered Thailand's rape laws gender non-specific (see Douglas Sanders' chapter in this volume). Second, a *phu-ying kham-phet* is legally able to marry only a woman. Such a marriage is a same-sex marriage in any practical sense of the term, which is cruelly ironic in view of the fact that same-sex marriage (and even civil union) is supposedly not recognized in Thai law. Any ceremonies of marital union in which she and her male partner participate (e.g. religious ceremonies over which a Buddhist monk presides) have no legal force. Transmen are in the same position.

Among *phu-ying kham-phet*, the numbers affected are large indeed. The vast majority of Thai *phu-ying kham-phet* (around 98 percent) appear exclusively attracted to men (Winter 2006c). Almost all *phu-ying kham-phet* are consequently deprived of the practical right to marry and to enjoy its emotional, financial, and legal benefits, including opportunities for a family life (perhaps involving adoption of a child). These are rights that the ICCPR, to which Thailand has acceded, appears to guarantee. The interim constitution promulgated in 2006, promising adherence to "international obligations", appears to guarantee these rights, too.

The Impact of Transprejudice in Daily Life

The undermining of the rights to work, to marry and found a family, and to privacy all have a further impact on *khon kham-phet* lives. For the *phu-ying kham-phet,* long-term unemployment reduces self-reliance and any capacity to contribute to the welfare of parents, grandparents, or younger siblings. It drags self-esteem down and drives many *phu-ying kham-phet* into sex work, including in specialized "*ladyboy*" bars.

Phu-ying kham-phet are not only pushed into sex work; there are also forces that attract them to this type of work. For some, it offers earnings beyond what is possible elsewhere, funding hormone treatment and surgery, and enabling support for parents and siblings. Work in specialized "*ladyboy*" bars may also provide a sense of community, especially for those who have migrated to the city. Finally, sex work provides some with the opportunity for nightly reaffirmation of an identity as female, as well as the possibility of meeting *farang* (foreigners), whom many Thai *phu-ying kham-phet* regard as more accepting towards gender diversity, and who may offer long-term financial support and take their *phu-ying kham-phet* girlfriends with them to their home countries, where marriage and a family may be possibilities. It is difficult to know how many *phu-ying kham-phet* are involved in sex work in Thailand. One study by Jenkins et al. (2005, 8) found that 15 percent were involved in full-time sex work, with an additional 50 percent supplementing their incomes elsewhere by way of occasional sex work. However, one has to be cautious about these sorts of figures. This research was conducted in Bangkok, Chiang Mai, Pattaya, and Phuket—all cities in which there are comparatively large sex-work communities. In addition, sex workers may be more "socially visible" and better networked and hence more likely, in an opportunistic sample, to become research participants than are those who make their livings outside sex work.

The *phu-ying kham-phet* sex worker is faced with a reality that is grim, even by the usually grim standards of sex work faced by natal females. Faced with pressures to take bar fines[23] and have sex with customers, they are left open to the risk of contracting sexually transmitted diseases, given that many customers are unwilling to use condoms[24] and that they may be the receptive participant in anal intercourse. Sex work, though widespread throughout Thailand, remains illegal. Police harassment can be a major problem, especially for those working on the streets. The widespread and misinformed police practice of using condom possession as presumed evidence of sex work has only added to the problem, discouraging the carrying of condoms by street sex workers. The less-attractive and older the *phu-ying kham-phet* is, the less power she has to insist on use of a condom anyway. Migrants from the countryside, often less educated and less well-informed than their urban counterparts, may be particularly at risk. Drug and alcohol use, disturbingly common among those involved in sex work, exacerbate the problem of unsafe sex.[25] Anti-impotence drugs used by customers add to the problem further, raising the risk of anal abrasions through repeated intercourse of long duration. For a more detailed discussion of the involvement of Thai (and other Asian) transwomen in sex work, see Winter and King (forthcoming).

Whether engaged in sex work or not, many *phu-ying kham-phet* find that intimate relationships go nowhere. They commonly report that partners, typically identifying as *phu-chai thae* ("real men" in Thai), leave them for relationships with women, with whom they can get married, have children, and thereby satisfy their expectations, and those of their parents, for them to enjoy a full family life. As Jenkins and others note, "The dream of many is to find a 'husband' and live their lives as wives. This seems to occur very seldom, however, and many katoey are quite cynical and sad about their chances at a normal life" (2005, 20). The difficulties are well illustrated in the quotation below:

> If I love a person I will love him completely. I will always take care of him. But I know he will turn away from me—he will disregard me— when he compares me with a real woman. I have to be the runner-up. I must try to deal with this situation. (Phi, university student and *phu-ying kham-phet*, Chiang Mai University, from Costa and Matzner 2007, 71)

My impression listening to *phu-ying kham-phet* talk about their romantic lives is that each broken relationship exacerbates insecurity. The result is often that a *phu-ying kham-phet* enters new relationships grasping at any sign of commitment (or any possibility thereof) in her partner, dispensing with the use of condoms long before caution would advise. Indeed, this may be partly responsible for the low usage of condoms apparent in research into *phu-ying kham-phet* sexual health.[26]

HIV research focusing on *phu-ying kham-phet* is scarce, a fact that has been described as "stunning" in one report (Jenkins et al. 2005, 5). Nonetheless, enough research exists to cause concern. Another recent study put HIV infection at 17.6 percent for *phu-ying kham-phet* (described in the study as "transgendered males"), compared with 15.3 percent among other MSM, and 11.4 percent among male sex workers.[27] One NGO head has even noted that "[i]t is quite probable that transgenders have higher infection rates than intravenous drug users in Thailand."[28] Yet Thai HIV/AIDS services have tended to focus on female sex workers and, more recently, gay men. Very little in the way of HIV/AIDS education or health care has been focused on the needs of the *phu-ying kham-phet*,[29] whose sexual patterns may little resemble either of the other two groups mentioned.

The absence of HIV/AIDS services intended specifically for transpeople reflects a more general absence of gender-related health services for them.

Apart from the profusion of doctors offering (to varying standards) cosmetic and genital surgeries (see Aren Aizura's chapter in this volume), little general health care intended specifically for transpeople is available. The widespread use of feminizing hormones by *phu-ying kham-phet* proceeds largely without any medical monitoring.[30] A research finding showing lower quality of life among hormone-takers (as opposed to non-hormone takers) gives cause for concern (Suja et al. 2005).

The problems in service delivery described above are just part of the health-care problem for *phu-ying kham-phet*. Government health workers are often seen as discriminatory, as described in the following first person account cited in Jenkins et al.:

> Once I had a motorbike accident. I was wounded and cried. They [medical staff] told me to be stable (and) try not to move. After that, the nurse yelled at me about getting injured and coming to the hospital. The doctor was nice but the nurse was impolite. She said that I deserved it because I drove fast. Then she cursed me, saying 'damn *katoey*' (18-year-old anonymous *phu-ying kham-phet*). (Jenkins et al. 2005, 15)

Moreover, *khon kham-phet* forced to leave home and migrate to the cities encounter another problem. Like all other Thais, each is allocated to a specific health-care centre for the so-called "30 baht" Universal Health Care scheme, a national programme, and migrants to the cities may not have the papers that would enable them to access the scheme in the place to which they have migrated (Jenkins et al. 2005, 22).

As if all this were not enough, all these challenges—in regard to privacy, employment, and legal status, as well as social and economic marginalization, sex work and related risks to mental and physical well-being, and the absence of appropriate health care—are sometimes exacerbated by estrangement from the family,[31] as well as by experience of sexual and physical violence, including that perpetrated by police (see Jenkins et al. 2005, 15–16). All these experiences contribute to a general malaise within the *phu-ying kham-phet* community. *Phu-ying kham-phet* commonly anticipate retro-transition back to a male gender presentation at a later date,[32] often become involved in drug use (Jenkins et al. 2005, 16–17)[33] and display a worrying propensity for suicidal thought and behaviour.[34] Little is known about the effect upon transmen, but one can assume that they, too, find their life circumstances less than ideal.

Transprejudice, Pathology, and Global Psychiatry

The picture I have painted is one of broad and sometimes systematic discrimination, oppression, and injustice against *khon kham-phet*. Why does this situation persist? One reason may be that, as in many other Asian countries, a culture of human rights is relatively poorly developed in the Thai case. It is worth recalling that Thailand only acceded to the two treaties discussed in this chapter in the late 1990s. Another reason is that in Thailand, as in other places in Asia, the fight for *khon kham-phet* rights has often been subsumed within the fight for gay and lesbian rights.[35] This has been both a blessing and curse. On one hand, *khon kham-phet* have benefited from alignment with a large and comparatively well-organized pressure group. However, their own specific concerns may have sometimes been overlooked. The construction of a non-discriminatory vocabulary of transgenderism, such as is used in this chapter, is an important step towards the effective promotion of the distinctive interests of *khon kham-phet*.

Of course, the fight for rights is necessary only where those rights are withheld. Seen in this light, the key question in regard to Thailand is, "Where does Thai transprejudice come from?" I recently led an international team of researchers to look at transprejudice in seven countries; the United States, the United Kingdom, China, the Philippines, Malaysia, Singapore, and Thailand.[36] The sample totalled 841 undergraduate students, all of whom completed a questionnaire that examined their attitudes and beliefs regarding transwomen, and whose responses represented a continuum running from transprejudice to "transacceptance". We identified five underlying components of transacceptance-transprejudice. They were: (1) mental pathology, the presumption that transwomen were mentally ill; (2) denial as women, meaning denial of the idea that transwomen are women or should be treated and have rights as such; (3) social rejection, the rejection of overall social contact with transwomen; (4) peer rejection, the rejection of any contact with transwomen among one's peer group, and (5) sexual deviance, the idea that transwomen are in some way sexually deviant.

Mental pathology was the most powerful underlying component, determining overall transacceptance-transprejudice more than any other factor. Moreover, it was closely correlated with all the other factors.[37] Across the seven countries as a whole, those who believed transwomen were mentally ill also tended to deny them any status and rights as women, reject social contact with them (overall and in their peer groups), and believe that they were sexually deviant. *In short, the presumption of mental pathology was closely linked to prejudicial attitudes that, expressed in behaviour, would result in discrimination against transwomen.*

What about Thailand? A large number of the Thai student respondents adopted a mental pathologization stance towards *phu-ying kham-phet*. Around half (51 percent) believed they are men who have something wrong with their minds (*pen phu-chai thi mi khwam-phit-pokati thang-jit-jai*); a third (31 percent) believed they have an unstable personality (*mi bukkhalikkaphap mai nae-norn*), and a quarter (28 percent) believed they needed psychological help (*torng-kan khwam-chuay-leua thang-jit-jai*). A smaller number (14 percent) went further, claiming they had a weak character (*mi bukkhalik orn-ae*). A substantial number of these young and educated Thais thus presumed *phu-ying kham-phet* have something mentally wrong with them—a stance towards transwomen familiar to many in the West (for example, in the United States) and, as we have seen, the official view of the Thai military until the recent change of policy. The links between mental pathology beliefs and the various other components of transprejudice were evident. Importantly, Thais who believed *phu-ying kham-phet* were mentally ill also tended to reject any social contact with them (among peers or more generally), and believed that they were sexually deviant. There was also an indication of a tendency to deny them treatment and rights as women.[38]

Given Thailand's previously gender-pluralist culture (Peletz 2006), with well-established *khon kham-phet* themes both historically (spirit mediums and healers) and culturally (Buddhist gender transformations, Northeastern Thai creation myths),[39] it is worth asking the question, "Where does a presumption of mental pathology come from?" In the West, the mainstream medical view is that gender identity variance is a mental disorder. Large numbers of transpeople are diagnosed as experiencing Gender Identity Disorder, often abbreviated as GID (in the American Psychiatric Association's manual)[40] or transsexualism (in the World Health Organization manual, 1992). That so many Western transpeople submit to these diagnoses, despite, in most cases, believing themselves mentally healthy (and appearing so to others), is a reflection of the role that mental-health professionals play in controlling access to transgender medical care. Without a professional diagnosis of GID or transsexualism, a person is often denied access to feminizing hormones and/or sex-reassignment surgery.

This mental pathology model has become subject to mounting critical scrutiny. In North America, transpeople, as well as researchers and clinicians, have increasingly called for reform, concentrating their efforts on the GID diagnosis promulgated by the American Psychiatric Association. While some have called for a revision of the diagnostic guidelines, others have sought the removal of the psychiatric diagnosis altogether.[41] Importantly, it is often argued that the GID diagnosis, by classifying the person as mentally disordered, ironically serves to exacerbate the intolerance and stigma already experienced by transpeople and undermines their mental health. It does this more than many other psychiatric diagnoses because it involves a pathologization of one's very identity (in contrast, for example, to diagnosis of obsessive-compulsive behaviour, which involves simply a pathologization of a person's behaviour).

Mainstream Western views in psychiatry may be shifting slowly. For example, a document recently issued by the United Kingdom Royal College of Psychiatrists states that terms such as transsexualism and GID are clinical labels for "atypical gender development", adding that "the experience of this dissonance between the sex appearance, and the personal sense of being male or female, is termed gender dysphoria. The diagnosis should not be taken as an indication of mental illness. Instead, the phenomenon is most constructively viewed as a rare but nonetheless valid variation in the human condition, which is considered unremarkable in some cultures" (Royal College of Psychiatrists 2006, Section 2.2).

Findings from our seven-nation study, noted above, add weight to the claim that mental pathologization adds to the stigma and discrimination experienced by transpeople. It underlines that the phenomenon is not limited to the developed societies of North America and Western Europe, but is also found in Southeast Asia, and, we may extrapolate, possibly elsewhere.

Of course, circumspection is needed here. Correlations do not imply any specific line of causation, particularly at the level of the individual. For many people a mental-illness view of transpeople may promote transprejudice. For others, the reverse may happen; existing transprejudice may promote the view that transpeople are mentally ill, and current views within mainstream psychiatry will provide them with support for their belief.[42] Regardless of the direction of causality, mental pathologization clearly spells bad news for transpeople worldwide. Whether it prompts or rationalizes transprejudice, it arguably facilitates the social and economic exclusion of transpeople, impairs their mental and physical well-being, and contributes to genuinely worrying pathologies of social isolation, social anxiety, depression, helplessness, hopelessness, and self-harm.[43]

Few if any of the undergraduate students in our seven-nation study had probably ever read DSM–IV, ICD–10, or any other psychiatric text. Even fewer of their compatriots would have done so. However, worldwide, ideas about the pathology of gender identity variance percolate into the general community, for example, by way of magazine articles, TV documentaries, and the Internet. In Thailand these ideas have been disseminated by another means—military service. As seen above, a large number of *phu-ying kham-phet* carry *Sor. Dor. 43* military discharge papers stating them to be victims of "a disease causing permanent psychological damage", a commonly understood reference to their gender identity variance. The effect has been to cultivate an impression, apparently absent in earlier Thai culture, that these individuals are mentally ill (and, of course, undermining *phu-ying kham-phet* chances of leading a normal life).

The implications of our seven-nation study are clear. *In Thailand (as elsewhere in the world) the idea that transpeople are mentally ill serves to promote or support transprejudice,* with probable effects on the social and economic marginalization of transpeople, and consequent effects on their well-being and health, including their mental condition.

Clearly, additional forces beyond psychiatry promote or support transprejudice. Across much of the Judaeo-Christian and Islamic worlds, religion probably plays an important role.[44] In Thailand, *phu-ying kham-phet* involvement in the sex industry no doubt reinforces stereotypical views that they are sexually provocative and sexually motivated.[45] Such ideas are unlikely to promote acceptance (especially as women) in a patriarchally conservative society that values sexual propriety in its women.[46] Moreover, the removal of "Gender Identity Disorder" and "Transsexualism" from the psychiatric manuals would, in any case, be unlikely to lead to a demise of the idea that transpeople are mentally ill. The case of homosexuality is instructive in this regard. Internationally, large numbers of people evidently persist in regarding it as a mental illness, even though it was gradually removed from psychology and counselling manuals in steps from as long ago as 1973.[47]

Notwithstanding these considerations, the message is clear. In the West the idea that transpeople are by their nature psychologically damaged is under sustained attack. Thai *khon kham-phet* appear to have an interest in the outcome of that struggle. With the American Psychiatric Association now engaged in a further revision of its Diagnostic Manual (the first since DSM–IV in 1994), the World Health Organization revising its International Classification of Diseases (the first since ICD–10 in 1992, see WHO [1992]), and the World Professional Association for Transgender Health (WPATH) setting about revising its widely used "Harry Benjamin Guidelines" for the mental and physical care of transpeople, it seems that interest may never have been greater.

The *khon kham-phet* of Thailand are becoming better organized, both socially and politically, within the existing Thai LGBT movement, and through their own transgender groups. They have already achieved victories in the domestic Thai context, for example, the *Sor. Dor. 43* issue, and reform of the rape laws. They have also linked with their counterparts across the region, playing an active role in setting up the Asia-Pacific Transgender Network (APTN). I believe that they also have a role to play in the resolution of international debates on the status of transgenderism and transsexualism.

Notes

Chapter 1

1. Information provided by Wipas Wimonsate, Medical Research Technologist/MSM Community Associate, Thailand Ministry of Public Health — United States Centers for Disease Control (MoPH — US CDC) Collaboration.
2. Or. Tor. Kor. is the Thai acronym for *Ongkan Talat pheua Kasettakorn*, the Marketing Agency for Agricultural Workers, a government agency whose office building is near this locale.
3. Source: National Economic and Social Development Board. Cited in the *Bangkok Post*, "Price pressure on rise, says NESDB", 27 May 2008, p. B1.
4. Chang Noi (a pseudonym), "Thailand's huge rich-poor divide", *The Nation*, 18 August 2003, p. 5A.
5. amfAR (Foundation for AIDS Research) MSM Initiative, "As AIDS conference opens, amfAR releases report exposing global failure to address HIV among MSM", media.amfar.org (accessed 5 August 2008).

Chapter 2

1. At that time the subject of transvestite Muay Thai boxers was not at the centre of my research, and the data here are largely from my field notes, in which I recorded my discussions with Thais about the phenomenon and their perceptions of it from local media coverage. Unfortunately, I have not had the opportunity to conduct a detailed analysis of local press and media accounts of the phenomenon of Thai *kathoey* kickboxers.
2. *Nong* Tum was, for example, invited in July 1999 to be a guest on a variety show on an Argentine television channel. Furthermore, he has been the subject of several articles in the foreign press, such as *The New York Times*, 4 April 1998, "Bangkok journal; Was that a lady I saw you boxing?" www.nytimes.com (accessed 10 December 2009); *National Geographic*, 25 March 2004, "Thai 'Ladyboy' kickboxer is gender-bending knockout", http://news.nationalgeographic.com (accessed 10 December 2009).
3. *Bangkok Post*, 17 February 2004, "Ruthless transvestite Apinya to debut against US boxer", www.bangkokpost.com (accessed 8 December 2009); *Bangkok Post*, 29 February 2004, "Apinya kicks into top gear", www.bangkokpost.com (accessed 8 December 2009); *The Nation*, 18 February 2004, "Another kratoey steps into the ring", http://www.nationmultimedia.com (accessed 8 December 2009); *The Nation*, 25 February 2004, "Transvestite fighter a winner", http://www.nationmultimedia.com (accessed 8 December

2009); *The Nation*, 9 June 2004, "No handbags allowed", http://www.nationmultimedia. com (accessed 8 December 2009).

4. *The Nation*, 26 February 1998, http://www.nationmultimedia.com (accessed 8 December 2009); *Bangkok Post*, 25 February 1998, "Transvestite slugger snatches manly points win at Lumpini", www.bangkokpost.com (accessed 8 December 2009); *Bangkok Post*, 1 March 1998, "Transvestite slugger dispels all doubt of his 'manhood'", www.bangkokpost.com (accessed 8 December 2009); *Bangkok Post*, 18 March 1998, "Parinya's fight delayed for a week", www. bangkokpost.com (accessed 8 December 2009); *Bangkok Post*, 29 March 1998, "Parinya too good for Danish challenger", www.bangkokpost.com (accessed 8 December 2009).

5. *Bangkok Post*, 3 March 1999, "Boxer prepares for new title challenge", www.bangkokpost. com (accessed 8 December 2009); *Bangkok Post*, 5 March 1999, "Is all change for better?" www.bangkokpost.com (accessed 8 December 2009); *Bangkok Post*, 9 December 1999, "Boxer's operation", www.bangkokpost.com (accessed 8 December 2009).

6. *The Nation*, 22 February 2006, "Nong Tum to have another go in the ring", www. nationmultimedia.com (accessed 8 December 2009); 23 February 2006, "Sex-change boxer back in the ring", www.nationmultimedia.com (accessed 8 December 2009).

7. The roundhouse kick is renowned to be the most devastating kick technique among the various martial arts. It is a chin blow that necessitates a rotation of the entire upper body. The movement is initiated by the shoulders (as in a rugby pass) and takes in successively the hips and then the leg, such that the kick will be delivered with maximum speed and power.

8. *The Nation*, 18 February 2004, "Another kratoey steps into the ring", http://www. nationmultimedia.com (accessed 8 December 2009).

9. *The Nation*, 26 February 1998, http://www.nationmultimedia.com (accessed 8 December 2009); "Transvestite slugger snatches manly points win at Lumpini", *Bangkok Post*, 25 February 1998, www.bangkokpost.com (accessed 8 December 2009).

Chapter 3

1. Thai New Wave Cinema is an unofficial label denoting movies produced since the Asian financial crisis of 1997. Dominated by advertising-based directors such as Nonzee Nimibutr and Pen-ek Ratanaruang, the strong visual style of these movies brought Thai audiences back into that nation's cinemas after a period of relative decline for Thai cinema.

2. *Tomboys* are masculine-dressing homosexual women, whereas their feminine counterparts are called *dee* (from the English "la_dy_").

3. Interview, Bangkok, 11 November 2007.

4. In 2005, the Thai film market was worth 4 billion baht a year and was made up of 60 percent Hollywood films, 35 percent Thai productions, and the rest comprising East Asian and other movies (Bamrung 2006).

5. In 2004, Tai Entertainment joined forces with GMM Pictures and Hub Ho Hin Films to form GMM Tai Hub (GTH). The chief executive of the newly formed company was quick to clarify that GTH was seeking a forty percent share of the domestic film market and thus "might not invest in alternative movie projects that could be risky in terms of profits" (Parinyaporn 2004).

6. Since there is no authority in Thailand that accurately reports box-office figures, the numbers used here are based on information circulated by the studios themselves and should not be taken as exact. However, they put the success of the films in a statistical perspective.

7. This reflects Jackson's findings about different degrees of *kathoey* acceptance. "The transgender males most criticised . . . are those considered loud-mouthed, aggressive or

lewd; qualities widely regarded as low-class. . . . In contrast, the most admired *kathoey* are those who appropriate and exhibit a high standard of feminine beauty" (1999, 230).

8. DVD, Bonus material.

9. For a more comprehensive discussion of *Tropical Malady*, see Ferrari, 2006, 47–62.

10. Films are coded "P" for "promotion" of educational films that all Thais are encouraged to see and "G" for general audiences. Age-restricted movies are divided into the categories "13+", "15+", "18+", and "20+" for audiences of the indicated age and above.

11. See www.bangkokpost.com/entertainment/movie/33160/learning-and-adapting (accessed 21 February 2010).

12. The sources for these audience responses are my own observations and conversations with other viewers that corresponded to media reports and Internet discussions. See http://bkkmindscape.blogspot.com/2007/11/love-of-siam-reaction-part-1.html (accessed 14 November 2007).

13. Pasuk Phongpaichit, speaking in the question-and-answer session at the seminar "Coup, Capital and Crown" on 13 December 2007. Information obtained through personal attendance.

14. The media impact on homosexual identities has been highlighted by Tom Boellstorff (2003, 33) in the case of Indonesia, where 95 percent of his informants cited mass media as the means by which they first understood themselves through the local concepts of *lesbi* or *gay*.

Chapter 4

1. The question of modernity's historicity and, in particular, its current and future status is notoriously vexed. Contrary to accounts that would proclaim modernity a process that has finished or even collapsed, this chapter proceeds from the understanding that modernity is by definition incomplete and ongoing. This is not so much in the classic Habermasian sense of an assertion of the continuing relevance and promise of Western modernity qua post-Enlightenment rationality, but, rather, more in the sense that the critical reconceptualization of modernity as a constellation of overlapping and competing processes and histories returns modernity as plural and continuously renewing. "To think in terms of 'alternative modernities'," writes Dilip Parameshwar Gaonkar (2001, 1), "is to admit that modernity is inescapable and to desist from speculations about the end of modernity. Born in and of the West some centuries ago under specific socio-historical conditions, modernity is now everywhere. It has arrived not suddenly but slowly, bit by bit, over the *longue durée*— awakened by contact; transported through commerce; administered by empires, bearing colonial inscriptions; propelled by nationalism, and now increasingly steered by global media, migration, and capital. And it continues to 'arrive and emerge', as always in opportunistic fragments . . . but no longer from the West alone."

2. Drawing on the revisionist critical theories of Oskar Negt and Alexander Kluge, Miriam Hansen explicitly argues for cinema as an adjunct or alternative public sphere. Cinema, she asserts, "functions both as a public sphere of its own, defined by specific relations of representation and reception, and as part of a larger social horizon, defined by other media, by overlapping local, national and global, face-to-face and deterritorialized structures of public life" (Hansen 1993, 198).

3. An alternative spelling of this director's name is Youngyooth Thongkonthun.

4. This director's name is also sometimes spelt as Poj Anon.

5. In this sense, as much as *Love of Siam* actively subverts the teen film's central convention of heteronormative coupling, it faithfully adheres to the genre's other core conventions,

notably an accent on *bildungsroman*-style narrative and melodramatic characterization. Studies of the teen film suggest that, for all its diversity, many, if not most, entries in the genre share a central concern with the dramatization of modern adolescence and its specific tensions and dilemmas, primarily the passage to adulthood and fully socialized identity played out, more often than not, as a classic coming-of-age narrative (Shary 2005). Rooted in the structural liminality, or in-betweenness, of adolescence, the coming-of-age narrative of the teen film makes a metaphor of the transition from childhood to adulthood as a symbolic drama of self-becoming, a crucial aspect of which is the development of sexual agency and the search for a stable sexual selfhood out of the irruptions and ambiguities of incipient teen sexual activity.

6. An earlier study by Wimal Dissanayake suggests that this type of accented familialism is, in fact, a defining element of Asian cinematic melodrama and one that serves to distinguish it from Western modes. Where "in Western melodramas", he writes, "it is the individual self in relation to the family that is explored . . . in Asian melodramas it is the familial self that is the focus of interest" (Dissanayake 1993, 4).

7. As an indication, below is a sample of comments from a single thread sourced virtually at random from on an English-language forum:

> "I don't get the ending! Why does it end that way? When he asked his mom about making decisions . . . didn't that mean that it was ok for him to do what he wants? Shouldn't it have ended differently? I am completely lost . . ."

> "I was loving the movie and everything seemed like we would get a happy ending but when Tong says . . . what he says, I was floored. Yes, I don't think it should have ended that way either because everything leading up to it made you think otherwise but, hey, I did not direct it. However, it was beautifully done and I have to say it took me awhile to stop crying after the end of the movie. I just did not understand or expect the ending."

> "I rewatched it twice today and just can't figure out why the hell it ended the way it did . . . made no kind of sense. Everything points to them being together . . . and when Tong is running to hear him sing, when he is smiling when the song is again actually being sung directly to him and when he runs through the crowd to catch up to Mew . . . and then you have to hear 'I cannot be with you as your boyfriend.' . . . WTF !! !!!!!!!!!!!!!!!!!!!!!!!!!!!!!!!!!!!!!!! I get so pissed and angry because it makes no damn sense. Everything that happened in the movie did NOT lead up to that ending."

> "The Love of Siam—Discuss." *Subscene*, 13–18 March 2008. http://subscene.com/forums/t/7433.aspx (accessed 27 April 2010).

8. Even Mew ultimately ends up in a position of family-coded queerness, assuming the very role performed by his grandmother in the prologue sequence as guardian of the family home and keeper of the romantic flame. In the film's beginning, a young Mew is shown having been left behind in Bangkok by his parents, who have relocated upcountry. Explaining that his role is to care for her, his grandmother says to Mew that she must stay on in the family home, and he by her side, to tend vigil should the spirit of her husband, Mew's grandfather, return. The film's final scene, with a teary-eyed Mew sitting in his house as he looks into an uncertain but hope-filled future of waiting for love's return, effectively puts Mew in this same role. It is a scene that equally buys into the insistent valorization of suffering as ennobling and life-affirming, identified by Dissanayake (1993, 4–5) and others as a distinguishing aspect of Asian film melodramas and one that is particularly prevalent in Thai melodrama. See also Serhat Ünaldi's account in this volume of the prominence of the moral value of "suffering" in early Thai queer films.

Chapter 5

1. This chapter is an edited version of a paper I wrote for the Southeast Asia Consortium on Gender, Sexuality, and Health at Mahidol University, in 2005. My research for Mahidol focused on the structuring process between gay places in Bangkok and performances of Thai gay identities.

2. The gay saunas that I describe are similar to gay bathhouses in North America. Thais have borrowed the expression "gay sauna", or *sauna ga*y in Thai, from gay communities in Australia, the United Kingdom, and Europe.

3. There has been considerable debate among scholars of queer genders and sexualities in Thailand on the new identities such as gay, *tom*, *dee*, etc. in the Thai sex and gender order. For further discussion on these debates see Jackson (1999a, 2000), Morris (1994, 1997), Sinnott (2004), and Storer (1999a, 1999b).

4. I thank Tong Tawalwongsri, a graduate student at Thammasat University, for interpreting and then transcribing the interviews.

5. For a fuller description of types of gay business establishments, see "The Purple Baht: History and Types of Thai Gay Businesses", *The Men of Thailand*. http://www.floatinglotus.com/tmot/gaybiz.html (accessed 1 November 2008).

6. The built environment of the gay sauna primarily facilitates and hosts anonymous sexual activities of various forms between men. The constructed landscape is a highly sexualized terrain suggesting an exclusive focus on sex. Typically, it consists of "fantasy environments" that recreate erotic situations that may be illegal or dangerous when performed in public locations. Orgy rooms encourage group sex, while "glory holes" recreate the setting of public toilets, and mazes take the place of bushes and undergrowth in public parks. Steam rooms and gyms are modelled after gym locker areas, while video rooms recreate the balconies and back rows of movie theatres. Sauna customers are regulated by a set of situationally defined norms, including restrictions on modes of communication, styles of behaviour, and regulations about the use of physical space. For example, different areas are designated as being either for sex or a "sex-free zone" (e.g. the television lounge, the area in the main entry, and the locker rooms). Sex occurs—at varying rates and to varying degrees—either inside private cubicles, in semi-private facilities such as the dry saunas and steam rooms, or in open orgy rooms, and, depending on the number of customers, in communal open facilities such as the pool. Bangkok gay saunas also regularly feature promotions such as discounted rates for students or early visitors, no-towel nights, underwear nights, and holiday parties.

7. At the time of writing, there were more than thirty gay saunas throughout the Bangkok metropolitan area.

8. Thai perceptions of class status do not necessarily mean actual socio-economic status. According to Jackson (1995), assignations of "upper" or "lower" class in the Bangkok gay community refer as much to a person's presentation or perceptions of style and may also reflect and individual's class aspirations as much as actual class status as such.

9. Siam, an abbreviation for Siam Square, is a downtown shopping precinct noted for its up-market youth-fashion stores. It is a very popular hang-out for middle-class Bangkok youth. See Brett Farmer's account of this precinct in his chapter here on the film *Love of Siam*.

10. The site of the old The Babylon has since been converted into a restaurant and a series of condominiums.

11. While the business name of the sauna is "The Babylon", the venue is widely known in gay communities in both Thailand and internationally simply as "Babylon".

12. See, for instance, the accounts of The Babylon on gay web sites such as www.dreadedned. com and www.squirt.org.

13. This idea was suggested by Gary Atkins (2005). Although Babel and Babylon are two different stories in the Old Testament of the Bible, where Babylon is represented as a city of debauchery, and while it is often associated with harlotry and whoredom, "the story of Babel as a cosmopolitan place is said to have inspired the architecture of The Babylon sauna.

14. The Babylon is close to the major area of Sathorn Road, which was one of four key zones of the city identified by international property consultancies in the 1980s as sites for developing high-status residential and business districts (Askew 2002). The neighbourhood of The Babylon is now composed of luxury condominiums, consular and embassy offices, and up-market residences. In recent years, the quiet neighbourhood has been gentrified into a gay residential place for upper middle-class Thai gay men and foreign gay expatriates. This information is based on the impressions of my informants as to the composition of the neighbourhood of The Babylon, as well as information from gay Filipino informants and other foreign expatriates who live in the condominiums that line Sathon Soi 1.

15. I borrow the idea of "homonormativity" from a lecture delivered by Dr. Martin Manalansan at the University of the Philippines in 2005, wherein he explained and critiqued the concepts of heteronormativity and homonormativity. According to Manalansan, homonormativity refers to the global landscape of Western gay culture that has created the sense that it is ever-present and has in fact entered the mainstream public domain, appropriating heteronormative values.

16. There is no evidence that Thai men who patronize The Babylon actually come from middle-class backgrounds. However, the projection of middle-class cultural capital is evident from Thai patrons of The Babylon, including those who were identified by my informants as "money boys". This is thus an instance of the performance of a class-inflected gay identity. As Tom Boellstorff (2007) notes, and as detailed by Peter Jackson in his opening chapters in this volume, Southeast Asian gay identities are inflected with an aspirational middle-class caché.

17. This is a reference to Tata Young's song of the same title.

Chapter 6

1. See http://learners.in.th/blog/mas-comed/62426 (accessed 1 April 2010).

2. The borrowed English word "stroke" here means masturbation.

3. Zeed-sard, written as *sit-sat* in the official Thai romanization, is an exclamation used to express intense pleasure, including sexual pleasure.

4. The study was originally reported in Thai in Ronnapoom Samakkeekarom, Pimpawun Boonmongkon and Wachira Chantong (2008).

5. These figures are based on observation of roughly 200 users in four chat rooms for 12 nights in three consecutive monthly periods, totalling approximately 7,200 cases. Some of these cases may have constituted regular users logging on several times.

6. Tha Nam Non is the Nonthaburi Pier, located in Nonthaburi Province in Central Thailand.

7. This means: "From Ramkhamhaeng Road, Soi 65 [in eastern Bangkok]; age 16, height 173 cm, weight 65 kg."

8. *Chak wao* (literally "to fly a kite") is Thai slang meaning "to masturbate".

9. *Ma Du K.* literally means, "come see p. (pricks)". The English letter "K" here stands for the romanized spelling of *khuay*, "cock, prick".

10. *Na-rak* means "cute".

11. *Krapok* means "testicles".
12. Y 2 K refers to the pre-millennium rumour of a collapse of computers worldwide in the year 2000. The letter "K" also refers to the Thai word *khuay*, "cock", as noted above.
13. *Kradae* means "to be affected".
14. Krung Thep is the Thai name for Bangkok.
15. Chiang Mai is a province and city in northern Thailand.
16. Isan denotes the northeastern region of Thailand.
17. For example, the name of the chat room Gay Ha Fan ("Gays Looking for a Partner") would communicate to experienced users that they have to divulge their age, weight, height, location, and sexual identity to comply with the rituals at work in this chat room, whereas in Gay Stroke, for example, this would not be required.
18. An IP (Internet Protocol) address is a series of numbers that identifies which particular computer or network is connected to the Internet.
19. A *wai* is a traditional Thai greeting that consists of placing one's hands, palms together, before one's face and bowing slightly. It is performed to show respect to a senior.
20. IM, "instant messaging", is an Internet service that allows for the quick exchange of written messages.

Chapter 7

1. This chapter forms part of a doctoral dissertation on the valorization of travel metaphors within gender-variant discourses. It is the product of many conversations with people interested in gender-variant travel practices, inside and outside of Thailand. I am grateful to Fran Martin, Vera Mackie and Peter A. Jackson; and in Thailand to Prempreeda Pramoj Na Ayutthaya, Nantiya Sukontapatipark, and Sitthiphan Boonyapisomparn for offering their expert knowledge on *kathoey* health care.
2. The expressions trans and gender-variant are used here to describe any cross-gender identifications or practices. Trans men include those who were assigned female at birth and who now live as men. Trans women include those who were assigned male at birth and who now live as women.
3. Interviews were conducted with trans women from the United Kingdom, the Netherlands, the United States, and Australia who obtained surgery at Thai gender reassignment clinics in 2006 and 2007 in Thailand and Australia.
4. The manager asked to remain anonymous. Interview, 15 July 2006.
5 In this chapter I use GRS, gender reassignment surgery, to denote both genital and non-genital procedures. It is sometimes referred to as SRS (sex reassignment surgery). The trans women participants in this project underwent many different surgical procedures, including castration, or orchiectomy; vaginoplasty, the construction of a neo-vagina; breast augmentation, or augmentation mammoplasty (AM), and facial feminization surgery (FFS).
6. See the English-language web site of Dr. Chettawut Tulayaphanich, www.chet-plasticsurgery.com (accessed 19 May 2007).
7. According to Dr. Preecha's estimates in a 2006 interview, less than one percent of patients at the Preecha Aesthetic Institute were Thai. The Suporn Clinic's manager noted in an interview that the vast majority of Dr. Suporn's patients were non-Thai. The Phuket Plastic Surgery Center had a clientele that was around 95 percent non-Thai clientele in 2006. I follow Thai etiquette in referring to the Thai surgeons by their given [names.
8. I use pseudonyms to identify research participants in this chapter to preserve their anonymity.

9. The Thai word *farang* here is generally understood to mean white non-Thais, rather than foreign visitors from other regions in Asia or other non-white, non-Thai people. To avoid any suggestion of Eurocentrism, in this chapter I use Thai-language terms to write about Thai gender-variant identities and practices. *Kathoey* can refer to male-to-female transgender or transsexual categories (Jackson 2003c, paragraph 2), but historically it has had many different connotations, including male homosexuality, a "third sex or gender" (*phet thi-sam*), and cross-dressers who are assigned male or female at birth (Jackson 1997b, 171). "Ladyboy" is a Thai coinage of English words to mean *kathoey*. *Sao praphet sorng* is a Thai term meaning "second type of woman". It is used by many gender-variant Thais to identify themselves in preference to the term *kathoey*.

10. Interview, Sydney, 18 February 2007.

11. Interview, Bangkok, 18 June 2006.

12. Interview, Brisbane, 30 July 2006.

13. "Trans masculine" here refers to masculine gender-variant identities or practices. Anecdotally, chest-reconstruction surgery is popular with *toms* and available in urban and provincial hospitals.

14. An excellent Foucauldian analysis of the medicalization of gender variance in the WPATH Standards of Care, as well as psychiatric frameworks such as the *Diagnostic and statistical manual of mental disorders*, can be found in Spade (2006).

15. Interview, 18 June 2006.

16. Thirty percent was the figure cited by Sitthiphan Boonyapisompam (Hua), a *sao praphet sorng* activist and health worker who coordinated a Pattaya-based drop-in centre for *sao praphet sorng* and *kathoeys*. Interview, Bangkok, 17 January 2008.

17. Interview, 18 June 2006.

18. Interview, Dr. Suporn, 24 June 2006.

19. Personal communication with the clinic manager at the Suporn Clinic, June 2006.

20. "Medical tourism for Saudi vacationers in focus." *Arab News*, 3 August 2006. www.arabnews.com/?page=1&section=0&article=85985&d=3&m=8&y=2006&pix=kingdom.jpg&category=Kingdom (accessed 1 October 2008).

21. The difference in estimates here may reflect the fact that most non-Thais who receive medical treatment in any given year are expatriate workers or tourists who did not travel to the country for medical purposes.

22. This fantasy is not limited to heterosexuality. Similar fantasies operate anecdotally within gay "rice queen" portrayals of Thai gay men. A rice queen is a white man who desires "Asian" men as partners.

23. Tourism Authority of Thailand, www.tatnews.org/emagazine/1983.asp (accessed 14 June 2007).

24. This is one Thai tourist-marketing strategy amongst many. Other narratives stress different aspects of Thailand, such as the "rugged adventure" of visiting hill tribes in the north of the country, or eco-adventures that promise to reveal the "real situation" to the tourist.

25. Interview, 18 June 2006.

26. Interview, 16 July 2006.

27. www.phuket-plasticsurgery.com (accessed 25 May 2008).

28. www.hygeiabeauty.com/sex-change.html (accessed 23 May 2008).

29. Interview, 19 February 2007.

30. Interview, 17 December 2007.

31. Interview, 17 December 2007.

32. The convention that one must obtain genital surgery to be a "real" man or woman has been

soundly critiqued within trans theory, beginning with Sandy Stone's "Post-transsexual manifesto" (1992).

33. See "Rebecca's life on Mars", http://hometown.aol.com/mches48837/ (accessed 12 July 2007).

34. http://hometown.aol.com/mches48837 (accessed 12 July 2007).

35. This situation seems consistent with more generalized labour relations in Thailand, particularly the ideological power of *bun khun* (reciprocal obligation), or family obligations, between employers and employees. Under the terms of *bun khun*, employers occupy a similar symbolic status to parents, and employees occupy the position of children who owe their employer-parents loyalty and obedience. See Mills (1999, 122–124).

Chapter 8

1. An earlier version of this chapter was published in 2007 in *South East Asia Research* (15 [2], 281–99). I would like to thank Andrei Aksana for taking the time to discuss his writing with me in Jakarta in December 2006. Thanks also to Pauline Khng, Sarah Hicks, Rachel Harrison, and an anonymous reviewer for *South East Asia Research* for their comments on earlier drafts of this article.

2. All quotations from this novel are taken from the 2004 edition. Translations are my own.

3. The book is now in its 4th printing, and sales have exceeded fifty thousand copies, which would suggest as many as 200,000 readers (Interview with Aksana, 10 December 2006). Aksana is probably one of the best-selling fiction writers in Indonesia today.

4. Following Tom Boellstorff, I recognize the Indonesian terms *gay* and *lesbi* to be distinct from the English "gay" and "lesbian" (2005, 8). The Indonesian term *normal*, which is used by *gay* and *lesbi* Indonesians, refers to dominant understandings of modern sexuality (Boellstorff 2005, 8) and should similarly be seen as distinct from the English term "normal".

5. See, for example, Fran Martin (2003) on Taiwan and Peter Jackson (2001) on Thailand.

6. Hill and Sen (2005, 57, 62) quote estimates of 12 million Internet users in Indonesia as a whole in 2004, with most access being via Internet cafes, workplaces, and schools or campuses. The number has undoubtedly increased significantly since that date.

7. This book has had twenty-nine reprints, and there is now a sequel, *Jakarta undercover 2: karnaval malam* (Jakarta undercover 2: night carnival), and a spin-off movie, Jakarta Undercover (2007, directed by Lance).

8. These follow a number of books that have taken lesbian love as their main theme, most notably *Garis tepi seorang lesbian* (The margins of lesbianism) by Herlinatiens (2003). Note also the *gay* content, even if it is not the central theme, of, for example, Dee's *Supernova* (2000) and *Jazz parfum dan insiden* (Jazz perfume and the incident) by Seno Gumira Ajidarma (1996). Seno's short story *Lelaki yang terindah* (The most beautiful man), first published in 1991 and included in his 2003 collection, *Sebuah pertanyaan untuk cinta* (A question for love), also has a *gay* theme.

9. While this might reflect the reluctance of Indonesians publicly to define themselves according to their sexuality, we should also note Boellstorff's findings that most Indonesian men would not identify with the idea of being "out" or "not out". Instead, they tend to talk about being open (*terbuka*) in particular spaces. *Gay* Indonesians do not necessarily see a contradiction in being open only in certain *gay* spaces. In other spaces, those of the *normal* world, it is neither desirable nor necessary to be open (Boellstorff 2005, 91). It seems that for the moment the *normal* world should probably be seen as including the world of publishing, or at least its public face.

10. Chris Berry (1997, 14) has argued this point with respect to the upsurge in the production of gay films in various Asian countries.

11. Andrei Aksana, born in Jakarta (19 January 1970), is the latest in the line of a somewhat prestigious literary heritage. Aksana's mother, Nina Pane, is a novelist and screenwriter, and Andrei is the grandson of the prewar writers Armijn Pane and Sanoesi Pane. His official web site is http://andreiaksana.blog drive.com.

12. He reportedly published his first novel, *Mengukir mimpi terlalu pagi*, when he was nineteen. After a break to concentrate on his education and career he returned to writing and his novels to date are *Abadilah cinta* (Let love be eternal) (2003a), *Cinta penuh air mata* (Love full of tears) (2003b), *Lelaki terindah* (The most beautiful man) (2004a), *Sebagai pengganti dirimu* (In place of you) (2004b), *Cinta 24 jam* (24 hour love) (2004c), *Pretty Prita* (Pretty Prita) (2005), *Karena aku mencintaimu* (Because I love you) (2006a).

13. The English-language title and chapter headings notwithstanding, the book is written in Indonesian.

14. See, for example, the discussion "Lelaki terindah karya Andrei Aksana" on *AjangKita Forum,* www.ajangkita.com/forum/viewtopic (accessed 10 April 2007); comment on *Lelaki terindah* on the *Kupunyabuku* blog, http://kupunyabuku.blogdrive.com/comments?id=7 (accessed 11 April 2007); reviews of *Lelaki terindah* on *A Feminist Blog,* http://afemaleguest. blog.co.uk/?tag=lelaki%20terindah> (accessed 12 April 2007), and "*Lelaki terindah*—the gay community exposed!" on *Agaauthor,* http://agaauthor.multiply.com/reviews (accessed 12 April 2007). The novel is also mentioned on various discussion boards on the Indonesian gay site *BoyzForum,* http://www.readybb.com/boyzforum/ (accessed 10 April 2007). For an example of a negative blog commentary, see Nanas Homo (2006).

15. All section headings are in English in the original.

16. See Peter Jackson (1999a) and Douglas Sanders (2002) for further details of this discussion.

17. See, for example, the entries on Bangkok on the popular gay web sites *fridae.com,* http:// www.fridae.com/cityguides/bangkok/bk-intro.php (accessed 10 April 2007), and *Utopia Asia,* http://www.utopia-asia.com/tipsthai.htm (accessed 10 April 2007).

18. *QueerCast #23: Pre-Party Bitching!,* http://mediac01m01.libsyn.com/podcasts/ a3f728811c8fb15b3cc2dfa244 a38b82/4628e794/queercast/queercast_23-pre-party_ bitching.mp3 (accessed 10 April 2007). *Queercast,* hosted by Ian Lee and Nicholas Deroose, describes itself as "Singapore's juiciest queer podcast".

19. In the novel, one of the first sights visited is Jatujak Market. DJ station, one of the most well-known gay nightclubs in Bangkok, is also the site of a key scene in the novel. Rafky and Valent have to return home to Jakarta before they are tempted to visit Babylon, perhaps the best-known gay spa/sauna in the Thai capital.

20. Texas being a play on the word *terminal,* the bus station being nearby, and Kalifor being a play on the *kali* (river) near which that location was sited (Boellstorff 2005, 24).

21. The text here hints that Valent has long been aware of his sexuality, though we are told little else of what he has experienced on previous visits to the city.

22. Certainly there are cases of forced marriage. Boellstorff (2005, 110) notes that for some *gay* men marriage is highly traumatic, with some choosing suicide rather than accepting a marriage forced upon them.

23. Aksana (Interview, 10 December 2006) claims that after having included this character, readers and his publisher asked him to write a book with a central gay character.

Chapter 11

1. I wish to thank Nantiya Sukontapatipark for her invaluable help in keeping me well stocked with articles, magazines, books, and theses during my time away from Thailand. I am very grateful for her insights and information. I also wish to thank Kallayanee Techapatikul for her help in checking translations and guiding me through difficult moments in writing. Financial assistance from Yale University's Gay and Lesbian Studies Program was essential in completing this research.
2. The influence of the Marxist concept of hegemony and of Foucault's concept of discourse is so widespread in anthropology, as well as queer studies, that it would be difficult to find many new publications without some appropriation of these concepts. I have cited a few well-known texts that focus specifically on these concepts, but an exhaustive list would prove nearly impossible.
3. For more on Thai NGO history, see Delcore (2003) and Ungpakorn (n.d., 2006).
4. Astraea: Lesbian Foundation for Justice is an organization based in the United States that provides small grants to LGBT and progressive organizations around the world. See www.astraea.org.
5. See Jackson (1997b) and (2004c) for a more in-depth discussion of the historical emergence of the term "gay" and its positioning relative to the category *kathoey*.
6. I use the phrase "Anjaree organizers" rather than giving specific names of individuals because not all of the members and organizers are public figures or have agreed to have their names used.
7. My thanks to Peter Jackson for this historical note. Jackson dates the emergence of these discourses to the work of Sut Saengwichian on *kathoey* in 1956. See Jackson (1997b, 60, n. 13, and 62, n. 15) for the early references to American publications from the 1930s and 1940s.
8. Lesla web site was www.lesla.com. It was inactive at the time of writing and the current status of Lesla is not clear.
9. See Sinnott (2004, chapter 6) for more detailed discussion of the relationship between these groups and the reaction of *toms* to Anjaree's gender-neutral discourse of "women who love women".
10. *LeslaZine*, No. 1, October 2000, pp. 7–10.
11. See Sinnott (2004, 29–30) for more discussion of the negative connotations of the term "lesbian" for *toms* and *dees*.

Chapter 12

1. The Social Order Campaign was concerned with ensuring that entertainment venues throughout Thailand observed legal closing hours, excluded minors, and discouraged the use of recreational drugs. The campaign was highly publicized during the time that Purachai was interior minister and was widely supported by the Thai middle class.
2. High-society hairdresser Pan Bunnak was a publicly gay figure in the 1970s, while scholar-turned-actor Seri Wongmontha was a public voice for Thai *kathoeys* and homosexuals in the 1980s (see Jackson 1995).
3. Interview, 20 September 2007.
4. "Thai LGBT activists fight for constitutional protection", International Gay and Lesbian Human Rights Commission, 11 July 2007. See www.iglhrc.org (accessed 20 September 2008).
5. Kultida Samabuddhi, "We've laid a foundation", interview with Saneh Chamarik, *Bangkok Post*, 13 July 2007, p. 2.

6. A number of politicians assumed that Naiyana was lesbian because of her advocacy in issues of sexual orientation and gender identity. She has a husband and at least one child.

7. Interview, Naiyana Suphapung, 20 September 2007.

8. "Gay women face higher risk: expert", *The Nation*, 29 November 2001, p. 6A.

9. Karnjariya Sukrung, "A Forgotten Minority", *Bangkok Post, Outlook*, 12 December 2001, p. 1. The "right to love" is a formulation popularized by Amnesty International in its publications and activism on LGBT rights.

10. *Bangkok Post, Outlook*, 12 December 2001, p. 1.

11. Annual Pride parades were held in Bangkok from 1999 to 2006. Figures at the meeting represented gay businesses and LGBT organizations. Some pride events occurred in 2007, but no parade was held.

12. Author's notes from the meeting. Translation by Timo Ojanen.

13. Wassana Nanuam, "Military scraps offending label against gays", *Bangkok Post*, 2 April 2006, p. 3.

14. "Gays take on Novotel in club row", *The Nation*, 28 June 2007, p. 1A; "Anti-Novotel campaign grows", *The Nation*, 29 June 2007, p. 1A.

15. "An historic victory for human rights", *The Nation*, 22 August 2007, p. 9A.

16. Most notably Anjana Suvarnananda, Natee Teerarojjanapongs, and the Rainbow Sky Association of Thailand and Sapaan NGOs.

17. Interview, Naiyana Suphapung, 20 September 2007.

18. Anjana Suvarnananda, e-mail transmission, 1 June 2007.

19. Sanitsuda Ekachai, "Activists want gay rights in charter", *Bangkok Post*, 26 May 2007, p. 4.

20. Alisa went on to run for mayor of Pattaya in April 2008, gaining 6,000 to 7,000 votes of a total vote of 30,000, not enough to win the post.

21. Anjana Suvarnananda, e-mail transmission, 10 June 2007.

22. The Thai-language document is available at www.sapaan.org/article/72.htm (accessed 10 March 2010). My thanks to Peter Jackson for his preliminary translation into English. I have modified his language slightly.

23. At the request of Anjana Suvarnananda of Anjaree, I drafted a background paper on how other countries handled the question of the sex indicated on the personal documentation of transgendered individuals. The examples were partly from the West but also from the jurisdictions in Asia that permit a change in documents for post-operative transsexuals (Indonesia, Japan, Korea, Singapore, Taiwan, and parts of China). I attended the planning meetings and the two National Legislative Assembly committee meetings that are described in this section.

24. Prapasri Osathanon, Wannapa Phetdee, "Draft 'ignores transvestites'", *The Nation*, 23 October 2007, p. 4A; Manop Thip-Osod, "Honorifics bill goes to cabinet for deliberation", *Bangkok Post*, 25 October 2007, p. 3.

25. Wannapa Phetdee, "Women to get choice of Mrs, Miss", *The Nation*, 8 February 2008, 4A.

26. Bhanravee Tansubhapol, "On the lookout for citizens' rights", *Bangkok Post*, 13 July 2007, p. 10.

27. Thongbai Thongpao, "NHRC selection is deeply flawed", *Bangkok Post*, 26 April 2009, p. 11. See also Supalak Ganjanakhundee, "Selection of new rights commissioners is a legal farce", *The Nation*, 23 April 2009, p. 2B; "Unearthing strange facts", *Bangkok Post*, 25 April 2009, p. 12; Achara Ashayagachat, "Selection of rights panel runs into flak", *Bangkok Post*, 21 April 2009, p. 4; Achara Ashayagachat, "Nominees for NHRC job have their say", *Bangkok Post*, 22 April 2009, p. 4.

28. Achara Ashayagachat, "A question of credibility dogs new panel already", *Bangkok Post*, 16 May 2009, p. 9.

29. "New NHRC embraces spirit of cooperation", *Bangkok Post*, 21 July 2009, p. 3.

30. Achara Ashayagachat, "Thailand seeks entry to UN rights council", *Bangkok Post*, 25 February 2010, p. 4.

Chapter 13

1. This chapter is based on a paper entitled "Transpeople in Thailand: Acceptance or oppression", presented at the Tenth International Conference of Thai Studies, "'Thai societies in a transnationalised world'", which was held at Thammasat University, Bangkok, in January 2008. In preparing this fuller version, I am grateful to Peter Jackson, Krissana Mamanee (Sana), Prempreeda Pramoj Na Ayutthaya (Bon), and Kosum Omphornuwat (Jigsaw) for their observations and patience in answering my questions.
2. http://www.globalgayz.com/g-thailand07-1.html (accessed 15 September 2008).
3. This expression is used, for example, on the "Transgender Women of Thailand" web site at http://www.thailadyboyz.net (accessed 15 September 2008).
4. Nada Chaiyajit of the ThaiLadyboyz group in e-mail communication with the author, 16 May 2008.
5. For a recent review of international transgender hate crime, see Kidd and Witten (2007) and TransGender Europe (2009).
6. Leaving aside the accuracy (or otherwise) of this figure, the prevalence of gender variance is almost certainly higher in Thailand than in many other cultures worldwide. I consider why this might be so in Winter (2002b).
7. For a critique of Thailand's reputation as a "gay paradise", see Jackson (1999).
8. See an in-depth discussion in Costa and Matzner (2007, 17*ff*).
9. Jackson, e-mail to author, 29 October 2008.
10. See, for example, Costa and Matzner (2007); Gallagher (2005); Jackson (1995); Jenkins et al. (2005); Luhmann (2006); Matzner (2001); Nanda (2000); Totman (2003); Winter (2006a); Cameron (2006).
11. See, for example, Jackson (1995).
12. For more detail on the rights of "people of diverse sexualities" in the current Thai constitution, see Douglas Sanders' chapter in this volume.
13. This appears to be the view of the United Nations Human Rights Committee, which declared in the 1990s that the Commonwealth of Australia had breached the ICCPR in allowing the state of Tasmania to persist in criminalizing homosexuality. The committee noted that the protected category of "sex" in ICCPR Article 2 is to be taken as including sexual orientation.
14. The other six nations were the United States, the United Kingdom, Malaysia, Singapore, the Philippines, and China. The research is reported in Winter et al. (2009). The Thai version of the questionnaire employed the term *"phu-ying praphet sorng"* ("second kind of woman").
15. Jackson, e-mail to the author, 29 October 2008.
16. I use the term "natal" (i.e. "birth") here. The more commonly used term, "biological" sex, is problematic. There is increasing evidence for a facet of biological sex called brain sex (or brain gender, as in Hines, [2004]), and that individuals may be hard-wired for sex-linked behaviour and personality differences at birth. This hard-wiring may extend to transpeople; they may be born with brains that are in a physical (biological) sense cross-sexed (GIRES, 2006). The implication is that transwomen may be viewed as biological women, as are their natal female counterparts (and that transmen may be viewed as biological men).
17. Worldwide, and perhaps in Thailand too, transmen may find it easier to pass socially than transwomen, if only because the cross-sex hormones available to them often induce physical changes faster, and sometimes with longer-term effects, than for transwomen taking female hormones.

18. See Cameron (2006, 29), and Jenkins et al. (2005, 14). Jenkins et al. note that this designation as psychologically damaged has also undermined the possibility of getting a passport. In August 2005, the Thai military, under pressure, indicated that it would no longer use this phrase. The decision appears not to be retrospective, i.e. does not make possible replacement of old *Sor. Dor. 43* papers with new ones.

19. See Jackson (2002). It appears that no follow-up study was undertaken to examine the effect of this affair upon the already low numbers of *phu-ying kham-phet* working as teachers.

20. In Asia, change of legal gender status (as evidenced in the right to a heterosexual marriage) is now possible in Japan, South Korea, the People's Republic of China, Taiwan, Singapore, Indonesia, Iran, Kyrgyzstan, Kazakhstan, and Saudi Arabia. Reports also suggest it is possible in Indonesia (Dédé Oetomo, e-mail to the author, 22 February 2008).

21. In the United Kingdom these legislative changes were incorporated into the Gender Recognition Act of 2004.

22. Until recently, the perpetrator of rape upon a *phu-ying kham-phet* could be tried only for physical assault (Cameron 2006, 27).

23. In British English, a "bar fine" is a fee that a customer pays the management of a bar or commercial sex establishment to take a sex worker off the premises. In Australian and American English, this is more commonly called an "off fee", which is a direct translation of the Thai expression *kha off*.

24. Cameron (2006, 19) reports anecdotal evidence suggesting that the willingness of partners of *phu-ying kham-phet* to use condoms is very low.

25. For more information see Jenkins et al. (2005, 17) and Cameron (2006, 17).

26. For example, Luhmann (2006) reports that among his *phu-ying kham-phet* research participants who had ever had a regular sexual partner, 28 percent had never used a condom with that partner.

27. From a presentation by F. Van Griensven, "Epidemiology of HIV and STI in MSM in the greater Mekong region: what do we know?" (PowerPoint presentation at the Regional Consultative Forum in Bangkok, 15–16 August 2005). Cited in Jenkins et al. (2005, 5).

28. Andrew Hunter, head of the Asia Pacific Network of Sex Workers, reported in Cameron (2006, 17). Research quoted by Cameron reveals that intravenous drug users are usually thought to be the group with the highest HIV infection rate.

29. See Jenkins et al. (2005, 22) and Cameron (2006, 31).

30. See Luhmann (2006), who found that only 50 percent of his sample had consulted a doctor prior to initiating hormone use, while only 28 percent had gone to a doctor to establish current dose levels. My 2007 study with Chaisuak Lertraksakun (report in progress) revealed that within our sample of 150 *phu-ying kham-phet,* 139 had taken cross-sex hormones at some time in their lives. Though the vast majority had taken advice before doing so, it was most often from other *phu-ying kham-phet*. Only 44 had taken advice from qualified nurses or doctors. The figures for medical consultation were hardly better after starting to take hormones; only 68 went to a qualified nurse or doctor for care.

31. Fathers typically appear less accepting than mothers towards their *phu-ying kham-phet* children. See, for example, Jenkins et al. (2005, 8); and Winter (2006a).

32. See Jenkins et al. (2005, 11) and Winter (2006c). This second study (a sample of 195 young *phu-ying kham-phet*) found that around 11 percent anticipated presenting themselves as male by the time they were fifty years of age.

33. Jenkins et al. (2005, 16–17).

34. In an unpublished study of 225 *phu-ying kham-phet* aged 15 to 55 (mean age 24.6 years), Winter and Vink found that 34.5 percent had at some time in their life thought about killing themselves (usually or all the time for 4.5 percent of them). Even more worrying, over

one in five (22 percent) reported having attempted suicide at least once in their lives; 12.6 percent of the sample had done so more than once.

35. Note, for example, the work done by broad LGBT groups such as Anjaree, the Rainbow Sky Association of Thailand, and Bangkok Rainbow for the promotion of *khon kham-phet* rights. See Megan Sinnott and Douglas Sanders in this volume.

36. The research team was comprised of Pornthip Chalungsooth (US), Yik Koon Teh (Malaysia), Ying Wuen Wong (Singapore), Anne Beaumont (UK), Loretta Man Wah Ho (Hong Kong, China), Francis "Chuck" Gomez and Raymond Aquino Macapagal (Philippines), Nongnuch Rojanalert and Kulthida Maneerat (Thailand), and me. See Winter et al. (2009).

37. Mental pathology correlated with denial as women at 0.55, with social rejection at 0.50, peer rejection at 0.64, and sexual deviance at 0.44. All these correlation co-efficients were statistically significant beyond the 99 percent level of confidence.

38. Mental pathology correlated with denial as women at 0.12, with social rejection at 0.26, peer rejection at 0.18, and sexual deviance at 0.42. The two highest correlations were statistically significant beyond the 99 percent level of confidence, the third-highest was significant beyond the 95 percent level. The lowest correlation fell slightly short of significance.

39. See Sherer (2006) and Matzner (n.d.).

40. American Psychiatric Association Task Force (1994).

41. See Bartlett et al. (2000); Hale (2007); Langer and Martin (2004); Newman (2002); Richardson (1999); Vasey and Bartlett (2007); Vitale (2005); Wilson et al. (2002); Winter (2007); Winters (2006).

42. Other possibilities also exist. Some individuals may hold to broad, "essentialist" belief systems about sex and gender (for example, that sex and gender are indivisible and unchangeable), which, in turn, lead them to believe that transpeople are mentally ill, and also to deny them gender rights, to regard them as sexual deviants, and avoid social contact with them.

43. See, for example, Clements-Nolle et al. (2006), and Grossman and D'Augelli (2007).

44. See, for example, the discussion of transwomen in Malaysia in Teh (2002).

45. In our 2007 study, 57 percent of Thai respondents believed that *phu-ying kham-phet* are sexually perverted (*wiparit thang-phet*). By contrast, only 22 percent of US students took this view about transwomen.

46. Costa and Matzner (2007) discuss the Thai feminine virtue of *khwam-riap-roi* at some length in their book on *sao praphet sorng* ("women of the second kind"). For further discussion of how perceptions of impropriety can dramatically undermine acceptance towards *phu-ying kham-phet* see Matzner (2001).

47. See the US research of Klamen et al. (1999), who found that a quarter century after depathologization, nine percent of second-year medical students still believed homosexuality to be a mental disorder.

A Glossary of Thai LGBT Terms

Chai rak chai (noun, formal) — men who love men; the Thai rendering of "men who have sex with men", or MSM.

Chao si-muang (noun) — "purple people" or "lavender people"; an older collective expression for the *kathoey*, gay, and *tom-dee* communities.

Chum-chon gay (noun, colloquial) — gay community.

Dee (noun, colloquial) — from "la<u>dy</u>", a feminine-identified woman who is the romantic and sexual partner of a *tom* (see below); a feminine lesbian.

Ee-aep (noun, slang) — a closeted gay man; a closet queen.

Fai rap (noun, colloquial) — "the receptive partner", in either male-male or female-female sex. Used in both gay and *tom-dee* communities.

Fai ruk (noun, colloquial) — "the active partner", in either male-male or female-female sex. Used in both gay and *tom-dee* communities.

Gay king (noun, colloquial) — sexually active partner in a gay relationship.

Gay queen (noun, colloquial) — sexually receptive partner in a gay relationship.

Kathoey (noun) — a transwoman; male-to-female transgender or transsexual. Derogatory in some contexts.

Kham-phet (adjective, formal) — transgender and/or transsexual.

Khwam-lak-lai thang-phet (noun, formal) — sexual and/or gender diversity.

Les (noun, colloquial) — from "<u>les</u>bian". In some instances denotes a woman who does not necessarily engage in gender role-play, as either a masculine *tom* or feminine *dee*, in a romantic and sexual relationship with another woman. In other instances *les* may be understood as a feminine lesbian and conflated with *dee*.

Les king (noun, colloquial) — from "lesbian" and "gay king", a *les* (see above) who is the sexually active partner.

Les queen (noun, colloquial) — from "lesbian" and "gay queen", a *les* (see above) who is the sexually receptive partner.

Phet (noun) — generic term for sex, gender, and sexuality.

Phet-saphap (noun, formal) — gender (literally "*phet* status").

Phet-withi (noun, formal) — sexuality (literally "*phet* orientation").

Phu-chai (noun) — a man; usually denotes a heterosexual man and is used in contrast to gay.

Phu-ying (noun) — a woman; usually denotes a heterosexual woman.

Phu-ying praphet sorng (noun, colloquial) — "a second type of woman", a more polite term than *kathoey* for male-to-female transgenders and transsexuals.

Rak phet diao-kan (formal) — same-sex love; to love the same sex.

Rak-ruam-phet (formal, academic) — a biomedical and often pathologizing term for "homosexuality". Now resisted by Thai LGBT groups and replaced by *rak phet diao-kan* ("same-sex love").

Sangkhom gay (noun, colloquial) — the gay scene, gay social life.

Sao praphet sorng (noun, colloquial) — "a second type of young woman", a more polite term than *kathoey* for younger male-to-female transgenders and transsexuals.

Si-muang (noun) — purple, lavender; historically a colour associated with *kathoeys* and gay men.

Si-rung (noun) — rainbow colours; now has queer connotations as a collective symbolic marker of all Thai LGBT identities and communities.

Tom (noun, colloquial) — from "tomboy", a masculine woman whose romantic and sexual partner is a *dee* (see above).

Ying rak ying (noun, formal) — women who love women.

Bibliography

Ahmed, Sara. 2006. *Queer phenomenology: Orientations, objects, others.* Durham, NC: Duke University Press.

Ajidarma, Seno Gumira. 1996. *Jazz parfum dan insiden* (Jazz perfume and the incident). Yogyakarta: Yayasan Bentang Budaya.

———. 2003. Lelaki yang terindah (The most beautiful man). In *Sebuah pertanyaan untuk cinta* (A question for love). Seno Gumira Ajidarma. 50–61. Jakarta: Gramedia Pustaka Utama.

Aksana, Andrei. 2003a. *Abadilah cinta* (Let love be eternal). Jakarta: Gramedia Pustaka Utama.

———. 2003b. *Cinta penuh air mata* (Love full of tears). Jakarta: Gramedia Pustaka Utama.

———. 2004a. *Lelaki terindah* (The most beautiful man). Jakarta: Gramedia Pustaka Utama.

———. 2004b. *Sebagai pengganti dirimu* (In place of you). Jakarta: Gramedia Pustaka Utama.

———. 2004c. *Cinta 24 jam* (24 hour love). Jakarta: Gramedia Pustaka Utama.

———. 2005. *Pretty Prita* (Pretty Prita). Jakarta: Gramedia Pustaka Utama.

———. 2006a. *Karena aku mencintaimu* (Because I love you). Jakarta: Gramedia Pustaka Utama.

———. 2006b. *Be a writer, be a celebrity; the secrets of best-seller novels*. Jakarta: Gramedia Pustaka Utama.

———. 2006c. Menanti pelangi (Waiting for a rainbow). In *Rahasia bulan* (Secrets of the moon). Is Mujiarso, ed. 211–21. Jakarta: Gramedia Pustaka Utama.

Altman, Dennis. 1996a. Rupture or continuity? The internationalization of gay identities. *Social Text*, 14: 77–94.

———. 1996b. On global queering. *Australian Humanities Review*, July 1996. Internet edition http://www.lib.latrobe.edu.au/AHR/archive/Issue-July-1996/altman.html (accessed 17 June 2007).

———. 2001. *Global sex*. Crows Nest, NSW: Allen and Unwin.

American Psychiatric Association Task Force. 1994. *Diagnostic and statistical manual of mental disorders: DSM–IV*. Washington DC: American Psychiatric Association.

Anchalee Chaiworaporn and Adam Knee. Thailand: Revival in an age of globalization. In *Contemporary Asian cinema: Popular culture in a global frame*. Anne Tereska Ciecko, ed. 58–70. London: Berg, 2006.

Anderson, Benedict. 1983. *Imagined communities*. London: Verso.

———. 1990. Murder and progress in modern Siam. *New Left Review*, 181: 33–48.

Anjaree. 1995. Going to the meeting for Asian women who love women in Taiwan. *Anjareesarn*, 2 (11): 11.

Anonymous. 2004. Cultural ministry irate over gay civil servants: Blaming TV media as a distributing source. *Utopia-asia.com*, 4 June 2004. www.utopia-asia.com/unews/article_2004_06_4_034037 (accessed 12 May 2007).

Anwar, Joko. 2004. 'Masterpiece' only good for a laugh. *Jakarta Post*, 30 May 2004. www.thejakartapost.com/yesterdaydetail.asp?fileid=20040530.ho1 (accessed 26 May 2005).

Armitage, J. and J. Roberts. 2002. An introduction to technology & society in the 21st century. In *Living with cyberspace, technology & society in the 21st century*. John Armitage and Joanne Roberts, eds. 1–16. London: Continuum.

Askew, Marc. 2002. *Bangkok: Place, practice and representations*. London: Routledge.

Atkins, Gary. 2005. Encountering Babylon: Pursuing beauty and sexual justice at a globalized gay sauna. Paper presented at Sexualities, Genders, and Rights in Asia, 1st International Conference of Asian Queer Studies, Bangkok, 7–9 July 2005.

Auge, Marc. 1995. *Non-places: Introduction to the anthropology of supermodernity*. London: Verso Press.

BBC. 2004. Transvestites rescue Thai movies. BBC broadcast, 23 March 2004. http://news.bbc.co.uk/2/hi/entertainment/3558637.stm (accessed 26 May 2007).

Badalu, John. 2005. Novel gay? Yang benar aja! (A gay novel? You can't be serious!) *Djakarta*, March 2005 (53): 68.

Bamrung Amnatcharoenrit. 2006. Film industry to grow 5%: New releases to help spur ticket sales. *Bangkok Post*, 19 January 2006, p. B3.

Barber, Benjamin R. 1996. *Jihad vs. McWorld*. New York: Ballantine Books.

———. 2007. *Consumed: How markets corrupt children, infantilize adults, and swallow citizens whole*. New York: W. W. Norton & Company.

Barmé, Scot. 2002. *Woman, man, Bangkok: Love, sex, and popular culture in Thailand*. New York: Rowan & Littlefield.

Barrioneuvo, Alexei. 2007. Macho Buenos Aires warming to gays: Luxury hotel is latest example of outreach to new market. *International Herald Tribune*, 1–2 December 2007, p. 2.

Bartlett, N. H., P. L. Vasey, and W. M. Bukowski. 2000. Is gender identity disorder in children a mental disorder? *Sex Roles*, 43 (11–12): 753–85.

Baumann, R. 1992. *Folklore, cultural performances, and popular entertainments*. New York: Oxford University Press.

Bell, C. 1992. *Ritual theory, ritual practice*. New York and Oxford: Oxford University Press.

Bernstein, Elizabeth and Laurie Schaffner, eds. 2005. *Regulating sex: The politics of intimacy and identity*. London and New York: Routledge.

Berry, Chris. 1994. *A bit on the side: East-West topographies of desire*. Sydney: Empress Publishing.

———. 1997. Globalisation and localisation: Queer films from Asia. In *The bent lens: A world guide to gay and lesbian film*. C. Jackson and P. Tapp, eds. 14–17. St. Kilda, Victoria: Australian Catalogue Company.

———. 2001. Asian Values, family values: Film, video, and lesbian and gay identities. In *Gay and lesbian Asia: Culture, identity, community*. Gerard Sullivan and Peter A. Jackson, eds. 211–31. New York: Haworth Press.

Berry, Chris, Fran Martin, and Audrey Yue, eds. 2003. Introduction: Beep – click – link. In *Mobile cultures: New media in queer Asia*, 1–18. Durham, NC, and London: Duke University Press.

Bhabha, Homi. 2004. *The location of culture; with a new preface by the author*. London: Routledge.

Bkkdreamer. 2010. Simply love. http://bkkmindscape.blogspot.com/2007/11/simply-love-love-of-siam-part-1.html (accessed 27 April 2010).

Blackwood, Evelyn. 1998. Tombois in West Sumatra: Constructing masculinity and erotic desire. *Cultural Anthropology*, 13 (4): 491–521.

———. 2007. Transnational sexualities in one place: Indonesian readings. In *Women's sexualities and masculinities in a globalizing Asia*. Evelyn Blackwood and Saskia Wieringa, eds. 181–205. New York: Palgrave.

Boellstorff, Tom. 2003. I knew it was me: Mass media, 'globalization', and lesbian and gay Indonesians. In *Mobile cultures: New media in queer Asia*. Chris Berry, Fran Martin, and Audrey Yue, eds. 21–51. Durham, NC: Duke University Press.

———. 2005. *The gay archipelago: Sexuality and nation in Indonesia*. Princeton, NJ: Princeton University Press.

———. 2007. *A coincidence of desires: Anthropology, queer studies, Indonesia*. Durham, NC: Duke University Press.

Bookman, Milica Z. and Karla R. Bookman. 2007. *Medical tourism in developing countries*. New York: Palgrave Macmillan.

Butler, Judith. 2000. Critically queer. In *Identity: A reader*. Judith Butler, ed. 33–59. London: Sage.

———. 2006. Undiagnosing gender. In *Transgender rights*. Paisley Currah, Richard M. Juang, and Shannon Price, eds. 274–98. Minneapolis, MN: University of Minnesota Press.

Caceres, C. F., M. Pecheny, T. Frasca, and R. R. Rios. 2008. *Review of legal frameworks and the situation of human rights related to sexual diversity in low and middle income countries*. Geneva: UNAIDS.

Cameron, L. 2006. *Sexual health and rights: Sex workers, transgender people and men who have sex with men: Thailand*. New York: Open Society Institute.

Cannell, F. 1999. *Power and intimacy in the Christian Philippines*. Manila: ADMU Press.

Centers for Disease Control and Prevention. 2006. HIV prevalence among populations of men who have sex with men, Thailand, 2003 and 2005. *Morbidity and Mortality Weekly Report*, 55 (3): 844–48.

Cheah, Pheng. 2007. Biopower and the new international division of reproductive labor. *boundary 2*, 34 (1): 79–113.

Ching, Yau. 2010. *As normal as possible: Negotiating sexuality and gender in mainland China and Hong Kong*. Hong Kong: Hong Kong University Press.

Choron-Baix, C. 1995. *Le choc des mondes. Les amateurs de boxe thaïlandaise en France*. Paris: Kimé.

Clements-Nolle, K., R. Marx, and M. Katz. 2006. Attempted suicide among transgender persons: The influence of gender-based discrimination and victimization. *Journal of Homosexuality*, 51 (3): 53–69.

Clift, Stephen, Michael Luongo, and Carry Callister. 2002. *Gay tourism: Culture, identity and sex*. London and New York: Continuum.

Clough, Patricia Tiniceto. 2007. Introduction. In *The affective turn: Theorizing the social*. Patricia Tinecito Clough, ed. 1–33. Durham, NC: Duke University Press.

Connors, Michael. 2007. *Democracy and national identity in Thailand*, revised edition. Copenhagen: NIAS.

Costa, L. and A. Matzner. 2007. *Male bodies, women's souls: Personal narratives of Thailand's transgendered youth*. Binghamton, NY: Haworth.

Cruz, Oggs. 2008. The love of Siam. http://oggsmoggs.blogspot.com/2008/04/love-of-siam-2007.html (accessed 27 April 2010).

Cruz-Malavé, Arnaldo and Martin F. Manalansan IV. 2002. Dissident sexualities/alternative globalisms: Introduction. In *Queer globalizations: Citizenship and the afterlife of colonialism*. Arnaldo Cruz-Malavé and Martin F. Manalansan IV, eds. 1–10. New York and London: New York University Press.

Dee. 2000. *Supernova: Ksatria, puteri dan bintang jatuh* (Supernova: Knight, princess and falling star). Bandung: Truedee.

Delcore, Henry. 2003. Nongovernmental organizations and the work of memory in Northern Thailand. *American Ethnologist*, 30 (1): 61–84.

D'Emilio, John. 1993. Capitalism and gay identity. In *The lesbian and gay studies reader*. Henry Abelove, Michèle Aina Barale, and David M. Halperin, eds. 467–76. New York: Routledge.

Dissanayake, Wimal. 1993. *Melodrama and Asian cinema*. Cambridge and New York: Cambridge University Press.

Drucker, Peter. 2000. Introduction: Remapping sexualities. In *Different rainbows*. Peter Drucker, ed. 9–42. London: Gay Men's Press.

Emka, Moammar. 2002. *Jakarta undercover: Sex 'n the city*. Yogyakarta: Galang Press.

———. 2003. *Jakarta undercover 2: karnaval malam* (Jakarta undercover 2: night carnival). Jakarta: GagasMedia.

Erni, John Nguyet. 2005. Queer pop Asia: Toward a hybrid regionalist imaginary. Paper presented at the 1st International Conference of Asian Queer Studies, Bangkok, 7–9 July 2005.

Ezinky. 2004. *Ini dia, hidup* (This is it, life). Jakarta: Kebun Ide.

Ferrari, Matthew P. 2006. Mysterious objects of knowledge: An interpretation of three feature films by Apichatpong Weerasethakul in terms of the ethnographic paradigm. M.A. thesis, College of Fine Arts, Ohio University, Athens, Ohio.

Formoso, Bernard. 1987. Du corps humain à l'espace humanisé: Système de référence et représentation de l'espace dans deux villages du nord-est de la Thaïlande (From the human body to humanized space: System of reference and representation of space in two Northeastern Thai villages). *Etudes rurales*, 107–108: 137–70.

———. 1994. Les Isan (The people of Isan). *Péninsule*, 29: 53–99.

———. 2001. Corps étrangers. Tourisme et prostitution en Thaïlande (Foreign bodies: Tourism and prostitution in Thailand). *Anthropologie et sociétés*, 25 (2): 55–70.

Foucault, Michel. 1980. *The history of sexuality volume 1: An introduction*. Robert Hurley, trans. New York: Vintage Books.

———. 1995. *Discipline and punish: The birth of the prison*. Alan Sheridan, trans. London: Vintage.

———. 2007. *Security, territory, population: Lectures at the Collége de France 1977–78*. Graham Burchell, trans. London: Palgrave Macmillan.

Francis Nandasukon. 2005. Morng phan lok gay yuk mai jak "phaphayon" (Looking at the modern gay world through "movies"). *Positioningmag*, April, 2005. www.positioningmag. com/Magazine/Details.aspx?id=31742 (accessed 28 July 2007).

Gallagher, R. 2005. Shifting markets, shifting risks: HIV/AIDS prevention and the geographies of male and transgender tourist-oriented sex work in Phuket, Thailand. http://bangkok2005. anu.edu.au/paper/Gallagher.pdf (accessed 3 March 2010).

Gaonkar, Dilip Parameshwar. 2001. *Alternative modernities*. Durham, NC: Duke University Press.

Garcia, Michael. 2004. More than just sex: Three women authors take the Indonesian literary world by storm. *Inside Indonesia* 80 (Oct–Dec). http://www.serve.com/~inside/edit80/p26-27garcia.html (accessed 10 April 2007).

GIRES (Gender Identity Research and Education Society). 2006. Atypical gender development: A Review. *International Journal of Transgenderism* 9 (1): 29–44.

Girling, John. 1981. *Thailand: Society and politics*. Ithaca, NY: Cornell University Press.

Gledhill, Christine. 1999. Rethinking genre. In *Reinventing film studies*. Linda Williams and Christine Gledhill, eds. 221–43. London: Arnold.

Gorton, Nick. 2006. Health care and insurance issues for transgender persons. *American Family Physician*, 73 (9): 1591–98.

Grossman, Andrew. 2000. 'Beautiful publicity': An introduction to queer Asian film. In *Queer Asian cinema: Shadows in the shade*. Andrew Grossman, ed. 1–29. New York: Haworth Press.

Grossman, A. H. and A. R. D'Augelli. 2007. Transgender youth and life-threatening behaviors. *Suicide and Life-Threatening Behavior*, 37 (5): 527–37.

Hale, C. J. 2007. Ethical problems with the mental health evaluation standards of care for adult gender variant prospective patients. *Perspectives in Biology and Medicine*, 50 (4): 491–505.

Hamilton, Annette. 1997. Primal dream: Masculinism, sun, and salvation in Thailand's sex trade. In *Sites of desire, economies of pleasure: Sexualities in Asia and the Pacific*. Lenore Manderson and Margaret Jolly, eds. 145–65. Chicago: University of Chicago Press.

———. 2002. The national picture: Thai media and cultural identity. In *Media worlds: Anthropology on new terrain*. Faye D. Ginsburg, Lila Abu-Lughod, and Brian Larkin, eds. 152–70. Berkeley: University of California Press.

Hansen, Miriam. 1993. Early cinema, late cinema: Permutations of the public sphere. *Screen* 34 (3): 197–210.

———. 1999. The mass production of the senses: Classical cinema as vernacular modernism. *Modernism/Modernity*, 6 (2): 59–77.

———. 2000. Fallen women, rising stars, new horizons: Shanghai silent film as vernacular modernism. *Film Quarterly* 54 (1): 10–22.

Harrison, Rachel V. 2005. Amazing Thai film: The rise and rise of contemporary Thai cinema on the international screen. *Asian Affairs*, 36 (3): 321–38.

Harrison, Rachel V. and Peter A. Jackson, eds. 2010. *The ambiguous allure of the West: Traces of the colonial in Thailand*. Hong Kong: Hong Kong University Press.

Herlinatiens. 2003. *Garis tepi seorang lesbian* (The margins of lesbianism). Yogyakarta: Galang Press.

Hill, David and Krishna Sen. 2005. *The Internet in Indonesia's new democracy*. London: Routledge.

Hines, M. 2004. *Brain gender*. New York: Oxford University Press.

Ho, Loretta Wing Wah. 2010. *Gay and lesbian subcultures in urban China*. London and New York: Routledge.

Hochschild, Arlie. 2003. *The managed heart: Commercialization of human feeling*. Berkeley: University of California Press.

Holmes, D., ed. 2001. *Virtual globalization: Virtual spaces/tourist spaces*. London: Routledge.

Homo, Nanas. 2006. Nanas Homo vs Andrei Aksana, *Sastrawan Jahat*. http://sastrawan-jahat.blogspot.com/2006/11/nanas-homo-vs-andrei-aksana_10.html (accessed 10 April 2007).

Hunter, Tim. 2005. Six-pack for the queer-hearted. *The Age*. Melbourne, 19 March 2005. www.theage.com.au/news/Film/The-queerhearted/2005/03/17/1110913717487 (accessed 27 April 2010).

Isaraporn Pissa-ard. 2009. Thailand in Australian fiction. Ph.D. dissertation, Department of English, University of Sydney.

Jackson, Peter A. 1995. *Dear Uncle Go: Male homosexuality in Thailand*. Bangkok: Bua Luang Books.

———. 1997a. Thai research on male homosexuality and transgenderism and the cultural limits of Foucaultian analysis. *Journal of the History of Sexuality*, 8 (1): 52–85.

———. 1997b. *Kathoey* <>gay<>man: The historical emergence of gay male identity in Thailand. In *Sites of desire/economies of pleasure: Sexualities in Asia and the Pacific*. Lenore Manderson and Margaret Jolly, eds. 166–90. Chicago: University of Chicago Press.

———. 1998. Male homosexuality and transgenderism in the Thai Buddhist tradition. In *Queer Dharma: Voices of gay Buddhists*. Winston Leyland, ed. 55–89. San Francisco: Gay Sunshine Press.

———. 1999a. Tolerant but unaccepting: The myth of a Thai 'gay paradise'. In *Gender and sexualities in Modern Thailand*. Peter A. Jackson and Nerida Cook, eds. 226–42. Chiang Mai: Silkworm Books.

———. 1999b. An American death in Bangkok: The murder of Darrell Berrigan and the hybrid origins of gay identity in 1960s Thailand. *GLQ: A Journal of Lesbian and Gay Studies*, 5 (3): 361–411.

———. 2000. An explosion of Thai identities: Global queering and reimagining queer theory. *Culture, Health and Sexuality*, 2 (4): 405–24.

———. 2001. Pre-gay, post-queer: Thai perspectives on proliferating gender/sex diversity in Asia. In *Gay and lesbian Asia: Culture, identity, community*. Peter A. Jackson and Gerard Sullivan, eds. 1–26. New York: Harrington Park Press.

———. 2002. Offending images: Gender and sexual minorities, and state control of the media in Thailand. In *Media fortunes, changing times: ASEAN states in transition*. Russell H. K. Heng, ed. 201–30. Singapore: Institute of Southeast Asian Studies.

———. 2003a. Performative genders, perverse desires: A bio-history of Thailand's same-sex and transgender cultures. *Intersections: Gender, History and Culture in the Asian Context*, Issue 9, http://intersections.anu.edu.au/issue9/jackson.html

———. 2003b. Gay capitals in global gay history: Cities, local markets, and the origins of Bangkok's same-sex cultures. In *Postcolonial urbanism: Southeast Asian cities and global processes*. Ryan Bishop, John Phillips, and Wei-Wei Yeo, eds. 151–63. New York and London: Routledge.

———. 2004a. The Thai regime of images. *Sojourn: Journal of Social Issues in Southeast Asia*, 19 (2): 181–218.

———. 2004b. The performative state: Semi-coloniality and the tyranny of images in modern Thailand. *Sojourn: Journal of Social Issues in Southeast Asia*, 19 (2): 219–53.

———. 2004c. *Gay* adaptation, *tom-dee* resistance, and *kathoey* indifference: Thailand's gender/ sex minorities and the episodic allure of queer English. In *Speaking in queer tongues: Globalisation and gay desire*. William L. Leap and Tom Boellstorff, eds. 202–30. Urbana IL: University of Illinois Press.

———. 2004d. The tapestry of language and theory: Reading Rosalind Morris on poststructuralism and Thai modernity. *Southeast Asia Research*, 12 (3): 337–77.

———. 2006. Why I'm a Foucauldian. *Sojourn: Journal of Social Issues in Southeast Asia*, 21 (1): 113–23.

———. 2009a. Capitalism and global queering: National markets, sex cultural parallels, and multiple queer modernities. *GLQ*, 15 (3): 357–95.

———. 2009b. Global queering and global queer theory: Thai (trans)genders and (homo) sexualities in world history. *Autrepart: Revue de Sciences Social du Sud*, 49 (March 2009): 15–30.

Jackson, Peter A. and Nerida M. Cook, eds. 1999. *Genders and sexualities in modern Thailand*. Chiang Mai: Silkworm Books.

Jackson, Peter A. and Gerard Sullivan, eds. 1999. *Lady boys, tom boys, rent boys: Male and female homosexualities in contemporary Thailand*. New York: Harrington Park Press.

Johnson, Mark. 1997. *Beauty and power: Transgendering and cultural transformation in the southern Philippines*. Oxford and New York: Berg.

Jakobsen, Janet R. 2002. Can homosexuals end Western civilization as we know it? In *Queer globalizations: Citizenship and the afterlife of colonialism*. Arnaldo Cruz-Malavé and Martin F. Manalansan IV, eds. 49–70. New York and London: New York University Press.

Jenkins, Carol, Prempreeda Pramoj na Ayutthaya, and Andrew Hunter. 2005. *Katoey in Thailand: HIV/AIDS and life opportunities*. Washington, DC: USAID.

Joseph, Miranda. 2002. Family affairs: The discourse of global/localization. In *Queer globalizations: Citizenship and the afterlife of colonialism.* Arnaldo Cruz-Malavé and Martin F. Manalansan IV, eds. 71–99. New York and London: New York University Press.

Jureerat Sudsom. 2008. *Fang phu-kamkap jap ao ma kradiat* (Listen to directors if you really want to understand). Bangkok: Popcorn.

Karyono, Wiwik. 2004. *Pacarku, ibu kosku* (My lover is the matron of my college halls). Yogyakarta: Galang Press.

Kasian Tejapira. 1997. Imagined uncommunity: The lookjin middle class and Thai official nationalism. In *Essential outsiders: Chinese and Jews in the modern transformation of Southeast Asia and Central Europe.* Daniel Chirot and Anthony Reid, eds. 75–98. Seattle: University of Washington Press.

———. 2001. The post-modernization of Thainess. In *House of glass: Culture, modernity and the state in Southeast Asia.* Yao Souchou, ed. 150–69. Singapore: Institute of Southeast Asian Studies.

Kidd, J. D., and T. M. Witten. 2007. Transgender and transsexual identities: The next strange fruit—hate crimes, violence, and genocide against the global trans-communities. *Journal of Hate Studies,* 6 (3): 31–63.

King, Dave. 2003. Gender migration: A sociological analysis (or the leaving of Liverpool). *Sexualities,* 6 (2): 173–94.

King, M., S. Winter, and B. Webster. 2009. Contact reduces transprejudice: A study on transgenderism and transgender civil rights in Hong Kong. *International Journal of Sexual Health,* 21 (1): 17–34.

Kittiwut Jod Taywaditep, E. Coleman, and Pacharin Dumronggittigule. 1997. *The international encyclopedia of sexuality: Thailand.* www.sexquest.com/IES4/IES1-3contents.html (accessed 1 June 2006).

Klamen, D. L., L. S. Grossman, and D. R. Kopacz. 1999. Medical student homophobia. *Journal of Homosexuality,* 37 (1): 53–63.

Klein, James. 2002. The evolution of Thailand's national human rights commission, 1992–2001. In *Thailand's new politics.* Michael Nelson, ed. 25–65. Bangkok: White Lotus.

Kong Rithdee. 2006a. A pair of new Thai films touch on the subject of homosexuality. *Bangkok Post,* 26 June 2006, p. 23.

———. 2006b. "Seasons change": No rain, no gain. *Bangkok Post,* 24 October 2006, p. 19.

———. 2007a. Filmmakers rise against censorship. *Bangkok Post,* 24 April 2007. http://www.bangkokpost.com/240407_News/24Apr2007_news07.php (accessed 24 April 2007).

———. 2007b. Just plain queasy. *Thai Film Foundation,* 11 October 2008. www.thaifilm.com/articleDetail_en.asp?id=104 (accessed 11 June 2008).

———. 2007c. In search of the next "Brokeback Mountain." *Bangkok Post,* 20 July 2007. www.bangkokpost.com/200707_Realtime/20Jul2007_real21.php (accessed 20 July 2007).

———. 2007d. Time to move forward. *Bangkok Post,* 4 May 2007. www.bangkokpost.com/Realtime/04May2007_real21.php (accessed 4 May 2007).

———. 2007e. Two gays, plenty of guns. *Bangkok Post,* 21 September 2007. http://www.bangkokpost.com/210907_Realtime/21Sep2007_real005.php (accessed 22 September 2007).

———. 2007f. Love, actually: "The Love of Siam." *Bangkok Post,* 23 November 2007, p. R6.

———. 2008a. Hope and fear for the coming year. *Bangkok Post,* 4 January 2008. http://pages.citebite.com/q1h3q2k1mcrd (accessed 25 May 2008).

———. 2008b. Bangkok shows 'Siam' love: Gay teen romance sweeps critics awards. *Daily Variety,* Bangkok, 5 March 2008, p. 12.

———. 2010. To show or not to show. *Bangkok Post,* 27 August 2010, http://www.bangkokpost.com/entertainment/movie/193152/to-show-or-not-to-show (accessed 28 August 2010).

Langer, Susan J. and James I. Martin. 2004. How dresses can make you mentally ill: Examining gender identity disorder in children. *Child and Adolescent Social Work Journal*, 21 (1): 5–23.

Leap, William. 1999. *Public sex, gay space*. New York: Columbia University Press.

Leap, William, and Tom Boellstorff, eds. 2004. *Speaking in queer tongues: Globalization and gay language*. Urbana: University of Illinois Press.

Leung, Helen Hok-Sze. 2008. *Undercurrents: Queer culture and postcolonial Hong Kong*. Vancouver: UBC Press.

Lewis, Glen. 2003. The Thai movie revival and Thai national identity. *Continuum: Journal of Media and Cultural Studies* 17 (1): 69–78.

———. 2006. *Virtual Thailand: The media and cultural politics in Thailand, Malaysia and Singapore*. London: Routledge.

Lim, Eng-beng. 2005. Glocalqueering in new Asia: The politics of performing gay in Singapore. *Theatre Journal*, 57: 383–405.

Lombardi, Emilia. 2007. Public health and trans-people: Barriers to care and strategies to improve treatment. In *The health of sexual minorities: Public health perspectives on lesbian, gay, bisexual and transgender populations*. Ilan H. Meyer and Mary E. Northridge, eds. 638–52. New York: Springer.

Loos, Tamara Lynn. 2006. *Subject Siam: family, law, and colonial modernity in Thailand*. Ithaca: Cornell University Press.

Lotex, Andy. 2004. *Kau bunuh aku dengan cinta* (You are killing me with love). Yogyakarta: Galang Press.

Lowy, Dina. 2007. *The Japanese 'new woman': Images of gender and modernity*. New Brunswick: Rutgers University Press.

Luhmann, N. 2006. *The health risk and health care seeking behaviors of male-to-female transgender persons in Khon Kaen, Thailand: First implications for targeted prevention*. Khon Kaen: Khon Kaen University.

Lyon, David. 2002. Cyberspace: Beyond the information society? In *Living with Cyberspace, Technology & Society in the 21st Century*. John Armitage and Joanne Roberts, eds. 21–33. London: Continuum.

Manalansan, Martin. 1997. In the shadows of Stonewall: Examining gay transnational politics and the diasporic dilemma. In *The politics of culture in the shadow of capital*. Lisa Lowe and David Lloyd, eds. 485–505. Durham, NC: Duke University Press.

———. 2003. *Global divas: Filipino gay men in the diaspora*. Durham, NC: Duke University Press.

Martin, Fran. 2003. *Situating sexualities: Queer representation in Taiwanese fiction, film and public culture*. Hong Kong: Hong Kong University Press.

Martin, Fran, Peter A. Jackson, Mark McLelland, and Audrey Yue, eds. 2008. *AsiaPacifiQueer: Rethinking gender and sexuality in the Asia-Pacific*. Urbana and Chicago: University of Illinois Press.

Mathana Chetamee. 1995. Withi-chiwit lae chiwit khrorp-khrua khorng ying rak ying (Lifestyles and family life of women who love women). M.A. dissertation, Department of Anthropology, Thammasat University, Bangkok.

Matzner, Andrew. n.d. Transgenderism and Northern Thai spirit mediumship. http://web.hku.hk/~sjwinter/TransgenderASIA/TGinThailandSpirit.htm (accessed 2 February 2010).

———. 2001. The complexities of "acceptance": Thai students' attitudes towards kathoey. *Crossroads: An Interdisciplinary Journal of South East Asian Studies* 15 (2): 71–93.

May Adadol Ingawanij. 2008. Disreputable behaviour: The hidden politics of the Thai film act. *Vertigo Magazine* 3 (8): 30–31.

May Adadol Ingawanij and Richard Lowell MacDonald. 2005. The value of an impoverished aesthetic: *The Iron Ladies* and its audiences. *South East Asia Research*, 13 (1): 43–56.

————. 2010. Blissfully whose? Jungle pleasures, ultra-modernist cinema and the cosmopolitan Thai auteur. In *The ambiguous allure of the West: Traces of the colonial in Thailand*. Rachel V. Harrison and Peter A. Jackson, eds. 119–34. Hong Kong: Hong Kong University Press.

McCamish, Malcolm, 1999. The friends thou hast: Support systems for male commercial sex workers in Pattaya, Thailand. In *Lady boys, tom boys, rent boys: Male and female homosexualities in contemporary Thailand*. Peter A. Jackson and Gerard Sullivan, eds. 161–91. London: Routledge.

McLelland, Mark J. 2006. Japan's original gay boom. In *Popular culture, globalization and Japan*. M. Allen and R. Sakamoto, eds. 159–73. London and New York: Routledge.

Mezzadra, Sandro. 2005. Taking care: Migration and the political economy of affective labor. Presentation, 16 March 2005, Goldsmiths College, University of London, Center for the Study of Invention and Social Process. www.goldsmiths.ac.uk/csisp/papers/mezzadra_taking_care.pdf (accessed 12 April 2007).

Mills, Mary Beth. 1999. *Thai women in the global labor force: Consuming desires, contested selves*. New Brunswick: Rutgers University Press.

Mohanty, Chandra Talpade. 1997. Women workers and capitalist scripts: Ideologies of common interests, domination and the politics of solidarity. In *Feminist geneaologies, colonial legacies, democratic futures*. M. Jacqui Alexander and Chandra Talpade Mohanty, eds. 3–29. New York: Routledge.

Morris, Rosalind C. 1994. Three sexes and four sexualities: Redressing the discourses on gender and sexuality in contemporary Thailand. *Positions*, 2 (1): 15–43.

————. 1997. Educating desire: Thailand, transnationalism, and transgression. *Social Text*, 15 (3 and 4): 53–79.

————. 2004. Intimacy and corruption in Thailand's age of transparency. In *Off stage, on display: Intimacy and ethnography in the age of public culture*. Andrew Shryock, ed. 225–42. Stanford: Stanford University Press.

Mujiarso, Is, ed. 2006. *Rahasia bulan* (Secrets of the moon). Jakarta: Gramedia Pustaka Utama.

Mukhopadhyay, Bhaskar. 2006. Cultural studies and politics in India today. *Theory, Culture & Society*, 23 (7–8): 279–92.

Mulder, Neils. 1997. *Thai images: The culture of the public world*. Chiang Mai: Silkworm Books.

Namaste, Viviane. 2000. *Invisible lives: The erasure of transsexual and transgendered people*. Chicago: University of Chicago Press.

Nanda, Serena. 2000. Transgendered males in Thailand and the Philippines. In *Gender diversity: Cross-cultural variations*. Serena Nanda, ed. 71–85. Illinois: Waveland Press.

Nantakwang Sirasoontorn. 2007. *Nang di-di thi cheu "Rak Haeng Siam"* (A great movie titled "Love of Siam"). *Krungthep Turakij*, 23 November 2007, p. 25.

Nantiya Sukontapatipark. 2005. Relationship between modern medical technology and gender identity in Thailand: Passing from "male body" to "female body." M.A. dissertation, Institute of Language and Culture for Rural Development, Mahidol University, Salaya.

National Human Rights Commission of Thailand. 2007. *Phu-ying pok-porng sitthi manutsayachon* (Women human rights defenders). Bangkok: National Human Rights Commission of Thailand.

Nattakorn Devakula. It's the love of Thailand: Rak Haeng Siam. *Bangkok Post*, 27 November 2007, p. 15.

Neale, Steve. 2000. *Genre and Hollywood*. London: Routledge.

Newman, L. 2002. Sex, gender and culture: Issues in the definition, assessment and treatment of gender identity disorder. *Clinical Child Psychology and Psychiatry*, 7 (3): 352–59.

O'Brien, Michelle. 2003. Tracing this body: Transsexuality, pharmaceuticals & capitalism. www.deadletters.biz/body.pdf (accessed 27 May 2007).

Ojanen, Timo T. 2009. Sexual/gender minorities in Thailand: Identities, challenges, and voluntary-sector counselling. *Sexuality Research and Social Policy*, 6 (2): 4–34.

Ong, Aihwa. 1999. *Flexible citizenship: The cultural logics of transnationality*. Durham, NC: Duke University Press.

Oradaol Kaewprasert. 2005. The very first series of Thai queer cinemas: What was happening in the 1980's? Paper presented at the 1st International Conference of Asian Queer Studies, Bangkok, 7–9 July 2005. http://bangkok2005.anu.edu.au/papers/Kaewprasert.pdf (accessed 18 April 2007).

Oranong Kittikalayawong. 1991. Phreuttikam thang-phet lae jetakhati khorng nak-rian way-run: korani seuksa phreuttikam rak-ruam-phet khet-kan-seuksa 3 (Sexual behaviors and attitudes of adolescent students: A case study on homosexual behaviors in the educational region 3). Master's dissertation, Department of Clinical Psychology, Mahidol University, Bangkok.

Ortner, Sherry. 1989. Gender hegemonies. *Cultural Critique*, 14: 35–80.

Paga Sattayatam 1973. Kan-priap-thiap khwam-samphan nai khrorp-khrua thi hai kan-op-rom liang-du khorng bukkhon thi rak-ruam-phet kap bukkhon pokati (A comparison of homosexual and normal people with respect to the relationships within their families). Master's dissertation, Chulalongkorn University, Bangkok.

Pantip.com. 2008. *Khun khit wa phaphayon Thai reuang "Rak Haeng Siam" pen "nang gay" reu mai?* (Do you think the Thai movie "Love of Siam" is a "gay movie" or not?") http://topicstock. pantip.com/chalermthai/topicstock/2008/03/A6429158/A6429158.html (accessed 27 April 2010).

Parinyaporn Pajee. 2004. Movie muscle. *The Nation*, 2 June 2004. www.nationmultimedia.com (accessed 17 May 2007).

———. 2007. Censorship. The director's cut. *The Nation*, 3 May 2007. www.nationmultimedia. com (accessed 3 May 2007).

Pattana Kitiarsa. 2005. Lives of hunting dogs: *Muai Thai* and the politics of Thai masculinities. *South East Asia Research*, 13 (1): 57–90.

———. 2007. Muai Thai cinema and the burdens of Thai Men. *South East Asia Research*, 15 (3): 407–24.

Pattaya Yaisoon. 1984. Family dynamic in child of male homosexuals. Master's dissertation, Department of Public Health, Mahidol University, Bangkok.

Patton, Cindy. 2002. Stealth bombers of desire: The globalization of 'alterity' .

Peletz, M. G. 2006. Transgenderism and gender pluralism in Southeast Asia since early modern times. *Current Anthropology*, 47 (2): 309–40.

Pellegrini, Ann. 2002. Consuming lifestyle: Commodity capitalism and the transformations in gay identity in emerging democracies. In *Queer globalizations: Citizenship and the afterlife of colonialism.* Arnaldo Cruz-Malavé and Martin F. Manalansan IV, eds. 134–45. New York and London: New York University Press.

Pfaff, Timothy. 2005. Out of the jungle and onto the big screen: Cult film from Thailand travels to U.S. *San Francisco Chronicle*, 9 July 2005. http://sfgate.com/cgi-bin/article.cgi?f=/ c/a/2005/07/09/DDG60DKJEQ1.DTL (accessed 16 May 2005).

Phermsak, Lilakul. 2002. Govt endorsement: Homosexuality "not a disease." 27 December 2002. www.nationmultimedia.com (accessed 10 March 2009).

Prempreeda Pramoj na Ayutthaya. 2003. Kan-chuang-ching attalak 'kathoey' nai ngan cabaret show (Contesting identities of *"kathoeys"* in cabaret shows). Master's dissertation, Faculty of Social Development, Chiang Mai University, Chiang Mai.

Prosser, Jay. 1999. Exception locations: transsexual travelogues. In *Reclaiming genders: Transsexual grammars at the fin de siècle.* Kate More and Stephen Whittle, eds. 83–116. London: Cassell.

Puar, Jasbir Kaur. 2002. Circuits of queer mobility: Tourism, travel, and globalization. *GLQ: A Journal of Lesbian and Gay Studies*, 8 (1–2): 101–38.

Rakkit Rattachumpoth. 1999. Foreword. In *Lady boys, tom boys, rent boys: Male and female homosexuality in contemporary Thailand*. Peter A. Jackson and Gerard Sullivan, eds. xi–xviii. New York: Harrington Park Press.

Rangan, Pooja. 2007. Transitions, transactions: Bollywood as signifying practice. In *Sarai reader 07: Frontiers*. Monica Narula, Shuddhabrata Sengupta, Jeebesh Bagchi, and Ravi Sundaram, eds. 273–85. Delhi: Sarai.

Rennesson, Stéphane. 2005. Muay Thai, une ethnographie de la filière de la boxe en pays issane (Nord-Est thaïlandais) (Muay Thai, an ethnography of the Thai boxing network in northeastern Thailand). Ph.D. dissertation, Anthropology Department, Paris Ouest Nanterre La Défense University.

———. 2007. *Violence et immunité. La boxe thaïlandaise promue en art de défense national* (Violence and immunity: Thai boxing promoted as an art of national defense). *L'Homme*, 182: 163–86.

Reynolds, Craig J. 2002. *National identity and its defenders: Thailand today*, revised edition. Chiang Mai: Silkworm Books.

Reynolds, Robert. 2007. *What happened to gay life?* Sydney: University of New South Wales Press.

Richardson, J. Response: Finding the disorder in gender identity disorder. *Harvard Review of Psychiatry* 7, No. 1 (1999): 43–50.

Ronnapoom Samakkeekarom, Pimpawun Boonmongkon and Wachira Chantong. 2008. *Phet-withi chai rak chai nai Camfrog pheun-thi saiber, khrongsang amnat lae sukkhaphawa thang-phet* (The sexuality of Thai men who have sex with men in Camfrog on-line web cam chatrooms: Cyberspace, power structures, and sexual health). In *Phet-withi nai seu niyom: boribot siang lae serm tor sukkhaphawa thang-phet* (Sexuality in popular media: Contexts constituting risks to or enhancing sexual health). Pimpawun Boonmongkon, Ronnapoom Samakkeekarom, Wachira Chantong, Phanupak Poompluk, and Chayanun Manokasemsuk, eds. 17–64. Bangkok: Women's Health Advocacy Foundation Thailand.

Roseberry, William. 1989. *Anthropologies and histories: Essays in culture, history, and political economy*. New Brunswick, NJ: Rutgers University Press.

Royal College of Psychiatrists, United Kingdom. 2006. Good practice guidelines for the assessment and treatment of gender dysphoria (draft document). London: Royal College of Psychiatrists.

Ruting, Brad. 2007. Is the golden mile tarnishing? Urban and social change on Oxford Street, Sydney. Paper presented at the Queer Space: Centres and Peripheries Conference, University of Technology, Sydney, February 2007.

Saithid Wiangmoon. 2006. Kan-jat-kan tua-ton khorng wai-run ying rak ying nai rong-rian mathayom-seuksa torn-ton (Self-management of a girl-loving girl teenager in Secondary School). Master's dissertation, Chiang Mai University, Chiang Mai.

Sandoval, Chela. 2002. Dissident globalizations, emancipatory methods, social-erotics. In *Queer globalizations: Citizenship and the afterlife of colonialism*. Arnaldo Cruz-Malavé and Martin F. Manalansan IV, eds. 20–32. New York and London: New York University Press.

Sanders, Douglas. 2002. Some say Thailand is a gay paradise. In *Gay tourism: culture, identity and sex*. S. Clift, M. Luongo and C. Callister, eds. 42–62. London: Continuum.

Sanitsuda Ekachai. 2001. *Keeping the faith: Thai Buddhism at the crossroads*. Bangkok: Post Books.

Sassen, Saskia. 2002. Women with/in cyberspace. In *Living with cyberspace: Technology & society in the 21st century*. John Armitage and Joanne Roberts, eds. 109–19. London: Continuum.

Schwartz, Barry. 2007. The kind of capitalism we want. *Re/view: The Australian Financial Review*, 4 May 2007, p. 10.

Shary, Timothy. *Teen movies: American youth on screen*. London and New York: Wallflower, 2005.

Sherer, B. 2006. Gender transformed and meta-gendered enlightenment: Treating Buddhist narratives as paradigms of inclusiveness. *Revista de Estudos da Religiao*. www.pucsp.br/rever/rv3_2006/p_scherer.pdf (accessed 2 February 2010).

Sinnott, Megan. 2000. The semiotics of transgendered sexual identity in the Thai print media: Imagery and discourse of the sexual other. *Culture, Health and Sexuality* 2 (4): 425–40.

———. 2004. *Toms and dees: Female transgenderism and same-sex sexuality in Thailand*. Honolulu: University of Hawaii Press.

Spade, Dean. 2006. Mutilating gender. In *The transgender studies reader*. Susan Stryker and Stephen Whittle, eds. 315–32. New York: Routledge.

Staiger, Janet. 1995. *Bad women: Regulating sexuality in early American cinema*. Minneapolis, MN: University of Minnesota Press.

Stoler, Ann. 2002. *Carnal knowledge and imperial power: Race and the intimate in colonial rule*. Berkeley: University of California Press.

Stone, Sandy. 1992. The empire strikes back: A post-transsexual manifesto. *Camera Obscura*, 29 (1): 50–176.

Storer, Graeme. 1999a. Rehearsing gender and sexuality in modern Thailand: masculinity and male-male sex behaviours. In *Lady boys, tom boys, rent boys: Male and female homosexualities in contemporary Thailand*. Peter A. Jackson and Gerard Sullivan, eds. 141–60. New York: Haworth.

———. 1999b. Performing sexual identity: naming and resisting "gayness" in modern Thailand. *Intersections: Gender, History and Culture in the Asian Context*, 2. http://intersections.anu.edu.au/issue2/Storer.html (accessed 1 November 2010)

Sucheera Pinijparakarn. 2004. Call to limit gay presence on TV. *The Nation*, 5 June 2004. www.nationmultimedia.com/search/page.arcview.php?clid=2&id=100073 (accessed 12 May 2007).

Sudarat Musikawong. 2007. Working practices in Thai independent film production and distribution. *Inter-Asia Cultural Studies*, 8 (2): 248–61.

Suja, S., S. Sutanyawatchai, and S. Siri. 2005. *Quality of life in male to female transsexuals using and not using female hormone therapies*. Chiang Mai: Chiang Mai University Press.

Sulaiporn Chonwilai. 2002. Tua-ton nai reuang lao: Kan-tor-rorng thang attalak khorng ying rak ying (Narrating selves: Negotiating lesbian identity). Master's dissertation, Anthropology Department, Thammasat University, Bangkok.

Sumalee Tokthong. 2006. Kan-hai khwam-mai lae kan-tor-rorng nai chiwit khu khorng ying rak ying (Women loving women's self-definition and negotiation in their "married" lives). Master's dissertation, Anthropology Department, Thammasat University, Bangkok.

Tanabe, Shigeharu, and Charles F. Keyes, eds. 2002. *Cultural crisis and social memory: Modernity and identity in Thailand and Laos*. London: Routledge.

Tasanee Thanaprachoom. 1989. Phreuttikam thang-phet lae jetakhati khorng nak-rian way-run: korani seuksa phreuttikam rak-ruam-phet khet kan-seuksa 5 (Sexual behaviors and attitudes of adolescent students: A case study of homosexual behavior in educational region 5). Master's dissertation, Department of Clinical Psychology, Mahidol University, Bangkok.

Tattelman, Ira. 1999. Speaking to the gay bathhouse: Communicating in sexually charged spaces. In *Public Sex Gay Space*. William Leap, ed. 71–94. New York: Columbia University Press.

———. 2000. Presenting a queer (bath) house. In *Queer Frontiers: Millennial Geographies, Genders, and Generations*. Joseph A. Boone, Debra Silverman, Cindy Sarver, and Karin Quimby, eds. 222–43. Wisconsin: University of Wisconsin Press.

Teh, Yik Koon. 2002. *The mak nyahs: Male to female transsexuals in Malaysia*. Singapore: Eastern Universities Press.

Terdsak Romjumpa. 2002. Wathakam kiao-kap "gay" nai sangkhom Thai Phor. Sor. 2508–2542 (Discourses on "gays" in Thai society: 1965–1999). Master's dissertation, History Department, Thammasat University, Bangkok.

Thanes Wongyannava. 2008. Policing the imagined family and children in Thailand: From family name to emotional love. In *Imagining communities in Thailand: Ethnographic approaches.* Shigeharu Tanabe, ed. 22–40. Chiang Mai: Mekong Press.

Thongchai Winichakul. 2000. The quest for 'siwilai': A geographical discourse of civilization thinking in late nineteenth and early twentieth century Siam. *Journal of Asian Studies*, 59 (3): 528–49.

Thossaporn Klinhom. 2007. Chookiat Sakveerakul: "Nang" Thai mai chai "rak" baep diao (Chookiat Sakveerakul: Thai movies don't have just one kind of love). *Krungthep turakij*, Bangkok, 12 December 2007. www.bangkokbiznews.com/2007/12/12/WW06_0616_news.php?newsid=210506 (accessed 12 December 2007).

Thunska Pansittivorakul. 2006. A conversation with Apichatpong Weerasethakul. *Criticine.com*, 30 April 2006. www.criticine.com/interview_article.php?id=24 (accessed 7 May 2007).

Tong, Chee Kiong, and Kwok Bun Chan, eds. 2001. *Alternate identities: The Chinese of contemporary Thailand*. Leiden: Brill Academic Publishers.

Totman, Richard. 2003. *The third sex: Kathoey: Thailand's ladyboys*. London: Souvenir.

TransGender Europe. 2009. Report of the transgender murder monitoring project. *Liminalis*, 9 (3). http://www.liminalis.de/project.html (accessed 1 February 2010).

Ungpakorn, Giles Ji. n.d. Challenges to the Thai N.G.O. movement from the dawn of a new opposition to global capital. www.istendency.net/pdf/NGO/pdf (accessed 10 March 2010).

———. 2007. The impact of the Thai "sixties" on the people's movement today. *Inter-Asia Cultural Studies*, 7 (4): 570–88.

Vail, Peter T. 1998. *Violence and control: Social and cultural dimensions of boxing in Thailand*. Ph.D. dissertation in Anthropology, Cornell University, Ithaca NY.

Van Esterik, Penny. 1996. The politics of beauty in Thailand. In *Beauty Queens on the Global Stage: Gender, Contests and Power*. Colleen Ballerino Cohen, Richard Wilk, and Beverly Stoeltje, eds. 203–16. New York: Routledge.

———. 1999. Repositioning gender, sexuality, and power in Thai studies. In *Genders and sexualities in modern Thailand*. Peter A. Jackson and Nerida M. Cook, eds. 275–89. Chiang Mai: Silkworm Books.

———. 2000. *Materializing Thailand*. Oxford: Berg.

Van Griensven, F., S. Thanprasertsuk, R. Jommaroeng, G. Mansergh, S. Naorat, and R. A. Jenkins, 2005. Evidence of a previously undocumented epidemic of HIV infection among men who have sex with men in Bangkok, Thailand. *AIDS*, 19: 521–26.

Van Griensven, F., A. Varangrat, W. Wimonsate, S. Tanpradech, K. Kladsawad, and T. Chemnasiri. 2009. Trends in HIV prevalence, estimated incidence, and risk behavior among men who have sex with men in Bangkok, Thailand, 2003–2007. *Journal of Acquired Immune Deficiency Syndrome*, 52 (November): 234–39.

Vasey, P. L. and N. H. Bartlett. 2007. What can the Samoan "Fa'afafine" teach us about the Western concept of gender identity disorder in childhood? *Perspectives in Biology and Medicine*, 50 (4): 481–90.

Veena Thoopkrajae. 2005. "Queer" conference attracts big response. *The Nation*, 5 July 2005. http://nationmultimedia.com/2005/07/05/headlines/index.php?news=headlines_17926558.html (accessed 15 May 2007).

———. 2007. If it isn't the censors, it's the special interest groups. *The Nation*, 5 May 2007. www.nationmultimedia.com/2007/05/05/opinion/opinion_30033445.php (accessed 15 May 2007).

Virno, Paolo. 2004. *A grammar of the multitude.* New York: Semiotext(e).

Vitale, A. 2005. Rethinking the gender identity disorder terminology in the diagnostic and statistical manual of mental disorders IV. www.avitale.com/hbigdatalkplus2005 (accessed 27 April 2010).

Vitaya Saeng-Aroon. 2007. Love in a hot climate. *The Nation,* 6 December 2007, www.nationmultimedia.com/worldhotnews/30058318/index.php (accessed 27 April 2010).

Wada-Marciano, Mitsuyo. 2008. *Nippon modern: Japanese cinema of the 1920s and 1930s.* Honolulu: University of Hawaii Press.

Waters, Malcolm. 1995. *Globalization.* London and New York: Routledge.

Weeks, Jeffrey. 2007. *The world we have won: The remaking of erotic and intimate life.* London and New York: Routledge.

Wekker, Gloria. 2006. *Politics of passion: Women's sexual culture in the Afro-Surinamese diaspora.* New York: Columbia University Press.

Weisman, Jan R. 2001. The tiger and his stripes: Thai and American reactions to Tiger Woods's (multi) "racial self." In *The sum of our parts: Mixed-heritage Asian Americans.* Teresa Williams-León, Cynthia L. Nakashima, and Michael Omi, eds. 231–44. Philadelphia: Temple University Press.

Wikipedia. 2010. Cinema of Thailand. http://en.wikipedia.org/w/index.php?title=Cinema_of_Thailand&oldid=204272376 (accessed 27 April 2010).

Williams, Raymond. 1977. *Marxism and literature.* Oxford: Oxford University Press.

Wilson, Ara. 2004. *The intimate economies of Bangkok: Tomboys, tycoons, and Avon ladies in the global city.* Berkeley: University of California Press.

———. 2006. Queering Asia. *Intersections: Gender, history, and culture in the Asian context,* No. 14 (Nov. 2006). http://intersections.anu.edu.au/issue14/wilson.html.

———. Medical tourism in Thailand. In *Asian biotech: Ethics and communities of fate.* Aihwa Ong and Nancy Chen, eds. Forthcoming. Durham NC: Duke University Press.

Wilson, Ian, Chris Griffin, and Bernadette Wren. 2002. The validity of the diagnosis of gender identity disorder (child and adolescent criteria). *Clinical Child Psychology and Psychiatry,* 7 (3): 335–51.

Winter, Sam. 2002a. Counting *kathoey. TransgenderASIA* web site. http://web.hku.hk/~sjwinter/TransgenderASIA/paper_counting_kathoey.htm (accessed 23 November 2008).

———. 2002b. Why are so many *kathoey* in Thailand? *TransgenderASIA* web site. http://web.hku.hk/~sjwinter/TransgenderASIA/paper_why_are_there_so_many_kathoey.htm (accessed 23 May 2003).

———. 2006a. Thai transgenders in focus: Their beliefs about attitudes towards and origins of transgender. *International Journal of Transgenderism,* 9 (2): 47–62.

———. 2006b. What made me this way? Contrasting reflections by Thai and Filipina transwomen. *Intersections: Gender, history, and culture in the Asian context,* Issue 14. http://intersections.anu.edu.au/issue14/winter.htm.

———. 2006c. Thai transgenders in focus: Demographics, transitions and identities. *International Journal of Transgenderism* 9 (1): 15–27.

———. 2007. Transphobia: A price worth paying for "gender identity disorder?" Paper presented at the First Biennial Symposium of the World Professional Association for Transgender Health, Chicago, 6–8 September 2007.

Winter, Sam, P. Chalungsooth, Teh Y. K., N. Rojanalert, K. Maneerat, Wong Y. W., A. Beaumont, L. Ho, C. Gomez, and R. A. Macapagal. 2009. Transpeople: A seven-country study of acceptance, prejudice and pathologisation. *International Journal of Sexual Health,* 21 (2): 96–118.

Winter, Sam and Mark King. Well and truly fucked: Transwomen, stigma, sex work and sexual health in South to East Asia. In *The prostitution of women, men and children: A global perspective.* Rochelle Dalla, ed. Forthcoming, Lanham MD: Lexington Books.

Winter, Sam, and L. Vink. Predictors of mental health in a sample of transwomen in Thailand. Forthcoming.

Winters, Kelley. 2006. Gender dissonance: Diagnostic reform of gender identity disorder for adults. *Journal of Psychology & Human Sexuality* 17: 71–89.

Wise Kwai. 2007. Review: *The Love of Siam. The Nation Weblog.* http://thaifilmjournal.blogspot. com/2007/11/review-love-of-siam.html (accessed 27 April 2010).

———. 2008. *Love of Siam* director's cut sold out, screenings extended. *The Nation Weblog.* http://thaifilmjournal.blogspot.com/2008/01/love-of-siam-directors-cut-sold-out.html (accessed 27 April 2010).

Witchayanee Ocha. 2008. Expounding gender: Male and transgender (male to female) sex worker identities in the global-Thai sex sector. Ph.D. dissertation, School of Environment, Resources and Development, Asian Institute of Technology, Bangkok.

World Health Organization. 1992. *Tenth revision of the international classification of diseases (ICD–10).* Geneva: WHO.

World Professional Association for Transgender Health. 2006. *Standards of care for gender identity disorders, sixth version.* http://wpath.org/Documents2/socv6.pdf (accessed 5 April 2008).

Yao, Souchou. 2001. Introduction. In *House of glass: Culture, modernity and the state in Southeast Asia.* Yao Souchou, ed. 1–23. Singapore: Institute of Southeast Asian Studies.

Zhang, Zhen. 2005. *An amorous history of the silver screen: Shanghai cinema, 1896–1937.* Chicago: University of Chicago Press.

Index